# CRUCIFIED
## AND RESURRECTED

# CRUCIFIED
# AND RESURRECTED

*Restructuring the Grammar of Christology*

# Ingolf U. Dalferth

*Translated by* Jo Bennett

**B**
**Baker Academic**
*a division of Baker Publishing Group*
Grand Rapids, Michigan

Originally published as *Der auferweckte Gekreuzigte*
© 1994 by J. C. B. Mohr (Paul Siebeck), Tübingen. All rights reserved.

English translation © 2015 by Ingolf U. Dalferth
Published by Baker Academic
a division of Baker Publishing Group
P.O. Box 6287, Grand Rapids, MI 49516-6287
www.bakeracademic.com

Printed in the United States of America

Library of Congress Cataloging-in-Publication Data
Dalferth, Ingolf U.
    [Auferweckte Gekreuzigte. English]
    Crucified and resurrected : restructuring the grammar of Christology / Ingolf U. Dalferth ; translated by Jo Bennett.
        pages cm
    Includes bibliographical references and index.
    ISBN 978-0-8010-9754-6 (pbk.)
    1. Theology, Doctrinal. 2. Jesus Christ—Person and offices. I. Title.
BT78.D25913 2015
232—dc23                                                                          2015025073

15   16   17   18   19   20   21      7   6   5   4   3   2   1

To Eberhard Jüngel

# Contents

# Translator's Preface

"The task of translating a German theological work is never quite straightforward," wrote Sir Edwin Hoskyns in the preface to his 1933 translation of Karl Barth's *Epistle to the Romans*. Perhaps I may be allowed to echo his magnificent understatement.

Despite the complexity of the task, it has been a privilege to have been invited to translate Professor Dalferth's scholarly, carefully argued, and deeply interesting work. I have gained much personal benefit from dealing with his theological thinking on a daily basis and am convinced that this text fully merits introduction to a wider, English-reading audience. In undertaking the task, I have sought to retain a balance between conscientious translation of Dalferth's argumentation and the need for the English version to be read with fluency and enjoyment.

The issue of gender is one that may not have confronted Hoskyns but is inevitable for today's writers and translators. Wherever possible I have used "humans" or "human beings" for *der Mensch* and thus have been able to avail myself of the plural pronoun "they," resorting only where absolutely necessary to the gender-specific "he" or the slightly clumsy "he or she."

Another issue faced by German-to-English theological translators in any era is the translation of *Glaube*. In agreement with Professor Dalferth, I have used "belief" whenever the object is a doctrinal proposition or doctrine, and "faith" whenever *Glaube* expresses an attitude toward or a relationship of trust in a person.

Biblical quotations are taken chiefly from the New American Standard Bible, except where a direct English translation gives the sense of the German quotation more accurately and therefore better supports the point the author is making.

Aware that some potential readers of the English text may not have Professor Dalferth's thorough acquaintance with classical languages, I have provided, within the limits of my abilities and subject to his review, translations of the Latin and Greek terms that occur fairly frequently within the text.

My use of italics follows the original, except for a very few instances where I felt that the introduction of italics in the English translation was the best way to enhance the reader's understanding of the text.

I would like to express my gratitude both to Bishop Michael Bourke, assistant bishop in the Anglican Diocese of Hereford and former cochair of the Meissen Commission, for his reading of my draft translation and his very helpful comments and suggestions; and of course to Professor Dalferth himself, whose thorough knowledge of the English language greatly simplified our discussions of various aspects of the translation process.

Jo Bennett
January 15, 2015

# Preface to the 2015 English Edition

## 1. Beyond *Mythos* and *Logos*

Every book has a history, and this book is no exception. Originally I did not plan to publish it separately but wrote it as the second part of a large study of the European strategy of orienting oneself in mental space by the contrast between *mythos* and *logos*, the mythical (narrative, temporal, meaning-constituting) and the rational (argumentative, atemporal, reason-giving), and the impact of this orienting strategy on Christian theology. The distinction between these different types of rationalities, experiences, and ways of thinking—variously conceived and contrasted and continuously reinterpreted since the beginnings of European philosophy, science, and theology in ancient Greece—is deeply entrenched in the history of European thought and has held a particular grip on philosophy and theology. My idea was to show that the mode and character of Christian theology can be understood neither in terms of this mental orienting strategy nor without reference to it. In antiquity Christian theology contrasted with both the *mythos* and the *logos* traditions by developing into a hybrid "third" that was different from both; in medieval Europe it tried to synthesize the mythical and the rational into a unity that transcended both, but this unity was always on the brink of breaking apart; and in modernity it redefined itself by reference to the mythical and rational strands within itself without completely identifying with either of them.

Christian theology emerged in a cultural setting in which it had no choice but to relate to the traditional orienting pattern of *mythos* and *logos* without ever fitting into it: because of its eschatological and soteriological orientation, and the christological and trinitarian ways of thinking that resulted from it, Christian theology became "the other" of both traditions by using modes of thinking derived from both of them. Later the contrast between Christian theology, on the one hand, and the ancient *mythos* and *logos* traditions, on the other, was turned into an internal distinction within Christian theology itself, which thereby became all-encompassing but at the same time precariously unstable, always in danger of losing its balance between the mythical and the rational by overemphasizing the one at the expense of the other. Enlightenment thinkers forced theology to rethink this internalizing strategy by insisting that it had to choose between either the one or the other: Christian theology is either an outdated mythology or an unfounded theism or—and most likely—both at the same time in different respects. Many critics in the eighteenth and nineteenth centuries agreed with the first or the third view, or with both, and turned their back on Christianity and Christian theology. Others opted for the second horn of the dilemma but tried to show that it was not an unfounded but rather a well-founded theism. However, neither the skeptical atheist's nor the rational theist's way out is convincing. Both wrongly accept the alternative posed by the Enlightenment against the backdrop of the medieval synthesis of the mythical and the rational. But this alternative offers a choice between the devil and the deep blue sea. Christian theology cannot identify with either the *mythos* or the *logos* strand, or simply combine them into some higher but inconsistent unity, without losing its characteristic identity as the unique thought form of the Christian faith. It is neither the mythology of a particular historical faith, nor a general philosophical theism unrelated to any particular faith, nor an inconsistent combination of both, but rather an intellectual endeavor sui generis. As Augustine made clear with reference to the Stoic pattern of theologies:[1] Christian theology is neither a form of natural theology (philosophical theism or *theologia naturalis*), nor a form of poetic or mythical theology (mythology or *theologia fabulosa*), nor a form of political theology (civil religion or *theologia civilis*), but a fundamental critique of all three. If anything, Christian theology bears a faint similarity to natural theology because it seeks knowledge and truth and is not merely a matter of human invention and social convention. But it would be best not to call it theology in any of three Stoic senses at all. It is neither a case of *mythos* nor of *logos*, nor a combination of both, but something sui generis.

It took a huge effort for Christian theology to recover this insight at the end of modernity, and it never completely achieved it in a way that left a noticeable imprint on contemporary culture. Where it succumbed to the lure of the Enlightenment alternative, it became rationalist, liberal, and modernist; and

1. *Civ.* VIII, 1 and 5.

where theology rejected modern rationalism, it restated the classical synthesis or became radically orthodox. However, neither is a way forward. In the light of the Enlightenment criticism, the precarious synthesis of the mythical and the rational cannot simply be continued, not even in a radically orthodox way; yet in the light of the origin of Christian faith and the beginnings of Christian theology, the Enlightenment alternative should not be accepted. Christian faith is not merely one religious belief among others (as Enlightenment rationality has it); by its own account, it is the awareness and acknowledgment that Christ's cross and resurrection mark the end of the old world and the beginning of the new. By unfolding, exploring, and thinking through this faith from its own point of view, Christian theology is neither a case of *mythos* or *logos* nor a combination of both, but something unique and sui generis.

It was only when Christian theology rediscovered its eschatological roots in the late nineteenth and early twentieth centuries that it became aware again of the uniqueness of its intellectual project and managed to posit itself in contrast to both the *mythos* and the *logos* strands within its own tradition. It did so—without turning into something different by trying to be both or by choosing between them—by becoming theological through and through. In order to meet the challenge to be true to the eschatological reality of faith in God's creative and renewing presence in creation through Christ and the Spirit, it had to avoid three dead ends: (1) the classical *aporia* of a metaphysical "both-and," of constructing itself as an incoherent metadiscipline of the rational and the mythical; (2) the Enlightenment *aporia* of a dogmatic "either-or," of allowing itself to be forced into the Procrustean bed of choosing between rationalism and obscurantism; and (3) the self-defeating *aporia* of a "neither-nor," of cutting all constructive ties to the surrounding culture by relating in a merely negative way to it. Theology is neither a "both-and" nor an "either-or" nor a "neither-nor" of the mythical and the rational; rather, it is a sustained intellectual effort to understand everything in a new way from the point of view of the eschatological breaking in of God's creative presence in the human reality of this life and world in and through God's Word and Spirit. By orienting itself toward this life- and world-changing event, theology distances itself from both the *mythos* and the *logos* strands in European culture, freely using aspects of both without being reducible to either of them in creating and elaborating its own christological, trinitarian, and pneumatological thought forms. Only in this way can it be true to what makes it unique: the eschatological event of faith in the creative, saving, and perfecting presence of God, the poet of the possible, as it becomes disclosed in Christ when humans are changed by the Spirit from their God-ignoring lives of nonfaith and unfaith to a life of faith, trust, hope, and love of God and God's neighbors.

This is no more than a rough sketch whose details need to be filled in before it will be convincing. But even so, it will be obvious why the test case for this view of Christian theology and its history is Christology, the distinctive form of Christian thinking about God, human existence, and the world. From the beginning, Christian theology had to face up to a threefold challenge. It had to define itself in contrast not only to the mythologies of the Greco-Roman world but also to the natural theology of Hellenistic philosophies and the prophetic theology of the Jewish tradition. It had to conceive God in personal terms, and as acting in history, without relapsing into myth; it had to conceive him as creator and ruler of the universe without reducing him to a metaphysical principle of the cosmos; and it had to conceive him as the eschatological Savior who had acted in Jesus Christ in a definite way, universally valid and relevant not only for the Jews but for everyone. None of the contemporary theological paradigms could combine all this in a convincing and consistent way. Thus Christian thinkers were forced to develop a new theological paradigm: *Christology*.[2]

The term *Christology* is understood here not in a narrow and specific sense but in a broad and foundational sense. It does not merely signify the doctrine of the person of Christ, or of the person and work of Christ, as distinct from the doctrine of the salvation achieved by Christ and appropriated through faith in Christ in the sacramental life of the church (soteriology and ecclesiology). Rather, it signifies the fundamental thought form of the Christian faith that has foundational import for all Christian theology. It informs its trinitarian thought about God as Father, Word, and Spirit; its soteriological accounts of human life in terms of sin, justification, and the church; and its eschatological views of world, life, and history as God's creation. All the characteristic teachings of Christian theology are manifestations of thinking about God, human existence, and the world in christological terms. These terms did not fit into the traditional pattern of *mythos* and *logos* in antiquity, and they do not fall prey to the criticism of both forms of rationality in modernity. It is true that the christological thought form did not develop independently of the orienting strategy of *mythos* and *logos*, and neither was it ever practiced completely unrelated to it. But it cannot be coherently stated or sufficiently understood in terms of it. It became something sui generis by using the pattern of *mythos* and *logos* to distinguish itself from both *mythos* and *logos*, thereby going beyond the whole European pattern of orientation and becoming something distinctly different and new.

2. I. U. Dalferth, *Theology and Philosophy* (Eugene, OR: Wipf & Stock, 2002), 36–37.

## 2. From Confession to Grammar

The first part of the book was published in 1993 under the title *Jenseits von Mythos und Logos: Die christologische Transformation der Theologie* (Freiburg: Herder). It traced the orienting strategy of *mythos* and *logos* through the European history of thought from Greek antiquity through the beginnings of Christian theology (Logos-Christology and trinitarian thought) to the medieval synthesis and its breakdown in modernity. I then analyzed in detail three attempts to turn this strategy on itself and thereby critically reenforce or overcome it: the hermeneutics of myths, from the late eighteenth-century to the twentieth-century attempts of demythologizing Christian theology; the structuralist efforts to understand the functioning of myths and rituals in strictly rational terms of *logos*; and the philosophical and theological attempts to spell out the sui generis character of the christological form of Christian thought in terms of grammar—Newman's grammar of assent, Wittgenstein's idea of theology as grammar, Austin Farrer's reconstruction of a grammar of revelation from the "Rebirth of Images" in the biblical tradition, and Luther's insistence on a *grammatica theologica* as the proper mode of a *theologia crucis*. The study ended with an outline of Christian dogmatics as a grammar of Christian life and the practice of faith. It restated the old (but controversial) insight that theology is best understood and practiced not as a theoretical or speculative discipline that aims at knowledge of God and of everything in relation to God (*scientia speculativa*) but as a practical discipline that studies actions, acts, and activities that change human life (*scientia practica*)—not, however, merely human actions (*de rebus operabilibus ab homine*, as Aquinas rightly insisted) or primarily the religious activities of humans (as nineteenth-century neo-Protestantism maintained), but the divine activity that changes human life from sin to salvation, from disregarding God's presence to orienting itself toward God's presence, from ignoring God to loving God and one's neighbor, from death to life.

The second part was meant to ground this conception of theology as a grammar of the life of faith in a detailed reconstruction of the beginnings of the christological thought form of Christian theology. Combining analytic and hermeneutical approaches and paying close attention to exegetical and historical findings, I explored and discussed the issues of incarnation, cross, and resurrection; the basic doctrinal problems of classical Christology and trinitarian thought; and the soteriological issue of understanding the salvific significance of the death of Jesus in terms of sacrifice and atonement. In the end the book was published independently and with a different publisher under the title *Der auferweckte Gekreuzigte: Zur Grammatik der Christologie*

(Tübingen: Mohr Siebeck, 1994). But the overall argument stayed untouched. I attempted to substantiate in *Crucified and Resurrected* what I had outlined in *Jenseits von Mythos und Logos*. And I did so by tracing the genesis of the fundamental pattern of christological thought from (1) the resurrection confessions through (2) the gospel account of the cross and the life and message of Jesus to (3) his understanding of God that (4) reworked, intensified, and sharpened the heritage of Israel in which Jesus grew up and (5) grounded the resurrection experience of his Jewish followers who became the first Christians. The rationale of this account is twofold: If, as I argue, the confession that Jesus has been raised by God is the starting point of christological reflection in the New Testament, then Christian theology stands or falls with the clear and careful conceptual exposition of this confession. Second, the method I use to do this is the hermeneutical strategy of asking for the question or questions to which a given text, idea, or view seeks to provide an answer; of exploring to whom this answer may be, has been, or may have been given; and of identifying the question or questions that either were raised or may and perhaps should have been raised, by the answers given: What is the problem posed by the resurrection confession of the first Christians that is answered by reference to the cross? What is the problem posed by the Gospel account of the cross that is answered by the New Testament narratives of the life and message of Jesus? What is the problem to which Jesus's proclamation of the coming of God's kingdom seeks to give an answer? What is the problem posed by understanding the references to God in the Gospel accounts of the cross in terms of Jesus's message of God's coming? What is the problem posed by Jesus's death on the cross that is answered by the resurrection confession of (some of) his followers? What is the problem posed by the Christian accounts of Jesus's death and resurrection for those who did not or do not see Jesus's life and death in this way? And what is the problem posed for Christians by the fact that most don't see or understand it in this way? In short, if we try to understand the emergence of the christological thought form, we have to interpret the resurrection confessions with respect to the cross; the cross with respect to the life and message of Jesus; the life and message of Jesus with respect to God; Jesus's message of God with respect to the cross, the life of those who confess God to have raised Jesus from death, the world that they confess to be God's creation, and the life of those who live in God's creation but ignore or deny all this. The result of this dynamic interpretative process is the emergence of a christological thought form about God, human life, and the world that is never finished but permanently in the making, driven forward by the life and practice of faith and the inquiring intellect that seeks to understand the life and practice of faith in the light of the self-presenting and self-communicating activity of God. Because of its christological thought form, Christian theology is essentially about the creative activity of God in creation and new creation, and about the creative passivity of human life as the locus where God's prior activity in creation becomes manifest in a way that transforms human life from a life of ignoring or denying God's presence to a life of faith in the love of God and all others as God's neighbors.

The book concentrates on reconstructing the grammar of this christological thought form, not on applying it to the complex and wide-ranging issues of Christian life and practice in a globalizing world. All this is no doubt important, but unless we are clear about the christological grammar enacted in Christian life, we cannot ensure that what we claim to be Christian is in fact so. The problems of our world are not solved in or by theology, but Christian theology aims at helping Christians to engage in identifying and solving the problems of our time by providing guidelines and signposts for orientation. A grammar book is not to be confused with a discourse or a practice that enacts that grammar, and while Christian theology seeks to outline the grammar of a Christian life of faith, it is in the actual practice of this faith in the manifold areas of human life in our contemporary world that this grammar is enacted. We must not expect theology to do what can only be done in the life and practice of faith. Theologies come and go, and no theological view ought to be confused with the eschatological reality that it seeks to unfold. In theology, there is always room for improvement and deeper insight, and there is always a chance of being wrong whereas others may be right. What is decisive about human life from a Christian point of view is not what we think and do but that this life is the locus of God's creative and transforming presence, whether we believe it or not. Accordingly, the crucial question is not about our theologies but rather the question of whether our life is actually transformed from a life of unfaith and self-love to a life of faith and the love of God and neighbor. If we are justified, then we are justified by faith and not by how we experience or think about faith or practice it. Faith is not something we can achieve by what we do or think ourselves, but a gift for which we may pray and give thanks but which we cannot give to ourselves or to anybody else. The christological thought form is the thought form of this gift, and Christian theology is unique and sui generis precisely by being christological through and through.

## 3. Further Reflections

The book left its mark on debates in Germany, Great Britain, Switzerland, and the Netherlands, but it was not the last thing I wrote on Christology. In the following years I deepened, defended, and elaborated what I had written in a number of areas, concentrating in particular on the following: the significance of the life and person of Jesus for the Christian faith ("Jesus Christus—Zeichen für Gottes Zuwendung: Die Bedeutung der Person Jesu für den christlichen Glauben," in *Theologie zwischen Pragmatismus und Existenz-denken: Festschrift für Hermann Deuser zum 60. Geburtstag*, ed. G. Linde, R. Purkarthofer, H. Schulze, and P. Steinacker [Marburg: N. G. Elwert, 2006], 231–44), the debate about Jesus's death and the empty grave ("Volles Grab, leerer Glaube? Zum Streit um die Auferweckung des Gekreuzigten," *ZThK* 95 [1998]: 379–402), the hermeneutics of the resurrection ("The Resurrection: The Grammar of 'Raised,'" in *Biblical Concepts and Our World*, ed. D. Z. Phillips and M. van der Ruhr [New York: Palgrave, 2004], 190–208), the importance of the christological dogma for Christian theology ("Gott für uns: Die Bedeutung des christologischen Dogmas für die christliche Theologie," in *Denkwürdiges Geheimnis: Beiträge zur Gotteslehre; Festschrift für Eberhard Jüngel zum 70. Geburtstag*, ed. I. U. Dalferth, J. Fischer, and H. P. Großhans [Tübingen: Mohr Siebeck, 2004], 51–75), and the outline of a critical Christology ("Weder Mythos noch Metaphysik: Grundlinien einer kritischen Christologie," in *En in een Heer Jezus Christus: Het Dogma van Chalcedon als Leesregel en Spreekregel*, ed. H. Rikhof [Utrecht: Najaarsconferentie Samenwerkingsverband voor theologisch onderzoek, 2002], 14–30). These writings should be taken into account when discussing the issues of this book. They are further stepping-stones toward a Christian theology that takes the christological thought form seriously and does not shy away from emphasizing that Christian theology, as deeply contextual and context dependent as it always is, has its beauty and significance precisely in being unique and sui generis: it explores something new that cannot sufficiently be understood in terms of something familiar, and although we have to make use of our available cognitive, emotive, and conceptual resources to understand it at all, we are well advised to use the christological thought form in theology in the way outlined: not as a definitive doctrinal statement of a truth that we cannot understand but only accept or reject, but as a hermeneutical guideline that inducts us into a process of reorienting our life toward the creative presence of God and helps us to move through the questions and answers posed and provoked by the gift structure of Christian faith again and again in our own way and at our particular place in history. It is not theory but practice that counts, and the practice of faith is not an economic exchange of goods in a relationship of mutual rights and duties but a free gift that exceeds anything we can receive and that creates its own recipients by making more of them than they could ever become by themselves.

## Acknowledgments

Grateful thanks are due to the original publisher, Mohr Siebeck (Tübingen), for permission to translate this book.

It is a pleasure to thank Jo Bennett, who has done an excellent job of translating the book into English. Without her the book would not have appeared in English at all.

I also thank David Chao, who put me in contact with Baker Academic, and Dave Nelson for his painstaking help in editing the manuscript and seeing it through to press. Without them the book would not have been published now.

The index was prepared by Sean Callaghan, and my research assistant Marlene Block has been of invaluable help in getting everything ready for print. Without them I would still be reading the proofs.

The book was originally dedicated to Eberhard Jüngel on the occasion of his sixtieth birthday. Twenty years later the English translation is now being published shortly after his eightieth birthday. If there is one thing I do not want to change in this book, then it is this dedication: *Ad multos annos*!

Ingolf U. Dalferth

# Preface to the 1993 German Edition

Christian theology finds its proper thought form in dogmatics. Beyond the boundaries of religious myth and philosophical logos, but in constant reference to faith imageries, life experiences, and the conceptualizing efforts of the thought process, dogmatics describes the inner rationality of the Christian way of life in the form of a christological grammar of the Christian life of faith. It re-creates the structures of faith imageries by undertaking a critical examination of the identity of faith in the multiplicity of its articulations. It clarifies the conditions of the identity of faith and the rationality of the Christian life of faith by establishing rules to govern its practice and the focus of its content. It unfolds this focus systematically by using argumentative discourse to analyze the Christian eschatological understanding of reality and by presenting its main features coherently. And it examines the reliability of this understanding of reality by shedding light on its grounds for validity in comparison with other concepts of reality and life orientations, and by testing whether its claims to truth and validity are justified in the light of those grounds. Dogmatic thought thus makes plain what it means to have reasons for advocating the Christian faith, by illuminating the ground of faith as the rationality of the life of faith and the validity of the confession of faith. In itself it is neither the ground nor the foundation for faith; instead, it shows that a reasoned faith is not impossible, because faith in Jesus Christ has a unique ground, so that the Christian life of faith, too, has its own rationality.

As the grammar of the Christian life of faith, dogmatics seeks to illuminate this rationality in a systematic way by reference to the ground of faith, the triune God. So it unfolds the specificity of the content of faith in christological terms by affirming God's saving activity in Jesus Christ as the basis of faith and as the foundation and criterion for true knowledge of God; it apprehends the existence and practice of the Christian life of faith pneumatologically, by tracing it back to God himself, who has revealed himself and allowed himself to be known in Jesus Christ as all-transforming, creative love; and it conceives of the ground of faith in trinitarian terms, since it is only on this basis that the rationality of the Christian life of faith can be disclosed and illuminated theologically in its christological specificity and its pneumatological basis.

This trinitarian approach means that the thought form of dogmatics is far from being an irrelevant, abstract theory. As a christological grammar, it is not just externally related to practical experience but is in fact practical in itself. It is not simply the theory of a specific religious practice in Schleiermacher's sense; it aims to be practical in the soteriological sense emphasized by Luther: that its theme is the presence of God in Jesus Christ, whose death is appropriated by faith.[1] Dogmatic theology itself can never be or accomplish this appropriation of faith; it is thus no substitute for faith. But it can lead to the appropriation of faith by using its tools of argumentation to guide thought and life onto the foundation to which faith, and everything else along with it, owes its existence. Hence, dogmatic theology is not only unequivocally distinct from faith but also intrinsically related to it, in that it distinguishes the ground of faith from faith itself and affirms this ground as the point of reference for the life of faith and for all else. It cannot formulate this ground apart from faith, but the dogmatic formulation of this ground of faith is no more the ground of faith itself than theology is a substitute for faith. Hence, theology must apply to itself the differentiation that it claims theologically for faith; this has always been the case, and is so now more than ever. This preserves it from the danger of a fundamentalism that takes itself too seriously, but at the same time underlines the realism with which it counts on the effective presence of God. By systematically differentiating faith from the ground of faith, and itself from both, it resists the temptation to make its fallible theological insights into a yardstick for the Christian life of faith; it is able, instead, as a christological grammar of the Christian life of faith, to guide this lifetime and again to orient itself anew toward what constitutes it: God's saving activity in Jesus Christ.

This present work sets out to do what I outlined last year in *Jenseits von Mythos und Logos*[2] as the task of Christian dogmatics. Guided by the question of the proper argumentational structure for dogmatic thought, it seeks to

---

1. *WATR* 1, no. 153.
2. I. U. Dalferth, *Jenseits von Mythos und Logos: Die christologische Transformation der Theologie* (Freiburg: Herder, 1993), 6.

unfold the main features of a grammar of Christology so as to state, clearly and systematically, the consequences of the christological transformation of theology. It does not claim to offer the only possible representation of even the main features of such a grammar. But it does seek to show that a dogmatic unfolding of the Christian faith has to follow a path of thought that leads from the resurrection to the cross, from the cross to the life of Jesus, and from there to the understanding of God, which, when given a new and remodeled form, leads to the understanding of salvation. Every attempt to curtail or avoid this christological line of argument leads down a side alley and, in neglecting the understanding of God, bypasses the Christian understanding of salvation and of reality as well.

Once again I would like to thank my friends and colleagues for a great deal of help of various kinds. Just before the start of the examination period, Philipp Stoellger, with some assistance from Franziska Mihram, undertook the time-consuming task of creating the index. He had already provided critical comments on the manuscript at many points, prompting me time and again to reconsider the positions I had adopted. I am inclined to doubt that I have convinced him. But I hope that I may be successful where other readers are concerned, at any rate.

This book is dedicated to Eberhard Jüngel on the occasion of his sixtieth birthday. As he once said, he was never in favor of theology based on the "rotary-fan principle," in which "everything is thrown into the air and given a vigorous whirl, producing the impression of a theological departure for new shores, although in the end it is impossible to identify any genuine advancement of knowledge." As a theological teacher, he always insisted that theology should never be negligently allowed to fall short of its proper intellectual level, and that the mere grouping together of fashionable buzzwords should be kept for formulating theological brainteasers. As its fruits attest, theology accomplishes its real task when, with eyes and ears open to the concerns of its age, it follows its course unwaveringly and is practiced in accordance with its true purpose: to be an introduction to the "logic of the gospel."

Frankfurt, November 1993
Ingolf U. Dalferth

# Abbreviations

## Apostolic Fathers

| | |
|---|---|
| *2 Clem.* | *2 Clement* |
| *Did.* | *Didache* |

### Ignatius

| | |
|---|---|
| *Eph.* | *To the Ephesians* |
| *Magn.* | *To the Magnesians* |

## Ancient Sources

### Augustine

| | |
|---|---|
| *Civ.* | *De civitate Dei* (*The City of God*) |
| *Trin.* | *De Trinitate* (*The Trinity*) |

### Epictetus

| | |
|---|---|
| *Diatr.* | *Diatribai* (*Dissertationes*) |

### Irenaeus

| | |
|---|---|
| *Haer.* | *Adversus haereses* (*Against Heresies*) |

### Josephus

| | |
|---|---|
| *Ant.* | *Jewish Antiquities* |

### Origen

| | |
|---|---|
| *Cels.* | *Contra Celsum* (*Against Celsus*) |

### Plato

| | |
|---|---|
| *Tim.* | *Timaeus* |

### Tertullian

| | |
|---|---|
| *Prax.* | *Adversus Praxean* (*Against Praxeas*) |

## Modern Sources

| | |
|---|---|
| AA | Immanuel Kant, *Gesammelte Schriften*, Ausgabe der Königlich Preußischen Akademie der Wissenschaften. |
| *ATR* | *Anglican Theological Review* |
| *BK* | *Bibel und Kirche* |
| BKAT | Biblischer Kommentar Altes Testament |
| *BSLK* | *Die Bekenntnisschriften der evangelisch-lutherischen Kirche*, 11th ed. Göttingen: Vandenhoeck & Ruprecht, 1992. |
| *BZ* | *Biblische Zeitschrift* |
| DS | *Enchiridion symbolorum, definitionum et declarationum de rebus fidei et morum*, ed. Heinrich Denziger and Adolf Schönmetzer. Freiburg: Herder, 1997. |
| EKKNT | Evangelisch-katholischer Kommentar zum Neuen Testament |
| *EKL* | *Evangelisches Kirchenlexicon*. Edited by Erwin Fahlbusch et al. 4 vols. 3rd ed. Göttingen: Vandenhoeck & Ruprecht, 1985–96. |
| *EvTh* | *Evangelische Theologie* |

| GCS | Die griechischen christlichen Schriftsteller der ersten (drei) Jahrhunderte |
| IKaZ | *Internationale katholische Zeitschrift* |
| JBL | *Journal of Biblical Literature* |
| KD | *Kerygma und Dogma* |
| MT | Masoretic Text |
| NIDNTT | *The New International Dictionary of New Testament Theology.* Edited by Colin Brown. 4 vols. Grand Rapids: Zondervan, 1975–78. |
| NTS | *New Testament Studies* |
| PRSt | *Perspectives in Religious Studies* |
| RGG³ | *Die Religion in Geschichte und Gegenwart.* Edited by Kurt Galling. Tübingen: Mohr Siebeck, 1957–65. |
| SNTSMS | Society for New Testament Studies Monograph Series |
| Theol | *Theology: A Journal of Historic Christianity* |
| ThLZ | *Theologische Literaturzeitung* |
| ThPh | *Theologie und Philosophie* |
| TQ | *Theologische Quartalschrift* |
| ThR | *Theologische Rundschau* |
| TWNT | *Theologisches Wörterbuch zum Neuen Testament.* Edited by Gerhard Kittel and Gerhard Friedrich. Stuttgart: W. Kohlhammer, 1932–79. |
| WA | *D. Martin Luthers Werke. Weimarer kritische Ausgabe.* 120 vols. 1883–2009. |
| WATR | *D. Martin Luthers Tischreden.* 6 vols. |
| WMANT | Wissenschaftliche Monographien zum Alten und Neuen Testament |
| ZKhT | *Zeitschrift für katholische Theologie* |
| ZNW | *Zeitschrift für die neutestamentliche Wissenschaft* |
| ZThK | *Zeitschrift für Theologie und Kirche* |

# 1

# Incarnation

## *The Myth of God Incarnate*

## 1. The Myth Debate

In July 1977 a relatively slim volume appeared in England under the title *The Myth of God Incarnate*. It was published, after three years of discussion, by a group of seven theologians from various denominations under the direction of John Hick.[1] The book triggered a shock wave. The first edition was already sold out before the release date. Over thirty thousand copies were sold within the first eight months. It gave rise to the stormiest discussion in ecclesiastical and theological circles since the publication of J. A. T. Robinson's book *Honest to God* fifteen years earlier. Conservative evangelical circles made just as little secret of their unanimous rejection of the ideas it set forth as did neoorthodox Roman Catholic theologians—who invoked Barth—or their even more traditionally minded Anglican cousins. The Church of England Evangelical Council called on the five Anglican authors to resign from their positions within the church. In the press, letters to the editor questioned whether the five could even be considered Christians. The book ignited a public

---

Some material in this chapter appears in a slightly different form in I. U. Dalferth, "Der Mythos vom inkarnierten Gott und das Thema der Christologie," *ZThK* 84 (1987): 320–44.

1. J. Hick, ed., *The Myth of God Incarnate* (London: SCM, 1977).

scandal. A few short weeks later an apparently very hastily written rebuttal edited by Michael Green and titled *The Truth of God Incarnate* was rushed onto the market.[2] A heated theological debate ensued, which precipitated an avalanche of literature.[3] What was the furor about?

In the first keynote chapter of the *Myth* book, Oxford patristic scholar Maurice Wiles formulated the problem as follows: "Could there be a Christianity without . . . incarnation?" or—to phrase it a little more precisely—without the belief that "Jesus of Nazareth is unique in the precise sense that, while being fully man, it is true of him, and of him alone, that he is also fully God, the Second Person of the coequal Trinity"?[4]

One might be tempted to reject this question as self-contradictory and therefore meaningless. Isn't belief in Jesus Christ by definition belief that the Second Person of the Trinity has taken human form? But this semantic gambit—fairly popular among theologians—doesn't yield us any progress if Christianity can exist, or indeed has existed, without it. Admittedly, we could insist that any such faith is not worthy of the name "Christianity," that we have here a heresy, a faith that is no longer—or, it might rather be said, not yet—Christianity. However, in order to arrive at such a judgment, it is theological arguments of substance that are called for, rather than semantic assertions. For the point at issue is no longer simply whether a supposedly

2. M. Green, ed., *The Truth of God Incarnate* (London: Hodder, 1977).

3. G. M. Newlands's literary review of *The Myth of God Incarnate* (*New Studies in Theology* 1 [1980]: 181–92) provides an overview of initial reactions. The most important contributions to the debate can be found in the following journals: *Modern Churchman*, *New Blackfriars*, *Religious Studies*, *Theology*, and *Modern Theology*. From among the countless books on the subject, I cite here in particular N. Anderson, *The Mystery of the Incarnation* (London: Hodder & Stoughton, 1978); D. Cupitt, *The Debate about Christ* (London: SCM, 1979); Cupitt, *Taking Leave of God* (London: SCM, 1980); Cupitt, *The World to Come* (London: Trinity, 1982); S. T. Davis, *Logic and the Nature of God* (London: Trinity, 1983), chap. 8; M. Goulder, ed., *Incarnation and Myth: The Debate Continued* (London: SCM, 1979); M. Goulder and J. Hick, *Why Believe In God?* (London: SCM, 1983); C. E. Gunton, *Yesterday and Today: A Study of Continuities in Christology* (London: SPCK, 1983); A. E. Harvey, ed., *God Incarnate: Story and Belief* (London: SPCK, 1981); R. T. Herbert, *Paradox and Identity in Theology* (Ithaca, NY: Cornell University Press, 1979); J. Hick, *God Has Many Names* (London: Macmillan, 1980); Hick, *The Metaphor of God Incarnate: Christology in a Pluralistic Age* (Louisville: Westminster, 1994); W. J. Hollenweger, *Umgang mit Mythen*, Interkulturelle Theologie 2 (Munich: Christian Kaiser, 1982); J. P. Mackey, *Jesus the Man and the Myth: A Contemporary Christology* (London: SCM, 1979); T. V. Morris, *The Logic of God Incarnate* (Ithaca, NY: Cornell University Press, 1986); S. M. Ogden, *The Point of Christology* (London: SCM, 1982); T. F. Torrance, ed., *The Incarnation: Ecumenical Studies in the Nicene-Constantinopolitan Creed A.D. 381* (Edinburgh: Handsel, 1981); K. Ward, *Holding Fast to God: A Reply to Don Cupitt* (London: SPCK, 1983); M. Wiles, *Faith and the Mystery of God* (London: SCM, 1982).

4. M. Wiles, "Christianity without Incarnation?," in *Myth of God Incarnate*, ed. Hick, 1–10, esp. 1.

Christian tenet, or one that calls itself Christian, falls within a predefined concept of what is Christian. The point at issue is rather our very concept of what is Christian, in other words, our understanding of what is essentially Christian. So we can rephrase Wiles's question thus: Does belief in the incarnation belong to the essence of Christianity? If so, then Christianity cannot exist without this tenet. But if Christianity can exist without it, then belief in the incarnation is not an essential constituent of Christianity. Precisely this thesis is put forward, using various arguments, by Wiles and the other authors of the *Myth* book: belief in Jesus Christ is not necessarily belief in the incarnation; Christology (the theological self-interpretation of belief in Jesus Christ) is therefore not necessarily incarnational Christology.

There is nothing new in that. Years before the *Myth* book was published, Wolfhart Pannenberg had stated, "In contrast to classical incarnational Christology, which took the idea of incarnation as its starting point and assigned the incarnation process a place in the sequence of factors for discussion, a practice of starting from the historical figure of the human Jesus of Nazareth seems to be gaining increasing acceptance today."[5] The outcry that greeted the thesis put forward by the *Myth* authors can therefore be correctly understood only against the background of the previous 150 years of Anglican theology. Since the Oxford Movement for restoration in the middle of the nineteenth century had focused Anglican spirituality and theology so rigorously on the mystery of the incarnation, the concept of incarnation had become something of a neo-Anglican "shibboleth, exempt from reasoned scrutiny and treated with unquestioning literalness."[6] Across the entire theological spectrum there was an environmental shift to a "religion of incarnation,"[7] with the concept of incarnation as the all-encompassing paradigm of theological thinking. This paradigm has four main structural elements:

1. The doctrine of the incarnation, as the most concentrated expression of the gospel, holds the dominant theological position among the articles of Christology.[8] In that God's Son, the Second Person of the Trinity, entered our human existence, God took on himself the human condition in such a

5. W. Pannenberg, "Christologie und Theologie," in *Grundfragen systematischer Theologie: Gesammelte Aufsätze* (Göttingen: Vandenhoeck & Ruprecht, 1980), 2:129–45, esp. 2:130–31.
6. Hick, *Myth of God Incarnate*, ix.
7. This was the subtitle of the influential *Lux Mundi* anthology edited by C. Gore: *A Series of Studies in the Religion of the Incarnation* (London: John Murray, 1889). Cf. R. Morgan, ed., *The Religion of the Incarnation: Anglican Essays in Commemoration of Lux Mundi* (n.p.: Bristol Classical Press, 1989).
8. Cf. R. J. Wilberforce, *The Doctrine of the Incarnation of Our Lord Jesus Christ* (London: John Murray, ³1850).

way that we humans are now in touch with God through the human nature
of Jesus Christ. It is therefore not the cross and the resurrection but the fact
that Christ became human that is the decisive soteriological message of the
Christian faith.

2. This has ecclesiological consequences. The incarnation is not simply a
past event, but "Christ is continuously incarnated in his church."[9] If Jesus
of Nazareth was the locus of God's becoming human, then the church is
the locus for the continuous presence of the incarnate one. It becomes this
locus by virtue of being a sacramental system, within which believers are
incorporated into the mystical body of Christ through the sacraments, the
instruments whereby grace is appropriated. "To be united with the church
and to be united with Christ are therefore identical processes."[10]

3. In the course of the debate with Darwinism, this incarnational-sac-
ramental approach was expanded, by the *Lux Mundi* group in particular,[11]
into a theology of creation immanentism.[12] The incarnation is not only the
foundation of the church; it is also the key to understanding the world. God
is to be sought in the world, not above the world. As the incarnate Logos
he is at work in the whole of creation, in nature as well as in human culture
and science. Contemporary phenomena such as socialism and the theory of
evolution are therefore to be viewed as allies, not opponents, of the Christian
faith, so that, in the light of the incarnational concept, there will eventu-
ally be a relationship of unbroken harmony between modern culture and
Christian faith.

4. If we had accentuated God instead of the world in this relationship of
immanence, then, taking the same premises as our starting point, we could
have arrived at propositions concerning the doctrine of God that would take
aspects of the Christian tradition that had hovered at the edges thus far and
draw them into a central position. This becomes evident especially in the Anglican theology of the suffering of God,[13] out of which there emerged a series
of significant works in the period during and after the First World War, and

9. F. Oakley, "Sacramental Confession," *The British Critic* 33 (1843): 314–15, quoted in
G. Gaßmann, "Die Lehrentwicklung im Anglikanismus: Von Heinrich VIII. bis zu William
Temple," in *Handbuch der Dogmen- und Theologiegeschichte*, ed. C. Andresen, A. Ritter, and
G. Benrath (Göttingen: Vandenhoeck & Ruprecht, 1980–84), 2:353–409, esp. 2:398.

10. Gaßmann, "Lehrentwicklung," 398.

11. The group included C. Gore, E. S. Talbot, H. Scott Holland, J. R. Illingworth, and R. C.
Moberly.

12. Cf. J. R. Illingworth, *Divine Immanence: An Essay on the Spiritual Significance of Matter* (London: Macmillan, 1903).

13. J. Moltmann, *The Trinity and the Kingdom: The Doctrine of God* (Minneapolis: Fortress, 1993), 30–36.

which was later recalled to mind by Jürgen Moltmann.[14] This theology, too, is indissolubly linked with the basic incarnational approach. If Christ is God made man, then his earthly life provides insight into God's being. The suffering of the Son on the cross, which the church commemorates in the eucharistic offering, is to be understood as the temporal realization of that which is done by God the Father in eternity: he is a suffering God, who suffers with us, for us, and because of us, and who, by his loving commitment to the affairs of the world, transforms the process of evolution into a process of redemption.

These brief comments give sufficient indication that the concept of incarnation characterizes neo-Anglican Christology and equally its ecclesiology and its doctrines of creation and of God.[15] It constitutes the foundation of its entire theological system and is itself grounded on a belief in the incarnation that is held to be fundamental. Since the *Myth* authors' thesis takes precisely this foundation as its point of reference, they remain unaffected by theological matters of dispute, such as those that might come up for discussion under this paradigm. Rather, it argues openly for a theological paradigm shift that was certain to have a considerable effect on the theological self-understanding of the new Anglicanism. The frenzied and acrimonious tone of the debate is therefore hardly surprising. What is more surprising is that it was conducted in such an ill-defined and superficial manner and was very quickly pressured into apparent contradictions.

For academic theology in England, however, this debate did not come as a total surprise. For years there had been increasing signs that the center of the theological debate was beginning to shift away from the question of God toward Christology. Since the end of the 1960s, there had been certain milestones on this path, such as the publications of the Cambridge Christology Seminar[16] and Don Cupitt's Stanton Lectures of 1969, which expressly endeavored to initiate a philosophical debate on Christology and were published in 1971 under the title *Christ and the Hiddenness of God*.[17] Then in 1974 there appeared, under the title *The Remaking of Christian Doctrine*, Maurice Wiles's Hulsean Lectures, given in Cambridge the previous year. These set out,

14. G. C. Morgan, *The Bible and the Cross* (London: Fleming H. Revell, 1909); C. E. Rolt, *The World's Redemption* (London: Longmans, Green, 1913); G. A. Studdert Kennedy, *The Hardest Part* (London: Hodder & Stoughton, 1918); V. F. Storr, *The Problem of the Cross* (London: John Murray, 1919); J. K. Mozley, *The Impassibility of God: A Survey of Christian Thought* (Cambridge: Cambridge University Press, 1926).
15. Cf. L. B. Smedes's account in *The Incarnation: Trends in Modern Anglican Thought* (Kampen: J. H. Kok, 1953).
16. S. W. Sykes and J. P. Clayton, eds., *Christ, Faith and History* (Cambridge: Cambridge University Press, 1972).
17. D. Cupitt, *Christ and the Hiddenness of God* (London: SCM, 1971).

in view of the difficulty of achieving a truly viable historical knowledge of Jesus using the sources available to us, to conduct a fundamental inquiry into incarnational Christology.[18] In 1977 the publication of Geoffrey Lampe's *God as Spirit* completed the shift from criticism to constructive counterproposal.[19] On the basis of a rigorously developed Spirit Christology, Lampe decisively opposes the idea of the preexistence and postexistence of the person of Jesus Christ, thereby pulling the rug out from under the traditional doctrine of the incarnation. This doctrine, however, is not simply discarded but reinterpreted as a continuous incarnation of God the Spirit in the human spirit. There is no dispute that this, God's incarnate presence, is uniquely represented in Jesus Christ. But this unique expression comes about not by simple virtue of the incarnation but by virtue of the manner and quality of this incarnation. Put briefly, Lampe's attempt no longer sets out to unfold the doctrine of incarnation christologically; now it does so pneumatologically. It is no longer to be restricted to one locus within the field of Christology; instead, Lampe locates Christology, in its entirety, within the context of a comprehensive pneumatological concept of incarnation that thematizes the self-mediation of the Spirit of God with the human spirit. This means that, whatever theological objections may be raised against Lampe's attempt, the metaphysical[20] misunderstanding, at any rate—that the doctrine of the incarnation and its unfolding in the classical two-natures doctrine is a theory of the *persona privata* [private person] of Jesus Christ—is overcome. Jesus Christ may be treated as a theological topic only when viewed in his specific relationships with God and with human beings—never abstractly, as an individual regarded in isolation. It is through these relationships that he is what he is, and he can therefore never be considered as a christological topic apart from them.

    *The Origin of Christology*, a thoughtful and carefully argued book by Cambridge New Testament scholar emeritus Charles Moule that appeared in the same year as Lampe's work, demonstrates that the individualistic misunderstanding of Christology can be overcome in quite another way.[21] Against the thesis that Christology had, as it were, developed in an evolutionary manner, by mutation and selection, from simple New Testament beginnings to ever more advanced christological concepts, Moule tries to show that the formation of ecclesiastical Christology in the early centuries is to be understood not as an evolutionary development but rather as the gradual unfolding of

18. M. Wiles, *The Remaking of Christian Doctrine* (London: SCM, 1982).

19. G. Lampe, *God as Spirit* (Oxford: Oxford University Press, 1977).

20. Cf. Wiles, "Christianity without Incarnation?," 9.

21. C. F. D. Moule, *The Origin of Christology* (Cambridge: Cambridge University Press, 1977).

an idea, the nucleus of which had already been set out in the New Testament by Christ in his bodily form. From the outset, and not just during its later phases, Christology has been the doctrine of the *persona publica* [public role] of Jesus Christ—as formulated by Luther—and has thus had an intrinsically soteriological structure. Jesus Christ's connection with us is just as much a constituent of his nature as is his connection with God.

It was onto this scene of a growing struggle toward a rethinking of traditional christological positions that the provocatively marketed *Myth* book exploded. The manner in which the book was presented, calculated as it was for the greatest possible public effect, forced the issue into a crude and superficial polarization, as is suggested, for example, by the two titles quoted at the beginning of this chapter: *The Myth of God Incarnate* and *The Truth of God Incarnate*. Practically every word in these titles is unclear: after all, what is meant by "incarnation," what is meant by "myth," and what is meant by "truth"? Small wonder that its overall treatment in the ensuing debate continued to be confused and unsatisfactory. It would not be particularly profitable to trace the individual threads of the discussion. I will focus instead on a critical identification of the essential dogmatic problem that was the original *quaestio disputata* [issue at stake] of the debate, first of all by clarifying the point of the proposition put forward by the *Myth* authors, and second by discussing these arguments in the light of the central question regarding the nature of the subject matter of Christology.

## 2. Thesis and Counterthesis

Belief in Jesus Christ is not necessarily belief in the incarnation; Christology is therefore not necessarily incarnational Christology—that is the basic thesis of the *Myth* group. But this only appears unambiguous. Terms such as *incarnational belief* and *incarnational Christology* can be understood quite differently, as is indicated by the bases put forward by the *Myth* authors for their proposition. These can in essence be summed up as a fundamental-theological argument, a historical argument, an exegetical-hermeneutical argument, and a theological argument:

1. The *fundamental-theological argument* emphasizes that belief in Jesus Christ is not the same as believing and assenting to certain doctrinal and credal formulas. It is true that the Christian faith can only ever be confessed in a certain linguistic format, but the linguistic form of the confession is not what is believed: faith in Jesus Christ is not the same as assenting to certain credal formulas.

2. The *historical argument*[22] argues that Christology has *not always* been incarnational Christology. "Incarnation" is a theological concept formed in the second century that only gradually became the dominant concept of ecclesiastical Christology. It is therefore historically inadequate to equate Christology with incarnational Christology, incarnational belief with Christian belief, or even faith in Jesus Christ with assent to certain doctrinal formulations: faith in Jesus Christ is not necessarily belief in the incarnation of the Second Person of the Trinity.

3. The *exegetical-hermeneutical argument*[23] emphasizes that Christology is *never purely* incarnational Christology. In the New Testament you will already find numerous statements that focus less on the incarnation of God in Christ than on his cross, his resurrection, and his presence in his community, and that are therefore clearer early indications of an ascent or exaltation Christology than of a descent or incarnational Christology. Incarnational Christology can therefore at best be regarded as one of several models of christological speech and thought; there is no question of equating belief in the incarnation with Christian faith: faith in Jesus Christ need not necessarily be articulated using the incarnational model.

4. The *theological argument*[24] argues that the incarnational Christology that has become the standard paradigm since Nicaea and Chalcedon and was given its classic presentation by Athanasius has never been satisfactorily explicated theologically. The idea of a being who, because God has taken human form, is fully human and fully God, is deemed self-contradictory. Every attempt to demonstrate its consistency, such as the Cappadocians' doctrine of an- and enhypostasia and its assimilation into modern (Protestant) theology; assumptus, habitus, and subsistence theories of Scholastic theologies; or the kenosis theories of Lutheran and Anglican origin, has called into question either the humanity or the divinity or the unity of the person of Jesus Christ. Years earlier, Pannenberg had concluded for similar reasons: "The impasse reached by every attempt to construct Christology by beginning with the incarnational concept demonstrates that all such attempts are doomed to failure."[25] Instead of constant radical reinterpretations of traditional incarnational Christology, which permit the retention of the word *incarnation*

22. Cf. Wiles, "Christianity without Incarnation?," 1–3; F. Young, "A Cloud of Witnesses," in *Myth of God Incarnate*, ed. Hick, 13–47, esp. 23–30.

23. Cf. Young, "Cloud of Witnesses," 14–23.

24. Cf. J. Hick, "Jesus and the World Religions," in *Myth of God Incarnate*, ed. Hick, 167–85, esp. 177–78; Hick, "Is There a Doctrine of the Incarnation?," in *Incarnation and Myth*, ed. Goulder, 47–50.

25. W. Pannenberg, *Jesus–God and Man*, trans. L. L. Wilkins and D. A. Priebe (Philadelphia: Westminster Press, 1968), 334.

at best but not its traditional semantic content, is it not therefore more appropriate, as Wiles urges, to attempt a theological recasting of what it was that this doctrine once sought to formulate?[26] For if legitimate criticism of the terminology of traditional incarnational Christology is not to become a problematic criticism of the Christian faith itself, there must be theological insistence that faith in Jesus Christ cannot be equated with a belief in the Nicene doctrine of the incarnation.

None of the arguments put forward is convincing. Certainly there is no denying that faith in Jesus Christ is something other than belief in certain doctrinal or credal formulas; that it has also been articulated in ways other than in the incarnational model; that it did not first appear in the second century; and that its express identification as faith in the incarnation was relatively late. But the fact that faith in Jesus Christ is a practical life relationship that differs from a doxastic assent to certain doctrinal statements does not mean that it did not always have a certain doxastic component.[27] The fact that the concept of the incarnation did not dominate christological discourse from the outset does not mean that the subject matter that this concept sought to comprehend was not already present. Just because it is not purely in a context of incarnational Christology that Jesus Christ is spoken of does not, in itself, exclude the possibility that we are dealing here with the early stages of (with variations on or equivalents to) a discourse giving expression to an incarnational Christology that leads to a concept to which these give only rudimentary and approximate expression. And the fact that there is as yet no theologically satisfactory analysis of the early church doctrine of the incarnation certainly does not mean, even if we were to accept this wholesale judgment, that there could not be such an analysis, as long as the self-contradictory nature of this conceptual model remains unproven and its meaningful interpretation is thus not yet established as impossible.

The arguments presented remain so unconvincing because they adopt the key terms *incarnational belief* and *incarnational Christology* but then oscillate continuously between different subject matters, failing to distinguish between *incarnation event, concepts of incarnation, credal declarations of belief in the incarnation, doctrine of the incarnation,* and *theories of the incarnation.* But it is by no means irrelevant to the crux of the thesis under discussion whether (1) "incarnation" refers to the event of the incarnation of God in Jesus Christ, in other words, the event that is therefore the *subject matter* of

26. Wiles, "Christianity without Incarnation?," 6–10.
27. Cf. I. U. Dalferth, "Über Einheit und Vielfalt des christlichen Glaubens: Eine Problemskizze," in *Glaube,* ed. W. Härle and R. Preul, Marburger Jahrbuch Theologie 4 (Marburg: Elwert, 1992), 99–137.

all christological confessions and all christological reflection;[28] or whether
(2) it refers to one of the various *conceptual forms* by which Christians have
affirmed their faith and its subject matter; or whether (3) one of the various
*representational forms* of the christological subject matter by means of which
faith in Jesus Christ was articulated, in the New Testament implicitly, and
later explicitly, is in dispute; or whether (4) it refers to the doxology of the
incarnation and the Nicene and Chalcedonian *doctrine of the incarnation*
that was developed from it and sought to protect the New Testament confession of Christ and its ecclesiastical repetitions from misunderstandings and
misinterpretations by means of binding confessional statements; or, finally,
whether (5) it refers to one of the various theoretical theological attempts—by
no means always in accord with one another—to analyze the early church
doctrine of the incarnation conceptually and to examine it systematically. For
although all these points are connected, we must on no account reject them
all just because we call some of them critically into question. It is therefore
important to clarify the target of our criticism: Is it the claim that the incarnation event is the fundamental subject matter of Christology? Is it the
incarnational-christological conceptual and representational forms of the
christological subject matter? Is it the doxology and doctrine of the incarnation? Or is it a (theological) theory of the incarnation?

If one tries to state the *Myth* authors' thesis more precisely in the light
of these distinctions, then the nub of their criticism can be summarized in
four points:

1. The christological topic is not an incarnation event; rather, incarnational
   Christology is one of a number of different representational forms of
   the christological topic. Christians have indeed articulated this subject
   matter in terms of incarnation, but they also have used other images
   and representations so that it not only can be understood as incarnation
   but also can always be understood and defined in other ways.
2. The incarnational-christological form of representation is mythological
   in that it applies the mythical motif of the incarnation of a god to Jesus

28. I use the terms *subject matter* and *content* in the sense current in the discourse-analytic
extension of C. F. Hockett's distinction between "topic" and "comment" (*A Course in Modern
Linguistics* [New York: Prentice Hall, 1958], 201) on the theme-rheme structure of texts. When
we speak, we state what we are talking about (topic) and then say something about it (comment).
If we begin speaking of something else, we have changed the subject, even if we want to say the
same thing about it. It is in this sense that the question of the subject matter of Christology is
the question of what Christology must deal with when it speaks about Jesus Christ if it doesn't
want to deviate from its subject matter, and when it wants to speak of something else, even
when it still seems to be saying the same thing.

in order to interpret his significance for us in a poetic way.[29] Today this traditional confessional language lends obscurity rather than illumination to the subject matter of Christology.

3. Our manner of speaking of the incarnation event demonstrates this very thing. Such an event cannot be the subject of Christology, since it owes the hypothesis of such an event to a hermeneutical misunderstanding: the misleadingly realistic interpretation of the mythological confessional statements that articulate faith in Jesus Christ as belief that God took human form in Jesus Christ.

4. Incarnational Christology is the result of this incorrectly realistic interpretation of such confessional statements and has led to the dogmatic conception of Jesus Christ as God incarnate, which is now no longer apprehended as myth.

Thus the charge brought by the *Myth* authors is directed, not wholesale against *that which* the Christian faith articulates in its christological confessions, but against one specific *manner in which* it articulates it: the representation of its subject matter as an incarnation event and the incorrectly realistic misunderstanding of these mythological confessional statements as an incarnational Christology.

The countercriticism has reacted strongly, insisting—as, for instance, in *The Truth of God Incarnate*—that the incarnation event is the indispensable christological theme: it is the central topic that must be dealt with by any Christology that does not want to miss its target. For those who argue thus, the charge brought by the *Myth* authors must inevitably be directed not merely against a specific conceptual and representational form of the christological topic but against the topic itself: *it is in fact what* the christological confessions articulate, and not simply *how* it is articulated, that is criticized as mythical.

Thesis and counterthesis appear to be mutually exclusive: *Is the incarnation event the fundamental subject matter of christological statements, or is incarnational Christology just one way—and a misleading way at that—of articulating the christological subject matter?* Is the incarnational concept therefore an indispensable theological representational form of the christological subject matter, or is it merely one such form, and one better avoided, at that? That is the question. It can be answered, and the theological position of incarnational Christology can thus be properly judged, only once there is clarity regarding the subject matter of Christology: With what are the christological confessions concerned, and with what, accordingly, must Christology

29. Hick, *Myth of God Incarnate*, ix.

concern itself in order to interpret the confessions of faith in Jesus Christ properly? We will now move on to examine this second question.

## 3. The Question of the Christological Subject Matter

"Ultimately Christology is no more than the exposition of the confession that 'Jesus is the Christ.'"[30] This sentence by Walter Kasper concerns the subject matter of Christology. It implies that all christological confessions, however different their individual content, converge thematically in the confession that Jesus is the Christ, which in turn finds its most appropriate and most fruitful expression in the "confession of Jesus as the Son of God," so that it can be said that "*Christian faith stands or falls with the confession of Jesus as the Son of God.*"[31]

But in the face of such a considerable difference in content, is the implication of an even greater thematic convergence justified, given the factual diversity of christological confessions? Don Cupitt in particular,[32] as one of the *Myth* authors, continually points out that it is by no means clear that confessions such as "Jesus is Lord," "Jesus is the Christ," "Jesus is the Savior," or "Jesus is the Son of God" can be understood as superficial variations of an identical fundamental christological theme. The implications are too various, the assumptions are too different, and the force of these confessions too divergent. One can confess Jesus as Lord and Savior without having to confess him as the Son of God. And one can confess him as the Son of God—as in *2 Clement* (1.1)—in order to emphasize the unity of God and Jesus, or conversely—as in the Pseudo-Clementine homilies from the third century (16.15)—to accentuate the difference between God and Jesus and to reject any incarnational-christological interpretation of this creed as heretical. Given these differences, one cannot simply take a broad-brush approach; rather, it must first be proven that the multiplicity of christological confessions can be traced back to a single underlying thematic structure, of which the confession that Jesus is the Christ is a typical example, and which culminates in the confession of Jesus as the Son of God. For the question is whether and to what extent the christological confessions all say *the same thing*. Here we are not considering whether their content is identical, since the statements "Jesus is Lord" and

30. W. Kasper, *Jesus the Christ* (London: Burns & Oates, 1976), 37.
31. Ibid., 163.
32. D. Cupitt, "Professor Stanton on Incarnational Language in the New Testament," in *Incarnation and Myth*, ed. Goulder, 166–69; Cupitt, "The Debate about Christ," in *Incarnation and Myth*, ed. Goulder, chap. 1.

"Jesus is the Son of God" are manifestly different in content. Rather, we are considering the *identity of their subject matter*: Are they all even speaking *about the same thing*?

John Hick—to pick him out as one example—disputes this. According to him, incarnational Christology itself is due to a momentous thematic change in christological confessions: the change from *reference to Jesus of Nazareth* to *reference to the Logos or Son of God* as the actual subject of christological predications. As "Christian theology grew through the centuries it made the very significant transition from 'Son of God' to 'God the Son,' the Second Person of the Trinity."[33] This step was significant because the transition from "Jesus is God's son" to "Jesus is God the Son" implied a *change of reference*. According to Hick, "Jesus is God's son" is a metaphorical statement about Jesus of Nazareth, while he interprets "Jesus is God the Son" as a metaphysical statement about God the Son. He explains this transition as a misguided attempt to place a metaphysical interpretation on a metaphor functioning as religious myth, thus understanding it no longer as a metaphorical statement about a figure within our historical, empirical reality but as a descriptive statement about a being from a transempirical reality.

Hick's argumentation is revealing in many respects. For one thing, it is based on a widespread but problematic structural analysis of christological confessions. For another, it connects this with a proper but no less problematic conception of myth. Let us give more-careful consideration to both points.

## 4. The Structure of Christological Confessions

The confession "Jesus is the Son of God" may be analyzed in different ways, depending on our interpretation of the little word *is*. Hick himself discerns four possible interpretations: as the "is" of *predication* ("Jesus is obedient"), of *class membership* ("Jesus is a human being"), of *definition* ("A human is a rational living being"), or of *identity* ("Jesus is the eldest son of Mary").[34] Of these possibilities the definition and class-membership interpretations are hardly worth serious consideration. The first does not claim to be an affirmation of truth; it simply provides information about how the confessing person wishes the word *Jesus* to be understood. In the second, on the other hand, a confessional statement would need to take the form "Jesus is a son

33. Hick, "Jesus and the World Religions," 175; cf. D. Cupitt, "Jesus and the Meaning of 'God,'" in *Incarnation and Myth*, ed. Goulder, 31–40, esp. 33, 37.

34. J. Hick, "Christ and Incarnation," in *God and the Universe of Faiths: Essays in the Philosophy of Religion* (London: Macmillan, 1973), 148–64, esp. 154.

of God" or "Jesus is Son of God." But this would be inconsistent with the factor of the uniqueness of Jesus Christ, which the christological confession expressly emphasizes by using the definite article.

Both the main analyses employed, either implicitly or explicitly, by the *Myth* authors thus attempt to understand the confession "Jesus is the Son of God" as a version of a statement of *identity* or of *predication*. The *Myth* authors are united in their premise that "Jesus" is the name of an actual historical figure, whereas the phrase "the Son of God" is not a name but a description or title.[35] In other words, "Jesus" is the name of a Jew who lived in Palestine at the beginning of the Christian era, was baptized by John, and was active for several years as a teacher, rabbi, and miracle worker in Galilee and as far as Jerusalem, where he was crucified. This Jesus is a historical figure whose story is known, at least in outline, although the historian is faced with considerable difficulties when he seeks to sketch a portrait of this Jesus on the basis of the material available to us in the New Testament. But none of the above applies to the expression "the Son of God." This is a description or a title, not a name. What it articulates is not something that could conceivably become the subject of historical research. The difficulties involved are not, as in the case of Jesus, purely factual but are of a fundamental nature, since the historian is not in a position to give an informed view concerning the Son of God.[36] What then, on these premises, is the significance of analyzing the confession "Jesus is God's son" as a statement of identity or of predication? Hick himself pursued two different analytical approaches in different phases of his thought, and I will briefly examine each of these in more detail.

### 4.1. Identity Analyses

If we understand "Jesus is the Son of God" *as a statement of identity*, then the expressions "Jesus" and "the Son of God" refer to the same individual. But whichever of the three possible ways of logically structuring this confessional statement is adopted, this understanding results in considerable theological difficulties:

1. If "Jesus" refers to the historical figure of the man Jesus of Nazareth, then, given this premise, "the Son of God" cannot possibly refer to anyone or anything other than this man. This analysis is surely unacceptable from a Christian point of view.

35. Cf. Cupitt, "Jesus and the Meaning of 'God,'" 31–40.
36. Cf. D. Cupitt, "One Jesus, Many Christs?," in *Christ, Faith and History*, ed. Sykes and Clayton, 131–44; Cupitt, *Debate about Christ*, chap. 8.

2. If, however, we come from the opposite direction and say that "the Son of God" here refers to the Logos, the Second Person of the Trinity, then "Jesus" cannot possibly refer to anyone or anything other than this Logos, and we arrive at an understanding no less unacceptable from a Christian point of view.

3. The orthodox teaching of the early church therefore insisted that "Jesus" refers to a very specific person and that "the Son of God" refers to the divine Logos. It was therefore compelled to identify the person of Jesus with the divine Logos and thus to regard the unity of the transhistorical Logos with the historical Jesus as free from contradiction. The various attempts to achieve this within the thought context of the time are not examined here. These attempts were always unacceptable, that is to say heretical, if either the full divinity of the Logos or the full humanity of Jesus was not assured, or—as with the charge leveled against the Nestorians—if it was thought that the Logos and Jesus neither shared nor could share an identity but rather that they remained juxtaposed.

But what kind of identity ought to be attributed to the unity between the Logos and Jesus so as to avoid such deficiencies? In an essay written in 1966, Hick considers two possibilities: *qualitative identity* and *numerical identity*. According to Hick, one could speak of qualitative identity if Jesus's agape toward his fellow human beings corresponded qualitatively to God's agape toward them. But such a qualitative correspondence is always a matter of degree of approximation. If one seeks to think of the incarnation in terms of this identity model, there is a blurring of the distinction between incarnation and inspiration, and one arrives at best, according to Hick, at a "Degree Christology," which cannot do justice to the uniqueness of the incarnation of divine agape in Jesus. It is therefore necessary to speak, in the Nicene and Chalcedonian sense, not only of a qualitative but also of a numerical identity.[37]

However, the principle of identity first formulated precisely by Leibniz asserts that two objects can be numerically identical only if each possesses all the attributes of the other, so that everything that can truly be said of the one is also true of the other and vice versa. But this clearly leads to difficulties in the above instance. We read in Luke 19:41 that Jesus wept at the sight of Jerusalem; this could not be said, however, of the eternal Logos, a point that led, according to Bishop Epiphanius, to the Orthodox Church erasing this sentence summarily from the Gospel. Again, whereas Jesus died, this by

37. Hick, "Christ and Incarnation," 156–57.

definition could not be said of the immortal Logos. Not until the advent of high Lutheranism was anyone bold enough to gaze at the cross and state, "God himself is dead."[38] This was why the Chalcedonian dogma insisted that both groups of attributes, the divine and the human, are properties of Jesus Christ "without confusion and without change," "without division and without separation." But this requires the conjunction of both groups of attributes, which by no means satisfies the Leibniz law. For Jesus must be held to be *totus deus* [fully divine] but not to be *totum Dei* [the whole of God]. The doctrine of the *communicatio idiomatum* [communication of properties] therefore tried to govern how and under what conditions the divine attributes of Jesus and the human attributes of the Logos may be stated without descending into total contradiction. Given the complicated nature of the resulting doctrinal statements, it is not surprising that there was an attempt to counter this somewhat epicyclic theory with a simpler concept that promised to resolve this problem more appropriately.

Two possible ways of doing this suggest themselves. One can stay with the analysis of the confession as a statement of identity, while clarifying the concept of identity in such a way that it can do justice to the differences that must be taken into account. Or one can seek to analyze the confession differently so as to avoid the difficulties encountered from the outset.

The first route is feasible only if one tries to conceive of the numerical identity between Jesus and the Logos other than according to the Leibniz law. This is because the law defines the concept of identity so specifically that there can be no relationship of identity between individuals at all. Only concepts are what they are, and nothing else; it is therefore only between concepts that there is sufficiently complete correspondence between their attribute groups for a relationship of identity to exist. The identity sentence formulated by Leibniz is thus a statement of the fundamental nonidentity of individuals, so that the concept of the numerical identity of individuals must be construed in some other way. But how?

Hick attempted this in 1966 by distinguishing three concepts of numerical identity: the concept of self-identity, the concept of identity through change over time, and the concept of identity through continuity or inclusion.[39] The

38. J. Rist, "O Traurigkeit, o Herzeleid" (1641), second stanza: "O grosse Not! / Gott selbst liegt tot. / Am Kreuz ist er gestorben; / hat dadurch das Himmelreich / uns aus Lieb erworben." Cf. E. Jüngel, "Das dunkle Wort vom 'Tode Gottes,'" in *Von Zeit zu Zeit* (Munich: Christian Kaiser, 1976), 15–63; Jüngel, *God as the Mystery of the World: On the Foundation of the Theology of the Crucified One in the Dispute between Theism and Atheism*, trans. D. L. Guder (Grand Rapids: Eerdmans, 1983), 63–100.

39. Hick, "Christ and Incarnation," 159–60.

first concept is logically trivial, since it brings the minimal reflexivity structure to the concept, such that if it is valid at all, it is valid for all. The second concept, on the other hand, transforms the problem of identity into a problem of identification, in that it formulates it as a question of identifiability and reidentifiability of the same object in different situations. Neither concept is particularly helpful for the problem under discussion. Hick therefore argues in favor of the third concept, that of *continuity*, which he interprets in the sense of the relation between part and whole, to explicate the relationship of identity between Jesus and the Logos.

Within the context of substance thinking, this is theologically comparatively unconvincing. Jesus Christ is recognized to be *totus deus* and not just a part of the divine substance. In seeking to explain this identity, Hick therefore tries to conceive of the relationship as "continuity of event" rather than a "continuity of entity"[40] and to replace the concept of *homoousia* with the concept of *homoagape*:[41] Jesus's agape is said to have been the continuation of the divine agape on earth, while he himself was the phenomenal correlation of a noumenal divine activity.[42] For—and this is how he illustrates the idea—just as the sun and its rays, as they warm the earth, constitute one single complex context, so God's love and Jesus's love constitute one single complex context, so that one can say, "Jesus was God's attitude to mankind incarnate."[43]

The problem with this attempt is that it once again reduces the concept of numerical identity to one of qualitative identity. For how should we conceive of such a continuity of context between noumenal divine love and phenomenal human love? Hick himself tries to explain it as the identity of a "moral pattern," which can be said to constitute numerical identity because a "direct causal connection," a causal continuity of event, has existed between them.[44] So instead of "incarnation" he uses a term borrowed from H. H. Farmer and speaks of "inhistorization,"[45] the finite mode of action of the infinite divine love.[46] Jesus is said to be fully and only human; but the love that determined the conduct of his life was God's love.[47]

40. Ibid., 160.
41. Ibid., 164.
42. Ibid., 162.
43. Ibid., 163.
44. Ibid., 162.
45. Ibid., 152.
46. Ibid., 159.
47. Ibid., 163. Similarly also E. Jüngel, "Zur dogmatischen Bedeutung der Frage nach dem historischen Jesus," in *Wertlose Wahrheit: Zur Identität und Relevanz des christlichen Glaubens*, Theologische Erörterungen 3 (Tübingen: Mohr Siebeck, 1990), 214–42, esp. 235–36n55.

The relationship of identity between the Logos and Jesus is thus construed by Hick as a "continuity-of-agapéing,"[48] with a clear accent on the "moral pattern" of the morality of love. However, his eventual conclusion was that this explained little more than the old terminology did. His suggestion that the word *homoagape* should be used in place of *homoousia* has, at best, the following to recommend it: no one knew exactly what was meant by *ousia* in this context, whereas at least everyone had a rough idea of the meaning of "agape."

It is unsurprising that in subsequent years he moved away from this interpretation to an increasing degree. Characteristically, the accent on the morality of love was retained, but he took the second of the two routes described above to resolve the problem: a logical analysis of the confession "Jesus is the Son of God" as *predication*.

### 4.2. Predication Analyses

If we analyze this confession as a *predication* rather than as a statement of identity, then we admittedly avoid the problems of interpretation raised by the concept of identity, but we exchange these for other difficulties. We must now ask what the subject of this predication is, and what exactly is predicated. There are two different possibilities.

1. If *Jesus* is the subject of the predication, then he is being said to be the Son of God, who therefore possesses all the attributes that are encapsulated in the Son-of-God predicate—however this is understood. If this is the case, the question of whether these attributes are correctly ascribed to Jesus is unavoidable. This question cannot be decided without examining whether Jesus of Nazareth actually demonstrated and possessed these attributes, and whether it was only he who possessed them and was capable of possessing them. Herein lies one of the principal motifs for the intensive research into the life of Jesus in the nineteenth century and for the revival of the kenotic Christologies within Lutheran and Anglican theology in the past hundred years and in the present.

2. One could, on the other hand, analyze the predication under discussion from the opposite angle, in the sense that "the Son of God" is "Jesus." In that case, it is not Jesus but the Son of God (i.e., "Son of God" according to the understanding of the term in classical incarnational Christology), the Logos, the Second Person of the Trinity, who is the subject and of

48. Hick, "Christ and Incarnation," 164.

whom it is said that he is Jesus of Nazareth. This analysis imposes, as it were, another subject on the life story of Jesus of Nazareth, with the result that this life story becomes the predicate of a divine person. If carried to the extreme we would be left not only with the problem of Monophysitism but also with the docetic heresy, according to which the Second Person of the Trinity took human form and a human life story, but only temporarily. But even the orthodox solution, as presented to us in the doctrine of an- and enhypostasia, leaves open the question of whether the full individual humanity of Jesus remains assured. For if what constitutes the person of Jesus is the Logos, the Second Person of the Trinity, so that Jesus is not a self-individuating human subject, then it is not surprising "that Christologies designed around the theme of incarnation have never ever led to the historical and concrete humanity of Jesus of Nazareth."[49]

Both of these ways of construing the confession "Jesus is the Son of God" as a predication lead merely to a theologically superficial antithesis of Christologies "from above" and "from below" and thus remain unsatisfactory. If "Jesus is the Son of God" cannot be satisfactorily understood either as a statement of identity or as a predication, how is this confession to be construed? Hick tries to characterize it as a special nondescriptive predication by arguing that "it is a basic metaphor functioning as religious myth."[50] This brings me to my second point.

## 5. The Mythological Character of Christological Confessions

Hick's thesis conveys a characteristic understanding of the relationship between myth, metaphor, and metaphysics.[51] This understanding is supported initially by the fact that, in contrast to the position implied by the title of the rebuttal, *The Truth of God Incarnate*, it does not simply play off myth

49. Pannenberg, "Christologie und Theologie," 134.
50. Hick, "Is There a Doctrine of the Incarnation?," 47–50, esp. 49.
51. J. Hick, "Incarnation and Mythology," in *God and the Universe of Faiths*, 165–79. Neither he nor the other authors of the *Myth* book distinguish between "mythical" and "mythological," or between "myth" and "mythical/mythological discourse," since they are interested—as so often in theological debates of this sort—not in myth but in Christology. This, together with a complete disregard of recent myth research, is a particularly unsatisfactory and much-criticized aspect of this debate (cf. M. Wiles, "A Survey of Issues in the Myth Debate," in *Incarnation and Myth*, ed. Goulder, 1–12, esp. 3). However, since this group of problems would require separate consideration that would not help to resolve the point at issue here, no special terminological significance will be attached to the above distinctions in what follows.

against truth as its antithesis. To write off mythical discourse as plainly untrue is not only to hold a simplistic concept of truth; it is to postulate a naïve
polarization between descriptive discourse as the only "true" discourse, and
all other forms of discourse, which may be presumed to be "untrue." But to
take the polarization between myth and truth as the starting point for one's
treatment of mythical or mythological discourse is to forgo from the outset
the possibility of a positive interpretation of the latter.

This is precisely what Hick seeks to do. But he too proceeds on the basis
of far too simple a distinction. When he speaks of the "truth of the myth,"
he means "a kind of practical truth consisting in the appropriateness of the
attitude to its object."[52] According to him, myths are intended "to express a
valuation and evoke an attitude,"[53] so they "express a commitment, or make
a value-judgment"[54] and are "not literally true."[55] He therefore defines myth
as "a story which is told but which is not literally true, or an idea or image
which is applied to someone or something but which does not literally apply,
but which invites a particular attitude in its hearers."[56] The "practical truth"
of the myth is thus reduced to the pragmatic function of prompting its hearers
to adopt an appropriate attitude to the subject of the myth. But the pragmatic
and semantic dimensions of the myth cannot be played off against each other
in this way. If the semantic dimension of the myth embodies no truth, then how
can any attitude prompted and evoked by the myth be considered appropriate?

Hick is more cautious when he suggests that mythological discourse is
metaphorical and not descriptive. It does not describe an empirical story,
subject, or person in an unusual way, and neither does it describe an unusual
nonempirical story, subject, or person. The relationship between theme and
content in such discourse (in other words, what it speaks about, and what is
said about it) is thus not a relationship in which an individual case is subsumed
under a set of general concepts; rather, it is a hermeneutical relationship
between *interpretandum* (that which is to be interpreted) and *interpretans*
(that which interprets it): this type of discourse conveys the significance of a
story, a subject, or a person and their relevance for us, and it expresses their
"meaning for us." This is what gives it its metaphorical quality. But this means
that discourse concerning the incarnate God is mythological in precisely the
following sense: it applies the universal mythical incarnation motif to Jesus,
not in order to describe or characterize him, but as a way of "expressing his

52. Hick, "Jesus and the World Religions," 178.
53. Ibid.
54. Ibid., 177.
55. Ibid., 178.
56. Ibid.

significance for us."[57] "Jesus is God's son" is not a statement about Jesus that could be true or false; it is a metaphor that uses a mythical concept in order to declare "his significance to the world": "He is the one in following whom we have found ourselves in God's presence and have found God's meaning for our lives."[58] This "basic religious metaphor"[59] is the subject of a metaphysical misunderstanding when it is perceived no longer as a metaphorical expression of Jesus's significance for us but rather as a descriptive statement concerning Jesus of Nazareth. According to Hick, this is just what has happened to incarnational Christology, which failed to understand the metaphorical nature of the confessional statement "Jesus is the Son of God" and interpreted it as a realistic and descriptive assertion of Jesus's divine sonship. Hick concludes that, as a result of this failure to grasp the hermeneutical internal structure of the confession, "the centuries-long attempt of Christian orthodoxy to turn the metaphor into metaphysics was a cul-de-sac. For the metaphor has always evaded the attempts to convert it into a coherent theory or hypothesis."[60]

The basic problem with Hick's analysis is its starting point: he characterizes "Jesus is the Son of God" as a metaphor because he uses a mythical concept for the historical figure of Jesus of Nazareth in order to express his meaning for us. This is a double misidentification: For one thing, this confession is not concerned merely with the tangible, historical Jesus of Nazareth, which is what Hick is clearly implying. For another, it is concerned with his *soteriological* significance, not with any significance he has for us. Hick perceives this in the fact that he is "our sufficient model of true humanity in a perfect relationship to God."[61] To emulate this model is our path to salvation. In contrast, however, we must here insist on the theological position that Jesus Christ is not merely the example but is above all the sacrament of our salvation.[62] We do not obtain salvation by emulating a model, even when the model is Jesus of Nazareth; we obtain it through justification by faith alone. Hick's Pelagianizing soteriology is the obverse of his inadequate Christology, which in turn is the direct implication of his unsatisfactory analysis of christological confessions. The only reason these confessions have soteriological significance is that they do not speak merely of Jesus of Nazareth; they speak of the *Jesus Christ who was raised from the dead by God*. "Jesus is the Son of God" is not a metaphor

57. Hick, *Myth of God Incarnate*, ix.
58. Hick, "Jesus and the World Religions," 178.
59. Hick, "Is There a Doctrine of the Incarnation?," 48.
60. Ibid., 48–49.
61. Hick, "Jesus and the World Religions," 178.
62. Cf. Wiles, "Christianity without Incarnation?," 8–9; E. Jüngel, "Das Opfer Jesu Christi als sacramentum et exemplum: Was bedeutet das Opfer Christi für den Beitrag der Kirchen zur Lebensbewältigung und Lebensgestaltung?," in *Wertlose Wahrheit*, 261–82.

because a mythological predicate is here being applied to a Jew who belongs to the distant past; rather, it is a metaphor because it attempts to speak of the one who has been crucified and raised in such a way that he is presented as the living one who is constantly present. Jesus Christ has soteriological relevance for us solely because he mediates our relationship with God *in the present*. So the principal flaw in Hick's analysis is that he equates the Christ to whom the christological confessions refer with the historical figure of the man Jesus of Nazareth. His underestimation of their theological reference thus causes him to deviate from their confessional character at the decisive point.

A further consideration leads inevitably to the same verdict. There can be no doubt that Hick's attempt to analyze "Jesus is the Son of God" as a basic metaphor functioning as religious myth emphasizes an important aspect of confessions: the confessing persons themselves are involved in the confession, in that they are articulating a commitment to action, as distinguished from statements or declarations. Anyone who "makes a confession of faith makes it known that he intends to act in a particular way and that he is prepared to render account for his actions in the light of his confession."[63] Given that confessions do not merely state a fact but express something that has validity for the confessing persons, they can be described, as they are by Hick, as articulations of value judgments and commitments to action.[64] But one cannot, as he does, declare this to be their single or decisive property and then pit the practical against the literal truth of the confession. Those who confess that "Jesus is the Son of God" are not merely declaring their commitment to action—to follow Jesus in keeping the double commandment of love, for example. Rather, they are indicating that they are committed to this course of action because they hold a specific belief, namely, that Jesus is the Son of God. The propositional and performative dimensions of the confession are indissolubly linked. The confessing person proclaims Jesus to be the one he truly *is*. It is not just one view of Jesus that he seeks to express; it is the *true* view, of which others ought to be convinced (evidence) and with which they should be able to agree (consensus), since it is not merely his private opinion but represents Jesus Christ's own being (correspondence). Whether the confession "Jesus is the Son of God" is both true and capable of attracting consensus depends on two things: (1) the appropriateness of the confessional *content* of the predicate "the Son of God" and, most importantly, (2) the correct understanding of the confessional *topic* "Jesus."

63. H. Kraml, *Die Rede von Gott sprachkritisch rekonstruiert aus Sentenzenkommentaren* (Innsbruck: Tyrolia, 1984), 142.
64. Hick, "Jesus and the World Religions," 177–79.

## 6. The Topic of Christological Confessions

The outlined analyses of the confession as a statement of identity and as a predication imply that "Jesus" refers to the Jesus of Nazareth who once lived on earth, which is the unanimous opinion of the *Myth* authors. But if the confession did indeed take this as its reference, it would be speaking in a very strange way about a historical figure. Admittedly, christological reflection would then have to begin "from below," with the historical figure of Jesus— which would follow the current christological trend—but it would never, or only superficially, advance to "above," to discourse concerning God, let alone be able to unfold God's saving activity. Wolfhart Pannenberg was therefore correct when he clarified that a "Christology from below" short-circuits when it "starts with the humanity of Jesus *as opposed to* his relationship with God."[65] Either God is already involved when we speak of Jesus, or else he is only superficially involved and is therefore of little significance. If one considers that the confession takes the historical figure of Jesus as its topic, then it would be making abstract reference to an empirical human story, initially isolated from God, whose relationship to God would remain an external interpretament (or interpreting image) in the story and would be spoken of merely in order to indicate the meaning it has for the speaker. But to propose this as the topic of the confession is to preclude from the outset any theologically adequate understanding of christological confessions, because preoccupation with the historical element will lead to a disregard for their eschatological and soteriological properties. The Christian salvation experience does not

---

65. Pannenberg, "Christologie und Theologie," 136. He attempts to conceive of this relationship in the light of Jesus's *human nature* by working with a "concept of human nature" that views the human being "in his inescapable being of referring to his divine origin and to his divine destiny." Jesus's fellowship with God is then surely just one special instance of a phenomenon common to all humanity, namely, the universal "human relationship with God" (ibid.). In contrast, we are attempting here to conceive of this relationship in the light of *Jesus's nature* as articulated in his *preaching* and manifested in the *conduct of his life*. This relationship is not simply a special expression of the overall human relationship with God, although of course Jesus participated in just such a relationship. Rather, it is an expression of God's special relationship with this man, which, although it does not fundamentally differentiate him from us, makes it possible for his relationship with God to be formed in such a way that it can be described as "bringing humanity as such into the truth" (ibid.). The theological accent is therefore not on an abstract characteristic of being human in general but on a concrete act on God's part. Only thus can it become clear that all discussion of the relationship between God and humans remains vague and therefore theologically unsatisfactory, as long as we do not differentiate precisely between God's placing of himself in relationship with us (grace) and our disrupted relationship to God (sin). In the perspective of this distinction, however, a Christology may be unfolded that retains its soteriological crux and does not become merely the "development of a Christology of God's self-actualization" (145).

stem primarily from *what* the christological confessions declare concerning
Jesus; it stems from the fact that they declare it *concerning him*. Christians
confess Jesus as Son of God, Lord, Savior, Word of God, and so on, for this
reason: they know him to be *the one who was crucified and whom God raised
from the dead*.

This means that, in order to give logical structure to christological confessions, their content must always be reconstrued as a statement *concerning the
one who has been crucified and raised*. In other words, it is not the tangible
historical Jesus in isolation who is the point of reference, and thus the topic,
of christological confessions, but Jesus Christ raised from the dead by God.
Faith in Jesus Christ focuses not on a figure from the past but on a present
person: the *Christus praesens* [Christ present] of the Christian proclamation.
From the very beginning this has been the Easter message and the proclamation
of the eschatological event: that God raised Christ as the firstborn from the
dead (1 Cor. 15).[66] All christological confessions and statements, all narrative
and discursive texts in the New Testament are concerned with this event, even
though they use very varied ways of unfolding its implications for us, for Jesus
himself, and for God.[67] This also applies to the Gospels, which are no more
and no less than interpretations of the resurrection message as proclaimed in
the events of Jesus's life—his words and his deeds as the evangelists recalled
them. By setting their entire narrative about Jesus within the context of the
cross and the resurrection, they emphasize that this narrative discloses its true
meaning only in the light of the Easter event. Briefly stated, the theologically
inescapable confession and the basic affirmation on which the Christian faith
is founded are this: God raised the crucified Jesus from the dead. When this
confession speaks of Jesus, it speaks of the *one who was raised by God*.

## 7. Methodological Consequences for Christology

But this sounds quite unspecific and could therefore be easily misunderstood
if we did not clarify who it is that was raised and what it means to affirm his
resurrection. Right from the outset, therefore, the Christian faith has never

66. The attempt by G. Kegel in his *Auferstehung Jesu—Auferstehung der Toten: Eine traditionsgeschichtliche Untersuchung zum Neuen Testament* (Gütersloh: Gütersloher Verlagshaus
Mohn, 1970) to demonstrate that the resurrection of Jesus occupies no central position within
Christian faith and doctrine is neither factually nor methodologically convincing. For a critical
appraisal of this work, cf. H. Hübner, "Kreuz und Auferstehung im Neuen Testament," *ThR*
54 (1989): 262–306, esp. 267–68.

67. Cf. C. F. Evans, *Resurrection and the New Testament* (London: SCM, 1970), particularly chap. 2.

doubted that the one who has been raised is *the crucified Jesus of Nazareth* (resurrection of *Jesus*) and that to speak of his having been raised by God is to acknowledge the occurrence of *an eschatological event that affects not only him but God himself and each one of us* (resurrection of Jesus *Christ*).

The significance of this may be summarized as follows: The question regarding the identity of the one who is proclaimed as the risen one in different confessions and in references to them may be answered by pointing explicitly to Jesus of Nazareth and his story. The theological nub of the story is Jesus's disclosure of the nearness of God, which he revealed, in word and deed, as the saving accessibility of God's mercy and forgiving, fatherly love. Jesus's proclamation of God, and the testimony of his life to the availability, trustworthiness, and transformative power of God's love, is the basis of the early Christian confessional statements. It is important to start here in order to understand how they speak of God (i.e., their understanding of God) and how they use the concept of resurrection, including how they understand God's saving activity. The announcement of the imminent advent of the reign of God, the merciful Father on whom Jesus called and whom he proclaimed, was central to his message. Jesus's message provided the first Christians with the background, the key, and the field of vision they needed in order to understand his passion, his cross, and his postresurrection appearances. By applying Jesus's message to his person and story, and to their experiences of him after his death,[68] the first Christians effected a hermeneutical transformation, changing something completely improbable into something so probable that a fundamentally contradictory experience was opened up to them as an eschatological certainty.

The use of the concept of resurrection in the early Christian confessions is testimony to precisely this process. In the light of Jesus's message, the first Christians came to understand their experience of the double outcome of Jesus's life by going back to a unique eschatological action by the Lord of life and death, which broke through the entire human experience of death and in which the reign of God has finally dawned. Given Jesus's message concerning the imminent approach of the kingdom of God, their experience—that the Jesus whose life had ended in death on the cross was the same Jesus whom

---

68. This reference to the early Christians' application of Jesus's message to his person does not mean—at any rate, not first and foremost—that they were consciously interpreting it in this way. Rather, his message gave them a field of vision within which they took for granted that the events they had experienced were to be understood in a specific way. From the very beginning the early Christians were convinced that they had not read this significance into their experiences, but that it had been revealed to them. They declared that they had not come to this understanding by themselves, but that the Spirit of God was its originator.

they subsequently experienced as their living Lord—was interpreted by them in a hermeneutically consequent way to mean that God, whom Jesus had invoked as the merciful Father, had faithfully stayed close to him even on the cross, maintaining his living fellowship with him right through death. If this was indeed true, then it was of fundamental universal significance, and not only for Jesus. The merciful love of God that Jesus proclaimed was, in that case, stronger than death itself and was thus more fundamental than the most fundamental reality that defines human life as we experience it: it was God, not death, who had the last word in Jesus's story. If death could not separate Jesus from the life-giving love of God, then it can never separate anyone from God's love. The resurrection of this one person controverts the universal claim of death on us all: because Jesus has been raised to God's eternal life, the compassionate reign of God has dawned. This unique event has universal salvific significance, since it establishes once and for all that the final and most fundamental reality is God's love and nearness, not our separation from God by sin and death. Our salvation is to be found in eternal, unbroken fellowship with God, the source of all life, a living fellowship initiated by God himself and sustained by him in the face of all opposition.

To confess that Jesus was raised by God gives concentrated expression to all of this. At the heart of what is confessed is God's eschatological saving activity, which has fundamentally altered our experience of the reality of Jesus's cross and death and thus also the reality of our world and our experience. To confess the resurrection of Jesus thus has an intrinsically soteriological force. When it speaks of Jesus Christ, such a confession speaks essentially of God as the author of our salvation and makes clear how he brings it about. This is plain, not simply from the descriptions of Jesus's death as an "offering" or "ransom" for us but also from the titles ascribed to him, such as Messiah, Son of God, and Savior. Each of these conveys, in its own way, that this Jesus, who announced the dawn of God's reign and who was the first to be raised by God, has opened the way for us too to enter into eschatological fellowship with God and has revealed this as our way of salvation. The Christian confession of the resurrection speaks, therefore, in its very essence, both of the cross of Jesus and of the faithfulness of God and our salvation, and it is thus a confession that God was at work in the story of Jesus Christ to bring about our salvation. Its theme is the crucified Jesus, who was the first to be raised by God and has finally made plain who and what God is and what the nature of our salvation is, because he himself demonstrated the reality of that which he proclaimed: eternal fellowship with God.

If this Jesus Christ, the first to be raised by God from death, is indeed the referent of all christological confessions and therefore the proper theme of

Christology, then this theme intrinsically includes a threefold reference to Jesus Christ, to God, and to us. None of these items is what it is independent of its relationship to the other two. Rather, they disclose themselves to the theological mind as *functions of a field, and it is the task of Christology and its derivative Christian theology to elucidate the structure of this field and the grammar of its internal relationships.* So, in attempting to explicate God's eschatological saving activity as the final and ultimate reality, Christian theology cannot speak of God without going on to speak of Jesus Christ. It cannot speak of Jesus Christ without speaking of the Spirit. It cannot speak of the Spirit without inevitably speaking of God and of Jesus Christ. It cannot speak of God, Jesus Christ, and the Spirit, without discussing Jesus Christ, God's firstborn raised from the dead, and thus involving us and our reality. It cannot speak of us, our reality, and our world without going on to speak of God and Jesus Christ. Whatever topic it takes up, it must link it to God, to Jesus Christ, and to us in order to convey the reality of God's eschatological saving activity. The question of the historical Jesus, the theological question of God (in its narrower sense), the soteriological question of our salvation, and the associated creation-theological question of the origin and purpose of the world are therefore no mere premises, codicils, or inferences but integral dimensions of Christology itself. If we abstract them from this context, we are left with abstract historical discourse about Jesus, abstract theological discourse about God, abstract soteriological discourse about salvation, and abstract creation-theological discourse about the world; and no combination of these abstractions will ever lead to a concrete Christology and theology.

They must be viewed in context, not in theological isolation. *Thus the resurrection must be interpreted with the cross in mind, the cross with God in mind, God with the message of Jesus in mind, and God's actions on the cross and in the resurrection of Jesus with us and our world in mind*—this is the line of argument that Christology and Christian theology should take in order to conform to the Christian confession of faith in Jesus Christ. On the one hand, when he raises the crucified, dead, and buried Jesus to life, God, whose compassionate nearness Jesus had proclaimed, demonstrates that he stands fast by his partnership with this Jesus even in death and, in so doing, endorses Jesus's proclamation of the inexorable saving nearness of God's love: in the resurrection God identifies himself with Jesus's identification of him as compassionate love, thereby making it clear that this specific human being (*totus homo* [fully man]) is a true manifestation and interpretation of God's whole being (*totus deus* [fully divine]). On the other hand, the resurrection is a saving action that has relevance for us all, because it affects Jesus not just as Jesus but as Jesus the Christ—in other words, as the one who proclaimed the dawning kingdom of God and brought it to fruition. His resurrection involves not only him (the resurrection of Jesus) but also God and, through him, all of us (the resurrection of Jesus Christ), and it will therefore find its completion in our resurrection.

The Christian faith confesses the resurrection of Jesus Christ as an eschatological saving event, simply because it proves that not even death prevents God from maintaining living fellowship with those with whom he wants to be together: it demonstrates unequivocally and irrevocably the life-giving power of God's desire for fellowship and his love for his creation. This is why the most important issue for the Christian faith is not *what* it confesses Jesus Christ to be (the content of the confession) but that the one it confesses *is the one whom God raised as the firstborn from the dead* (the topic of the confession). For it was Jesus Christ who was singled out by God himself before all others to reveal the ultimate irreversible and unsurpassable truth of God's nature: ultimate, and irreversible and unsurpassable, because each change, revision, or enhancement in our time and history would necessarily have to take place in our time and history and thus before death—the death that in principle has been overcome by the resurrection of Jesus. The time is fulfilled in Jesus Christ, not only in the sense that God's promises have been realized, but also in the sense that this realization of God's promises makes it clear that the bounds of time and history are set by God's eternal life instead of by death. Anyone who confesses the one whom God did not cast off from living fellowship with him, even in death, claims Jesus's destiny, including God's unswerving care and presence, as his own. His faith in Jesus as the Christ and his hope in him as the mediator of God's life-giving presence will allow him to participate in Jesus's resurrection to continuous fellowship with God.

## 8. The One First Raised by God and Theological Method

Our examination of a wide range of Christian confessions shows the christological subject matter to be based on the recognition that *the risen Jesus Christ* was and continues to be the referent of christological confessions, statements, and narratives. The very consistency of this theme helps to integrate the varied and diverse content of the confessions. It is important, however, that the topic of christological confessions not be equated with particular terminology or wording, not even with the wording "Jesus Christ was raised." Indeed, the topic of the confession must be distinguished both from its *content* and also from the *way it refers* to this topic. A proper confessional hermeneutic must therefore always bear in mind two distinctions: the distinction between *topic* and *content*, and the distinction between *topic* and *formulation of topic*. What does this mean?

There is more than one way in which the risen Jesus Christ can be made the topic of a christological confession. In fact, different confessions use different linguistic devices to refer to this topic: names, titles, nominal clauses, images, metaphors. To the extent that these linguistic devices are expressions with their own semantic content (i.e., they do not merely indicate the topic but explore it in some particular way), they allow for specific interpretations of the topic of the confession that are not necessarily similar. This can produce difficulties or even logical contradictions if no distinction is drawn between the topic and its exploration, or between the referent of the confession and its designation within the confession. This applies to the expression "God's firstborn raised from the dead": here too, the topic and its designation do not coincide, so that the term itself must not simply be equated with the way it is explored. What distinguishes it from other thematizations is purely the fact that it establishes the original historical and factual reference point for christological confessions and thus functions as a paradigm for the Christian faith: to speak of the raising of the crucified one is to fix the topic of Christian confessions by defining their original reference point. In Christian thinking it functions as a topical rule—in other words, as the example against which it is decided whether a confession deserves to be described as Christian. In order to be considered Christian, a confession must make reference to the one to whom the resurrection confession refers: Jesus Christ, God's firstborn raised from the dead.

This does not mean that there must be an explicit reference to the resurrection of Jesus. The decisive factor is the identity of the referent, not the nature of the reference, since the identity does not proceed from the reference but precedes it. Thus, in some way, a confession must be about the one who was and is acknowledged as God's firstborn raised from the dead, and this will also be the case where the referent in question is that of the resurrection confession itself. Explicit mention of Jesus's resurrection is thus not essential to the subject matter of a confession in such a way that it would be impossible to articulate the latter without mentioning Jesus's resurrection. Rather, the primary purpose of affirming the resurrection is to nail down, in a way binding on Christians, the subject to which Christian confessions refer. But establishing the reference point of a confession is not the same thing as describing and giving a conceptual definition of the referent,[69] and neither is

---

69. On the difference between establishing a reference and describing or descriptively characterizing the referent, cf. S. Kripke, *Naming and Necessity* (Oxford: Wiley-Blackwell, 1980), and H. Putnam, *Representation and Reality* (Cambridge, MA: MIT Press, 1988), 36–42.

the declaration of the topic of Christian confessions the same thing as the formulation of their content.

This should be borne in mind when analyzing the content. The predicate components of christological confessions are thus not descriptive characterizations of the one whom they take as their topic (i.e., God's firstborn raised from the dead); they are a hermeneutical attempt to give succinct expression to the implications of Jesus's resurrection for Jesus himself, for God's relationship with his creation, for the life of the confessing person, and for all other people and created beings, as viewed from the perspective of the confessing person. They are interpretaments of (or interpreting images for) the one who has been raised, and they interpret God's eschatological saving activity in Jesus's cross and resurrection in accordance with the perception and experience of those who confess Jesus as the Christ.[70] The predicate components of christological confessions summarize the experiences encountered in God's saving activity as revealed in Jesus Christ. They indicate the diversity of Christian salvation experiences from the perspective of different areas of life and experience, which may be unified and integrated, though not without further qualification. Their unity lies—though not primarily and originally—in the one of whom they speak, not in what they say. Their unifying principle is their common point of reference: God's eschatological saving activity in the raising of the crucified one. This is the *interpretandum* that christological confessions seek, in their various ways, to interpret, and that Christology needs to explain and clarify.

The same applies to incarnational Christology. It is true that references to incarnation and references to resurrection are both interpretations of God's eschatological saving activity from particular experiential contexts and therefore cannot be simply identified with divine saving activity. But whereas statements

70. The German term *wahrnehmen* can be used in both a theoretical (or cognitive) and practical (or performative) sense. In the first sense it means "taking or accepting something as true," in the practical sense "performing (a task), taking (a chance or an opportunity), keeping (an appointment)," etc.—that is, turning a possibility into an actuality (*wahrnehmen* in the sense of *wahr machen*). I use *perceive* and *perception* in this and similar contexts as a general term for our cognitive activities, not only of our bodily senses (seeing, hearing, tasting, smelling, feeling) but also of all cognitive relationships to our environment, that are (1) primarily receptive rather than imaginary or merely constructive, and (2) are true of a concrete individual or group (experience in the sense of *erleben*) rather than of everybody who fulfills certain general conditions (experience in the sense of *erfahren*). Not every perception has the character of an experience that can be generalized (for all $x$, if $Fx$, then $Gx$), but all perceptions are concretely located ways of being aware of oneself (self-perception) or of something in one's environment (there is an $x$, such as $Fx$). Moreover, since there is no perception that is not informed by some constructive cognitive activity, all perception will also be construction. But—and this is the decisive point here—we can only perceive if there is something that can be perceived and whose perceptibility and intelligibility are not due to our perceiving but precede it, insofar as perception is the way in which reality discloses itself to us in a way we can notice and understand.

concerning the *raising of Jesus by God* belong to the primary historical and epistemological definition of the topic of christological confessions, to state that *God has taken human form* is a continuation of this primary definition. Incarnational Christology—and this confirms its early Christian origins—is a secondary interpretament of the resurrection confession, which seeks to explore the implications of specific interpretations of the resurrection for Jesus's life story, and to explain how it is integrated into fellowship with God's community of life. It provides supplementary interpretation of the christological topic, but it is not the christological topic. If we are to avoid both the problems caused by the *Myth* authors' underestimation of the topic of Christology and the even greater problems caused by their incarnation-christological opponents' overestimation, it is important not to blur the distinction between what God has done in raising Jesus from the dead and our interpretation of what he has done—including our interpretation of it as resurrection. Admittedly, we neither can refrain from making Jesus Christ the topic of our confessions in some way or other (e.g., as God's firstborn raised from the dead), nor can we refrain from acknowledging him as something or someone specific so that we construe him in some specific way (e.g., as Son of God). But if Christian faith is to remain faith in Jesus Christ and not be distorted into a belief in a particular method of confessing faith in Jesus Christ, it is essential that we confront each interpretation with an insistence on maintaining the critical distinction between the topic of the confession intended by the term *Jesus Christ* (God's eschatological saving activity) and its content. No confession, not even a confession of the divine sonship, can by its content exhaust the topic of the confession or substitute for what is referred to when the name of Jesus Christ is uttered. For even the confession of the divine sonship does not convey the christological topic but points in its own way to the risen Jesus Christ and thus to God's eschatological saving activity in the cross and resurrection of Jesus Christ as the subject and foundation of the Christian faith, which transcends even this interpretative attempt.

True, this confirms the thesis that incarnational Christology is not necessary, but not in the way envisaged by the *Myth* authors: the real subject matter of Christology is not, as they allege, the historical, tangible Jesus of Nazareth and his exemplary ethical and religious significance for us. The real subject matter is rather *God's firstborn raised from the dead*, meaning that *Christian faith stands or falls with the confession that Jesus has been raised by God*—and Christian theology stands or falls with the clear and careful conceptual exposition of this confession.

If theology adheres to the basic recognition that such an exposition demands, by interpreting the resurrection with the cross in mind, the cross with

God in mind, God with the message of Jesus in mind, and God's actions on the cross and in the resurrection of Jesus with us and our world in mind, this will provide a basic structure for theological doctrine and an argumentational sequence for the three dogmatic fields of Christology, theology (in its narrower sense of the doctrine of God), and pneumatology. This involves three steps.

The first step is to think through the resurrection in the light of the cross on which the life of Jesus ended, and to ask, What does it mean for Jesus, and therefore for a correct understanding of Jesus, that God raised him from the dead?[71] This is the fundamental *christological question*. The central problem is that of reconciling a knowledge of Jesus's life and death with the experience that Jesus lives—in other words, of considering the unity of his person, given the eschatological difference between death and new life in his story. The answer to this question lies in the Christian confession of Jesus as the Christ (Lord, Son of God, Savior, etc.), which finds its most concise form when the name Jesus Christ is uttered as a confession. It is the task of theology to unfold the Christian confession summarized and condensed in this utterance by considering its various aspects. The aspect of Jesus himself is dealt with by the doctrine of Jesus as *vere homo* [true man] and *vere deus* [true God] (christological dogma), that of ourselves in the doctrine of human being as *creatura* [creature] and *homo reus ac perditus* [man guilty and lost] (doctrine of creation and sin), and that of God in the doctrine of the *deus creator* [the creator God] as *deus justificans vel salvator* [the justifying and saving God] (doctrine of justification). Each of these doctrinal fields develops the whole of the basic Christian confession from a different standpoint. Not only does Christian dogmatics provide a systematic context for these individual doctrinal statements; in each doctrinal field the whole of the Christian faith is stated from a particular perspective and with a specific accent. The essence of Christian dogmatics lies not in the Christian doctrinal context as such but in the orderly transition between the different perspectives from which the whole of the Christian faith must always be carefully considered.

The second step, then, is to ask, What do the cross and resurrection mean for God and therefore for a proper understanding of the God proclaimed by Jesus? This is the fundamental issue that confronts the *doctrine of God*. The central problem that must be addressed is how to represent the God of Jesus's message in the light of the resurrection of the crucified Jesus, and how

---

71. These questions should always be linked theologically. The question as to what it meant for Jesus himself that God raised him from the dead belongs within the same epistemic-hermeneutical horizon of theological reflection as the question of its significance for our correct understanding of Jesus. The first question elicits the truth conditions on which the right answer to the second question will be based.

to do this in such a way that both God's action in raising Jesus, and also the relationships this action sets up between God and Jesus and between God and us and our world are included as constituent elements of our portrayal of him. This requires us to view God's resurrection activity, creating new life as it does, as a *divine action*; it demands that we define the essence and basis of this action as *love*, that we conceive of this God who thus acts from and through love as *trinitarian*, and that we accept the basis on which we recognize this trinitarian God as an activity of the self-revealing Spirit. On this basis,

- *God's identity* ("Who is God?") can be adequately perceived, in the light of Jesus's cross and resurrection, only in the distinction between *Father, Son, and Spirit*. This is because Christians cannot state who is meant by "God" without identifying him as the one whom Jesus called his Father and our Father, and because no one can say with certainty that Jesus was right to address God in this way, and that he was right to behave as the Son of this Father, unless he or she has been assured of this by the Spirit of God. This also means that

- *God's being* ("What is God like?") can be envisaged only as original activity, that is to say, activity that is without prerequisites and draws on nothing else; and that this activity in turn—the activity of the Father, Son, and Spirit—may be defined more precisely as the *trinitarian action of God* in creation, reconciliation, and consummation, which is made possible (immanent Trinity) and actual (economic Trinity) only in God himself.[72] This also means that

- *God's nature* ("What is God?"), viewed against the background of his eschatological defeat of death by new life, is defined as inexhaustible, creative love. It is *inexhaustible* love because its efficacy has no external or internal limit but is always defined as love that determines itself to love: on the basis of his activity, God, Father, Son, and Holy Spirit, interprets himself as inexhaustible love—inexhaustible because, as creative love, this love is the source of its own renewal. This love is *creative* because God lives it out both by distinguishing himself from an other and also by constituting this other as different from himself. In so doing, he relates to something that only exists in a state of comparative independence because God distinguishes himself from it: God, as God, expressly permits the other to exist by distancing himself from it, by allowing it space and time for its own life with God, and, where this space and time appear to be lost, by recovering them. In all of this, God demonstrates himself

72. Cf. Christoph Schwöbel, *God: Action and Revelation* (Kampen: Peeters, 1992), 42–45.

to be *love* in that he does not reserve his divine life for himself, living out his Godhood in Aristotelian self-sufficiency, undisturbed by Jesus's death on the cross. On the contrary, he opens up his life for this Jesus by participating in his life, suffering, and death, and thereby ushers in for him a new and eternal life. Not only is this proof of God's relationship to Jesus but it also reveals love for the other to be the whole point of the divine life and activity: in giving himself to the other, and in effacing himself for the benefit of others, God increases the efficacy of his life in support of other lives in such a way that everyone can always and everywhere depend on the effective presence of God and on his help, even when one no longer expects it or is unwilling or unable to rely on it.[73] And finally, this means that

- *God's knowability* ("How can God be known as God?") and every *real knowledge of God* ("As what is God truly known?") is to be understood in reference to *God himself* and thus to the *self-revealing activity of the Spirit of God*, which shows us how he knows himself in his being and his nature. That God can be known (the possibility of knowing God), that we can know God (our capacity for knowing God) as what we know God (the reality of our knowledge of God), and that we know God as the one who he truly is (the truth of our knowledge of God)—it is only thanks to God himself that all these are possible. So God can be known by us only because, and to the extent that, he allows himself to be known by us, enables us to know him, and helps us to know him. The Christian's faith in Jesus Christ convinces him or her of all this, and the *possibility of knowing God* through the truth of Jesus's proclamation of God is corroborated when, through the work of the Spirit and in the light of Jesus's message, his life, suffering, and death are understood in a manner that concurs with the resurrection confession (God's self-revelation). In the same way, our *capacity for knowing God* is corroborated by the fact that Jesus knew God, demonstrating that God created this human being, and therefore all human beings, as his partners in creation (the doctrine of humanity created in the image of God). The *reality of our knowledge of God* is demonstrated in that we, no less than Jesus, are always living in the perspective of a real understanding of God that we have inherited, even though we dispute or ignore it. And the *truth of our knowledge of God* is demonstrated in that the factual understanding of God imparted to us by his Spirit

---

73. Cf. I. Dalferth, *Existenz Gottes und christlicher Glaube: Skizzen zu einer eschatologischen Ontologie* (Munich: Christian Kaiser, 1984), 194–237.

is constantly being shattered and corrected as the Spirit assures us of God's revelation of himself in Jesus Christ (assurance of faith). In short, true knowledge of God is to be found in *our factual understanding of God, as it is constantly adjusted by the Spirit through God's revelation of himself in Jesus Christ*. Jesus Christ made this clear through the testimony of his life: as the fulfillment and climax of the Old Testament understanding of God, he proclaimed the gospel, revealing through his words and actions the good news of God's loving saving presence, and this good news continues to be imparted whenever the Spirit convinces human beings of the truth of the gospel through the channel of their factual comprehension (or incomprehension) of God.

In short, apart from Jesus Christ and the Spirit there can be no true knowledge of God that knows God as he knows himself, since the Christian faith holds that God's self-knowledge and self-understanding can be revealed only by the Spirit in and through Jesus Christ. God is recognized as God within the sphere of God's activity as Spirit; in a balanced combination of God's activity in Jesus Christ (who communicates God to us as merciful love) and through the Spirit (who discloses Jesus as the true witness to and communicator of God's love). God reveals his self-knowledge as divine love in Jesus Christ who through his personal testimony, message, and actions interprets and communicates God as merciful love to his people and all humanity. Humans understand Jesus Christ in the light of his testimony and message as the self-revelation and self-communication of God's merciful love if and insofar as the Spirit opens their hearts to trust Jesus's enactment and communication of God's love and enables them to accept it as the ultimate truth about God. Thus, only through the Spirit and by reference to Jesus Christ can God be known in his trinitarian Godhead as the creative power of merciful love for his creatures. Through this process God comes to be known as he knows himself (and not merely as we construe God to be): God is the one who reveals and communicates his self-knowledge as divine love in Jesus Christ and through the Spirit to us.[74]

The third and final step is to ask, What does God's activity in the cross and resurrection of Jesus mean for us and our world, and therefore for our correct understanding of ourselves and our world? It is the task of *pneumatology* to provide the answer to this question. As the doctrine of the Holy Spirit, this

---

74. Cf. I. U. Dalferth, *Kombinatorische Theologie: Probleme theologischer Rationalität* (Freiburg: Herder, 1991), 99–158.

is the doctrine of God's (economic) *activity as Spirit* in respect of that other which he distinguishes as different from himself (the creation); God's activity as Spirit within creation and as it affects the creation is explained by theology as an intrinsically *soteriological activity* on the basis of God's work on the cross and in the resurrection of Jesus. This is true

- in respect to the world as a whole, which, in its natural and cultural dimensions, is seen as the creator Spirit's field of operation (doctrine of creation);
- in respect to the life of Jesus Christ, which, in the light of the cross and the resurrection, is treated as the central manifestation of and the key to a knowledge of God's Spirit and his salvific activity (Christology); and
- in respect to human life itself, which, in terms of both individuals (personal faith) and social structures (community and church), is viewed as the saving Spirit's field of operation (soteriology); and finally also
- in respect to our ability to recognize God's activity in creation, reconciliation, and consummation, and thus to see our world, our life, and the life of Jesus Christ just as God sees them (doctrine of knowledge).

In this way *Christology* reflects on the significance of the raising of the crucified one for our understanding of the person of Jesus, and it explicates the basis on which the triune God can be known. The *doctrine of the Trinity* explores the meaning of Jesus's cross and resurrection for the concept of God and explains the objective basis of *pneumatology*. As the doctrine of God's activity as Spirit within the creation as distinct from God himself, pneumatology constitutes a doctrinal framework for all other theological fields of doctrine, since it reflects on God's activity in Jesus's cross and resurrection and its significance for our world as a whole (creation), for human life in general (soteriology), for Jesus's life in particular (Christology), and for our ability to understand God's work of creation, reconciliation, and consummation. The theological argumentation begins with Christology and leads us by way of the doctrine of the Trinity to pneumatology. Not only does pneumatology take as its theme the whole of creation, the sphere of God's activity as Spirit, whose self-revelatory disclosure illuminates the divine field of operation as encompassing everything; it also provides the basis for christological understanding and the epistemic trigger for the theological insight that the unity of divine activity is rooted in the trinitarian unity of the divine being and in the consummation of God's trinitarian life in its irreducible distinction between Father, Son, and Spirit.

This argumentational progression from Christology by way of the doctrine of the Trinity to pneumatology, and from there back to Christology and the doctrine of the Trinity, allows theology to summarize, at a doctrinal level, the self-understanding that Christians articulate when they confess their faith, namely, that they ascribe the foundation, content, and realization of their faith to God alone. By confessing their *faith in God's saving presence* in terms of *faith in Jesus Christ*, they are emphasizing that they are able to make this confession not by their "own reason or strength" but *solely through the Holy Spirit*.[75] Only a faith that believes that it does not believe in its own strength is a faith that justifies, since such a faith is governed wholly by God's life-giving presence as communicated by Jesus Christ and continuously experienced through his Spirit. Christian theology holds firmly to the understanding expressed in this confession, by teaching an understanding of God that is consistently and fundamentally trinitarian. Christians are therefore not distinguished from other people by the proximity of God, which is true for all; they are distinguished by the recognition, expressed in the confession, that Jesus Christ experienced this proximity irreversibly as God's saving presence, a presence that is continually mediated and revealed afresh through his Spirit.

The remaining chapters of this book will expand on the basic structure of Christian doctrine outlined above, developing it along the lines of the three steps enumerated. I will begin with Christology.

75. Cf. M. Luther, *Der kleine Katechismus*, BSLK 511–12.

# 2

# Cross and Resurrection

## The Word of the Cross

The fundamental Christian confession is that God raised Jesus from the dead. But what is actually being confessed is by no means obvious. The theological exposition of the confession must therefore focus on clarifying what it actually means when it affirms that Jesus was raised by God and on critically examining its origins and the bases of its validity. For the criteria and the unity of Christian confessions, in all their detail, variability, and diversity, derive from the fact that they all focus on the resurrection of God's firstborn from the dead; this would remain quite vague and open to misunderstanding if there were no clarification about who this risen one is and what it means to confess his resurrection.

What is required is not merely a semantic clarification of the term *resurrection* and an analysis of the associated clusters of ideas and images both within and outside the New Testament.[1] In order to render Christian confessions intelligible, the way in which they *use* these ideas and images

---

Some of the material in this chapter appears in slightly different form in I. U. Dalferth, "Das Wort vom Kreuz in der offenen Gesellschaft," *KD* 39 (1993): 123–48.

1. For a discussion of New Testament use of language, see J. Kremer, "Die Auferstehung Jesu Christi," in *Handbuch der Fundamentaltheologie*, vol. 2, *Traktat Offenbarung*, ed. Walter Kern, Hermann J. Pottmeyer, and Max Seckler (Freiburg: Herder, 1985), 175–96 and the literature cited therein.

needs to be clarified. To do this we must explicate both the sense of the predicates (What does resurrection mean?) and also their referent (Who is the God who raised Jesus?), the identity of the one who is confessed as the Risen One (Who is this Jesus who was raised?), and, last but not least, the nub of the confession (What is being affirmed when the resurrection of Jesus is confessed? Why is it being affirmed?). This can be done correctly only by using the rule set out above, so that one does not answer these questions one by one in an abstract way but rather answers by considering them within an interpretative sequence, looking at the resurrection with the cross in mind, the cross with God in mind, God with Jesus's message in mind, and God's actions on the cross and in the resurrection of Jesus with ourselves in mind. In this chapter we will focus first of all on the context of the cross and the resurrection.

## 1. The Cross and the Word of the Cross

"The sole distinguishing feature that radically separates Christianity and its Lord from other religions and their gods is the cross."[2] Ernst Käsemann's assertion reminds us emphatically that the decisive difference between Christians and non-Christians does not lie in the divergence between their resurrection hopes or ideas of God, their distinctive concepts of reality or expectations of salvation, their attitudes to life or their lifestyles, but that any differences in these areas are due to one fundamental distinction that is symbolized by the cross and is articulated sharply and unequivocally in the word of the cross. We can reach an understanding about concepts of God; together we can admit our awareness of the utter dependence of our existence; we do not dispute the role of the religious dimension in helping us to cope with the contingency of human life; and we can come to an arrangement concerning organized religion and church. But at the cross there is a parting of the ways. Before the cross all our deductions and conclusions; our efforts to illuminate, clarify, and provide metaphysical explanations; and our attempts at moral legitimization and aesthetic assessment come to naught. The cross is an affront: it contradicts all our expectations and all that we take for granted. It demands that we revise our ideas about God and about our life and our world. If the word of the cross is true, then the moral and religious coordinates of good and evil, God and the world, salvation and perdition—these coordinates by which we steer our lives—are inaccurate. This means that our wisdom is

2. E. Käsemann, *Der Ruf der Freiheit* (Tübingen: Mohr, ⁵1972), 90.

foolishness,[3] our search for meaning is meaningless, our good deeds are well intentioned at best, and our religion is organized unbelief. Paul knew that. Luther discovered it. Barth reaffirmed it. It is vital that christological reflection bear this constantly in mind.

Now, theology and the church have always had problems with the word of the cross. Even among the Corinthians there were those who had trouble coming to grips with this type of Christianity. And nothing has changed since then. It is not only today that the word of the cross is sidelined. And it is not simply because the cultural conditions of the first, fifth, or sixteenth centuries do not pertain today that the word of the cross has lost its attraction for church and society. When it has had an effect, it has been in spite of, rather than because of, the prevailing climate, or by breaking through, correcting, and reforming this climate—with profound individual and cultural consequences. As a result, Christians have never taken credit for any such effect; they have attributed it to God alone and given him the glory. He alone brings to effect the word of the cross, not our theological and ecclesiastical efforts. So to wish for a return to times supposedly much more favorable for the Christian faith is completely misguided. Now as then, the church is faced with the same basic problem: ensuring that the word of the cross is recognized in its words and actions, its λειτουργία, μαρτυρία, κοινωνία, and διακονία [its worship, witness, fellowship, and service]. Now as then, it is paramount that we differentiate clearly between the cross and our own actions so that we continually allow it to correct us. And this presupposes that we acknowledge it and pay heed to it.

What is this "word of the cross" that Paul speaks of (1 Cor. 1:18)? It is no theological dogma, even if it may be formulated as such: the word of the cross is the proclamation of the crucified Jesus Christ as God's ultimate saving action, valid for all. That sounds familiar enough. But what is it that is being proclaimed as salvation? In terms of trinitarian theology, when Jesus the Jew dies, the Son of God dies just as we will die. And he dies, indeed, a death far worse than that which any of us would hope for: condemned, rejected, forsaken, outcast, afflicted, alone. Can this really be the Christian answer to our archetypal human search for salvation, for wholeness and goodness, godliness, companionship, and happiness? No, instead it is the paradoxical correction and remodeling of all these expectations, longings, and hopes:

3. The word σοφία used by Paul in 1 Cor. 1:18–31 is not (philosophical) wisdom in the general sense but a soteriologically loaded and therefore fatally overloaded wisdom theology (*theologia gloriae*) that he counters with the "word of the cross" (*theologica crucis*). Cf. F. Lang, *Die Briefe an die Korinther* (Göttingen: Vandenhoeck & Ruprecht, 1986), 27–32. Theological tradition has generalized this contrast and has thus trivialized it into a rhetorical topos.

here on the cross the Son of God dies like one of us. He makes himself like us, and in so doing he makes us like him.

The old creation myth in Genesis tells of our first temptation from the mouth of the serpent: "You will be like God [or, more precisely: like gods]" (Gen. 3:5). In fact there is nothing to which we are more receptive and susceptible. Luther's seventeenth thesis, "Against Scholastic Theology" (1517), was absolutely correct: by nature, humans are unable to want God to be God. Indeed, they themselves want to be God and do not want God to be God.[4] And this is how we actually behave: like little gods, continually trying, in new and different ways and with more and more obvious consequences, to be lords of life and death.[5] But according to biblical insight and our own experience, we have achieved precisely the opposite: true death instead of overcoming death once and for all, and a more radical alienation from God than we had ever dared to envisage. We are not God. We are not even like God. Rather, we are so far from God that we do not even know what it is that we truly want when we want to be like God. But our lives and our actions are evidence that we are clinging unwaveringly to the serpent's whisperings. We want to be like God—whatever that means.[6] And in order to achieve this we are all prepared to do whatever it takes—even to kill God, as Nietzsche noted with horror.

The New Testament is aware of this sad truth. But in contrast to contemporary euphoria over the purported perfectibility of humanity, it is also aware of the futility of simply countering this situation with the vision of a more humane ethos: "Stay human and become humane." Such moral appeals neither will nor can move us to surrender what lies within us: the desire to

4. WA 1:225. The following attempt to unfold the *theologica crucis* [theology of the cross] will show that it can be developed from within the basic dilemma of human activity without having to start from the classic Reformation model of fear of judgment and the comfort of justification, together with the traditional doctrine of sin and judgment.

5. The truth of Luther's thesis does not depend on each individual *consciously* wanting to be like God. We can want to be like God even when we do not make an explicit decision to want it. The point is that we all *behave in reality* as if this were what we wanted. In other words, at every moment of our lives we ask ourselves whether we would not prefer it if God were not God and we ourselves were God instead. In all honesty, we would have to answer yes.

6. Since we do not know God as he knows himself and as he intends us to know him, we create our own images of God. So our wanting to be like God can take many different guises: we want to be like the God we have imagined for ourselves. Or we want not to be like others imagine God to be. Or we imagine God to be how we would like to be. In failing to reflect this dialectic, the protest mounted by feminist theology against the concept of sin as hubris—that this is a patriarchal construction that "bypasses women's experience" because "only in exceptional cases do they actively participate in the hubris of the powerful, tending more to see themselves as innocent victims when dealing with the powerful"—falls far short of the mark (L. Schottroff, "Sünde/Schuld II. Neues Testament," in *Wörterbuch der feministischen Theologie*, ed. E. Gössmann et al. [Gütersloh: Gütersloher Verlagshaus Mohn, 1991], 385–87, esp. 386, passim).

be like God. Nor can any well-intentioned prohibition or law, even one given by God himself, prevent us from continuing to act out the arrogant drives of our nature in the atrocities that blight our history. We cannot act differently, even when we want to.

The New Testament takes an entirely realistic view. To be like God, to manage without God, and to take the place of God—these are fundamental and indelible human drives, anchored in our very nature and characteristic of what we really are. As *human beings*, therefore, we are distinguished by the fact that we are capable of being like God, but as *sinful* human beings we are marked out by our desire to be like God and the ways in which we seek to achieve this. It is typical of our humanity that we want to be like God, whether we strive for this explicitly or whether it is simply implicit in our lives: we live and act *etsi deus non daretur* [as if there were no God]. It is a fixed element of our human nature that we not only desire to be like God but also are able to be like him, even if this ability is perverted by the manner of our life. For our very nature involves the ability to be like God—in the words of the Bible—to be *imago Dei*.[7] But this is not an ability we can actively develop. To be capable of being like God means that it is possible for us to be like God, but not that we have the ability to make ourselves like God. The modal possibility of Godlikeness is not the same as a natural capability for Godlikeness, and "it is possible that human beings are like God" does not imply that "human beings are capable of making themselves like God."[8] But this is just how we misunderstand ourselves and our nature, of which we have so little knowledge. We want to realize the modal possibility by natural means—to make ourselves like God, instead of allowing God to make us like him—and we can achieve this only by setting, or trying to set, ourselves up in his place.

But our attempt is destined to fail—at our death if not before. Can our Promethean arrogance end in anything but Sisyphean self-exhaustion and self-destruction? Is our insatiable urge to be like God not in fact an unrecognized drive toward separation from God and the absence of God in death, a grim death wish disguised as a yearning for deification? Is it clear from the way in which our life today is endangered, not only as a result of our capability to obliterate ourselves a thousand times over but also of our almost unlimited

7. If our nature involves the ability to be like God, then it is fulfilled when we are like God. But our *imago Dei* is accomplished not by what we do but by what God does. Luther expresses this when he follows Paul in describing the fulfillment of human nature, that is, of the *imago Dei*, using the theological definition "*hominem iustificari fide* [person justified by faith]" (M. Luther, *Disputatio de homine*, prop. 32, in *Lutherstudien*, ed. G. Ebeling, vol. 2, *Disputatio de homine*, part 1 [Tübingen: Mohr, 1977], 22).

8. On the difference between modal possibility and natural ability, cf. I. U. Dalferth, *Gott: Philosophisch-theologische Denkversuche* (Tübingen: Mohr, 1992), 140–41, 150–52.

ability to preserve life, that we are close to satisfying these urges? Our very actions have rendered us incapable of acting because we want our actions to dominate *everything* and are now beginning to see that we are in the process of removing the foundations for any action whatsoever. What actions, what moral code, what ethical principles can come to our aid in this dilemma? It is as if we are incapable of doing good *because* we know what evil is.[9]

That would be all that could be said of us if it were not for the word of the cross. Our actions lead to death whatever we do. But we can achieve our aim of being like God, albeit in a completely different way from what we had envisaged: not because of our own knowledge, planning, and activity but because God quite literally comes to meet us. This is the meaning of the cross. On the cross God responds to our deepest desire—and turns everything upside down. We want to be like God: immortal and knowing about good and evil. Now we are like God because he became like us on the cross, mortal and without any answer to the final question why: "*lema sabachthani . . .*" (Matt. 27:46). No answer broke the deathly God-forsaken silence that followed this question, and Jesus died with a loud cry. Is this the Godlikeness for which we would do anything, and for which, according to the myth, we are even prepared to ruin paradise and kill God? Small wonder that the word of the cross is a scandal and an offense for Jews and Greeks and for people of religious sensitivity and moral seriousness—not to speak of others. It only seems to take us, in our deepest human yearnings, and make us appear absurd. Can this be what we strive for, individually and as an entire human race?

Our religious sensitivity resists this fiercely. It looks for an escape route: belief in the resurrection! The "wisdom of the world" may find the cross a stumbling block and an offense. And it may have problems with the idea of the resurrection. But religious feeling and moral sensitivity are better able to deal with belief in the resurrection and even attempt to support it with metaphysical and moral arguments—in the form of proofs of the soul's immortality. In this way they also manage to neutralize the word of the cross. After all, surely this is essentially speaking of the resurrection of Jesus Christ as well.

Certainly, but not in such a way that the offense of the cross is blunted by a higher religious wisdom, that is the message of the resurrection. That would disarm the cross and make it a mere staging post on the route to the resurrection, turning the Stoic motto *per aspera ad astra* [through hardships to the stars] into a basic statement of the theology of the cross. This, though, is not the word of the cross but the *theologia gloriae* [theology of glory] prevalent in today's pulpits and on today's gravestones: a pious invocation of hope,

9. Cf. H. Blumenberg, *Matthäuspassion* (Frankfurt: Suhrkamp, [3]1991), 98–99.

though there is nothing left to invoke. But the resurrection is not a miracle that retroactively turns the life of Jesus, or any other life, into something different from what it was before. Admittedly there is no *word* of the cross without resurrection. But the resurrection does not belong to the *cross*. The cross is silent and renders all silent. God was silent. Jesus died. The disciples ran away. The cross provides us with no further understanding of human experience. There is no route from here to the resurrection message. The cross is soteriologically silent.

Its first utterance takes place in an entirely different context when it is set *right at the heart of the life of God* and *thus right at the heart of our life.* Only then is the eschatological significance that the cross holds for God, and therefore for us, revealed. This is the subject of the Christian resurrection message. It sets the cross within the context of the life of God and thus within the context of our life. This does not negate, surpass, or invalidate the cross. The cross retains its identity as the cross and, against the horizon of God's life, reveals more than could ever have been expected or expressed in our own horizon of experience. This "more" does not mean that the cross is superseded by the resurrection or that the historical event is carried forward by a further miraculous occurrence. It is the identification and interpretation of the cross of Jesus Christ, consummated in the word of the cross as the *saving event* that changes everything. The word of the cross shows that the cross is a saving event by interpreting it in the context of the life of God and by interpreting our life in the context of this interpretation of the cross. This interpretation also involves reference to the resurrection, which affirms the truth of the cross in God's life and in ours. It speaks of no other event after or alongside the cross, but only of this one, and it does so in a way that is far removed from the perspective of our experience: what happened there does not leave God unaffected; it brings him so close to us that he is with us, and we are with him, even in death. Nothing, writes Paul, neither death nor life, neither present nor future, neither height nor depth, can separate us from God's love (Rom. 8:38–39). So Christian resurrection discourse not only takes God's life and our life as its essential frame of reference; it also is constitutively and indissolubly related to the cross. Correctly understood, the Christian resurrection message is no more and no less than the word of the cross, which affirms the cross as saving event, as Paul never tired of emphasizing.

It is the *word* alone that accomplishes this. The cross as such is silent and renders all silent. Not until it is interpreted by the word of the gospel in the context of the life of God does it begin to speak. Then it discloses itself, from a theological point of view, to be the revelation of God's nature *sub contrario* [hidden beneath its opposite]. The word of the cross shows us that the most difficult and obscure question is not who and what God is but who and what we, the world, and death are. We think we know the answer, but we do not. Contrary to popular wisdom, the God question is the simplest question of all.[10] We, with our supposed knowledge of the world, life, and death, are the real problem. In this one realm we think we know the answers when we have not even understood the question correctly. In the other realm we complain that we can find no answer but overlook the fact that we have no need to search for it, because God, who either discloses himself to us or cannot be found at all, has revealed the answer in the word of the cross.

The word of the cross neither revises nor abrogates the cross. To locate the cross within the life of God does not void the fact that on the cross of Jesus Christ God makes himself like us, sharing our God-forsakenness, our death, our silence, our lack of answers to the ultimate questions. But it reveals something quite decisive about God: it makes plain the nature of the *godliness* of this God whom we are so determined to be like and who has now made himself like us. The word of the cross demonstrates God's godliness not to be the omnipotent self-preservation, unrestricted self-assertion, and omniscient self-sufficiency that we had expected, that we had developed as a metaphysical concept or had defended polemically, but rather to be *gratuitous self-abasement for our sakes*, a free commitment of himself to us in our remoteness from him, and selfless compassion for us in the face of our fundamental dilemma—that we cannot help wanting to be like him, even though of ourselves we can never be like him. Even as we, driven by our urge to be like God, unintentionally but inexorably flee from him into the arms of death, so God comes intentionally and unreservedly to us where we are. The word of the cross makes it plain that it is God himself, and not nothing, who awaits us at death, that our life, for all its imperfection and lack of fulfillment, its unexploited opportunities, and the guilty reality of the suffering it has caused so many, is not simply extinguished and abandoned but ends with God and in his presence. The word of the cross not only endorses our deepest human yearning to be like God; it simultaneously defines God's divinity as the unconditional selflessness that affirms us in our yearning. The New Testament uses several different terms for this divine selflessness toward us: the Johannine writings use the word "love" (ἀγάπη); the Pauline word is "righteousness" (δικαιοσύνη); and Luke uses "merciful" (οἰκτίρμων), and speaks of God's compassion toward us. This is what distinguishes God's divinity and is articulated in the word of the cross.[11]

10. Cf. Dalferth, *Gott*, 1–22.

11. Because the words and ideas employed occur in other contexts, the word of the cross could seem unspecific, interpreting the particular by reference to the universal. However, this is a hermeneutical misunderstanding. Interpreting the word of the cross in this way takes the love,

The New Testament word of the cross provides a double clarification of the serpent's utterance in the Old Testament. It confirms it to be true, though not at all as we had expected. And it gives precise meaning and content to our archetypal human striving to be like God. The serpent's utterance is not true because we are able to make ourselves like God; rather, it is true because he made himself like us on the cross of Jesus Christ. This does indeed define our nature to be like God, though as a result not of our actions but of God's: our Godlikeness results from God making himself like us. For us, to be like him means to be just as he showed himself to be on the cross: as selfless love, grounded in self-sacrificial compassion for others, not in its own self-preservation. In the New Testament "You will be like God" becomes "Be merciful, just as your Father is merciful" (Luke 6:36).

"Be merciful" is neither an empty appeal nor an impossible command. It asks nothing of us that we cannot do and be. Rather, it invites us to become what we are—what we are from God's point of view, and what we ourselves want to be—by freely appropriating in our own life what God has done for us in the life of Jesus Christ. For when we appropriate this Godlikeness, which we

---

righteousness, or mercy that constitutes God's selflessness toward us to be a particular form of a universal concept. But the word of the cross is not to be logically subsumed beneath a general concept and understood as a predicative definition of a particular in terms of a universal. Such a process expresses what is unique in terms of a universally valid norm, using semantic means intended to orientate us within our confusing life situations by helping to reduce complexity to simplicity. The word of the cross uses precisely the opposite semantic and hermeneutical processes: something unique is expressed in quite diverse ways; something entirely simple is interpreted in the context of a wide variety of life situations. These interpretations are to be understood from the point of view of *what* they interpret, not merely or primarily from the point of view of *how* and *as what* they interpret it. Thus the word of the cross has the semantic structure not of a terminological definition but of a metaphor, an image, a story, or an allegory. It conveys something eschatologically new, unique, and incomparable, and it does this in a variety of ways suited to the recipients so that it can be appropriated time and again within fresh forms of faith. There is no way of determining what is conveyed without reference to its appropriation (*fides facit deum*). For it is only in this individual appropriation, and thus in the plural formalization of faith, that the equivalence of the subject matter and the identity of the word of the cross can be ascertained. Thus one can arrive at a clear perception of what the word of the cross is and says only on the level of individual reception and appropriation, not on the abstract level of the defining concept: to realize what the word of the cross is, one must first appropriate it. The semantic formats of the word of the cross are not identical with the gospel but rather are to be understood as stimuli and challenges to appropriate the gospel. The ideas they use (love, righteousness, mercy, etc.) are thus to be interpreted not as more or less accurate terminological references but as helpful incentives to the reception of the gospel. They only take on this role when the comprehension process ties them back into the cross and resurrection of Jesus and interprets them in the light of those events. It is not religio-historical derivation and comparison that disclose their theological sense but this "eschatological reduction" to Jesus Christ. For this makes clear how the word of the cross must be understood in order for it to be received and appropriated as gospel.

could not accomplish for ourselves, only then will we be what, each in our own way, we strive to be and what in fact we already are because God has reached out to us: to become the *imago Dei* that we really are, we must receive from God the Godlikeness that he has accomplished for us. But we only receive this Godlikeness by appropriating it by faith, and we realize it only in the context of the life of faith. So the reference from the Gospel of Luke expresses what it means for us to be like God, as a result of God having made himself like us on the cross of Jesus Christ. It does not say that we could all be like God, as he has made himself like us, from and of ourselves. Rather, it expressly states the criterion on which this is decided and without which the invitation to become like God would be meaningless: God must have made himself our *Father*. Those, and only those, who know God as Father—who know and acknowledge him as their loving Father by faith in Jesus Christ—cannot help but take on God's likeness in such a way that they seek to reflect God's fatherly mercy in their own lives. This is not primarily because of any action of their own, which would entangle them anew in the impasse of such actions, but because they surrender their entire lives, with all their successes and failures, their happiness and suffering, to God's mercy: "Father, I commit my imperfect life to your perfect love. May your will, not mine, be done."

None can know and address God as Father of their own accord. This is why the word of the cross is foolishness and a scandal to us all, and why it can be interpreted only by the Holy Spirit. But where interpretation by the Spirit brings about recognition, provoking faith and penetrating our understanding of God, the world, and self, there we are transplanted from a notional relationship with God that is at best theoretical into a practical, living relationship with the Father of Jesus Christ, in which we no longer talk about God but rather talk to him and with him. At this point a radical transformation of position and perspective occurs, which enables us to comprehend our life as *creatio ex nihilo* (creation from nothing; Rom. 4:5, 17) and to shape it in accordance with the double commandment of love. Our conformity with the Father's mercy leads us from serving death into the service of life. For it is not self-assertion at the expense of others but selflessness for the benefit of others that is the path to life into which the cross directs us—both as individuals and as a church.

## 2. Theological Consideration of the Cross

If this is the word of the cross in broad outline, then the following is true in principle: the word of the cross is properly envisioned when it triggers the change from a self-centered to a God-centered life, provoking us to root our lives not merely in a theoretical and notional relationship with God but in a practical, living relationship with the Father of Jesus Christ. It can give this stimulus only if it is communicated to us with semantic clarity. This cannot occur if we speak of God, creation, and life after death in a manner that has now become acceptable again in a context of postmodern gnosis. We must speak of the *cross*, and we must speak of it in a way that makes it clear we are not dealing with speculative truths of the third kind but are seeking to initiate something completely new by making a concrete event in our history present within ourselves. We are giving the life of God a chance in our own life and death so that we become truly free amid the incompleteness of our lives: like God, in fact, just as we desire to be by nature.

If the word of the cross is to have this effect, four widespread tendencies within the church that belittle the message of the cross and thus distort and obscure the soteriological distinctness of the λόγος τοῦ σταυροῦ [word of the cross] must be avoided.

1. The *historical belittlement* of the message of the cross presents the cross primarily or exclusively as an event in the life of Jesus—the final event of his earthly life. This turns it into an event that recedes further and further into the distance as the years go by and is, at best, kept in mind through the church's acts of remembrance. It becomes one of the innumerable crosses that burden and besmirch our history. This avoids the danger of piety in explaining the meaning of the cross. But it leaves us in the dark about what distinguishes this cross from other, often far more gruesome, deaths inflicted by human beings on other human beings. It puts the cross on a level with Socrates's cup of hemlock, the murder of Caesar, deaths in war, the extermination of concentration camp prisoners, and the slaughter of those seeking asylum. This makes it a landmark in our history but certainly not a symbol of salvation.

2. The widespread *ethical belittlement* of the word of the cross in promulgating the cross primarily or exclusively as an ideal or a model of Christian behavior also fails to accord it this salvific status. The ethical causes that use and misuse the cross for their support are legion: sacrifice for one's neighbor, an example of resolute courage in the face of death, a protest against the oppression of true humanity, speaking up selflessly for the wrongdoers alongside us instead of egoistically saving ourselves, a challenge to carry our own cross and to crucify our flesh, practicing solidarity with sufferers. . . . It is not only feminist theologians for whom the cross, used this way, becomes a cross to bear.[12] It is all too clear that the cross readily becomes an instrument of our ethical

12. E. Valtink, ed., *Das Kreuz mit dem Kreuz*, Hofgeismarer Protokolle (Hofgeismar: Evangelische Akademie, 1990).

convictions and desires. It stands not for salvation but for our conventional, patriarchal, or feminist desires and hopes; not for what God has done for us but for what we ought to do for each other, depending on our current insights.

3. Such an approach to the cross leads to its *symbolic belittlement* in circumstances that are not limited to moral actions but cover the whole of human experience and behavior. The cross then becomes a symbol that occurs in a variety of forms in cultural contexts and functions as a central symbol attracting other symbols, thus weaving an interpretative network. It is represented as the tree of life,[13] as a sign of life and wholeness, with its arms pointing in the four directions of the compass, as a symbol of the humane, a mark of the connection between politics and religion, as an image of the crucified woman, an indicator of the "presence of the unspeakable," of the "dangers threatening humanity, the criminal dimension, suffering, isolation in situations of injustice and death, a sign that God is hidden and mankind is mute," as an allusion to the "dimension of the cross in world problems."[14] It is considered to be a symbol that is thought provoking for many and full of associations for all. This symbolic belittlement of the cross certainly follows current religious trends, which love the unspecific and appear ready to take on board anything that stirs the emotions and panders to the imagination.[15] But it ignores the link between the cross and the word of the cross and fails to recognize that "the hard historical fact of the crucifixion of Jesus of Nazareth *sub Pontio Pilato* is indissolubly" linked with the word of the cross.[16] Just as it is impossible to reinterpret or neutralize this hard fact as a necessary truth of reason, so

13. L. Schottroff, B. von Wartenberg-Potter, and D. Sölle, *Das Kreuz: Baum des Lebens* (Stuttgart: Kreuz, 1987).

14. H. May, "Theologie des Kreuzes in den Evangelischen Akademien," *KD* 39 (1993): 100–107, esp. 101.

15. Or, by contrast, anything that triggers negative associations and distinctions because it does not allow emotional identification. Cf., for instance, M. Kassel, "Tod und Auferstehung," in *Feministische Theologie: Perspektiven zur Orientierung*, ed. M. Kassel (Stuttgart: Kreuz, 1988), 191–226. The uncritical adoption of questionable depth psychology theories has resulted in the disastrous consequence that anything that flashes through the mind in connection with the cross is mistaken for theology: There are some who can find nothing better to say about the "once for all" of Pauline "cross and resurrection theology" than, "This theological expression brings to my mind disciplinary maxims I used to hear as a child, such as, 'I'm telling you this once and for all' or 'This must stop once and for all!'" (219), or can only respond with "such a religious 'once for all' is, however, not very deeply rooted in me emotionally and experientially" (219), or can produce a hasty generalization to the effect that "linear religious thinking is typical of masculine consciousness" (218), while cyclical thinking represents the "soft feminine solution" in contrast to "lethal masculine consciousness" (220–21)—not to mention the even more abstruse observations on the problem of sin (207–8) and of blood (210–13). Such people spin themselves into the corner of a web of associations with the cross while completely losing sight of the word of the cross.

16. O. Bayer, *Autorität und Kritik* (Tübingen: Mohr, 1991), 119.

it is also impossible to defuse it by transforming it into a universally available symbol without losing its point. But both church and theologians are in danger of attempting this in their current approach to the cross. True, such approaches connect with the spirit of the age, but they have nothing more to say to it and nothing with which to counter it, because they concentrate on the *symbol* of the cross instead of the *word* of the cross. If the church wants to proclaim the cross as a symbol of salvation, however, it cannot legitimately preach the cross without the word of the cross, nor the events of Golgotha without the theological nub of the gospel.

4. The fourth and final belittlement of the cross is its *religious belittlement*. It goes back a long way—as far as Corinth. Its most common form is a devaluation of the cross in favor of the resurrection. Christians should not discuss the cross, it is correctly maintained, separately from the resurrection. But this approach proceeds to the more problematic assertion that to view the cross and the resurrection in combination means "that Christian virtue does not consist in passive patience and the endurance of unjust violence; rather, it consists in the resurrection out of death, grief, and impotence."[17] This alternative not only suppresses the fact that it is the crucified one who is raised, and that the exalted one remains the crucified one; it is in fact only a small step away from shifting the emphasis wholly to the resurrection and viewing the cross as a path to exaltation at best. But, as Ernst Käsemann rightly emphasizes, "If the cross is merely the dark entry to heaven, the final extreme obstacle to victory, then the Christian message is barely different from that of its religious competitors." If so, then Christianity provides

nothing more than the fulfillment of a pious or a carnal longing for victory over the grave. Anthroposophy (or one of the many other speculative views of postmortal existence that are currently so popular) is much more appropriate for this purpose. If Christ is only the model on which our hope rests, then all is lost. Others have other models and are indeed able to support them with evidence. Precisely here we must indicate what is in fact rarely indicated by the average funeral sermon: our God comes to our aid against our will and our desires, never without offense, always in such a way that the third petition of the Lord's Prayer is honored.[18]

The fact that we find any talk of God's judgment so completely alien demonstrates how difficult it is for us to accept God's will in preference to our own desires. Stirring up our sense of sin in a moralizing or sentimental way is of

17. E. Stöffler, ed., *Feministische Theologie: An-stöße, stich-worte, schwer-punkte* (Munich: Christian Kaiser, 1992), 43.
18. Käsemann, *Ruf der Freiheit*, 90.

no help. We must find another way of treating our pious, carnal longings for resurrection. Whenever these lead us to imagine that we can manage without the cross, we are still unable to come to grips with the idea of judgment; we can conceive of the brokenness and imperfection of our life only in terms of something that, even if it cannot be overcome in our day-to-day living, must at least be surmounted by focusing our thoughts on wholeness and salvation. Paul, on the other hand, was able to talk about judgment and to deal with the imperfection of his life, because the cross stood at the heart of his doctrine of resurrection. The Christian proclamation of the resurrection is part of the proclamation of the cross—only thus can it be a proclamation of salvation.

Theology has a duty of care to take all possible steps to counter the above four ways in which the word of the cross is belittled. *Christian thought and Christian discourse concerning the cross need to be constantly aware of the fourfold caveat against treating it as a mere historical, moral, or religious symbol or as a royal road to life after death.* They must simultaneously make clear—and here there is an actual ongoing problem with the church's proclamation—

- that the word of the cross is not simply history but is rooted in a contingent historical event;
- that it does not merely preach morality but is intended to have life-changing effect;
- that it is not a universal add-on, a symbol of life or death in general, but opens up a specific perspective on life and death; and
- that it does not gratify our longing for an afterlife but rather functions as a message of judgment on our life before God and as a message of salvation about the life of God for us, in order to correct this longing and transfer its focus away from our own desires and longings onto God's actions and promises.

In order to defend itself against these ways of belittling the word of the cross, theology must be constantly and critically accountable for the underlying principles of Christian preaching about the resurrection of the crucified one. This requires explicit christological reflection and the training of those in teaching positions, which should bear the following in mind.

## 3. The Word of the Cross and the Proclamation of the Resurrection

It is central to the Christian confession that Jesus was *crucified*. It is the unanimous testimony of the New Testament, from its earliest strata (1 Thess.

1:9–10; 4:14; 1 Cor. 15:3–5, 7; Rom. 10:9; Phil. 2:6–11) and on throughout its divergent traditions, that the crucified one was not forsaken by God but was *raised from the dead.* This became in itself the objective basis for the Christian confession and the Christian community. How should we understand that central Christian confession of the resurrection, which forms the basis for all other statements of the Christian faith: "The crucified Jesus was raised from the dead by God"?[19]

In one of his last publications, Hans W. Frei distinguished between four prevalent answers to this question in recent theological discussion:[20]

1. The *mythological answer* argues that this confession gives mythological expression to the fact that the first Christians perceived and acknowledged the cross of Jesus as an effective symbol of salvation. A "miraculous resurrection" had happened, not to Jesus but to his disciples; and this miracle consisted, not in an unnatural phenomenon but in the fact that they began to have faith in Jesus Christ. What is crucial is that the confession therefore tells us something about the confessing persons, not about Jesus.[21]

2. The *historical-realistic answer*, on the other hand, emphasizes the very opposite: the New Testament confession is a faithful description of what actually happened on Easter morning. Jesus's resurrection is said to be a historical event that happened to Jesus himself prior to and independently of the disciples' faith.

3. The *critical-realistic answer* falls between these two viewpoints in asserting that the resurrection was indeed an event that happened to Jesus, but one that is not literally described in the New Testament texts. The event on which the fundamental Christian confession is based goes beyond anything that can be historically described. Thus the confession should be understood

---

19. This key question pursues a systematic rather than a historical issue. Thus we are not dealing here with the historical question of the factual origin of belief in the resurrection of Jesus, on which R. Pesch and the discussion he initiated concentrated (cf. R. Pesch, "Zur Entstehung des Glaubens an die Auferstehung Jesu," *TQ* 153 [1973]: 201–28; G. Lohfink, "Der Ablauf der Osterereignisse und die Anfänge der Urgemeinde," *TQ* 160 [1980]: 162–76; H. W. Winden, *Wie kam und wie kommt es zum Osterglauben? Darstellung, Beurteilung und Weiterführung der durch Rudolf Pesch ausgelösten Diskussion* [Frankfurt: Peter Lang, 1982]; I. Broer, "'Der Herr ist wahrhaft auferstanden' (Luke 24:34): Auferstehung Jesu und historisch-kritische Methode; Erwägungen zur Entstehung des Osterglaubens," in *Auferstehung Jesu—Auferstehung der Christen: Deutungen des Osterglaubens*, ed. I. Broer et al. [Freiburg: Herder, 1986], 39–62). Instead, we are dealing with the question of the correct *understanding* of this belief, on the one hand, and of its *objective basis*, and thus its *correctness*, on the other.

20. H. W. Frei, "How It All Began: On the Resurrection of Christ," *Anglican and Episcopal History* 58 (1989): 139–45. The descriptive terms for the four answers are my own.

21. Among the authors representing this point of view are P. Winter, *On the Trial of Jesus* (Berlin: De Gruyter, 1961), 149; G. D. Kaufman, *Systematic Theology: A Historicist Perspective* (New York: Scribner, 1968), 428–29, 433–34.

realistically, but the reality of the event it confesses is inadequately described
in the New Testament texts because it goes beyond anything capable of being
described.

4. The fourth, the *biblical-realistic understanding*, represents the viewpoint
that the resurrection is an event to which Jesus did indeed testify and that the
biblical testimony faithfully records—although not as "accurate report" but
as "adequate testimony" for "the abiding mystery of the union of the divine
with the historical."[22]

In distinguishing between the four viewpoints, Frei is guided by the presumed referent of the relevant resurrection confession. According to him, to
identify this referent either with the confessing Christian or with the historical Jesus of Nazareth is to lead to an inappropriate diminution that sees the
confession purely as an illustrative statement about the significance of Jesus
for believers[23] or as a mere factual historical statement about the crucified
Jesus.[24] In both cases there is no consideration that primarily and above all
a specific action by God is being confessed. In the third case this receives its
proper emphasis, but in such a way that the point of this action is seen only
with respect to Jesus. Frei argues for the fourth view, since this gives the clearest
statement of both the "the *truth* claim" and "the *mystery* of this message."
He finds the truth claim and the mystery of this message in two elements. For
one thing, the confession articulates the "continuity of the identity of Jesus
through the real, complete disruption of death": "He is the same before and
after death."[25] For another, it confesses that "his identity as this singular, continuing individual, Jesus of Nazareth, includes humankind in its singularity. He
is the representative and inclusive person."[26] According to him, therefore, the
nub of the Christian resurrection confession is to be found in its affirmation
of the *personal identity of the crucified one* and the *universal inclusiveness of
this person*: the crucified Jesus is the same as the risen Christ, and the risen
Christ embraces the whole human race within himself.

We must agree with Frei that no understanding of the resurrection confession is adequate unless it is interpreted both christologically (in relation to the

22. Frei, "How It All Began," 141.
23. This approach, which follows that taken by Bultmann and Marxsen (see below at n. 31),
is taken by J. Becker, "Das Gottesbild Jesu und die älteste Auslegung von Ostern," in *Jesus
Christus in Historie und Theologie*, ed. G. Strecker (Tübingen: Mohr, 1975), 105–26; Becker,
*Auferstehung der Toten im Urchristentum* (Stuttgart: Katholisches Bibelwerk, 1976).
24. This approach is to be found in G. R. Habermas, "The Resurrection of Jesus: A Rational
Inquiry" (PhD diss., University of Michigan, 1976); Habermas, *The Resurrection of Jesus: An
Apologetic* (Grand Rapids: Baker, 1980).
25. Frei, "How It All Began," 143.
26. Ibid., 143–44.

person of Jesus) and soteriologically (in relation to us). But one cannot stop there, for both these elements must be related to a third decisive factor, one that Frei himself fails to consider fully: the *action of God*, which determines the christological identity and the soteriological inclusiveness of the person of Jesus Christ in the first place. Unless one takes the *theological* dimension into account, the christological and soteriological dimensions of the resurrection confession remain mysteries, and the statements of transmortal identity and universal inclusiveness of the crucified one, held by Frei to be absolutely central, remain unjustifiable claims. But they are certainly elements or implications of a *confession* that relates first and foremost *to God*, that is, one that confesses and testifies to an *action by God* that affects both Jesus and us in a specific way. But what does this mean in reality?

## 4. God's Action as the Topic of the Resurrection Confession

In his contribution to the Bultmann-Barth discussion of the resurrection problem, H. G. Geyer has pointed out that, according to Bultmann, the resurrection confession is not a "reality judgment that gives linguistic (i.e., generally intelligible) articulation to certain facts in independence of the judging subject . . . , but a reflective judgment, in which the judging subject confesses a principle that he has encountered . . . from a source outside himself, and whose possibilities, or whose significance for all sorts of subjects, he is communicating."[27] This distinction between reality judgment and reflective judgment seeks to do justice to the confessional element involved when the resurrection of Jesus is spoken of, as well as to the soteriological dimension of the confession, so as not to reduce it to a quasi-factual assertion of a miraculous event that happened to the dead Jesus of Nazareth. This does not deal with the reality problem, however, but shifts it onto the issue of how we should understand the experience of the subject who believes that he is being directed by something outside himself. As G. Wenz asks, is this a question of "a precondition conditional upon itself, or, when all is said and done, a precondition that is presumed to be a precondition,"[28] of an acknowledged *reality* or only of *a confessed* reality?

Barth recognized the risk Bultmann ran of failing to distinguish the reality of the resurrection confessed by faith from the formation and act of faith

27. H. G. Geyer, "Die Auferstehung Jesu Christi: Ein Überblick über die Diskussion in der gegenwärtigen Theologie," in *Die Bedeutung der Auferstehungsbotschaft für den Glauben an Jesus Christus*, ed. F. Viering (Gütersloh: Gütersloher Verlagshaus Mohn, ⁴1967), 91–117, esp. 96.

28. G. Wenz, "Vom apostolischen Osterzeugnis: Notizen zu Gedanken Hans-Georg Geyers," in *Wahrheit und Versöhnung: Theologische und philosophische Beiträge zur Gotteslehre*, ed. D. Korsch and H. Ruddies (Gütersloh: Gütersloher Verlagshaus Mohn, 1989), 167–89, esp. 172.

within the disciples, and he insisted on the "actual occurrence of Jesus's resurrection" as distinct from the disciples' Easter faith, even if the resurrection itself cannot be recognized and acknowledged independently of faith.[29] But to speak of the *resurrection event* as distinct from *resurrection faith* is not a solution to the problem; it merely focuses it on the question of how we are to determine the topic of the resurrection confession. Does the latter refer to the "event of Jesus's resurrection,"[30] or is the term *resurrection* used merely as an "interpretament," as Marxsen emphasizes,[31] in other words, an "expression that alludes to the sense people give to certain events and phenomena"?[32] If the confession relates to a resurrection event, why does the New Testament tradition, "for all its tendency toward an interpretative elaboration of the Easter message," consistently refrain from "a narrative account of the event that the confession calls 'resurrection'"?[33] And if this formulation is only an interpretament, what *interpretandum* then is being explained thereby? The disciples' experiences? The empty tomb? The appearances of the crucified one? And why is the *interpretandum*, however it is identified, interpreted using resurrection terminology? Is the "resurrection statement" an "interpretament of the appearance event,"[34] or, on the contrary, are the appearance statements to be treated as "confirmation of the resurrection statement," as indeed are other potential candidates for the alleged *interpretandum*?[35]

The emerging dilemma is similar to the problem discussed in relation to the incarnational confession,[36] and it has a similar solution: the topic of the resurrection confession (i.e., what is expressed by the resurrection terminology is not an empirical fact or a historical event, however these might be identified, that is interpreted in a certain way; it is an *action by God*, which as such is not described but can be confessed only by those who

---

29. K. Barth, *Die kirchliche Dogmatik* II/2:531–37, esp. II/2:535.

30. This is a view put forward by P. Stuhlmacher, "Das Bekenntnis zur Auferweckung Jesu von den Toten und die biblische Theologie," in *Schriftauslegung auf dem Weg zur biblischen Theologie* (Göttingen: Vandenhoeck & Ruprecht, 1975), 128–66 and elsewhere.

31. W. Marxsen, *Die Auferstehung Jesu als historisches und als theologisches Problem* (Gütersloh: Gütersloher Verlagshaus Mohn, 1964), 141.

32. B. v. Iersel, "Auferstehung Jesu: Information oder Interpretation?," *Concilium* 6 (1970): 696–702, esp. 696.

33. L. Oberlinner, "Zwischen Kreuz und Parusie: Die eschatologische Qualität des Osterglaubens," in *Auferstehung Jesu*, ed. Broer, 63–95, esp. 63.

34. G. Kegel, *Auferstehung Jesu—Auferstehung der Tote: Eine traditionsgeschichtliche Untersuchung zum Neuen Testament* (Gütersloh: Gütersloher Verlagshaus Mohn, 1970), 22.

35. A. Vögtle, "Wie kam es zum Osterglauben?," in *Wie kam es zum Osterglauben?*, ed. A. Vögtle and R. Pesch (Düsseldorf: Patmos, 1975), 9–131, esp. 47.

36. Cf. above, 12–13.

know themselves to have been drawn by this action into this action). What is being interpreted here as God's act of resurrection is not a historical event or phenomenon, still less the subjective opinions and explanations of the first Christians. On the contrary, what is being confessed is an act of God that can be predicated as such and becomes the factual and verbal basis of the resurrection confession, substantiated and explained by means of a threefold identification process:

- It relates constitutively to the story of the crucified Jesus of Nazareth and as such necessitates *the reality statements of Christology in the past tense.*
- It relates this story constitutively to the life of God himself and as such necessitates *the theological reality statements of the doctrine of the Trinity.*
- By relating the story of the crucified Jesus to the life of God, it relates constitutively to the story of every human being—indeed of every created being—and as such necessitates the *universal reality statements of the doctrine of justification.*

The referent of the resurrection confession is therefore an act of God that is substantiated when it is interpreted in relation to the cross, when the cross is interpreted in relation to God, and both are interpreted in relation to ourselves. When the topic of the resurrection confession is thus correctly identified, there are two significant implications.

1. The first is that we are able to clarify what is meant by an "act of God": the activity manifested on the cross as divine creative activity on our behalf. By calling the crucified Jesus from death to life in eternal fellowship with himself (Rom. 4:24; 6:9; 10:9; 1 Cor. 15:4), God reveals the following in and through Jesus:

- the unshakable permanence of his creative presence ("it is always and everywhere true that God is present");
- the essence of his divine presence ("it is always and everywhere true that God is present as original and inexhaustible creativity");
- the character of his divine creativity ("it is always and everywhere true that God is love"); and
- the presence of his original and inexhaustible love even at the most extreme moment of our existence: in death ("it is always and everywhere true that God's creative love is present even in death").

God's *activity* thus reveals itself on the cross and in the resurrection of Jesus fundamentally and in every sense as *creative activity*,[37] and God's *nature* as inexhaustible *creative love*. So God is always and everywhere *creator*: "God's nature is to make something from nothing," as Luther says.[38] This creative God acts always and everywhere, in accordance with his nature, *as love* and *from love*. And God demonstrates this love by acting as the creator, redeemer, and consummator of all that is other than he is.[39] From the above basic theological conclusions we can deduce

- the *basic creation-theological statement* that God is the one who calls into being things that were not (Rom. 4:17);
- the *basic soteriological statement* that God is the one who, by grace alone and not because of any merit, calls that which is other than himself into life, preserves it in life (Rom. 4:2–8), and allows it to live as itself in his presence, granting it salvation; and
- the *basic eschatological statement* that God is the one who gives life to the dead (Rom. 4:17). Therefore, by his grace alone, he calls into being things that were not and preserves them in life; and what is more, he does not abandon that which no longer exists to its nonexistent state; he calls it back into his creative presence.

If we speak of creation strictly in relation to God's activity, and if we consider this activity strictly from the point of view of Jesus's cross and resurrection, to the extent that this reveals his fundamental nature, which takes nothing and makes something new from it, then the concept of creation will be theologically understated if it is described only as the "creating and sustaining of interdependent connections between natural and cultural areas of life, both those accessible to us and those inaccessible."[40] The point is rather that on each occasion God's action—formally stated—connects a starting position with a target position, without them being causally related to each

37. H. Kessler, "Der Begriff des Handelns Gottes: Überlegungen zu einer unverzichtbaren theologischen Kategorie," in *Kommunikation und Solidarität: Beiträge zur Diskussion des handlungstheoretischen Ansatzes von Helmut Peukert in Theologie und Sozialwissenschaften,* ed. H. U. v. Brachel and N. Mette (Fribourg, Switzerland: Edition Exodus, 1985), 117–30, esp. 123–24.

38. WA 1:183, lines 39–40.

39. Creation, redemption, and consummation are thus not three fundamentally different types of divine activity in the sense of the orthodox distinction between the three *actio Dei generalis, specialis,* and *specialissima* [general, special, and exclusive acts of God] but are three concrete forms, not reducible to each other, taken by the creative love that God is.

40. M. Welker, "Was ist 'Schöpfung'? Genesis 1 und 2 neu gelesen," *EvTh* 51 (1991): 208–24.

other in any way,[41] whether in the sense of the one-sided causal or dependence model criticized by M. Welker, or in the sense of the interdependence model favored by him. God's creative activity cannot be adequately defined within the perspective of the Aristotelian alternatives of accidental and substantial change, and neither can it be adequately conceived of as the creation of un-specified plural interdependence connections. For whether or not situations, circumstances, or contexts thus linked by God's activity are such that they are in one-sided causal relationships or mutual interdependence relationships, the decisive factor is that in each case God's action brings about something that in no way could have been derived or have originated from the start-ing position, however subtle the emergences: being from nonbeing, a new being from the old being, a being-with-God from a being-far-from-God, an eternal-being-with-God from a being-without-God. God's action is therefore fundamentally, and not merely in one respect, *creare ex nihilo*. And the crux of this classical doctrine of God's creative activity is by no means grasped if one seeks to understand it in the context of the prevalent alternatives: either God created something from "nothing," or he transformed chaos into cos-mos; either God created once (*creatio primordialis*), or his creation is to be understood as a continuous event (*creatio continua*);[42] or one seeks to over-come the logical contradictions of these alternatives by countering them with a model of plural emergent interdependencies. Instead, the decisive factor is that God's activity is always and everywhere to be comprehended as *creare ex nihilo* because it binds together *through nonbeing* all circumstances and coherences that it directs, calls forth, evokes, or correlates within the entire world, in heaven and on earth or forming part of the natural and cultural spheres of the world: God's activity is always mediated through nonbeing, whether this occurs in the form of the emergence within existing reality of what has not yet been, or of a truly new being (not just another being) in the old being or of a no-longer-being in eternal-being-with-God. Wherever God acts, new comes forth from nothing. And God is in action always and every-where where there is something, in every age and in every place in the world.

41. Even when causal dependence or interdependence relationships exist between them, God's activity is not what brings this about.

42. Ibid., 209–10. It is just as misleading to envisage God as having created the world once and for all at some point as to believe that he inaugurated emergent interdependencies. The doctrine of *creatio ex nihilo* means instead that God is to be distinguished from all that is called "world," that everything connected with the world owes its existence wholly and exclusively to God, so that if he were not present nothing would exist, and that God is the one who permits it to exist alongside him as something distinct from him. Cf. K. Ward, *A Defence of Traditional Theism* (unpublished paper, 9th conference of the ESPR on "Traditional Theism and Its Modern Alternatives," Aarhus, 1992).

2. Second, identifying the topic of the resurrection confession clarifies both what is meant by an "*act* of God" and also what is meant by an "act of *God*": that activity that is adequately defined as creative activity only when we explain it christologically with Jesus in mind, theologically with God in mind, and pneumatologically with ourselves in mind, thus understanding it as an essentially *trinitarian activity*. God defines himself as God in his creative, redemptive, and consummative activity by differentiating in relation to Jesus between the Father and his Son, in relation to God between the Son and the Father, and in relation to us by means of the distinction between the Father and the Son as creative Spirit, on the one hand, and his creatures, on the other. *God* is thus essentially, and as regards all his activity, trinitarianly defined as Father, Son, and Spirit as distinct from the creation. This means that not only the creation-theological but also the soteriological and eschatological statement of the Christian faith must be trinitarian in essence: creation, reconciliation, and consummation are not three separate acts of God; they constitute the threefold diverse manner in which the triune God carries out his trinitarian work.

If the topic of the resurrection confession is the activity of God understood in this sense, then all statements about the historical Jesus, his life, teaching, and death, as well as all statements about our experience and our world, can be fittingly expressed only as elements of this far more all-embracing reality.[43] If we disregard this and treat them in isolation as bare reality statements we will reach the erroneous conclusion described by Whitehead as a "fallacy of misplaced concreteness."[44] It is fundamental that historical and empirical statements about the world as nature, culture, and history, or about specific natural, cultural, and historical phenomena, whether they are based on everyday perceptions or are presented as the results of scientific experience, do not constitute independent principles and undisputed facts to be extrapolated into ever more controversial religious interpretations

43. H. G. Geyer expressed this when he said that although the death of Jesus was "the destiny of a Jewish prophet in Palestine during the principate of Augustus, and as such was the fate of an individual Jew whose public impact under the particular prevailing religious and political circumstances aroused the opposition of the established order and brought the death penalty upon him," nevertheless all this could "only *be properly viewed as one element of his wider reality*" ("Anfänge zum Begriff der Versöhnung," *EvTh* 38 [1978]: 235–51, esp. 240, italics mine), which becomes apparent in the Easter event and is decisively "attributable to the fact that this was brought about by God" ("Auferstehung Jesu Christi," 103–4). This implied relationship between a historical event and the wider reality of divine activity must be applied more broadly to all theologically relevant circumstances.

44. A. N. Whitehead, *Process and Reality: An Essay in Cosmology*, corrected edition, ed. D. R. Griffin and D. W. Sherburne (New York: The Free Press, 1978).

and theological explanations.[45] As they stand, they are instead *abstractions* of the underlying reality of divine activity, the results of specific selective products of our sensory perception and the relevant output of the rational capability with which we access the world of our experience, together with its scientific intensifications and refinements via methodological and mechanical tools. Understood abstractly and in reality, these aspects can come about only because and to the extent that they are essential elements of this divine activity. They would not exist without it, but it too would not be what it is without them.

This means that all our ordinary and scientific perceptions of reality have theological relevance. But this relevance takes a specific form: not as *evidence* or data, from which we can conclude that divine action is the probable explanation of the fact that they exist or are as they are; nor as historical, empirical, natural, or other *grounds* for theological statements about divine action; but as elements to be given theological consideration because they help to reveal conditions under which the Christian faith and the theological statements it formulates could be demonstrated to be self-contradictory and therefore impossible. Thus, for example, it is impossible to base theological statements about humankind on anthropological experience statements, and unnecessary to try to explain anthropological matters using theological theses. If, however, it were the case that human beings are not or could not possibly be as the Christian faith says and implies, then what Christians believe and confess would be impossible and a self-misunderstanding. Accordingly, Christian talk of God cannot be satisfactorily grounded on philosophical arguments for God's existence, and neither can our experience of the world be reliably explained by recourse to God. If, however, it could be shown that God does not or cannot exist, or that he is not or cannot be the God whom the Christian faith confesses, then Christian faith in God would be impossible and a self-misunderstanding. Precisely this applies to the resurrection confession also: if it could be shown that Jesus never existed, or that he was nothing like the Christian description of him, then "the historical cognizance of the person of Jesus Christ would make the homology 'I believe in Jesus' *impossible* and belief in Jesus Christ would be self-contradictory."[46] It is in

45. This is the viewpoint espoused by John Hick in his religious epistemology: *Faith and Knowledge* (London: Macmillan, 1974); Hick, "Seeing-as and Religious Experience," in *Problems of Religious Pluralism* (London: Macmillan, 1985), 16–27. In connection with this problem, cf. I. U. Dalferth, *Theology and Philosophy* (Eugene, OR: Wipf & Stock, 2002), 53–59.

46. E. Jüngel, "Zur dogmatischen Bedeutung der Frage nach dem historischen Jesus," in *Wertlose Wahrheit: Zur Identität und Relevanz des christlichen Glaubens*, Theologische Erörterungen 3 (Tübingen: Mohr Siebeck, 1990), 214–42, esp. 218.

this sense also that we should consider the historical problems raised by the resurrection confession.


## 5. The Experiential Basis of the Resurrection Confession

It is an indisputable historical fact that Christians have confessed and proclaimed the resurrection of the crucified one from the very beginning. Even before Paul's day they were declaring, "God has raised Jesus from the dead" (cf. Rom. 10:9; 1 Cor. 6:14; 15:15; 1 Thess. 1:10), and have accordingly proclaimed God as the one who "has raised Jesus from the dead" (cf. Rom. 4:24; 10:9; 1 Cor. 15:14–15; 2 Cor. 4:13–14; Col. 2:12). The confession of the resurrection of Jesus by God is the key statement as far back as the oldest Christian preaching.[47]

But it is historically just as indisputable that from the very beginning this message was regarded as incredible (cf. Matt. 28:17; Mark 16:14; Luke 24:41; Acts 17:32). Luke records that when Mary Magdalene, John, and Mary told the disciples what they had experienced at Jesus's grave, their words seemed to them like idle tales, and they did not believe them (Luke 24:11). Thomas, the proverbial doubter, is recorded in John's Gospel as having refused to believe the other disciples' report ("We have seen the Lord"), preferring to wait for Jesus himself to convince him of its truth (John 20:24–29). The resurrection message has never been a self-evident or even a probable kind of truth. On the contrary, all concerned—especially all who were present when Jesus died on the cross—found it utterly incredible.[48] So what prompted the first Christians to openly spread this unbelievable message that the crucified Jesus had been raised from the dead by God? And how did they plead the case for this unbelievable declaration of faith in the face of the incredulity, doubt, and ridicule with which it was received?

They did not appeal to the general possibility of resurrection or put forward analogous arguments based on other cases of resurrection, and neither did they introduce well-known, irrefutable, probable (or at any rate not impossible)

47. Cf. K. Wengst, *Ostern—Ein wirkliches Gleichnis, eine wahre Geschichte: Zum neutestamentlichen Zeugnis von der Auferweckung Jesu* (Munich: Christian Kaiser, 1991), 36.

48. This is not contradicted by the fact that the contemporary view held the resurrection of a dead person to be highly unusual, though not, as would be considered today, downright impossible. On the one hand, this does not make the resurrection of Jesus any more probable: there is in this particular instance no direct route from a possibility that is not wholly ruled out to a concrete reality. On the other hand, the predominant view would have had to support acceptance of the Christian message rather than suggesting, in line with the prevalent reaction, that it was an idle tale. But it was not just the educated Athenians on the Areopagus who burst into derisory laughter when they realized what Paul was telling them (Acts 17:32): even the first disciples reacted in much the same way to the appearance stories.

circumstances as evidence for their message. What they proclaimed was, according to their own conviction, so unique that it could not be communicated in this way (John 3:3). Hence they did not seek to prove their message to be true; instead, they testified to it. For both what they declared (the raising of Jesus by God) and their declaration itself (their testimony to the raising of Jesus by God) and the fact that their message met not solely with unbelief, but also, in many instances, with faith (the certainty of the truth of the resurrection message) were perceived by them to be *exclusively God's doing*. God alone had raised Jesus from the dead (Rom. 10:9); God alone had chosen and called those who now testified to this unbelievable act of God (Gal. 1:15–16); and God alone, through his Spirit, makes it possible to believe this testimony and to assent to the resurrection confession (1 Cor. 12:3). The content, realization, and spread of the resurrection message are therefore understood as the *free act of God's creative love*; human corroboration is neither necessary nor possible for the advancement of this message, nor would its persuasiveness be enhanced thereby in any way. It remains utterly incredible or else chooses its own way of making itself convincing. Faith in the resurrection message admittedly is produced not without human proclamation, though also not by it (Rom. 10:14–18), but only by the δύναμις θεοῦ [power of God] (Rom. 1:16), which constitutes the content, realization, and causal ground of the message.

### 5.1. The Credibility of the Resurrection Confession

This on no account means that Christians presented or testified to this message without recourse to arguments. In fact, the New Testament authors expressly emphasize that they and their sources are credible and reliable. Paul, for example, refers in 1 Corinthians 15:5–8 to original eyewitnesses such as Simon, the twelve disciples, more than five hundred brothers at the same time, James, "all the apostles," and, last of all, Paul himself. And they underline the fact that their witnesses were neither random nor frivolous, pointing out that what they bore witness to had taken place "according to the Scriptures" (1 Cor. 15:4) and just as Jesus had said (Matt. 28:6; Luke 24:6).[49] Nowhere does the New Testament contend that the eyewitness accounts of these witnesses prove the "fact" or "process" of the resurrection as such, only that Jesus appeared after his crucifixion as the living Lord to the persons quoted: they are named as witnesses to the appearances, not to the resurrection.[50]

49. Cf. Kremer, "Auferstehung Jesu Christi," 175–96, esp. 193–94.
50. Cf. also F. Mußner, *Die Auferstehung Jesu* (Munich: Kösel, 1969), 63–74, 121–24; R. Pesch, "Das 'leere Grab' und der Glaube an die Auferstehung," *Communio* 11 (1982): 6–20; Pesch, *Das Markusevangelium* (Freiburg: Herder, 1977), 2:519–43; Pesch, *Zwischen Karfreitag und*

The existence and the trustworthiness of these appearance witnesses do not make their resurrection message any more credible, probable, or acceptable to others, as the story of Thomas demonstrates. Only those whom God himself encounters through Jesus are persuaded of the truth of the resurrection message: in other words, those who come to faith firsthand, not secondhand. Neither is this invalidated by the Johannine ending of the Thomas story, which commends as blessed those who believe without seeing (John 20:29). In fact this has a double emphasis: there can be faith in the truth of the resurrection message only where the risen Jesus himself brings it about. But it is only in this exceptional (apostolic) instance that he does so by appearing in person. Normally he instills faith through the "Spirit of truth," who will take Jesus's place and will guide those who hear the message "into the whole truth" and in this way will "glorify" Jesus (John 16:13–14). In other words, the only kind of assurance of the truth of the resurrection message is the assurance of faith; assurance of faith comes only as a gift of the Spirit bestowed by Jesus; Jesus gives the Spirit only in the context of the congregation gathered for worship (cf. John 20:26), that is, where two or three are gathered in his name (Matt. 18:20); and the Spirit communicates the message of Jesus in a specific way (John 16:13), by interpreting it to each individual in a way that he or she finds intelligible, appropriate, and convincing (Acts 2:1–11).

So, if the resurrection message is accepted as true, this is not because of whatever witnesses are brought forward or any other external testimony. Their trustworthiness is not a sufficient argument in favor of the trustworthiness of the message, but neither would the message be refuted by their untrustworthiness. The central problem of the Christian resurrection confession—what makes it so incredible, not just then but now—lies in its content, not in its witnesses' poor powers of persuasion. This problem may be perceived more precisely if we profile it against the background of what is historically not (or barely) open to question—not in order to form a basis for proving or increasing the probability of the truth of the resurrection confession, but to set out the historically verifiable facts with which this confession must agree if it is to establish a serious claim to be true.

### 5.2. The Basic Problem of the Resurrection Confession

There are two facts that stand out historically: Jesus's crucifixion in Jerusalem, and the emergence of a rumor, spread by Jesus's followers, that he had appeared

---

*Ostern: Die Umkehr der Jünger Jesu* (Zurich: Benziger, 1983), 88; Pesch, "Zur Entstehung des Glaubens an die Auferstehung Jesu: Ein neuer Versuch," *Freiburger Zeitschrift für Philosophie und Theologie* 30 (1983): 87.

to them alive after his death. It can thus be considered historically secure that Jesus was crucified by the Romans in Jerusalem and that he died on the cross and was buried by his followers. There is evidence that at least some of them, shocked by Jesus's death, returned to Galilee. It is also likely that there existed a connection between several of the women who had followed Jesus and his grave (Mark 15:40–41, 47), but whether it was they to whom Jesus first appeared is difficult to substantiate, as is the view that such appearances occurred initially or exclusively in Galilee.[51] The only historical information beyond dispute is that after Jesus's death several of his followers claimed that they had encountered him alive, that they began to preach openly that God had raised the crucified Jesus from the dead, that a Jesus community began to gather in Jerusalem as a result of this preaching, that even skeptics such as Jesus's brother James joined this group, that similar communities soon started up in other places, and that these Jesus communities were persecuted by the Jews as sects. Our knowledge of the identity of the people to whom Jesus appeared is purely secondhand except for one instance (1 Cor. 15:5–8): Paul's own testimony (Gal. 1:15–16; 1 Cor. 9:1; 15:8). In no case can we say with certainty where these appearances took place, and neither do we have an authentic description of any of them. Paul himself speaks only of having "seen [ἑόρακα] Jesus our Lord" (1 Cor. 9:1), and even the pre-Pauline traditions say simply that Jesus "appeared [ὤφθη]" to the disciples (1 Cor. 15:5, 7; Luke 24:34). Nevertheless, two things are evident. For one, this "seeing" and "appearing" was not experienced and understood by those involved as a mere factual perception of Jesus that would have been available to anyone in a similar situation. They believed that God himself was responsible for initiating this awareness and that he was in fact showing Jesus *as* his Son to them. Paul speaks explicitly of God "revealing his Son" to him (ἀποκαλύψαι τὸν Υἱὸν αὐτοῦ), a revelation (ἀποκάλυψις) of Jesus as God's Son that had been granted specifically to him in a foreordained manner (cf. Gal. 1:15–16). For another, those who "saw" understood that in "seeing" they were simultaneously being commissioned to proclaim the one who was seen; in other words, they believed that God was calling them (1:16). Nowhere, however, are there claimed to have been any eyewitnesses to Jesus's actual resurrection. Even the tradition concerning the empty tomb (Matt. 27:62–28:15; Mark 16:1–8; Luke 24:1–12; John 20:1–18) gives us no well-founded historical facts. It is highly probable that this did not form part of the oldest resurrection narratives and thus belongs more to the consequences than to the presuppositions of the Easter tradition.[52]

51. Cf. Wengst, *Ostern*, 93–94.
52. According to K. M. Fischer, the "tradition of the finding of the empty tomb . . . is inherently completely independent of the appearance tradition" (*Das Ostergeschehen* [Göttingen:

This is not to deny that in the contemporary Jewish context a reference to the resurrection of a dead person implied that the body was no longer in the tomb, or that early Christian preaching took this for granted, especially as they would otherwise scarcely have found believers in Jerusalem. Jesus's burial place was known (Mark 15:42–46), and the Christians' Jewish critics did not question its emptiness (Matt. 28:13–15; John 20:15). But history does not indicate that this played any particular role as an argument in early preaching of the resurrection,[53] for which, taken on its own, it provides no factual basis. The fact that the tomb was empty does not prove that Jesus had been raised (cf. Matt. 28:13–15);[54] and Jesus's having been raised does not necessarily mean that his earthly body could no longer be in the tomb,[55] though his contemporaries—and indeed many theologians today[56]—would concur with this view.

The decisive historical fact on which the resurrection message is based is not the resurrection of Jesus but the disciples' Easter experience.[57] Their testimony

---

Vandenhoeck & Ruprecht, [2]1980], 55); cf. F. J Niemann, "Die Erzählung vom leeren Grab bei Markus," *ZKTh* 101 (1979): 188–99.

53. U. Wilckens, *Auferstehung: Das biblische Auferstehungszeugnis historisch untersucht und erklärt* (Stuttgart: Kreuz, 1970), 64. This is not to say that it cannot be understood and employed as a theological argument against a docetic view of the resurrection of Jesus as the survival of an incorporeal soul. See, for example, G. O'Collins, *The Resurrection of Jesus Christ* (London: Judson, [2]1980), 94–95.

54. G. O'Collins, *Jesus Risen* (London: Darton, Longman & Todd, 1987), 121–27. It is worth emphasizing this vis-à-vis M. Dummett, "Biblische Exegese und Auferstehung," *Communio* 13 (1984): 271–83; and R. Spaemann, "Religion und 'Tatsachenwahrheit,'" in *Wahrheitsansprüche der Religionen heute*, ed. W. Oelmüller (Paderborn: Ferdinand Schöningh, 1986), 225–34, esp. 232–34.

55. Kremer, "Auferstehung Jesu Christi," 187–88.

56. W. Pannenberg, "Response to the Debate," in G. Habermas and A. Flew, *Did Jesus Rise from the Dead? The Resurrection Debate* (New York: T. L. Miethe, 1987), 125–35, esp. 130–31.

57. According to G. Vermes, it is the early Christian witnesses' "collective conviction of having seen their dead teacher alive, combined with the initial discovery of the empty tomb, that provides the substance for faith in Jesus's rising from the dead" (*Jesus the Jew: A Historian's Reading of the Gospels* [London: SCM, [2]1977], 41). But in the light of Jesus's death on the cross, the *appearances of the living crucified one, taken on their own* even without the associated discovery of the empty tomb, provided the first Christians with sufficient grounds to adduce an act of resurrection by God in order to reconcile a set of circumstances that in human terms was irreconcilable. The empty grave on its own would not have provided grounds, since it could doubtless be readily explained in other ways (cf. Matt. 27:62–66; 28:2–4, 12–15; John 20:15). On the other hand, the appearances were in themselves sufficient to confront them with a fundamental problem. Either they must choose between two equally convincing (but from a human point of view irreconcilable) experiences, neither of which they could call into question without calling their very selves into question, or they must seek a different solution that would allow them to hold fast to their irreconcilable experiences. They found this solution as they applied Jesus's message of the reign of God that had dawned in his life to their own lives and experiences, leading them to the conviction that God had acted conclusively and eschatologically in raising the crucified one.

that the crucified one had appeared to them communicates this experience.[58] In speaking of Jesus's resurrection, on the other hand, they are speaking of what is for them the foundation of the appearance experience and of their testimony to it. For this testimony is characterized by a fundamental tension between two sets of circumstances, both of which were beyond dispute for the appearance witnesses, since they were certain that they had experienced both: (1) that Jesus had died on the cross and (2) that he had appeared to them as living Lord. Taken together, these experiences constitute a fundamental cognitive dissonance necessitating two irreconcilable statements concerning Jesus: "He has died" and "He lives." For the appearance witnesses these two statements were not so dependent on each other that the second corrected, canceled out, or disproved the first. The appearance experiences did not cause the confessing disciples to come to the conclusion that they were mistaken in their belief that Jesus had actually been killed on the cross. On the contrary: precisely because they had no doubt that he had died, the appearance of the living crucified one shattered the unity of their experiential context and with it their identity as experiential subjects in this world, thus presenting them with a fundamental problem of consistency. There are in principle three solutions to this problem of consistency, all of which have been available to their followers, now as then.

### 5.3. Three Ways of Solving the Basic Problem

First, one can question the crucifixion experience, maintaining that Jesus was not really dead. This may be reinforced historically by indications that the Israelites drew the boundary between life and death rather differently, as is clear from Psalm 86:13 and other texts, which count seriously ill or outcast persons as already dead.[59] Or a more scientific position can be adopted, saying that Jesus did not really die on the cross but only appeared to be dead, as has been repeatedly alleged, first by Basilides, later by H. E. G. Paulus, and more recently by J. D. M. Derrett.[60] But there have always been too many

58. This is the systematically decisive point: the identification of the crucified one with the one who appeared to the first witnesses—not precise information as to what these individual appearances might have comprised (cf. W. L. Loewe, "The Appearances of the Risen Lord: Faith, Fact and Objectivity," *Horizons* 6 [1979]: 177–92). R. Pesch's theory that the appearances were visions of the Son of Man (cf. "Zur Entstehung des Glaubens an die Auferstehung Jesu," 87–96; Pesch, *Zwischen Karfreitag und Ostern*, 61) should be judged as a *historical* theory—and, as such, unlikely in view of the multiplicity of christological statements in the New Testament textual sources alone (cf. H. Giesen, "Zu Entstehung und Inhalt des Osterglaubens," *Theologie der Gegenwart* 27 [1984]: 41–46; Oberlinner, "Zwischen Kreuz und Parusie," 87–90).

59. Kremer, "Auferstehung Jesu Christi," 29–30.

60. J. D. M. Derrett, *The Anastasis: The Resurrection of Jesus as a Historical Event* (Shipston-on-Stour: Peter Drinkwater, 1982).

well-documented historical facts countering both these lines of argument, as set out in the detailed Gospel accounts of the crucifixion.[61] The early Christian confessions and Jewish anti-Christian polemic were equally certain that Jesus had indeed died on the cross.

Another solution involves questioning the appearance experiences, dismissing them as hallucinations, for example,[62] or a fraudulent fabrication by the disciples,[63] as an unintentional misinterpretation of natural phenomena,[64] as purely subjective visionary experiences or wishful thinking on the part of the disciples,[65] as an interpretation arising out of their faith in the salvific significance of the cross,[66] or as "a shorthand way of saying that Jesus is the Christ of God."[67] There are, however, a whole host of objections to explanatory attempts of this type. For one thing, there is no basis for ascribing to the disciples any intention to deceive or mislead. As with the women on Easter morning (cf. Mark 16 and parallel passages in the other Gospels), they had not expected anything of the sort. In Paul's case we have his word that he was taken hold of by Christ (Phil. 3:12) against his expectation and against his will, and that he distinguished his encounter with the risen one from other ecstatic experiences and revelations (2 Cor. 12:2–4). Finally, it should be said that sometimes such appearance experiences were reported not just by individuals but by whole groups (1 Cor.

61. Cf. M. Hengel, "*Mors turpissima crucis*," in *Rechtfertigung*, ed. J. Friedrich et al. (Göttingen: Vandenhoeck & Ruprecht, 1976), 125–84; H. R. Weber, *Kreuz: Überlieferung und Deutung der Kreuzigung Jesu im neutestamentlichen Kulturraum* (Stuttgart: Kreuz, 1975), 25–31.

62. Cf. J. Carmichael, *The Death of Jesus* (New York: Dorset House Publishing, 1962), 210–18; Kaufman, *Systematic Theology*, 423–24; I. Wilson, *Jesus: The Evidence* (San Francisco, CA: Harper & Row, 1984), 141–42.

63. Cf. Matt. 27:26–28:15; John 20:1–18; Origen, *Cels.* 2.55; and in modern times especially H. S. Reimarus, "Über die Auferstehungsgeschichte," in G. E. Lessing, *Sämtliche Schriften* (Leipzig: K. Lachmann, ³1897), 12:397–428; Reimarus, "Vom Zwecke Jesu und seiner Jünger," in Lessing, *Sämtliche Schriften*, 13:221–327. The fraud hypothesis is no longer seriously advocated since it was critically examined by D. F. Strauß, *Das Leben Jesu kritisch betrachtet* (Tübingen: Osiander, 1835–36), 2:654.

64. Cf. D. Cupitt, *Christ and the Hiddenness of God* (London: SCM, 1971), 145.

65. Cf. D. F. Strauß, *Leben Jesu*, 655. The psychological explanatory approach is critically discussed in H. Kessler, *Sucht den Lebenden nicht bei den Toten: Die Auferstehung Jesu Christi in biblischer, fundamentaltheologischer und systematischer Sicht* (Düsseldorf: Patmos, 1985), 161–73.

66. Cf. the approaches adopted by R. Bultmann, "Neues Testament und Mythologie: Das Problem der Entmythologisierung der neutestamentlichen Verkündigung," in *Kerygma und Mythos*, ed. H. W. Bartsch (Hamburg: Reich & Heidrich, ⁴1960), 1:15–48, 1:46; and W. Marxsen, *Die Auferstehung Jesu als historisches Problem* as well as *Die Auferstehung Jesu von Nazareth* (Gütersloh: Gütersloher Verlagshaus Mohn, 1968); and also the critique by Kessler, *Sucht den Lebenden*, 173–81.

67. Cupitt, *Christ and the Hiddenness of God*, 165.

15:6; Mark 16:12–20), so that both individual and collective experiences must be taken into account.[68]

If neither of the two incompatible experiences, of Jesus's death and of his being alive, can be eliminated, the only remaining option is to seek an accommodation between them. There are two possible ways of achieving this. The first option would be to dispute the identity of Jesus, arguing for a different referent and a change of subject in the predication of both experiences. But if Jesus was dead and someone else, however similar to Jesus, was experienced as alive, then the Christian faith would be worthless, as Paul emphatically underlines in 1 Corinthians 15:14–19. The New Testament witnesses unanimously emphasize the *identity* of the crucified one with the one who appeared to them, thus confirming the identity of Jesus, whose death they had experienced and who had subsequently encountered them as the living one: "I was dead, and behold, I am alive" (Rev. 1:18). The only remaining option, as far as they could see, given the premise of Jesus's identity and the irreconcilability of his experiences, was to seek a solution, and this solution finds its expression in the Easter confession: *raised by God*.

The confession of the resurrection of Jesus does not articulate a historical fact, nor is it in itself the direct consequence of historical circumstances (such as the empty tomb or the Jesus appearances). It is the—thoroughly reasoned[69]—answer given by the first Christians to a *dilemma* between two incompatible sets of historical circumstances that could not be resolved in any other way: the experience that Jesus had died and the experience that he was alive. Succinctly stated, this answer results from the *application of Jesus's message concerning God's saving and life-giving presence to Jesus himself*,[70] so that it interprets the incompatible experiences of his death and his being alive in the light of God's message, which Jesus proclaimed and in consequence of which he had lost his life. This early Christian answer therefore speaks firmly *of God* and means precisely that God whom Jesus had proclaimed. In referring back to God, it

68. This emphasis is not in accordance with the hypothesis put forward by Ph. Seidensticker, that the "assembled church in its apostolic format, represented by more than 500 brothers" had been "confronted by the risen one and been convinced by him" (*Die Auferstehung Jesu in der Botschaft der Evangelien: Ein traditionsgeschichtlicher Versuch zum Problem der Sicherung der Osterbotschaft in der apostolischen Zeit* [Stuttgart: Katholisches Bibelwerk, 1967], 38).

69. Cf. Cupitt, *Christ and the Hiddenness of God*, 163.

70. "Application" here simply means that it is Jesus's message of the dawning reign of God that provides the field of vision and the means whereby his own story may be understood. This is not necessarily to be understood in terms of a conscious interpretative process, though a reflective consideration of the experiences of the death of Jesus on the cross and of his appearances need not exclude such a process. What is more fundamental is the self-explanatory understanding or "experiencing," so to speak, of these experiences in the light of Jesus's message: this is not a secondary interpretative context but the primary experiential context of these experiences.

does not convey any further historical facts, since these would not have resolved the fundamental experiential dilemma; rather, it conveys an *act of God* that transcends anything that can be grasped historically. It is an answer that is not given or experienced directly but revealed as the basis on which reconciliation of these two otherwise irreconcilable experiences becomes possible. For this act of God must elucidate how both "Jesus is dead" and "Jesus lives" can be confessed together in such a way that the two statements do not cancel out, negate, or modify each other to the point where they are unrecognizable, but justify the fundamental Christian confession "The crucified Jesus of Nazareth lives, *for he has been raised*" (cf. Mark 16:6). The reference in the confession to God's action functions as a way of explaining how Christians can confess two apparently incompatible statements about Jesus at one and the same time, holding each to be an experience-based fact that is individually indisputable. Every attempt to explicate the fundamental Christian confession theologically must thus be measurable against the position that neither of these two statements nor their sequence is to be abrogated, so that the fundamental tension they express between the historical death and the eternal life of Jesus is preserved. Accordingly, no attempt at theological explication can be convincing unless one of its central considerations is that the resurrection confession owes its existence not merely to a story from the past but always to a present experience as well:[71] the origins of Easter faith are rooted equally in the story of Jesus and in the story of the confessing community. Hence it cannot refer back to God's act of resurrection to resolve any cognitive and emotional dissonances without qualifying *both* points of reference in the light of this act, in other words, acknowledging Jesus *as Christ* and its own faith as the *work of God's Spirit*, and thus perceiving—initially implicitly but before long explicitly as well—the *trinitarian differentiation* within God's action.

## 6. The Verbal Format of the Resurrection Confession

God's activity, like God himself, evades all observational assessment and conceptual description.[72] Thus we can speak of him only figuratively, with the aid

---

71. P. Carnley (*The Structure of Resurrection Belief* [Oxford: Clarendon, 1987], chap. 1) deserves credit for having placed this at the heart of his observations.

72. On the problem of God's activity, cf., among recent discussions, T. F. Tracy, *God, Action and Embodiment* (Grand Rapids: Eerdmans, 1984); V. White, *The Fall of the Sparrow: A Concept of Special Divine Action* (Exeter: Paternoster, 1985); Kessler, "Begriff des Handeln Gottes"; M. Wiles, *God's Action in the World* (London: SCM, 1986); W. Härle and R. Preul, eds., *Vom Handeln Gottes*, Marburger Jahrbuch Theologie 1 (Marburg: Elwert, 1987); K. Ward, *Divine Action* (London: Collins, 1990); M. J. Hansson, *Understanding an Act of God: An Essay*

of images and thought and speech models taken from our experience, in order to render God's activity intelligible and to make it possible to communicate the experience of his actions verbally.[73]

### 6.1. The Epistemic Structure of Speech Models of God

The epistemic structure of this model may be briefly described as follows: something familiar from experience—and this is also true when we speak of God's *actions*—is applied to something not (yet) familiar or something new in a way that makes it clear that this something new is not to be understood simply as a further instance of the already familiar, so that *God's* action is not simply one instance of the actions we know from our own experience. Conceptual thinking takes a specific concept and from it produces a universal concept under which further specifics can be subsumed; model-based or figurative thinking, on the other hand, uses the specific to illuminate the individual, regarding which it initially (or permanently) remains open whether and how it can be subsumed as a specific within a universal concept. Model-based thinking therefore has a heuristic, not a classifying, function, which is clear on a verbal level because the chosen model is modified or qualified in such a way that its nondescriptive usage is evident. In speaking of God this occurs formally in that the chosen model is clarified negatively ("God is *not . . . but . . .*") or by means of a qualifying comparison ("God is *like . . . but . . .*"). Thus, for example: "God is not a shepherd who abandons his sheep when the wolf comes, but one who goes after a single lost sheep until he finds it" or "God is like a father, but not like an earthly father but a heavenly, eternal father." The models the Christian tradition uses to help it speak about God and God's activity have the following basic characteristics:[74]

1. They are *culturally conditioned*; that is to say, they all derive from the Christian sociocultural world and help Christians to speak of God: Old Testament images (king, messiah, sacrifice, righteous one, atonement, father, judge, covenant) play a crucial role in early Christian confessions of faith in the New Testament. This biblical imagery links into other similar imageries from the theological traditions found in areas where Christianity has gained a foothold in the course of its history: Greek, Slavic, Germanic, Oriental, African, Asian, and such.

---

*in Philosophical Theology* (Uppsala: Almqvist & Wiksell International, 1991); but especially Chr. Schwöbel, *God: Action and Revelation* (Kampen: Peeters, 1992).

73. Cf. I. U. Dalferth, *Religiöse Rede von Gott* (Munich: Christian Kaiser, 1981), 482–94.
74. Cf. Dalferth, *Theology and Philosophy*, 196–203.

2. They are *experience-conditioned*,[75] in that the selection of images from our cultural repertoire of images takes place through the specific experiences and situations within which Christians become Christians through the Spirit as a result of an encounter with the gospel. The assimilation and accentuation of the Old Testament images in Christian confessions of faith are conditioned by the specific manner in which the first Christians—who were of course Jews—experienced salvation (savior, reconciler, loving father, righteous judge, new covenant, end of the law). The image complexes used to think and speak of God (Son of God, liberator, leader, creator of the world, cosmic spirit, eternal will) change over the course of history to coincide with other non-Jewish experiential contexts in which Christians find themselves.

3. They are *christologically conditioned*, in that the point of all these models is that they are used to illuminate and open up the experience of faith in Jesus Christ that is brought about by the Spirit (Lamb of God, good shepherd, high priest, sin offering, true life, eternal love).

4. They are *theologically conditioned*, in that the thought and speech models each of us chooses from our own realm of experience in order to articulate the experience of faith in Jesus Christ must be qualified so that, in referring to Jesus Christ, they can always be understood simultaneously with reference to the even greater mystery of the inexhaustible goodness, truth, love, and power of God.

It is crucial that these four conditionalities within Christian models of God always be held together without a reductive bias to one or the other. The process of Christian language learning therefore requires a constant effort to create semantic links between the new and the old images without distorting or blurring their original heuristic and faith-oriented force. Then as now, this occurs first and foremost through liturgical use during worship and through theological reflection on and semantic elucidation of these image complexes. However, neither can fully prevent the aberrations and deviations that result from the one-sided overuse or questionable interpretation of individual images in the course of the semantic development of the imagery of faith. The Christian church realized quite early on, therefore, the necessity of formulating some *rules* to give guidance for the use of images in public practice within

75. K. Ward rightly says that Christian images of God "are founded on certain originative events which are taken as giving decisive clues to the nature of reality. And this is not an inferred reality, depicted as it is in itself, apart from all relation to our experience or our conceptual forms. It is reality as it is disclosed to the creative imagination and apprehended through conceptual forms available to us in our culture" (*The Concept of God* [Oxford: Basil Blackwell, 1974], 213).

the Christian community. Church teaching established the ground rule that to be acceptable in Christian contexts (i.e., to be concurrent with the basic experiences attested in the New Testament), all thought and speech models must be qualified or qualifiable in relation to ourselves (anthropologically), in relation to Jesus (christologically), and in relation to God (theologically). As far as Christian discourse regarding God is concerned, this is formulated in the *doctrine of the Trinity*, so that we are speaking legitimately of God only when we speak of him with reference to Jesus (the Son), with reference to our experience of Jesus as the Christ (the Spirit), and with reference to the fundamental premise of all this (the Father). Similarly, as regards Jesus, christological dogma states that we speak adequately of him in theological terms only when we consider him with reference to the story of Jesus of Nazareth (as a specific human being within history), with reference to God (theologically as true God), and with reference to us (soteriologically as truly human). Further, the Reformers' doctrine of justification drew from this the necessity of adequate theological discourse about humanity, which must constantly involve reference to God (created beings and sinners) and to Jesus Christ (belief and unbelief) in order to critically assess and assimilate the diversity of our actual experiences of ourselves and our world. This manner of speaking about God, Jesus Christ, and humanity does not result in observational (descriptive) statements of a comparatively general kind; instead, despite their contingent references, it results in absolutely localizing and therefore orientating model statements of universal validity:[76] God is not just that than which nothing greater can be conceived, meaning that he is still greater than anything we can think about him, as Anselm of Canterbury reasoned. But God is the one about whom nothing greater can be conceived than that which can be conceived of him in relation to Jesus Christ (christological) and thence in relation to us and the world (soteriological). This also means that Jesus Christ is the one whom we begin to conceive of adequately only when we conceive of him in relation to God (theologically) and in relation to ourselves and the world (soteriologically). Finally, our conception of what it means to be human is inadequate until we contemplate it both in its relative singularity in the context of evolving life and also in relation to God (as creation) and in relation to Jesus Christ (as creation destined for salvation). However, in no case are the resulting theological statements descriptive statements about a metaphysical reality; they are always heuristic expressions of an orientation

76. On the problem of absolute localization and comprehensive orientation, cf. Dalferth, *Religiöse Rede*, 590–92; Dalferth, *Existenz Gottes und christlicher Glaube: Skizzen zu einer eschatologischen Ontologie* (Munich: Christian Kaiser, 1984), 47–74; Dalferth, *Theology and Philosophy*, 204–23.

in our world that derives its standpoint and its perspectives from what is presented in the fundamental Christian confession of the raising of the crucified one: the ever-greater love of God, who reveals his presence eschatologically as the presence of the original creativity of inexhaustible love, by which he makes all things new.

### 6.2. The Strengths and Limitations of the Resurrection Model

This outline structure for model-based discourse about God also applies to the specific case of the fundamental early Christian confession "God has raised the crucified Jesus from the dead." It is evident that this manner of speaking is to be understood figuratively and not descriptively because the action of God to which it refers is also represented using other images that are in no way either equivalent semantically or interchangeable. Admittedly, God's actions cannot be spoken of without figurative terminology, but the image of waking/raising/rising is not the only model used by the first Christians to articulate God's action in respect to the crucified Jesus. The Jewish tradition from which this resurrection image derived also offered such images as the exaltation of the servant of God (Isa. 52:13–53:12),[77] the rapture of the righteous to heaven (Gen. 5:24; 2 Kings 2:1–18), the installation of a human being as "Son of God" and ruler in God's stead (Ps. 2), or the heavenly intercession of the eschatological prophet[78] as thought forms, and these too were drawn on to assist with the interpretation of God's actions experienced in the Christophanies (cf. Acts 1:1–11; 5:31).

But the use of the resurrection image possessed several advantages. For one thing, it referred not to an unusual event restricted to a local tradition but to a set of circumstances that was familiar to all: a sleeper waking, an invalid, or someone who is lying down, standing up. Second, it conformed to the Jewish view that God makes alive and wakens the dead to life (1 Sam. 2:6; Acts 26:8; Rom. 4:17–25): God gives life to the dead. Third, it picked up the apocalyptic expectation of a general resurrection of the dead that had been

77. Cf. L. Ruppert, *Der leidende Gerechte: Eine motivgeschichtliche Untersuchung zum Alten Testament und zwischentestamentlichen Judentum* (Würzburg: Echter, 1972); Ruppert, *Der leidende Gerechte und seine Feinde: Eine Wortfelduntersuchung* (Würzburg: Echter, 1973); K. Th. Kleinknecht, *Der leidende Gerechtfertigte: Die alttestamentlich-jüdische Tradition vom "leidenden Gerechten" und ihre Rezeption bei Paulus* (Tübingen: Mohr Siebeck, 1984).

78. Cf. K. Berger, *Die Auferstehung des Propheten und die Erhöhung des Menschensohnes: Traditionsgeschichtliche Untersuchungen zur Deutung des Geschicks Jesu in frühchristlichen Texten* (Göttingen: Vandenhoeck & Ruprecht, 1976); J. M. Nützel, "Zum Schicksal des eschatologischen Propheten," *BZ* 20 (1976): 59–94; H. Giesen, "Zu Entstehung und Inhalt"; D. Crump, *Jesus the Intercessor* (Tübingen: Mohr Siebeck, 1992), chap. 8.

carried forward from the prophetic tradition into contemporary Judaism: the end-time resurrection of the dead had already begun with Jesus.[79] Finally, it was particularly appropriate to apply Jesus's preaching about God's new creation and his life-giving presence to Jesus himself by using the image of his own resurrection by God. Death could not hold him, but God in his creative love raised him into his eternal presence, thus reinforcing his message and glorifying him to be the firstborn of all creation.

But here the usefulness of this model reaches its limits. The apocalyptic expectation of the resurrection of the dead focused on a universal and conclusive act of God. Christians, however, declared that this act applied only to the crucified Jesus, not to the whole of humanity.[80] Since they had not abolished the universal expectation, however, they now had two problems. They had to say and think something that was valid only for Jesus and not (yet) for others. The notorious problem of representing something unique in words was solved within the chosen image complex of the resurrection by representing this uniqueness as *firstness*: Jesus is the first one to be raised, but he will be followed by others. But this gave rise to the second problem. If what is already true of Jesus is not yet true for others (although it will and must be true of them if it is to be legitimately true of Jesus), then we are faced with an *eschatological stretching of time* between God's raising of the dead as it applies to Jesus and as it applies to all other known resurrection events. The universality of God's unique action in this first instance required that an internal time structure be drawn into it, which puts into effect universally the new life begun with Jesus: confessing the resurrection of Jesus requires Christians to identify not only the universal realization of this act at the end of time but also ways in which it is fulfilled between the already and the not yet. The first found its fulfillment in the last judgment, the second in God's faith-awakening activity through word and Spirit in the proclamation of the gospel. None of them is to be understood as a different kind of action by God; instead, they are fulfillments of God's resurrection activity under the eschatologically stretched time conditions between the completed past event as it happened to Jesus Christ and the future event as it will happen to each one of us.

79. Cf. W. Pannenberg, *Jesus–God and Man*, trans. L. L. Wilkins and D. A. Priebe (Philadelphia: Westminster Press, 1968), 66–73.

80. As a comparison between 1 Thess. 4:13–18 and 1 Cor. 15 shows, even Paul, who as a Pharisee was no stranger to the hope of the resurrection of the dead, took some time to achieve theological clarity concerning the soteriological implications of the resurrection of Jesus for believers. Cf. J. Becker, *Auferstehung der Toten im Urchristentum* (Stuttgart: Katholisches Bildungswerk, 1976), and the differing critique by G. Lüdemann, *Paulus, der Heidenapostel*, vol. 1, *Studien zur Chronologie* (Göttingen: Vandenhoeck & Ruprecht, 1980), 229–30, 263–64; and H. Hübner, "Kreuz und Auferstehung im Neuen Testament" *ThR* 54 (1989): 262–306, esp. 294–306.

## 7. The Reality Content of the Resurrection Confession

In the early Christian resurrection confession, God's action at the cross of Jesus is described figuratively, using words from our experience-based, everyday language to say that Jesus was *awakened* or *stood upright*. Such expressions suggested themselves because they provided a rudimentary explanation for the incomprehensibility of what God had done for Jesus, using the image of waking a sleeper or lifting someone lying down to his or her feet, without including God himself in the figure of speech in an inappropriate way. On the one hand, this way of explaining what had happened was not unreasonable given the absolute reality, for the confessing persons, of the outcome of God's action: Jesus had been killed, but they had experienced him alive. On the other hand, it was clear that the raising of the dead Jesus was *more than* the waking of a sleeper,[81] meaning that this element of the confession could not be considered to be an adequate description of God's action. The New Testament witnesses are united in their certainty that Jesus did not return to the transitory life he had left behind at death but entered on a new and im-mortal—in fact, a divine—life. As Paul says, he was raised not into his old body but into a new "spiritual body," to life in the glory of the divine life. "Jesus is dead" and "This man, who was killed, lives" thus constitute quite different types of experience statements: The first is in no way different from other experiences of death and justifies the well-founded, experience-based conclusion that Jesus, like all dead people, will not come back to life. The second, however, requires a declaration of faith, not in the least experience-based, that this living crucified one will never die again: if he lives in spite of being dead, then he lives, no longer as we live (oriented toward death) but as only God lives: eternally, and beyond the alternatives of death and life.

This does not merely imply that we must envisage such an eternal life as distinct from the life we experience; it further implies that we must envisage this life in a way that does not erase the distinction between creator and created being. The difference between God's life and our life is not principally that God's life is entirely without end. That would be nothing more than a miserable endlessness. But God's life is more than the mere opposite of a finite life. Its principal difference from ours is that it can allow another to participate in this eternal life without its own termination: it is not reserved for itself, but as divine life it is open to the other. But—and this is just as crucial—the other is drawn into God's eternal life only as a result of God's activity and not by

---

81. On the hermeneutical structure of this argumentation, cf. Dalferth, *Theology and Philosophy*, 198–203.

its own action. Just as death gives the most striking expression to this total "creaturely passivity," so the "resurrection from death" reveals this exclusively divine activity. The resurrection is therefore not a particular instance of waking or setting upright; it is the explicit expression of a plainly incomparable process: the divine creative activity (Rom. 4:17), which, in the eschatological event of the raising of the crucified one, unveils its own foundation as the inexhaustible love of God. In preserving the identity of Jesus along with the indescribability of God's action, the declaration that Jesus was raised by God communicates the irreconcilability of our experiences of Jesus in such a way that, on the one hand, the distinction between God and Jesus is preserved and, on the other, divine life can be predicated of Jesus on the basis of an action attributed to God and to him alone. It is therefore possible to confess in truth, "The dead Jesus lives—through God and with God, as the one through whom God identifies himself irrevocably as *God for us*," in other words, as Paul puts it, the God who, out of his inexhaustible love, gives life to the dead and calls into being things that are not.

This entails consequences for the Christian understanding of God and of our reality. So the broadening of the divine life, as expressed in the resurrection confession, to those who are other than God makes it theologically necessary for us not just to envisage God as other than finite life but also to accept that within the life of God there is a difference that makes it possible for God to draw another into his eternal life without abrogating the other's uniqueness and without thereby making himself, as God, indistinguishable from that other. Soon after the end of Jesus's preaching and the testimony of his life, this difference began to be expressed as the difference between *Father* and *Son*, with their divine unity in all its differentiation being conceived of as through the *Spirit*, and thus arose the doctrine of the Trinity.

On the other hand it was clear that God's action did not make it possible to accommodate the two resurrection confession statements "Jesus is dead" and "Jesus lives"—Jesus's deadness and his aliveness—on the level of our normal experience of the real world and its history, by combining them miraculously somehow or other against all experience, holding together two irreconcilable sets of circumstances *in* our world by some kind of divine fiat. The life-giving nearness of God and its expansion was experienced instead as an *eschatological qualification of our world as a whole*, affecting the entire world and not just some elements of it: it brought to light, *within* this world, the ultimate truth and destiny *of the world as a whole*. But since the whole cannot be an object of experience, this eschatological qualification of our world as a whole can be experienced only as each potential and actual experiential element is moved into the self-mediating and self-interpreting presence of God. It is seen in an irreducibly double perspective: not only as we discover it ourselves but also as it is disclosed to us due to the nearness of God, which in turn is disclosed to us by Jesus Christ and the Holy Spirit.[82] Our experience of the world, however, is fundamentally altered as a result of the irreducibly double perspective on each fact or circumstance, so that the eschatological qualification of the world as a whole is experienced within our world as a fundamental *difference* between our world, the *old world*, in which there are both death and life, and the *new world*, in which there is only life, and death no longer reigns. But the old world and the new world thus distinguished are not interrelated, like two phases of a unified experiential context, so that Jesus's eternal life could be understood as a continuation of his life after his death by other means. Rather, the old world and the new world are—as the old world would express it—totally discontinuous, or—as the new world would express it—held together through nonbeing by nothing other than God's creative power to make new. So the "continuity" lies solely in God's creative activity, not in creation. It is precisely thus that God shows himself to be the *one* God and creator of the old and the new world: he creates the new, connecting with the old world in such a way that he eliminates the old but retains whatever good creation he considers worth preserving because it can and will survive in the new world he is in the process of making. Within the processes of our world, he is thus already engaged in establishing a permanent distinction between the old and the new worlds, by which our world as a whole is being eschatologically qualified and gradually transformed into the new world. From the outset the resurrection confession has therefore had an eschatological relevance not only as regards Jesus but also for us and the entire world: God raised Jesus not to our transitory life but to his immortal life. However, he has not just singled him out from within our world but has thereby established through him alone a new world over against our world, so that our present world is fundamentally differentiated into "the old" and "the new" and is to be understood by tracing the new within the old.

82. God's nearness reveals itself to us by a process whose structure can be summarized using a typical example as follows. The nearness of God was a specific element of Jesus's preaching of the dawning kingdom of God. Inasmuch as Jesus's preaching became the interpretative horizon for his own life and death, it revealed the extent to which he was caught up into the life of God, and it made known the divine life as a life of love. The Christian proclamation communicates this in the form of the gospel. The gospel is experienced as true when it is received in faith by the work of the Spirit and is appropriated in one's own life. The key to this appropriation lies in perceiving the presence of the life-giving love of God by experiencing and recognizing this divine love at work in one's own life. God's presence cannot be perceived without this sounding board: it is revealed only by going back into one's own (both individual and shared) life story and viewing it in the light of the message of Jesus Christ.

The resurrection of Jesus by God is thus not a historical fact, however incomparable its uniqueness. All historical events take place in our world and are thus essentially worldly, while the resurrection of Jesus is essentially divine. It marks the boundary and the end of our world, which it qualifies as the old world by placing it in contradistinction to God's new world. What God did for the dead Jesus of Nazareth is an eschatological act of creation that qualifies the entire world anew. It does not establish a causal relation between "Jesus died on the cross" and "Christ, being raised from the dead, dies no more" (Rom. 6:9), nor does it connect them to each other in any way as cause and effect. The first is in principle a verifiable historical fact; the second is not. The resurrection of the crucified one does not mean that he came back to the life in this world that he had left on the cross: what God did for the crucified Jesus resulted in new life, not in a new version of the old life; and the new life into which the crucified one was raised by God is a kind that cannot become old any more. It is *eschatologically new*. "New" in this sense, though, is not a predicate belonging to the world we experience but "without doubt a predicate of divine action."[83] As such it has "a *conclusive* character,"[84] a *universal validity* and—as the definition of the intrinsically creative activity of God—a *renewing*, that is, a *restoring* character.[85] The outcome of God's act of resurrection is, accordingly, a new life for Jesus, which is *conclusively* removed from the power of death and is therefore recognized as having taken place once and for all, which possesses *universal validity*, meaning that it is recognized as the principal victory over the power of death, and which intrinsically holds the *power of effective renewal* and is thus recognized as a new life that makes other life and the lives of others new.

So in this sense the resurrection of Jesus is not a historical event that happens *in* the world and could stand, as such, alongside and among other historical events. Rather, it is an eschatological event that happens *to* the world, affecting all world events and, indeed, the world as a whole: a fundamental change to its frame of reference that converts the entire world of historical events into "the old world" by placing it in the light of "the new world" and the new life.[86] The experience of Jesus's death and the experience of his being

83. E. Jüngel, "Das Entstehen von Neuem," in *Wertlose Wahrheit*, 132–50, esp. 142.

84. Ibid., 144.

85. Cf. ibid., 147.

86. That goes unnoticed if the resurrection of Jesus is regarded as a miracle—however central and uniquely important—*in* the world. As a result, it is not treated seriously and with full theological appreciation but is robbed of its soteriological significance. For one thing, the objection is raised that "such reliance on past miracles as guarantors of future salvation is nothing new in the Jewish world." And for another, the nature of its particular revelatory quality remains obscure if it is purely one more instance of God's saving activity in history: "If all the

alive were indeed both experiences in the historical continuum of events, but what was experienced was historically fundamentally discontinuous and only interconnected through the activity of God as creator. The transition from "Jesus is dead" to "Jesus lives" denotes therefore neither a continuation of nor a further event in Jesus's life story, nor indeed the elimination of his identity, but a fundamental change to the frame of reference, within which Jesus is experienced and within which we speak of him and of his cross: the change from our perspective as creatures ("Jesus is dead") to the perspective of the divine creator ("Jesus lives"). Neither of these perspectives is mediated through creaturely continuity or development, meaning that no intensification of our creaturely perspectives, however great, could lead on to the perspective of the divine creator. On the contrary, the divine perspective is distinguished by the way it relates our creaturely perspective ("Jesus is dead") and the creator's perspective ("Jesus lives") to each other, so that it becomes possible to see through Jesus's life, suffering, and cross to an implicit truth that is impenetrable from a historical perspective alone yet explicitly articulated in the confession of faith in the resurrection of Jesus as the central eschatological turning point of world history:[87] the crucified Jesus, who by his words and deeds proclaimed the dawning βασιλεία τοῦ θεοῦ, now lives through and with the God on whose love and nearness he based his life. The continuity and unity of Jesus's life are grounded solely in God's relationship with him. The *creator himself is the only mediator* between the creation and the new creation; he reveals this by setting his seal on the crucified Jesus as the one who has been raised, and by confirming himself as author of his creation.[88]

The appearances are exemplary instances of this. It is true that these are earthly experiences, but faith recognizes them as experiences not of what is worldly but of what is divine: *God the creator's perspective on Jesus is imparted* by God the Spirit. This is why Paul calls them revelations (ἀποκάλυψις; Gal. 1:12). This revelation has threefold significance: it is the ἀποκάλυψις Ἰησοῦ

---

Resurrection meant was that God could intervene in history if He chose, what did it add to the Ten Plagues and the parting of the Red Sea?" (D. R. Schwartz, *Studies in the Jewish Background of Christianity* [Tübingen: Mohr Siebeck, 1992], 25). Every attempt to understand it in this or a similar way—as nothing more than a wonderful historical event—completely overlooks its eschatological character and loses sight of its soteriological significance, so that the claim articulated in the resurrection confession that the salvation experience possesses universal validity is met with nothing but incomprehension.

87. Cf. J. Roloff, "Neuschöpfung in der Offenbarung des Johannes," *Jahrbuch für biblische Theologie* 5 (1990): 119–38, esp. 120.

88. Because this eschatological event affects the world as a whole, it must be true that in the realm of the created there is *no direct identity and unity.* Rather, each being, each event, and each life, with all its different elements, is given its unity *by God himself.* It is what it is only because God is with it, making it what it truly is.

Χριστοῦ, the revelation of the fact that Jesus is the Christ, the Son (Gal. 1:16), who has come to us in accordance with the will of God to reconcile us with God (Gal. 1:4–5). On the one hand, it is the revelation of God as the Father who has raised Jesus from the dead (Gal. 1:1–5) and thereby assured us of his absolutely steadfast purpose of grace and peace (Gal. 1:3). On the other hand, it is the revelation of the deity of the Spirit, given that it is through the Spirit that God discloses himself as the ground of the revelation of Christ and God.[89] This Spirit-given *revelation of the Sonship of Jesus, the Fatherhood of God,* and *the deity of the Spirit* opens our eyes to the divine view of Jesus, of ourselves and our world, and of God himself, showing us the truth about our reality under the conditions in which we exist as created beings and as sinners. On our own we find this truth inaccessible and unrecognizable, since, as members of a world that has turned away from God, we deny and evade it. We can discern it only when we hear it in the gospel (Gal. 1:16), in the "word of the cross" (1 Cor. 1:18). From a worldly point of view it is indeed foolishness, but faith knows that this "foolish" word of God speaks wisdom, because it speaks to us, here and now, in our sinful existence in this world, telling us what one day will be manifest to all: that the crucified one has been raised by God into his eternal life, that he, who is the first to live eternally with God, wants to draw all others after him and that we are therefore right to confess this Jesus as the Son of God and the God he proclaimed as the loving Father who is near at hand.

So the transition from the cross to the resurrection of Jesus is not a sequence of worldly events but the eschatological manifestation, as perceived in our world, of the essential difference between creator and created being. This is perceived as a fundamental change of perspective on Jesus's life and death, a change that confirms God's view of the truth as opposed to our view of it. This is something that affects not only Jesus but primarily God and, from the outset, us also: it is a *divine process of revelation* and, because it affects Jesus, always affects us too.[90] However, its effect on us is not to reveal hidden things about Jesus, God, and ourselves that we could have discovered for ourselves somehow, sometime. Instead, it draws us into God's eternal life[91] and opens up to us a way of seeing that, as sinful created

89. The use of the images Son, Father, and Godhead is conditioned by the specific context of this revelation: Jesus's proclamation of the reign of God and of the dawn of his kingdom. These are not themselves the revelation but the (verbal) means by which God reveals himself to us.

90. Cf. Dalferth, *Religiöse Rede,* 470–73; Dalferth, *Philosophy and Theology,* 39–46.

91. Paul conceives of this process as *justification,* giving it tangible form as *baptism,* in which, while still in this life, we become a "new creation," so that the old has gone; the new is here (2 Cor. 5:17).

beings, we could never have had access to by ourselves: God's creative view of himself and of his creation as it really is. By drawing us into the environment of his life and consciousness, God introduces into our created lives his view of our reality as creator, opening our eyes not only to his status as creator and our status as sinful created beings but also to his forgiving love in the face of our sinfulness. In God's eternal life we exist soteriologically as "justified sinners" and eschatologically as "new creations," and this has cognitive and practical consequences for our lives as created beings. Thus we can neither concur with nor comprehend this divine view against the background of our creaturely way of seeing things without having to observe certain fundamental distinctions: as regards Jesus (*vere homo*—*vere deus* [true man—true God]), as regards ourselves (*simul peccator et creatura* [at once sinner and created being] or *simul iustus et peccator* [at once justified and sinner]), as regards the world (old creation—new creation), and as regards God (*deus absconditus*—*revelatus* [God hidden and revealed]). We cannot acknowledge these basic distinctions without applying them in practice, so that we orientate our experience and lifestyle by striving to live the new life within the environment of the old world, yet in accordance with our insight into God's distinction between the old world and the new.

This is apparent from the New Testament appearance stories. They confirm that those involved did not just recognize Jesus theoretically (Luke 24:13–31; John 20:14–16; 21:4b, 9, 12–14) but also recognized that they were charged above all with the practical proclamation of the message (Matt. 28:16–20; Luke 24:36–49; John 20:19–23) and that, as they took on this task, they would be beginning a radically new life. According to the New Testament testimonies, the appearances of the resurrected crucified one lead not merely to a theoretical recognition of the life-giving nearness of God but to a new way of living in the awareness that his nearness has changed everything. Where God breaks in on one's life, where the presence of the crucified one is experienced in such a way that the Spirit grants incontrovertible certainty of the nearness of God's love, one's whole life is radically redefined by the presence of this divine love. Its every aspect and activity are then shaped by the free appropriation of this love: love for God, our neighbor, and our enemy. This is manifested verbally in thanks to God (doxology), in confession of the resurrection of the crucified one (confession of Christ), and in the proclamation of the word of the cross (gospel). Furthermore, it is part and parcel of this new Christian life to try to secure theologically the content, basis, and expression of this thanksgiving, confession, and proclamation (*fides quaerens intellectum* [faith seeking understanding]) by focusing one's thinking on the one who brought and continues to bring God into one's life: *Jesus Christ.*

# 3

# Jesus Christ

*Fundamental Problems in Constructing a Christology*

Every theological attempt to explicate the resurrection confession must, in its statements about Jesus Christ, give due consideration to three fundamental facts that the confession claims to be true: the historical truth, "Jesus was crucified and died"; the eschatological truth, "Jesus has appeared to us as Lord and is alive"; and the theological truth, "The crucified Jesus lives through, in, and with God as the one through whom God has irrevocably identified himself as *God for us*, confirming this by the work of the Spirit."[1]

From the very beginning Christian theology has faced the soteriological challenge of integrating these three truths when *constructing a Christology*. Over the course of history, this has taken many shapes and forms. But three basic problems have always played a critical role: *Who* is this Jesus? *What* is this Jesus *for us*? *How* can he be what he is for us? The first question addresses the personal identity of the crucified one, the one who has been raised; it is the issue of the being of Jesus Christ. The second question addresses the universal salvific significance of this person; it is the issue of the being of Jesus Christ for us. The third question addresses the necessary and sufficient premises of

---

1. The first two truths constitute the kerygmatic core of the Christian message: "Jesus, who was crucified and died, has appeared to us as Lord and is alive." The third forms the basis of the attempt to give a theological answer to the questions raised by the first two.

the identity and salvific significance of Jesus Christ; it is the issue of the divine basis of the being of Jesus Christ for us. Each of these questions requires us to refer back to God by working out the answers we seek from within our understanding of God. While this understanding is a prerequisite, it will also be crucially redefined in the process, as we will show in this chapter and the next. Both the fact that it is presupposed and the fact that it becomes redefined confirm the chosen path toward the unfolding of the resurrection confession: in the light of the cross, the only theologically satisfactory interpretation of the resurrection traces its route via the cross and the life story of Jesus back to God himself. It is only by taking God himself as the reference point that the content of the confession of Jesus Christ's resurrection is opened up. It is inevitable, however, that such a reference pathway back to God himself via the cross and story of Jesus's life will leave its traces within our understanding of God, fleshing it out and extending it into a trinitarian concept.

## 1. The Personal Identity of Jesus Christ

The first problematic area concerns the question of the *personal identity of Jesus Christ*. This is a key question for Christian theology, and it may be answered in a variety of ways. But each of these answers restates the question, leading via a series of reflective levels to ever more fundamental answers. Four of these levels are particularly relevant from a methodological and factual point of view. When we begin from the resurrection confession, it is the question of identity that arises first: "Who is the one whom God raised from the dead?" It is answered by means of a *historical* reference: "the crucified Jesus of Nazareth." On the basis of this answer the question then metamorphoses into "Who is this Jesus of Nazareth?" which is answered with the *eschatological* reference "the one whom God raised from the dead." This provokes the third form of the question, "Who is the crucified one who has been raised?" to which the *soteriological* response is, "the one through whom God has irrevocably identified himself as God for us"—in other words, the Christ, the Lord, the Son of God. If the question is asked again on the level of "Who is the Son of God, the Christ, the Lord, through whom God has identified himself as God for us?" the reply can take the form either of a circular reference back to the historical statement, "Jesus of Nazareth," or of a *trinitarian* statement, "the Second Person of the Godhead." But this reply does not allow us to reframe the identity question in any meaningful way, since it could be answered only by reiterating the trinitarian response. So it means simply, "The Second Person of the Godhead is who he is—in other words, the one through whom God has irrevocably identified himself as God for us by raising the crucified Jesus of Nazareth." It thus refers all further questions back to the historical, eschatological, and soteriological answers that it summarizes. Taken on its own, none of these answers is theologically adequate. The question of the personal identity of Jesus Christ can be answered only on the historical, eschatological, soteriological, and trinitarian levels, that is, only with reference to Jesus of Nazareth, to God's saving activity for and through him, to us as the ones affected by, and recipients of, this salvation, and to the triune God as the ultimate ground of all of this. Each of these aspects must be considered in order to arrive at a theologically satisfactory answer, both to the identity question "Who is Jesus Christ?" and also to the corresponding identity questions "Who is God?" "Who am I?" and "Who are you?" In each case our answer is theologically dependent on the historical, eschatological, soteriological, and trinitarian network presented in the christological model. Let us therefore look at this network in more detail.

### 1.1. The Jesus of the Gospels

The question of the personal identity of Jesus Christ has its theological origin in the question of the identity of the one of whom it is said, "He died" and "He is alive." In the early days of the formulation of Christian confessions, this question was answered by saying that the one who has been raised was explicitly identified as the *crucified one*. This does not mean that only Jesus's death on the cross had significance for the identity of the one of whom the confession speaks. Rather, Jesus's complete life path, culminating in the cross, is what is relevant to this identity. Because christological thinking is focused on the crucified one, it is intrinsically and unavoidably linked with historical reality—a reality accessible to historical research—and, to be precise, with the life story of a very specific person: the story of Jesus of Nazareth.[2]

The New Testament model for this fundamental historical connection is to be found in the Gospels.[3] They trace the life path of the crucified Jesus from a kerygmatic point of view, their chief—though not their sole—response to the christological identity question being a *narrative* one: the one whom we confess as having been raised from the dead by God is Jesus of Nazareth, and

2. Cf. E. Jüngel, "Zur dogmatischen Bedeutung der Frage nach dem historischen Jesus," in *Wertlose Wahrheit: Zur Identität und Relevanz des christlichen Glaubens*, Theologische Erörterungen 3 (Tübingen: Mohr Siebeck, 1990), 214–42.

3. Cf. R. A. Burridge, *What Are the Gospels? A Comparison with Graeco-Roman Biography* (Cambridge: Cambridge University Press, 1992).

this is his story. The Gospels provide—albeit to some extent in passing—a
number of fairly reliable pieces of historical information concerning this
Jesus.[4] Jesus came from Nazareth in Galilee, as is borne out by his cognomen. The time and place of his birth are obscure; it is uncertain whether
he was really born in Bethlehem in Judaea. His mother's name was Mary,
and his father, a carpenter, was called Joseph. Jesus had several siblings; we
know the names of his brothers James, Joseph, Judas, and Simon, but not
the names of his sisters (Mark 6:3). It is not possible to establish with any
degree of certainty whether Jesus learned and practiced his father's trade.[5]
What is clear is that he himself never married. As a Galilean Jew he spoke
the Aramaic dialect of that region, though he could also read and write,
and understood the Hebrew of the Scriptures. His later preaching shows
that he had grown up in the traditions of Israel and probably also had come
into contact with the apocalyptic ideas of his period. However, he had not
received special training as a teacher of the law, even though he was later
addressed as "Rabbi" on account of his teaching—at that time the title was
in widespread use as an honorific form of address and not exclusively as an
occupational designation.[6] Jesus was a layperson, neither a scholar nor a
priest nor an ordained teacher of the law. He taught as a layperson, and in
fact—as far as we know from the Gospels—not primarily in the traditional
Jewish didactic format of scriptural exposition,[7] but in the manner of a
charismatic lay preacher, in parables and stories from his listeners' everyday
world, confronting them with his eschatological message of the dawning
reign of God and its practical consequences for their way of life. To begin
with, he probably belonged for a while to the followers of John the Baptist,
by whom he was baptized. It was to him that Jesus presumably owed his
message of the kingdom of God, which John announced and whose dawn
Jesus proclaimed. Before long he began his own preaching ministry and appeared publicly in Galilee as a charismatic wandering preacher, miraculous
healer, exorcist, and proclaimer of the dawning reign of God. He had considerable success among the simple Jewish populace of Galilee but seems to
have avoided the nearby Hellenistic towns. Before long he "could no longer
enter a town openly but stayed outside in lonely places. Yet the people still

4. G. Bornkamm, *Jesus of Nazareth*, trans. I. and F. McLusky with J. M. Robinson (Minneapolis: Fortress, ⁹1971), 53–63; K. Niederwimmer, *Jesus* (Göttingen: Vandenhoeck & Ruprecht,
1968), 27–31; G. Vermes, *Jesus the Jew: A Historian's Reading of the Gospels* (London: SCM,
²1977).
    5. Cf. Vermes, *Jesus the Jew*, 21–22.
    6. J. Jeremias, *Jerusalem zur Zeit Jesu*, Kulturgeschichtliche Untersuchungen zur neutesta-
mentlichen Zeitgeschichte (Göttingen: Vandenhoeck & Ruprecht, ³1963), 268.
    7. Vermes, *Jesus the Jew*, 26–29.

came to him from everywhere" (Mark 1:45 NIV). Through his teaching and ministry Jesus called into being an eschatological lay movement of simple Galilean fishermen, farmworkers, craftsmen, tax collectors, and women, who did not form part of any of the predominant groups (Zealots, Pharisees, Sadducees, or Essenes, or of the circle of John the Baptist). Their heterodox impact,[8] their permissive approach to the Sabbath commandment and the purity and dietary laws, together with their increasing numbers, inevitably attracted the attention of the political and religious authorities in Galilee (Herod Antipas) and in Jerusalem (the high priest and Pilate). For one thing, Galilee was the birthplace of many of the anti-Roman movements of the period,[9] particularly of the Zealots, whose agenda was the violent liberation of the Jews from Roman occupation.[10] Anyone who had influence on the masses and gathered a considerable following around him must expect to be viewed as a potential political rebel and condemned, as is borne out by the fate of John the Baptist.[11] For another thing, Jesus's free approach to the law brought him increasingly into conflict with the Jewish authorities, especially as the Galileans were in any case despised by the religious elite in Jerusalem on account of their lack of religious education and latent heterodoxy.[12] Accused of being a political agitator and messianic pretender by the Roman authorities, Jesus was sentenced to death on a cross by the Romans between AD 30 and 33 under Pontius Pilate and executed. He died in Jerusalem and was buried there.

However, the Gospels do not state all of this plainly by setting it out in narrative form. Their primary interest is not the historical data and details, since they do not consider that these, in isolation, hold the answer to the question of the identity of Jesus Christ. The question of the identity of Jesus Christ becomes increasingly exigent given the unremarkable nature of the available historical data, which make it particularly clear how, against the background of contemporary Jewish charismatic movements, Jesus is barely distinguishable from other Galilean miracle workers and Jewish Hasideans. If it was this Jesus of Nazareth whom God raised, who was this Jesus really? What makes him so special that God chose him from among the whole of

8. Cf. Niederwimmer, *Jesus*, 30.

9. S. Dubnow, *History of the Jews* (London: Oak Tree Publications, 1967), 1:74.

10. Cf. M. Hengel, *Die Zeloten: Untersuchungen zur jüdischen Freiheitsbewegung in der Zeit von Herodes I. bis 70 n. Chr* (Tübingen: Mohr Siebeck, 2011); S. G. F. Brandon, *Jesus and the Zealots: A Study of the Political Factor in Primitive Christianity* (New York: Charles Scribner's Sons, 1967).

11. Cf. Josephus, *Ant.* 18.117–118; Vermes, *Jesus the Jew*, 50–51.

12. Cf. S. W. Baron, *A Social and Religious History of the Jews* (New York: Columbia University Press, ²1952), 1:278. But cf. Vermes, *Jesus the Jew*, 57.

humanity to be raised as the firstborn from the dead? This is the key question that preoccupies the writers of the Gospels.[13] They seek to answer it
by telling their story in such a way as to make it clear why God singled out
this insignificant figure, Jesus of Nazareth, in such a unique way for his
eschatological purpose. Through the content and arrangement of the story
of Jesus, they give their readers or listeners hints, clues, comments, and explanations that indicate why it was specifically Jesus who was raised from
the dead. They have different ways of doing this. Mark's Gospel stresses the
concealment of Jesus's actual identity during the pre-Easter period, though
of course it was known to the Gospel writer, who uses narrative means to
make his readers and listeners fully aware of it. John's Gospel, on the other
hand, takes this identity as a starting point and attributes its historical concealment to the hardness of heart of Jesus's contemporaries. None of the

---

13. In the light of the answers they give to this question (Jesus is the Christ, the Son of God
[Mark 1:1], the promised Messiah from the house of David [Matt. 1:1–17], the end-time Messiah and ruler of God's chosen people [Luke 1:26–38; 2:1–20], the eternal Logos and Son of
God, sent by the Father into the world to redeem humanity [John 1:1–18; Phil. 2:6–11]), a whole
series of further questions arises. They attempt to answer these, in particular the question of
why this Messiah, the Christ, the Son of God, found so little welcome among his own people
and had to die in such ignominy on the cross. Given the identification and recognition of his
true identity, Christians in general, and the evangelists in particular, find that the comparative
lack of significance and impact of the historical Jesus and his shameful death on the cross pose
a theological problem to which they offer various solutions: that it is not Jesus in his fleshly
form but only the risen Christ who is of soteriological interest and significance (2 Cor. 5:16);
that everything happened exactly as the Scriptures had foretold (1 Cor. 15:3–5; Rom. 1:2–6;
Matt. 1:23, passim); that, as Luke observes, it is precisely this exploration of the lowly existence
of simple and apparently unimportant women, shepherds, fishermen, farmers, tax collectors,
etc., that portrays God's mercy toward the whole spectrum of the humble, the hungry, the
outcast, the disenfranchised, and the marginalized (after all, this is the theme of Mary's song,
the Magnificat); that the hearts of the Jews had been hardened in order that the whole world
might be saved (Rom. 9–11; John 8:21–58, passim) and that Israel in its turn might be provoked
to a jealous desire for salvation once more (Rom. 10:19; 11:1–16); that atonement for sins and
the restoration of fellowship with God could become possible only by this perfect sacrifice
(Hebrews); etc. Each instance represents yet another attempt to resolve the tension between
the true identity of Jesus Christ and the eventual destitute collapse of his historical existence;
in the end, one of two solutions is adopted. Either (1) they attribute no significance at all to
the destitution of Jesus's life, concentrating entirely on the Christ who was raised from the
dead—thereby adopting the Christian gnostic, docetic, and monophysitic manner of handling
the facts. Or (2) they seek to explain this destitution theologically by endeavoring to interpret
it as the expression of the divine intention and purpose: Jesus's life followed an insignificant
course because God wanted it that way in order to achieve what he intended for us. This is the
approach adopted by the early confessions, continued by the New Testament authors (each in
his own way), and concluded, with varying results, by the church Christologies. They defined
and interpreted Jesus Christ's earthly life as *status exinanitionis* [a state of self-emptying],
*oboedientia activa und passiva* [active and passive obedience], *kenosis*, redemptive acceptance
of the lowest into the life of God, revelation of God *sub contrario* [hidden under its opposite],
expression of the all-transforming love of God with its power in weakness, etc.

Gospels, however, offers a historical account of the life of Jesus; rather, they answer the identity question by linking together its historical, eschatological, and soteriological levels.

Thus, the Gospels are far from being biographies of Jesus. They do not answer the question of the risen one's identity by telling Jesus's life story as accurately as possible from a historical point of view, leaving it to us to draw the appropriate theological conclusions. Rather, each tells Jesus's life story in its own way, but with the aim of identifying Jesus with the one who has been raised and of highlighting the fact that his soteriological significance for us was already clear during the course of his life. In this respect, both *what* they present and *how* they present it distinguishes them from historical biographies, whether in the ancient or the modern sense. They are not just telling the story of a life; they are pursuing kerygmatic purposes and their own individual theological programs. At the level of the information presented, this is evident from the fact that none of them unfolds a historical context of biographical facts. Instead, by organizing the material available to them, each according to his own narrative style, the evangelists present *implicit Christologies* that can be theologically explicated. At the level of the manner of presentation, this is evident from the fact that their narratives are characterized not by a remote descriptive style *sine ira et studio* [without anger and partiality] but by theological commitment and by potential or *emergent Christologies* that are starting to manifest themselves in specific and to some extent divergent christological statements in the texts themselves, and to demand explicit acceptance and continuance.[14] The Gospels relate the story of Jesus in such a way that they present what they know of him in terms of a life that, right from the start, leads to the cross and resurrection, so that in all its aspects it therefore has christological value (implicit Christologies). They use various means to indicate the theological nature of their narratives and their post-Easter standpoint, from the structuring of their overall material to focus on the passion to the explicitly christological format of certain passages that refer back to Old Testament promises and images (cf. Matt. 12 and parallel passages in the other Gospels) and forward to Golgotha and Easter (messianic secret) and to the explicitly christological elements (genealogical record, birth, and baptism stories, lordship title, miracles, teaching authority of Jesus) that are

14. If they were simply presenting historical facts, they would have to supplement and substitute for each other. But since they are evolving an implicit Christology, each in his own way, with his own emphases and in the form of different emergent Christologies, the proper ground for comparisons between the Gospels is not the historical sequence of events unfolded in their narratives but the different ways in which their presentations of the life of Jesus demonstrate it to be the life of the one whom God raised from the dead.

early indications of later, specifically christological patterns and figures of thought (emergent Christologies).

So the Gospels answer the question of the personal identity of Jesus Christ, but not with a series of dogmatic assertions and doctrinal statements; they offer an *introduction to a hermeneutical mode of understanding* that turns out to be also a *christological process of recognition*. The tension between the implicit Christology of the Gospels' subject matter and the emergent Christologies of their narratives leads the readers or hearers of the Gospel texts back and forth along the path from the explicit and emergent to the implicit christological dimensions of the Gospel stories, within the context of their own life experience. As they read or hear these texts, they are not confronted with ready answers, but, within the environment of their own understanding, thinking, and day-to-day living, they are helped to acquire an increasingly better appreciation of the identity of Jesus Christ. They do so by understanding and accepting explicit christological expressions and their theological perspectives, thereby acquiring new christological insights into the material handed down and into their own life experiences, and thus becoming able to bring further theological depth to the elements of Christology already within their grasp.[15]

This process of christological acceptance and recognition happens inwardly and can only ever be undertaken by the person concerned, since it targets his or her own faith conviction and way of life. When the latter are manifested in clear christological statements and confessions, without which there can be no shared Christian life and confession, they do not provide others with answers as such but act as a stimulus and a challenge to them to embark on their own process of acceptance and recognition. Such personal responses are not arbitrary as long as we follow the inherent logic of the Gospel narratives and allow ourselves to be guided by the set of questions with which these texts confront us. At the very least—to select only one central and vital element—the material to be considered if the identity of Jesus Christ is to be disclosed on this journey from emergent to implicit Gospel Christologies must include *Jesus's own life testimony*. The answer to the question, "Who is the crucified one who was raised by God?" cannot be found without recourse to Jesus's *own* proclamation, in word and deed, of the dawning reign of God; to his understanding of God and his relationship with God as articulated in this proclamation; and to his associated claim to authority.

15. This is precisely what John 20:30–31 articulates when it says that all that has been recounted about Jesus has been written "that you may believe that Jesus is the Messiah, the Son of God, and that by believing you may have life in his name" (NIV).

## 1.2. The Testimony of the Life of Jesus

According to the Gospels, Jesus first appeared in public as a wandering Jewish preacher from the circle of John the Baptist.[16] The Gospel narratives, however, claim that his true identity is not revealed in this outward, public context, where he was, it is true, distinguished from other wandering Jewish preachers of the period by the radicalism that led the religious establishment to accuse him of blasphemy and heresy (Mark 2:7; 14:64). Who he really is first becomes apparent in the inner context of his particular relationship with God that was not accessible to the public. The baptism pericopes (Mark 1:9–15; Matt. 3:13–17; Luke 3:21–22) illustrate this in a narrative image intended to show Jesus himself wholly in the light of the essence of his public discourse and activity: the *proclamation of the dawning reign of God and the nearness of his love*. This message, which Jesus fleshed out through his discourse and actions, should form the basis of any answer to the question of his identity. What does this message mean?

Mark 1:14–15 summarizes it, stylized as the "gospel of God," which Jesus proclaimed in his public ministry as the good news about God: "The time is fulfilled, and the kingdom of God is at hand; repent and believe in the gospel."[17] This summary of Jesus's preaching is illuminating from three points of view: it gives the central content of his preaching (the proximity and dawn of the reign of God); it links the fulfillment of this preaching with the person of the preacher, Jesus himself (cf. Mark 1:1); and it describes and characterizes them both in the same terms (as good news). I shall begin with the last point.

At the *representational* level the "gospel" terminology functions as a Markan summary and interpretation of Jesus's eschatological proclamation of the βασιλεία ("The time has come"). It is an interpretative summary of Jesus's message by the author of Mark's Gospel, who uses this description to shift the preaching, life, and person of Jesus into a perspective that would have been inaccessible to Jesus and his original listeners: the perspective of

16. Cf. J. Murphy O'Connor, "John the Baptist and Jesus: History and Hypotheses," *NTS* 36 (1990): 359–74.

17. Cf R. Schnackenburg, *Gottes Herrschaft und Reich: Eine biblisch-theologische Studie* (Freiburg: Herder, ³1963); E. Jüngel, *Paulus und Jesus* (Tübingen: Mohr Siebeck, ⁶1986); Jüngel, "Zur dogmatischen Bedeutung," 219–21; Fr. Beisser, *Das Reich Gottes* (Göttingen: Vandenhoeck & Ruprecht, 1976); H. Kessler, *Suchet den Lebenden nicht bei den Toten: Die Auferstehung Jesu Christi in biblischer, fundamentaltheologischer und systematischer Sicht* (Düsseldorf: Patmos, 1985), 79–92; H. Merklein, *Jesu Botschaft von der Gottesherrschaft: Eine Skizze* (Stuttgart: Katholisches Bibelwerk, 1983); Merklein, *Die Gottesherrschaft als Handlungsprinzip: Untersuchungen der Ethik Jesu* (Würzburg: Echter, 1978); Merklein, "Jesus, Künder des Reiches Gottes," in *Traktat Offenbarung*, vol. 2, *Handbuch der Fundamentaltheologie*, ed. W. Kern and H. J. Pottmeyer (Freiburg: Herder, 1985), 145–74.

the end of Jesus's life at the cross and the resurrection. This "gospel" terminology—which is unlikely to go back to Jesus himself or to his pre-Easter
ministry[18]—applies a post-Easter perspective that shows that the author (and
thus also the attentive reader and hearer) knows more than the characters in
his story. While we begin to see use of the term *gospel* in early Jewish and
rabbinic sources, although not in the Septuagint,[19] Christian usage is drawn
from the early Christian language of mission and its content is clearly defined,
as the Pauline Epistles show: "The word 'gospel' denotes the basic Christian
formula 'God raised Jesus from the dead.'"[20] The content of the εὐαγγέλιον
θεοῦ of Romans 1:1 is thus spelled out in Romans 1:3–4 as the message of
Jesus's resurrection and ascension to power, and this is announced as the
message of salvation because everyone who assents to this confession, by
declaring with the mouth that "Jesus is Lord" and believing in his or her
heart that "God raised him from the dead" (Rom. 10:9), will be saved. This
definitive identification of the "gospel" as the message of the resurrection is
confirmed in 1 Corinthians 15 and in other key passages, so that W. Schenk
is correct to state "that the semantic content of the early apostolic gospel
terminology to be found in the writings of Paul is always and only rooted in
the Easter tidings."[21] In drawing on this concept to summarize Jesus's message,
Mark is commenting on his proclamation of the dawning reign of God in the
light of the significance it was afforded by Jesus's own story: this message is
the announcement of the dawn of the eschatological reign of God, brought
about conclusively in the resurrection of the crucified Jesus. The resurrection
of the crucified one (the "gospel" or "good news") is thus declared to be the
normative horizon of understanding for the βασιλεία—preaching of Jesus,
defining it as τὸ εὐαγγέλιον τῆς βασιλείας—as it is in Matthew's consistent
terminological usage (Matt. 4:23; 9:35; 24:14). The Gospels set the preaching,
life, and person of Jesus against the background of the resurrection message
from the start, and thus from the outset they construe the dawn of the reign
of God as proclaimed by Jesus within the context of his story, in other words,
*christologically.*[22]

---

18. W. Marxsen, *Der Evangelist Markus* (Göttingen: Vandenhoeck & Ruprecht, ²1959), 83;
W. Schenk, *Evangelium—Evangelien—Evangeliologie: Ein "hermeneutisches" Manifest* (Munich:
Christian Kaiser, 1983), 47–58; P. Stuhlmacher, "Evangelium 1. Biblisch," *EKL* 1:1217–21, esp.
1:1218; A. Jäger, "Evangelium 2. Dogmatisch," *EKL* 1:1221–22, esp. 1:1221.
    19. Cf. Stuhlmacher, "Evangelium 1," 1:1218.
    20. Schenk, *Evangelium*, 22.
    21. Ibid., 26.
    22. The various christological models they follow show that they each use their own way of
doing this. They share the conviction that if the resurrection of Jesus illuminates the truth of
his life, his preaching, and his person, then it must have been relevant from the outset and must

If we turn from there to the *subject matter* (i.e., the message of Jesus presented by Mark: "The time has come, and the kingdom of God has come near. Repent and believe in [God's saving nearness, which has been definitively revealed in the resurrection of Jesus]"), then it is obvious that Mark sees the core of this message in the *coincidence of the proclamation and the proclaimer*. What Jesus proclaims becomes reality in and with him: his person realizes his message.[23] The crucial element of the message of Jesus is not the preaching of the kingdom of God in itself but rather that this good reign of God *is now dawning*: "The time has come." Jesus uses the image of the kingdom of God (βασιλεία τοῦ θεοῦ) to link into the expectation of exilic and postexilic salvation prophecy that in the last days the reign of God will be visible to all nations (Isa. 52:7; Mic. 2:12–13; Zeph. 3:14–15; Zech. 14:9, 16–17). Jesus probably inherited this message from John the Baptist, to whose circle he is thought to have belonged for a while at least, and from whom he also received the baptism of repentance and purification that demonstrated the desire of the baptized to be converted and that would preserve them from the coming fire of God's judgment. Like John, Jesus takes up the Jewish apocalyptic contrast between the present age and the coming time of salvation when he announces that the kingdom of God *has come* or *is near* (ἤγγικεν). But in contrast to the Baptist, he not only foretells this time of salvation but proclaims its arrival: its advent is not imminent; it has now dawned. Also in contrast to the Baptist, the purification rite of baptism and withdrawal from the world into the wilderness

---

have defined his life, teaching, and being from the very beginning. But they choose different ways of expressing this "relevance from the outset" within their narratives: For Mark the christological anticipation of the Easter event occurs at Jesus's baptism, for Matthew and Luke at his virgin birth, while John anticipates Easter in his prologue, with its hymn to the preexistence and incarnation of the Logos, which acts as a reader's guide to the whole Gospel, as do Mark 1:1–3 and the genealogical record of Jesus in Matt. 1:1–17. These different narrative techniques go hand in hand with different christological models: Mark's appointment Christology, Matthew's revelation Christology, Luke's epiphany Christology, and John's sending Christology. They should not be compared directly, nor played off one against the other. Rather, they must each be related to a third element: the Easter message of the resurrection of the crucified one. A theological assessment from that perspective will show whether and to what degree their narrative techniques do justice to the message.

23. The gospel therefore treats the semantic (content-related) and pragmatic (situation-related) dimensions of Jesus's preaching—*what* he preached, *how* he preached it, and that *he* was the preacher—as interconnected. "Gospel" is not simply a Christian designation for the content of Jesus's message, and one cannot be said to be preaching the gospel just because one is proclaiming what Jesus proclaimed. Much more, the integration of the preacher and his message is crucial to the gospel, so that the person of Jesus himself forms part of the content of the message. Jesus's preaching and Christian preaching are not simply synonymous. To be saying the same as Jesus, Christian preaching must say more than he did: it must include Jesus himself, as well as his message, in the subject matter of its preaching. So it is not the message of Jesus that Christians proclaim *but the good news of Jesus Christ*.

were not Jesus's way of preparing for these epoch-making changes to the times and to world dominion. On the contrary, he lived among the people as a charismatic wandering preacher without possessions and without a family or a fixed abode,[24] and in his own way—without using the terminology of the apocalyptic conceptual world[25]—he gave tangible form to the apocalyptic expectations of the new age in his message of the dawning reign of God. The following elements are worth highlighting:

1. *The time of salvation.* The reign of God is the time of salvation; its advent makes everything new. Jesus makes it clear what this means when he defines this reign as overwhelming fatherly love, which he describes in the parable of the prodigal son and teaches us to pray for in the Lord's Prayer, where he details some of its aspects. When this love takes up its rule, God's justice and mercy will be established and God's will will be carried out in every circumstance. So God's reign is not a heavy yoke: it comes unconditionally to the poor, the outcasts, the despised, and the guilty. For them it marks the beginning of the time of salvation in which their present need is to be radically removed. This is why they are called blessed (Luke 6:20–23; Matt. 5:3–12)—not because they are poor but because the advent of the reign of God means the end of their destitution and the beginning of their salvation.

2. *Universality and individuality.* Because God's reign makes everything new, it brings with it a radical transformation in the lives of individuals and of whole peoples. The apocalyptic thought of the second century BC included not just Israel but the entire world in its expectation of a cosmic catastrophe and the new creation of the whole earth. "All nationalistic and theocratic tendencies disappear in Jesus's preaching. There is no talk either about the annihilation of the ungodly world power [i.e., Rome] or about the coming rule by Israel. On the contrary: Gentiles and Samaritans are held before the impenitent people of God as examples of true repentance and love."[26] When God's reign comes, it comes unconditionally, without any particular (ethnic or religious) preconditions and to everyone alike. But this certainly does not mean that it has the same consequences, the same effect, or the same significance for everyone. In itself it is the same for everyone, but it affects everyone individually.

3. *Judgment.* How God's reign affects an individual depends crucially on how it encounters him or her, and what it achieves depends on the condition

24. Cf G. Theißen, *Sociology of Early Palestinian Christianity*, trans. J. Bowden (Philadelphia: Fortress, 1978), 8–16.
25. He was after all "a layman. He had no training in 'Jewish wisdom,'" as K. Niederwimmer correctly observes (*Jesus*, 42).
26. M. Hengel, *Christ and Power* (Minneapolis: Fortress, 1977), 17.

in which it finds them. It always makes everything new, bringing about a fundamental transformation that changes the life and circumstances of those affected in a variety of ways. For the poor, the outcast, the despised, and the guilty, God's reign means the end of their destitution. For many, on the other hand—for the ruling classes in Israel; for the large landowners from the upper stratum of feudal society, who placed more emphasis on money than on God (Matt. 6:24); for the Sadducean priestly hierarchy in the temple, who had made God's house into a den of robbers (Mark 11:17); for the scribes and Pharisees, who had concealed and obscured the simple, clear, and unfettered loving will of their Father God with their scrupulous interpretation of the Torah—for all these the advent of the rule of God meant the end of their own rule, advantages, and privileges. Luke, in sharp contrast, counters the beatitudinal blessings with curses on those who, as a result of their religious, social, or economic advantages are comfortable in this Godless world and have come to terms with their unjust, heartless, and loveless way of life. For them the coming of the reign of God signifies not salvation but criticism, correction, and judgment, for self-righteousness, heartlessness, and lack of love have no place in the kingdom of God.

4. *Decision time.* The dawn of the reign of God is therefore a moment of distinction and decision. It is true that God's reign always comes in the form of compassionate, fatherly love, but not everyone it encounters will allow himself or herself to be affected and governed by it. This is why Jesus's parables constantly issue urgent calls to prepare for God's coming and to expect his appearance: God can come as unexpectedly as a householder on a journey, whose servants must hold themselves in constant readiness for his unanticipated return (Mark 13:33–37; Luke 12:36–38); or as a thief who breaks into the house unexpectedly (Matt. 24:43–44; Luke 12:39–40); or as the bridegroom for whose arrival the ten virgins were waiting (Matt. 25:1–13). But this expectant vigilance is only one element. The other element is to have the right reaction to the arrival of the reign of God. Mark sums it up in the concept of μετάνοια, conversion, which plays a central role not only in the preaching of the Baptist but also in several of the Jesus sayings (Matt. 11:21 // Luke 10:13 // Matt. 12:41; Luke 11:32; 13:3, 5; 15:7, 10; 16:30). In contrast to the Baptist, Jesus does not seem to have linked conversion with a particular outward rite like a baptism of purification. Instead he called people to follow him, both in the positive sense of placing themselves at the disposal of the dawning reign of God and thus also in the negative sense of relinquishing all family, social, and economic ties with the passing world and its structures. One who becomes involved with the reign of God cannot continue to live in the same way as before. Like the prodigal son, he must radically alter and reorient his

life (Luke 15:17). God does not compel this conversion and reorientation. It must be entered into voluntarily and on one's own initiative because God's fatherly love achieves its objective only in response to love freely returned. Even when one encounters God's reign and his love, this conversion does not happen inevitably or automatically. For Zacchaeus it happened (Luke 19:8), but not for the rich young ruler (Mark 10:17–22), who neither could nor would relinquish his wealth. Hence it is far more difficult for property owners, the rich, and the privileged than it is for the poor and those with few possessions, who have nothing to lose. Essentially, this radical reorientation of one's life can take place only when one encounters the kingdom of God with the impartiality, openness, and spontaneous joy with which children react to presents, without asking whether they are entitled to them or worthy of them, and without insisting on their own status or importance (Mark 10:15; Luke 18:17; Matt. 18:3).

5. *It comes of itself.* God's reign can thus be received only as a gift that one has not procured for oneself and cannot demand. It comes as and when God wishes. Its arrival cannot be forced by a messianic uprising: it comes in its own way and at the time determined by God himself. People can and should recognize the signs of the times (Mark 13:28–29; Luke 12:54–56) and participate in God's reign through conversion and amendment of their lives, but they can neither hasten nor delay its arrival. People must indeed reach a decision regarding the reign of God, but their decision is not what establishes it. They can accept and participate in it (faith), or they can reject and ignore it (unbelief), but nothing they do can bring it into being. They can radically change their lives in the light of the nearness and love of God, or they can ignore the chance of salvation that is being offered to them and cling to their present privileges and advantages, but they can neither hinder nor further the coming of God's reign. They can link their lives to the old era that is passing or to the new era that is dawning, but they cannot influence either the end of the old era or the arrival of the new.

6. *The time has come.* Jesus's preaching is not a statement about something expected to happen sometime in the future but a matter-of-fact, enthusiastic proclamation of current events: God's reign is coming now; it is very near; it is already dawning; the era of salvation has begun and is casting its unmistakable shadow across Jesus's activity and preaching. "Blessed are the eyes that see what you see. For I tell you that many prophets and kings wanted to see what you see but did not see it, and to hear what you hear but did not hear it" (Luke 10:23–24 NIV; cf. Matt. 13:16–17). In Jesus's preaching, God's reign is no remote, future reality, for the combined presence of the preacher and the proclamation is already making it present to his listeners (Luke 17:20–21).

Its reality is evident in its effects, as Jesus performs exorcisms and casts out demons (Luke 11:20; Matt. 12:28), and as he deprives Satan of his power (Luke 10:18). Jesus uses images such as the wedding feast (Mark 2:18–20), putting new cloth on an old garment (Mark 2:21) or new wine into old wineskins (Mark 2:22), as well as the parables of the treasure hidden in the field (Matt. 13:44), the pearl of great price (Matt. 13:45–46), or the harvest (Matt. 9:37–38), to communicate the concealed but effective and urgent presence of the reign of God. The era of salvation has begun; the time of waiting is coming to an end. It is no longer a time to hesitate but a time to set forth, unconditionally and regardless of existing ties: anyone who is reluctant to be swept along in the current of the dawning reign of God is not for it but against it. A duty of piety toward the dead (Matt. 8:22), the family, or even to oneself (Luke 14:26–27) does not constitute an argument against following the call to discipleship. In the light of the transforming and all-surpassing riches available under the reign of God, such arguments are as inappropriate as is concern about safeguarding one's own life (Luke 12:22–30). There is now only one commitment and concern: "Seek his kingdom, and these things will be given to you as well" (Luke 12:31 NIV). The coming of God's kingdom pervades the whole of the present and is the one and only reality that counts. But since it is not a tyrannical rule but the presence of the inexhaustible love of God, it does not crush and overpower people; instead, it provides everything they need. It is the age of peace, righteousness, and abundance, the time of salvation that is now dawning through the actions of Jesus himself and is motivating everyone, men and women from all levels of society, and by no means just Israelites, to reorient and reshape their lives.

It is this eschatological intensification and soteriological decisiveness, rather than its zealous urgency, that make Jesus's preaching so remarkable.[27] John the Baptist's preaching of judgment and repentance was also characterized by its expectation of the imminent dawn of the time of salvation. But while John was announcing the imminent start of the age of judgment (Matt. 3:10), Jesus was proclaiming the beginning of the reign of God here and now (Matt.

27. In the light of Easter, this eschatological intensification, together with the way in which Jesus's message and its expression in his own life, teaching, and ministry defined the substance of the kingdom of God, inevitably gave rise to the development of christological doctrines. If God's reign was just as Jesus's entire life had proclaimed it to be, in word and deed, then this reign had arrived to great effect in his words and actions. It provided the message of God's kingdom with the eschatological backdrop that allowed the death of Jesus on the cross and the appearances of the crucified one to be understood within the context of the raising of the crucified one by God as the eschatological saving action par excellence. Given these circumstances, it was inevitable that their implications for the person of Jesus Christ, the one who has been crucified and raised, would be thought through and developed christologically.

12:28). And while John was issuing a call to conversion, repentance, and baptism in view of the impending judgment, Jesus was proclaiming the start of the righteous reign of the God who vindicates the disenfranchised, a reign that takes effect only when God's saving nearness is accepted as the source of all things and that radically alters people's lives by aligning them completely with God, going beyond all religious rules, regulations, and traditions and transforming their lives so that they become the very places where God's saving will is realized. God's kingdom comes on its own terms and does not depend on human behavior. It is not God's reaction but his action that draws near to people to help them and to set their lives to rights because they are unable to help themselves and set themselves to rights. The dawning reign of God thus opens up possibilities of life that we could never have obtained for ourselves. We need do no more than allow ourselves to be drawn into God's nearness and be directed by it so that we love God and our neighbor as ourselves. Jesus shows us what this means by the whole practice of his life, in which his words and actions brought healing, help, fellowship, and joy to the sick, the outcasts, and the disadvantaged. It is thus with good reason that Mark characterizes Jesus's preaching not as a message of judgment but as good news. Viewed in the light of Easter, it does indeed reflect what the resurrection of the crucified one proved eschatologically: God will not allow anything to prevent him from accomplishing his saving will for us.

The Gospels present Jesus's proclamation in a way that allows these elements to be traceable throughout. Jesus uses his parables and parabolic actions in particular—what he says and what he does—to explain the image of the dawning reign of God. With the arrival of God's kingdom, something enters the world "that is in no way part of it but that can be experienced only as an *intrusion* into, or a fundamental *interruption* of, the world as a whole."[28] But this kingdom comes, as Jesus's parables explain, in an entirely *this-worldly manner*, in familiar events of everyday life, not in an exclusive sphere of religious experience, an ascetic existence, or a life in the desert, far removed from human society. So it does not merely have a religious aspect, involving the salvation of an individual's soul, but it brings salvation to the whole person, increasing all of his or her opportunities for life.[29] Accordingly, it comes chiefly to those who live and suffer in hostile environments, in underprivileged, disastrous circumstances, to the poor, the hungry, and the sick, to the crippled, the blind, and the lame, to sinners, tax collectors, and

---

28. Jüngel, "Zur dogmatischen Bedeutung," 220.
29. Cf. W. Schrage, "Heil und Heilung im Neuen Testament," in *"Auf Hoffnung hin sind wir erlöst" (Rom. 8:24): Biblische und systematische Beiträge zum Erlösungsverständnis heute*, ed. I. Broer and J. Werbick (Stuttgart: Katholisches Bibelwerk, 1987), 95–117.

outcasts.[30] Jesus specifically emphasizes the fact that God's kingdom comes without any help from us (Mark 4:27–29), that it cannot be forced to come, but that its coming can only be prayed for (Luke 11:2), that its arrival cannot be discerned from outward signs (17:20), but that it breaks into each life as a thief in the night, that anyone who does not want to sleep through it is therefore called on to be vigilant (Mark 13:32–36), and that it is more readily perceived by the poor and by social outcasts than by the rich and socially privileged.

First and foremost, however, Jesus makes it clear that the coming of God's kingdom is *directly linked with himself*. He does not merely announce it; he makes it present through his own words and actions (Matt. 12:28). He is not just its messenger but its agent. His listeners' relationship with himself as a person is therefore decisive for their relationship with the kingdom of God: no one can allow himself to be directed by it without allowing himself to be drawn into it. Hence Jesus's parables do not necessarily need to speak explicitly of God in order to mediate God's nearness. Jesus can therefore focus attention on this by means of actions that have no specific religious quality and even expressly contradict established religious behavior patterns: by eating, drinking, and celebrating with sinners, prostitutes, and tax collectors; by breaking Torah laws or prevalent interpretations of the Torah, such as the Sabbath commandment and the purity laws; or by the provocative freedom with which he countered the authority of Moses and the established understanding of the law with his "But I tell you" (Matt. 5:21–48). For Jesus the presence of the kingdom of God and the saving nearness of God are not tied to particular holy seasons, places, or rules, or to a cult or a priestly caste, or to religious rituals or ceremonies. They come about through his actions and take effect through him as a person.

This becomes especially apparent through the miracles Jesus is said to have performed. According to the Gospels, Jesus drew attention to himself as a miracle worker and exorcist. Admittedly, the Gospels are not interested in this in the same way that modern apologetic discussion of miracles is. The point of their accounts is not "*that there are miracles* (they take that as self-evident, without reflecting on it), *but that Jesus performed some.*"[31] This conviction probably goes back in essence to pre-Easter testimonies about Jesus. "The miracle tradition of the Gospels would be completely and utterly inexplicable if Jesus's earthly life had not left behind a general impression and a general recollection of a sort that later made it possible to proclaim Jesus a miracle

---

30. Cf. H. Kessler, "Überlegungen zur biblisch-christlichen Heilshoffnung," *Theologische Akademie* 12 (1975): 27–51, esp. 44.

31. Niederwimmer, *Jesus*, 33.

worker."[32] This is true, regardless of the fact that the Gospels show a tendency to "intensify, magnify, and multiply the miracles"[33] (cf. Mark 1:34 with Matt. 8:16; Mark 5:35–43 with Luke 8:49–56; Mark 8:5–9 // Matt. 15:34–38 with Mark 6:31–44 // Matt. 14:13–21 // Luke 9:10–17; and Mark 8:19–20 with Matt. 14:18–20 // Luke 9:12–17), that this development is already in evidence during the period before the Gospels were written, that the miracle narratives pick up motifs and analogies from Jewish and Hellenistic miracle stories, that the presentation of the healing miracles in particular follows a fixed literary structure, and that a whole series of miracle narratives (e.g., the stilling of the storm, Jesus walking on the water, the feeding of the five thousand Jews or of the four thousand gentiles in the Decapolis, the transfiguration, the raising from the dead of Jairus's daughter, of the widow of Nain's son, and of Lazarus) turn out, "in the light of form criticism to be projections of the experiences of Easter back into the earthly life of Jesus, or anticipatory representations of the exalted Christ."[34] Even though it can hardly be disputed that the nature miracles (the multiplication of the loaves, the turning of water into wine, the walking on the water, and the stilling of the storm) are formulated as legends, two facts can be established with a degree of certainty, nonetheless. First, Jesus, in contrast to many of his contemporaries, did no miracles of sensation or judgment, and neither did he perform healings and exorcisms for money, but he expressly protected himself against any such demands (cf. Mark 8:12; Luke 11:29–30 // Matt. 12:39–41 // Mark 8:12). Second, however, like many of his contemporaries, Jesus healed the sick and liberated the possessed, so he did indeed perform miracles of healing and exorcisms.[35] This made him well known in Galilee and beyond (cf. Mark 1:28, 39, 45; 7:37), contributed significantly to his popularity with the simple country people (Mark 2:1–12),

32. W. Kasper, *Jesus the Christ* (London: Burns & Oates, 1976), 90.

33. Ibid., 89.

34. Ibid., 90.

35. This historical assessment is correct, regardless of the question of whether these healings and exorcisms can be thought of according to the Enlightenment understanding of miracles as violating the laws of nature. Even if Jesus did not actually perform *miracles in this sense* or (if it is held that there can be no exceptions to the laws of nature) could not, in principle, have performed miracles, this would not alter the fact that he worked as a thaumaturge and an exorcist and was known and criticized for this. His activities as a thaumaturge and an exorcist would then have to be understood as being in harmony with the laws of nature but as a source of amazement and consternation to his contemporaries nevertheless. Conversely, there is nothing to be gained from the spurious apologetic argument that, in the light of the changes to our understanding of the laws of nature that have taken place within our century, the "violation of the laws of nature" is by no means nonsensical or inconceivable, so that it would be not at all impossible for Jesus to have worked miracles. This debate resorts to an interpretation of the term *miracle* that contributes nothing, either positive or negative, to an understanding of Jesus's activity.

but also provoked criticism from quite early on (cf. Matt. 12:28; Luke 11:20). His activities laid him open to the charge of being in league with the devil (Mark 3:22; Matt. 9:34; Luke 11:20). The criticism thus involved an evaluation of his healings and exorcisms rather than a questioning of the fact of their occurrence. Even his opponents did not dispute the latter. That Jesus really did perform such miracles, even on the Sabbath, was in itself one of the reasons for his conflict with the Jewish authorities (Mark 1:23–28; 3:1–6; Luke 13:10–17).

For the writers of the Gospels and for Jesus's contemporaries, it thus was not whether he worked miracles but the assessment of their significance that was the real problem. It is clear that verdicts varied widely from the outset, depending on the context in which Jesus's activity as a thaumaturge and an exorcist was considered. Jesus's miraculous deeds caused his family to regard him as, quite simply, mad (Mark 3:21). For the (Levite) temple lawyers ("scribes"),[36] they were demonic activities (Mark 3:22; Matt. 12:24). For the Christians (and for Jesus himself), on the other hand, such a view was blatantly self-contradictory: "How can Satan drive out Satan?" (Mark 3:23). Of course, the self-contradictory nature of this view was not immediately apparent from the events themselves, but only when they were seen in the context of Jesus's other actions. Taken in isolation, they could indeed be insane or demonic activities. But once one considers the whole picture, this changes. The Gospels insist that Jesus's miracles are not phenomena to be considered and judged in isolation. They are aspects of a broader picture. So the Gospels never describe these acts of Jesus purely as miraculous wonders (τέρατα) but as works of power (δύναμεις) and signs (σημεῖα). These descriptions make it plain that such acts point to something other than themselves, so that they can be understood only when it is clear *what* they demonstrate and *of what* they are signs. This becomes evident when they are understood *in the context of Jesus's whole message* and, in particular, of his *proclamation of the dawning reign of God*.[37] When they are isolated from the latter context, they are indistinguishable from the miraculous deeds of the Hellenistic miracle

36. Cf. D. R. Schwartz, "'Scribes and Pharisees, Hypocrites': Who Are the 'Scribes' in the New Testament?," in *Studies in the Jewish Background of Christianity* (Tübingen: Mohr Siebeck, 1992), 88–101; D. Lührmann, "Die Pharisäer und die Schriftgelehrten im Markusevangelium," *ZNW* 78 (1987): 169–85; E. S. Malbon, "The Jewish Leaders in the Gospel of Mark: A Literary Study of Marcan Characterization," *JBL* 108 (1989): 259–81.

37. They are viewed from an incorrect interpretative perspective theologically if one says, "They can only be understood against the background of the basic human hope for something totally different and totally new, for the coming of a new and reconciled world" (Kasper, *Jesus the Christ*, 95). They are to be understood theologically not within this anthropological context but rather in the christological context of the preaching and life of Jesus.

workers, which is why they drew censure from the temple theologians and the Pharisees on the grounds that they were demonic. But when they are understood in the context of Jesus's message, they function as evidence for this message and demonstrate what it means when God's reign dawns: disease, suffering, social isolation, religious discrimination, and separation from God are abolished where God's reign establishes itself.[38]

Viewed in the context of Jesus's βασιλεία-preaching, his miracles are the materialization of his preaching, works of power that are conclusive signs that God's kingdom has arrived. They give God's dawning reign visible contours and practical shape within human life. Further evidence of this focus on the reign of God is provided by Jesus's practice of *forgiving sins*, which plays a significant role in the miracle stories. In contrast to Jesus's activities as a thaumaturge and an exorcist, this practice, together with his criticism of the Torah, his provocative treatment of the Sabbath (Mark 2:23–28; 3:1–6), and his emancipated attitude to the requirements of the law (Mark 2:18–22) and to social outcasts (Mark 2:13–17), constituted a major stumbling block for the scribes (cf. Mark 2:5–12). On the one hand, it is a key aspect of the kingdom of God: without the forgiveness of sins, there can be no participation in the kingdom of God (Matt. 18:23–35; Luke 7:41–43; 15:11–32) or in true life (Mark 10:17; Luke 18:18). On the other hand, forgiveness of sins is the privilege of God alone: anyone who forgives sins is taking on himself a right reserved for God (Mark 2:7). Both these elements are characteristic of Jesus's preaching and ministry. Jesus thus makes it clear that the coming of the kingdom of God signifies victory over sin and the demonic powers (Matt. 12:28; Luke 11:20), the end of Satan's rule (Luke 10:18), and the beginning of the righteous reign of God (Luke 10:23–24), when God's saving will is to be accomplished and his purposes achieved. It is with good reason that Jesus's signs and acts of power are also understood, in the context of his preaching, as the eschatological fulfillment of the Old Testament promises: the blind receive sight, the lame walk, lepers are cleansed, the deaf hear, the dead are raised, and the good news is proclaimed to the poor (Matt. 11:5; cf. Isa. 29:18; 35:5–6; 61:1). The Gospels' conclusion is that God's eschatological kingdom has come in Jesus's activity, in word and deed, through his life and his person. This conclusion mirrors Jesus's claim that the coming of the reign of God is accomplished in his own activity (Mark 1:15) so that he is empowered to call others to discipleship (Mark 1:16–20; 2:14), to teach

38. G. H. Twelftree (*Jesus the Exorcist: A Contribution to the Study of the Historical Jesus* [Tübingen: Mohr Siebeck, 1993]) has shown that this close association between message and eschatology is a distinguishing aspect of Jesus's exorcisms.

with authority (Mark 1:21–27), to bring physical and psychological healing to people (Mark 1:29–31), to forgive sins (Mark 2:1–12), to associate and even eat with social outcasts (Mark 2:13–17), to take liberties with the law (Mark 2:18–22), to act as Lord of the Sabbath (Mark 2:23–28), to put an end to demonic control (Mark 3:22–27), and to make eschatological salvation dependent on him (Luke 12:8).

It was not only Jesus's listeners who were astonished, frightened, and dismayed by Jesus's claim to authority (Mark 1:27; 3:21–22; Luke 5:26).[39] In the Christians' view, it was no accident that the religious authorities of Israel perceived Jesus's claim as blasphemy and made it their central charge against him. By his words and actions Jesus was in fact placing himself above the Torah; he dared to "affirm God's will in such a way that he himself stood in God's place";[40] he ate with tax collectors and sinners and had already begun to celebrate the eschatological love feast;[41] he issued authoritative calls to people to follow him rather than waiting, as the teachers of the law did, until they asked him to admit them as disciples;[42] he drove demons out, healed, and forgave sins.[43] Anyone who places himself above God's law, exercises eschatological functions, controls demons, and forgives sins is presuming to have rights reserved for God alone. Inasmuch as Jesus did these things, he was claiming that God himself was at work in his actions. At any rate, his followers and his opponents unanimously understood him in this way. John's Gospel picks up this idea and states it more precisely (John 10:22–39); God himself is present in Jesus's words and actions, for he and the Father are one (ἕν) (John 10:30). "Jesus and the Father are not one single person—that would call for εἷς—but are one, meaning that Jesus does exactly what God does."[44] Jesus's actions accomplish God's actions (John 5:17–20). What Jesus does and proclaims is thus understood correctly only by those who comprehend his actions as mediating God's presence, as realizing God's saving activity, and as bringing in the righteous reign of God. Jesus is not only the one who

39. K. Scholtissek, *Die Vollmacht Jesu: Traditions- und redaktionsgeschichtliche Analysen zu einem Leitmotiv markinischer Christologie* (Münster: Aschendorff, 1992).

40. E. Fuchs, "Die Frage nach dem historischen Jesus," in *Zur Frage nach dem historischen Jesus*, Gesammelte Aufsätze (Tübingen: Mohr Siebeck, ²1965), 2:143–67, esp. 154.

41. J. Jeremias, *Neutestamentliche Theologie*, vol. 1, *Die Verkündigung Jesu* (Gütersloh: Gütersloher Verlagshaus Mohn, 1971), 117.

42. Kasper, *Jesus the Christ*, 100–104; W. Rebell, *Alles ist möglich dem, der glaubt: Glaubensvollmacht im frühen Christentum* (Munich: Christian Kaiser, 1989), 14:25–33.

43. In Qumran texts and in the Gospels, "heal" and "forgive sins" function as synonyms, as is shown by Vermes (*Jesus the Jew*, 67–69). This does not necessarily prove that they are *generally* to be understood as synonyms when used by Jesus.

44. E. Haenchen, *Das Johannesevangelium: Ein Kommentar, aus den nachgelassenen Manuskripten* (Tübingen: Mohr Siebeck, 1980), 392.

proclaims the reign of God; he is the place and instrument of its tangible realization, the kingdom of God in person or αὐτοβασιλεία, to quote Origen.[45]

### 1.3. The Son of the Father

Jesus did not refer to himself thus. Nevertheless, in the Gospels the Christology implicit in his words and actions becomes a more explicit and nascent Christology when he is challenged to identify himself with the aid of specific titles and images. According to Mark 8:27–29, the people saw him as John the Baptist, Elijah, or another prophet; Peter gave him the title of Messiah (and—according to Matt. 16:16, 22—"Son of the living God" and "Lord" as well); and Jesus himself used the title Son of Man. Only this latter appellation was in all likelihood used by Jesus himself.[46] According to G. Vermes, in everyday speech its basic Aramaic form functioned not as a title but as a diffident self-appellation by the speaker "out of awe, reserve, or humility."[47] In none of its occurrences (Mark 8:38 // Matt. 16:27 // Luke 9:26; Mark 13:26 // Matt. 24:30 // Luke 21:27; Mark 14:62 // Matt. 26:64 // Luke 22:69) is it likely that a reference to the eschatological collective figure (i.e., the figure in Dan. 7:13) goes back to Jesus himself.[48] It is far more likely "that the apocalyptically-minded Galilean disciples of Jesus appear to have 'eschatologised' [Jesus's neutral Aramaic manner of speaking] by means of a midrash based on Daniel 7:13."[49]

But neither the expression "Son of Man" nor the other titles referred to above could have been used exclusively of Jesus and not of others. None of them could have expressed his uniqueness without the use of additional designations. Almost all of these were first ascribed to Jesus in the light of Easter. And when, as with the title of Prophet, Jesus was already called this in his lifetime, he himself did not want others to know that he was called this, so that the community later insisted that Jesus represented something "more" and "greater" than a prophet (cf. Matt. 12). No christological inferences may therefore be drawn from any of these appellations in themselves, other than from their application to Jesus. Every attempt "to derive even a moderately clear Christology from the names of Jesus," taking the history of their pre- and non-Christian use as a starting point for christological statements, encounters

---

45. Origen, "In Matthew Tom XIV 7 [On Matt. 18:23]," GCS 40:289.
46. Cf A. J. B. Higgins, *The Son of Man in the Teaching of Jesus*, SNTSMS 39 (Cambridge: Cambridge University Press, 1980), 123–26.
47. Vermes, *Jesus the Jew*, 186.
48. Ibid., 182–86; cf. N. Perrin, *Rediscovering the Teaching of Jesus* (London: Harper & Row, 1967), 173–81; H. E. Tödt, *Der Menschensohn in der synoptischen Überlieferung* (Gütersloh: Gütersloher Verlagshaus Mohn, 1959).
49. Vermes, *Jesus the Jew*, 186.

"problems that are not readily surmountable."[50] These titles and appellations are christologically significant not in themselves or because of their provenance but by virtue of their use in the Christian community as reflected in the New Testament texts.[51] In some cases (Messiah, Lord, Son of God), though by no means in all (prophet, teacher), this usage has established christological traditions in which these appellations fundamentally altered their inherited semantic profile as a result of their application to the risen Jesus Christ. They provided aids for the articulation of something absolutely new and were thus subject from the outset to the rule that they could be understood, not descriptively, but in the traditional, customary way. The Christian community emphasized these hermeneutical changes from the beginning by subjecting the use of these appellations to the rule of augmentation ("Something greater than Jonah is here"; Matt. 12:41), reinterpreting them against the background of the story of Jesus's passion (e.g., the title of Messiah: Mark 8:31–33 // Matt. 16:21–23 // Luke 9:22), and ultimately by regulating them within a trinitarian framework. It is not the semantic content of the individual appellations, titles, and images as such that is decisive christologically; it is their Christian use for confessional purposes, packaging together (semantically explicable) references to Jesus, to God, and to the confessing persons.[52] Admittedly, this confessional use always results, according to Christian conviction, from the work of the Spirit—not only in the past but also, and indeed principally, in the current experience of individuals or the community. But this is the very reason why such use constantly stimulates us to ask what it is in Jesus's own words and actions that prompts us, in the light of Easter, to speak of him in this way.

The answer to this question is to be found in considering how Jesus vindicated and substantiated the claim to authority demonstrated by his words and actions. According to the Gospels he legitimized it on the basis of his relationship with God or, to be more precise, God's relationship with him.

50. Fr. W. Marquardt, *Das christliche Bekenntnis zu Jesus, dem Juden: Eine Christologie* (Munich: Christian Kaiser, 1990), 1:148.

51. Their provenance is only important when it hints at why these appellations in particular and no others were taken up for christological purposes. But they are not taken up as concepts under which Jesus Christ is subsumed as a special case. Rather, they constitute a semantic portfolio that makes it possible to formulate the being of Jesus Christ by giving clues and indications, using these concepts christologically in a way that breaks through and surpasses their traditional semantic significance so as to open them up to the awareness of God's unique saving activity in Jesus Christ. Cf. I. U. Dalferth, *Theology and Philosophy* (Eugene, OR: Wipf & Stock, 2002), 198–203.

52. Without doubt, however, the semantic content of these images also plays a role here. In fact, this usage actually determines its content—in continuity with, and in contrast to, its previous history. But only the newly constituted content of these images is christologically relevant.

Jesus appeals not to himself, but to the will of God, which he is accomplishing in his preaching and his actions.[53] This is especially true of the antitheses in the Sermon on the Mount (Matt. 5:21–48), where Jesus introduces a better righteousness to counter the Old Testament law by removing the restrictions and conditions surrounding the will of God and focusing it in a way that allows no escape, no reservations, and no excuses. The "But I tell you" does not counter the Old Testament commandments cited with an interpretation of the law that distances Jesus from other scribal interpretations. Rather, it affirms God's word and will *without recourse to any authority*—whether it be Moses, the scribes, or even Jesus himself[54]—in their absolute eschatological claim on his listeners: the content and not the source of the word is what matters. The absoluteness of the claim is not based on the fact that it is Jesus who makes it—after all, who is likely to accept it on the authority of

53. Jesus expressly rejected the title of Good Master with the comment that no one but God deserved to be addressed thus (Mark 10:18). He performs miracles and forgives sins, not on his own authority, but on the authority of his Father in heaven. This is indeed the charge leveled against him: that he professed to be acting on behalf of God, claiming God's authority and not merely his own, and that he blasphemed the name of God thereby.

54. The ἐξουσία that the earthly Jesus claimed in the Gospel of Mark and elsewhere, and on which he based his call to discipleship, his criticism of contemporary interpretations of the law, and his forgiveness of sins, was an authority he asserted not in his own name but in the name of God: Jesus claimed that what he said and did expressed the definitive will of God, even when this ran counter to the interpretation of the law held as binding in Israel. This inevitably provoked Jesus's opponents to accuse him directly of blasphemy: anyone who equates the codifying of the will of God with God's will itself is bound to view Jesus's treatment of the law as blasphemous arrogance. One must already have submitted oneself to what Jesus says and does if one is to hold a different view, and the sources make clear that this is far easier for the theologically uninitiated layperson than for those who have dedicated their whole lives to understanding and following the will of God as codified in the law. Nevertheless, it was almost inevitable that Jesus's self-effacement vis-à-vis his message would be construed by his opponents as self-promotion. *Precisely by relying wholly on the kingdom of God without appealing to any other authority to legitimate his preaching, he placed himself in a dubious light as a preacher.* Mark's Gospel makes it plain that even Jesus's followers were unable to submit themselves wholly and exclusively to his message during the pre-Easter period: even their eyes were not opened until after Easter. For only in the light of the death and resurrection of Jesus can his authoritative actions be understood as legitimate and not blasphemous, because God, whose rule he proclaimed, had vindicated both the message and the messenger. Jesus's authority is therefore not to be defined "*as participation in God's saving and kingly power*" that culminates "*in his laying claim to divine authority*" (Scholtissek, *Vollmacht Jesu*, 285–86) but as Jesus's consistent self-effacement right up to his own death, in order to make room for *God himself alone.* Jesus participates in God's authority not by claiming for himself what is God's alone but by making it known through his teaching and his life that God himself is asserting his authority absolutely, exclusively, and effectively. It is not participation in God's kingly power that singles Jesus out, but the fact that he is the locus of the self-mediation and self-revelation of the saving nature of this power.

this carpenter's son? No, it is because it expresses God's will, which anyone who has ears to hear can confirm for himself or herself.[55] In the antitheses in particular, the person of the preacher withdraws behind his message: the kingdom of God itself, not the preacher of the kingdom, confers legitimacy on its eschatological claim to validity.[56]

The principle clarified here applies across the board: "It is not Jesus who brings the kingdom—a conception that was completely foreign to Jesus himself; on the contrary, the kingdom brings him with it."[57] God determines his relationship with Jesus, not the other way around:[58] Jesus himself lives entirely within the relationship that God has established with him. The Gospels illustrate this with various images and strategies. Mark's Gospel, for instance, defines the start of Jesus's ministry as his baptism by John in the Jordan, when God's Spirit descends on Jesus in the form of a dove and God appoints him as his representative (Son of God) both in Israel and for humanity as a whole (Mark 1:9–11). Matthew emphasizes this with a further image, indicating that Jesus's life had already begun when he was conceived by the Holy Spirit (Matt. 1:18). John follows these images through to identify Jesus as the one and only Son who has shared God's own life and been at his side from the very beginning (John 1:18). Each of them is making the same point. Jesus did not establish his relationship with God: God himself took the initiative, entering into a quite distinctive relationship with Jesus, a relationship for which the evangelists unanimously use the image of the *Son*.

The choice of this particular image to describe Jesus's relationship to God and its significance for the later development of Christology is due to the interplay of a number of factors. To a greater degree than almost any other image, it picks up key elements of Jesus's own preaching, links into significant Old Testament traditions, connects with the conceptual worlds of Hellenistic Greece and ancient Judaism, and proves particularly apt for expressing the uniqueness, conclusiveness, and universality of the early Christian salvation experience within the process of theological reflection. It is not surprising that all of the above led to not a one-dimensional but a diverse and complex development of the conceptual content associated with the image of the Son.

55. Cf. H. Weder, *Die "Rede der Reden": Eine Auslegung der Bergpredigt heute* (Zürich: Theologischer Verlag Zürich, 1985), 99–102, 153–55.
56. The fact that the coming of the kingdom of God proclaimed by Jesus is to be understood as in no way the result of human activity but as the eschatological future that originates with God alone was the seminal insight of J. Weiß, *Die Predigt Jesu vom Reiche Gottes* (Göttingen: Vandenhoeck & Ruprecht, 1892), 63–67.
57. R. Otto, *Reich Gottes und Menschensohn: Ein religionsgeschichtlicher Versuch* (Munich: Beck, ³1954), 75.
58. Jüngel, "Zur dogmatischen Bedeutung," 230–31.

But this is not the place for a detailed reconstruction.[59] Here we are concerned solely with the objective basis for the application of this title to Jesus according to the testimony of his own life.

All critical exegetes agree that Jesus did not refer to himself as God's Son.[60] Even so, one of the decisive reasons for applying the image of the Son to him lies in the specific way in which Jesus himself expresses his relationship to God: the way in which he addressed God as Father or *Abba*. So it is not Jesus's designation of himself as Son but his *proclamation of God as Father* that forms the basis for the use of the image of Son to describe his relationship to God. Taking this as the starting point for the analysis of the image, there are three main issues to bear in mind.

### 1.3.1. FATHER AND SON

First, it must be stated systematically that to speak of the Son (of God)[61] is to speak of God as Father: it is only our designation of God as Father that affords theological significance to our reference to the Son. But if the Son image depends for its substance on the Father image of God, then it is an implication of this particular God concept and, as such, tells us first and foremost something about God himself. The decisive theological factor is thus neither the image nor its application to Jesus in themselves but what is being said *about God* in applying it to Jesus. The Christian use of the Son image is a formulation of the concept of God that constitutes a double hermeneutical reference device, in that an initial designation process (the application of the image to Jesus) implements a second designation (the description of God). Thus the Son image, which originated in the royal ideology of the Jewish Old Testament and was familiar from the Hellenistic θεῖος ἀνήρ tradition, is crystallized in terms of the theology of the cross by its application to Jesus, while the crystallization of the Son image in Jesus results in the Father image of God being given eschatological orientation and trinitarian substance. The Father image tells us what "God" means; the story of the "Son" fleshes out the meaning of "Father"; the testimony of the life of Jesus unfolds the meaning

59. Cf. especially M. Hengel, *The Son of God: The Origin of Christology and the History of the Jewish-Hellenistic Religion*, trans. J. Bowden (London: SCM, 1976); Vermes, *Jesus the Jew*, chap. 8.

60. Bornkamm, *Jesus von Nazareth*, 206; H. Conzelmann, *Grundriß der Theologie des Neuen Testaments* (Munich: Christian Kaiser, 1968), 147–49.

61. The absolute use of "the Son" (principally in the Gospel of John) and the various messianic and Hellenistic ways of using and understanding "the Son of God" in the Gospels will be treated here as variations of the same image. This does not mean that the differences between them are to be obliterated or challenged. But these different versions of the Son image tell us more about the evangelists and the confessing communities than about Jesus himself.

of "Son"; and the Spirit gives substance to the Fatherhood of God by illuminating the story of Jesus as that of the Son and as the key to understanding the Fatherhood of God.

### 1.3.2. THE SON AND HEIR

Second, it is a historical fact that Jesus's use of the Father image for God is not quite as unusual as has sometimes been maintained. The Father-Son image was already being used for God in the Old Testament (Isa. 64:8 [64:7 MT]; Ps. 103:13; Sir. 51:10), both collectively in relation to the whole nation (Deut. 14:1) and also in relation to the individual supplicant (Ps. 89:26 [89:27 MT]). No biological relationship is intended: aspects of both paternal and maternal care can receive equal emphasis in prophetic interpretations of the image (Ps. 103:13; Isa. 49:15; 66:10–11). Rather, it refers to an *enactment of a legal right* that was absolutely fundamental for Israel: the installation of the Davidic king, or—as in Deutero-Isaiah—of the whole people of God into their inheritance rights, the inheritance of the Promised Land (2 Sam. 7:14; Ps. 2:7; Jer. 3:19). The background of the covenant of inheritance lies behind both the reference to the *Father* (in Israel's patriarchal family system, the father is the one who passes on the inheritance [Deut. 21:15–17]), and the reference to the *Son* (the firstborn son [of the primary wife] is the heir; daughters only have inheritance rights if there are no sons [Num. 27:1–11], and even then they must marry within the tribe so that the family inheritance is not lost [36:1–13]). This background of inheritance, with its specific fields of association,[62] lies behind the biblical grammar of the Father-Son image in later times as well.[63] Whenever the exilic prophets use the Father image formally, as a way of addressing God in prayer (Isa. 63:16–19), they are following the deep grammar of the image, especially when they also recall that Israel is heir to God's promise and beg him to treat his people as such in spite of their guilt: the deep grammar of the Father-Son image associated with the Davidic covenant of inheritance determines not just the use of the image but also the thematic ideas that this image complex addresses and (potentially) expresses.

---

62. Father, fatherly love (Hos. 11:1), compassion (Jer. 31:20), blessing, son, firstborn (Exod. 4:22), heir, land, the son's gratitude to the father, bond with the father, service (Jer. 3:19), honor (Mal. 1:6), etc., until "lord" and "servant" replace "father" and "son" (Isa. 41:8–9 and elsewhere) in a manner suggestive of the economic system of the ancient world, which broadens the field of imagery still further into the economic sphere. Cf. W. Zimmerli, "παῖς θεοῦ A/B," *TWNT* 5:653–76.

63. A mythical background to the Father image, still discernible in the biblical texts, that views God as the father of heavenly sons or angels (cf. Gen. 6:2, 4; Deut. 32:8; Pss. 29:1; 89:7; Dan. 3:25), plays no role (or only a negative one) in the main biblical tradition and in Christian use of the Father image.

This did not begin to change until, in the course of the growing internalization and individualization of piety that began in the fifth century, the Father image of God became increasingly detached from the inheritance background that lay behind the special covenant between God and Israel and was given a creation-theological association with the creation of all human beings by God (Isa. 64:8; Mal. 2:10). This was of course an entirely possible generalizing development of the image complex. But the migration from a deep grammar that was linked primarily with the covenant of inheritance to one that was essentially creation-theological changed more than just the field of association of this image complex within the biblical tradition. It accentuated the biblical Father form of address for God so strongly that it became connected with the cosmological designation of the creator god as father in the Platonic (*Tim.* 28c) and the Stoic tradition (Cleanthes's *Hymn to Zeus*):[64] Philo, for example, took it up and linked it with Jewish and Christian thought.

But the custom of addressing God as Father was relatively common, not only in the older prophetic traditions and in Alexandrian Judaism but also in the Pharisaic and Hasidic Judaism of Jesus's time.[65] This is true even for the intimate family form "Abba," which can be seen as typical of Jesus's close, informal relationship with God and expresses his childlike certainty that God is near him as a helpful and loving father and that he cares for everyone, good or bad, just as a loving father does (Matt. 5:45).[66] Even this form of address for God is not unique to Jesus; it is used in a similar way by other pious, charismatic figures of his time.[67] While it is likely that Jesus addressed God as "Abba," it is just as likely that others did so too.

Jesus's manner of addressing God as "Abba" does not therefore, in itself, manifest either a new concept of God or an exclusive and unique relationship to God.[68] This is indicated only when Jesus's way of speaking to God is

64. Cf. Epictetus, *Diatr.* 1.9.6–7.

65. A. Strotmann, *"Mein Vater bist du!" (Sir. 51,10): Zur Bedeutung der Vaterschaft Gottes in kanonischen und nichtkanonischen frühjüdischen Schriften* (Frankfurt: Josef Knecht, 1991). Cf. K. H. Schelkle, "Gott der Eine und Dreieine," in *Wort und Schrift: Beiträge zur Auslegung und Auslegungsgeschichte des Neuen Testaments* (Düsseldorf: Patmos, 1966), 81–95, esp. 87.

66. Cf. J. Jeremias, "Abba," in *Abba: Studien zur neutestamentlichen Theologie und Zeitgeschichte* (Göttingen: Vandenhoeck & Ruprecht, 1966), 15–67; R. Hamerton-Kelly, "Gott als Vater in der Bibel und in der Erfahrung Jesu: Eine Bestandsaufnahme," *Concilium* 17 (1981): 247–56; Hamerton-Kelly, *God the Father: Theology and Patriarchy in the Teaching of Jesus* (Philadelphia: Fortress, 1979); R. Feneberg, "Abba—Vater," *Kirche und Israel* 3 (1988): 41–52.

67. Cf. Vermes, *Jesus the Jew*, 210–22.

68. In the Gospels Jesus consistently differentiates between "my Father" and "your Father," although he nowhere embraces himself and those whom he is addressing in an "our Father"; however, this probably documents the "christological style of the community" rather than being a distinguishing mark of his preaching (Conzelmann, *Jesus von Nazareth*, 123). For Jesus, God

considered and interpreted together with his other words and actions in the light of Easter. But this always takes place from a particular standpoint or in a particular context, so that what it highlights and how it is presented vary with the perspectives and narrative techniques of the onlooker. The Gospels give evidence of both, with their many and variously accentuated stylizations of the Father and Son imagery. The New Testament use of this image complex is not only diverse but exhibits different levels of integration and extension of these usages. It is possible to distinguish at least five levels.

1. Jesus's own use of the Abba form of address in the context of his preaching highlights two things in particular. First, it underlines *Jesus's differentiation between himself and God*[69] and thus the distinction between Jesus and the Father to whom he prays—however he may have understood himself. Second, it demonstrates that Jesus was charismatically convinced of the *eschatological nearness of God*, the presence of the heavenly Father and the dawn of God's saving reign. From both points of view, Jesus's use of the Abba image tells us first and foremost something about God, and only indirectly and implicitly something about himself.

2. After Easter this changes. In the light of the resurrection of the Jesus who had been crucified as "King of the Jews," the implications of the image he had used for God were drawn out as far as he himself was concerned. It is clear that this was initially guided by the deep grammar of this Old Testament image complex, with its origins in the covenant of inheritance: Jesus is "appointed the Son of God in power" (Rom. 1:4 NIV); he is "called the Son of God" (Luke 1:35). The nub of the matter is surely here: the one thus described was killed, was in fact crucified, convicted of blasphemy by the

---

is the Father of "the evil and the good, . . . the righteous and the unrighteous" (Matt. 5:45; cf. 21:28–32). The tendency to restrict the "your Father" to the disciples probably originated in the community. This is problematic when it is thought to exclude and is used as such: God is and desires to be the Father of all. However, accentuating the idea that only those who allow God to be their Father, and who address him as such, can *speak* of "our Father" does in fact bring a proper emphasis to bear: no one is a child of God by nature, as it were, but becomes one by a "legal enactment," through which God makes him or her his child. Only such a one can and will address God as "Father" in this sense. Viewed in this way, the reference to Jesus is not "christological narrowness" but is factually incontrovertible for two reasons. First, anyone who calls God Father is aligning himself with Jesus. To do the one without wanting the other is self-contradictory. Second, only in the account of Jesus's cross and resurrection does it become clear what it means to call God Father. So one cannot turn to God as Father *in this sense* without reference to Jesus. It is therefore with good reason that Paul specifies that Christians know and address God as the "Father of our Lord Jesus Christ" (e.g., 2 Cor. 1:3). Furthermore, it is with good reason that he makes it unequivocally clear that *in this sense* no one can know and address God as "Father" or "Abba" except by the Holy Spirit (Rom. 8:15; Gal. 4:6).

69. This is rightly emphasized by W. Pannenberg, *Systematic Theology* (Grand Rapids: Eerdmans, 1988–93), 1:263–64, 2:372–79.

Jews, and put to death by the Romans as the "King of the Jews" and therefore a messianic pretender. That he was the one whom God had raised from the dead was understood as divine confirmation of his message and confutation of his adversaries. The ancient confession in Romans 1:3–4 emphasizes both the human birth and the Davidic descent of the Jesus crucified as the Messiah and also his appointment as the Son of God in power through the Spirit by and since his resurrection from the dead. This utilizes and intensifies the underlying field of imagery in a way that makes its extension and reworking inevitable.

3. It was possible in the process to link into pre-Christian developments, which connected and combined the imagery of God as Father and God's Son with other fields of imagery. Thus, following Micah 5:1 and Psalm 110:3, links were made between the apocalyptic identification of the Messiah with the Son of Man (1 En. 48.10; 52.4; 4 Ezra 13), the Son of Man with the Son of David, the Son of Man with the Son of God,[70] and the Son of God (υἱὸς θεοῦ) with the Servant of God (παῖς θεοῦ), and crucially the concept of preexistence was introduced into these fields of imagery with the emphasis on the existence of the Son of Man (1 En. 48.6; 62.7), the Redeemer (Mic. 5:2 [5:1 MT]; Ps. 110:3), the Messiah (and his name),[71] and Wisdom (Prov. 8:22–31; Sir. 24) with God before the creation of the world. Paul is thus treading a well-trodden path when he links the confession of the raising of the crucified one and his appointment as the Son of God in power with the concept of the preexistent Messiah[72] and describes it as the sending of the eternal Son (i.e., the one destined as the Messiah from the beginning): "But when the set time had fully come, God sent his Son, born of a woman, born under the law" (Gal. 4:4 NIV; cf. John 11:27). Paul's further comments (Gal. 4:5–7) show that his development of this field of imagery is still crucially guided by the background metaphor of the covenant of inheritance.

4. The prologue to John's Gospel, on the other hand, demonstrates how this field of imagery is no longer to be combined with others but is replaced by another. He links the Son image and its inheritance metaphor ("Firstborn") with the Hellenistic Logos concept and contemporary wisdom speculation in such a way that the divinity of the Logos is unreservedly transferred to Jesus, so that the uniqueness of this Son of God ("the one and only Son") can be affirmed (John 1:1, 14, 18). God's firstborn from the dead thus becomes the one and only Son of God. He is not just *called* the Son of God after his resurrection: he *is*

70. Cf. Hengel, *Son of God*, 64–66.
71. Ibid., 66–76.
72. Cf. Vermes, *Jesus the Jew*, 137–55.

the Son of God from the beginning (cf. Mark 1:1). This means that—initially at any rate—what has happened is not so much a change of level of the statements made about Jesus (the one who is appointed to the role of God's Son and heir *is* the Son by right of inheritance) but rather an adjustment to the level of the background metaphor guiding these statements. The Old Testament field of imagery is replaced by the imagery of the Hellenistic Logos and wisdom speculation with its entirely different possibilities for development—right up to the Nicene affirmation that Jesus is "lumen de lumine, *Deum verum de Deo vero, genitum, non factum, consubstantialem patri* [Light from Light, *true God from true God, begotten, not made, of one being with the Father*]."

This has two important consequences in particular. First, it was not until the Logos, or Sophia, imagery[73] came into play that the *ultimate and unparalleled* nature of the salvation revealed in the story of Jesus could be expressed. As the preexistent Logos-Son, who came into the world and has now returned to his Father, Jesus Christ is not only exalted above all the angels[74] and all powers in heaven, on earth, and under the earth (Phil. 2:10; 1 Tim 3:16). He attracted to himself the whole "functions of Jewish Wisdom as a mediator of creation and salvation," and is confessed as the one in whom "are hid all the treasures of wisdom and knowledge (Col. 2:3)."[75] There is therefore no truth, no revelation, no wisdom, and no knowledge that does not emanate from the Logos-Son Jesus and his Spirit. And there is no activity of God in creation, reconciliation, and consummation in which he is not involved: God's activity and the activity of the Logos-Son are inseparably linked, for "I and the Father are one" (John 10:30).

Second, the Kyrios title, used as a form of address for God, can now be applied to Jesus too. It is true that in Aramaic- and Greek-speaking Judaism

73. On the Sophia imagery, cf. F. Christ, *Jesus Sophia: Die Sophia-Christologie bei den Synoptikern* (Zürich: Zwingli, 1970); R. L. Wilken, ed., *Aspects of Wisdom in Judaism and Early Christianity* (Notre Dame: University of Notre Dame Press, 1975); G. Schimanowski, *Weisheit und Messias: Die jüdischen Voraussetzungen der urchristlichen Präexistenzchristologie* (Tübingen: Mohr Siebeck, 1985); B. Lang, *Wisdom and the Book of Proverbs: An Israelite Goddess Redefined* (New York: Pilgrim, 1986); D. Georgi, "Frau Weisheit oder das Recht auf Freiheit als schöpferische Kraft," in *Verdrängte Vergangenheit, die uns bedrängt: Feministische Theologie in der Verantwortung für die Geschichte*, ed. L. Siegle-Wenschkewitz (Munich, 1988), 243–76; S. Schroer, "Jesus Sophia: Erträge der feministischen Forschung zu einer frühchristlichen Deutung der Praxis und des Schicksals Jesu von Nazareth," in *Vom Verlangen nach Heilwerden: Christologien in feministisch-theologischer Sicht*, ed. D. Strahm and R. Strobel (Fribourg, Switzerland: Edition Exodus, 1991), 112–28.
74. On the influence of biblical exegesis on the development of the doctrine of angels, cf. S. M. Olyan, *A Thousand Thousands Served Him: Exegesis and the Naming of Angels in Ancient Judaism* (Tübingen: Mohr Siebeck, 1993).
75. Hengel, *Son of God*, 72.

at the time of Jesus, the term *Lord* was used not just for God but also for earthly dignitaries, figures of authority within the family, recognized teachers, charismatic miracle workers, and so on.[76] And it is highly probable that the Gospels are picking up a pre-Easter use of language when they address Jesus as "Kyrios" in his capacity as a charismatic miracle worker (as Matthew and Mark do) or as a religious teacher (as Luke, in particular, does). But in the Gospel of John it is not just this everyday courtesy title; it is the Kyrios title used for God in the Septuagint that is transferred to Jesus. The confession of Thomas provides the clearest confirmation of this, when he addresses the risen Jesus as "My Lord and my God" (John 20:28). The transfer here of this divine form of address to the one who has been crucified and raised is rooted in the Easter doxology celebrating God's act of resurrection and is the basis on which it became possible for the Christian community to address prayers to Jesus Christ (Rom. 10:12; 1 Cor. 1:2; 2 Cor. 12:8). This inevitably raises the question not only of Jesus's divinity but also of the uniqueness of God, which both Jewish and gentile Christians upheld unwaveringly, in accordance with the Jewish foundational confession of faith. These two questions could be answered only by reworking the understanding of the unity of God while continuing to uphold the uniqueness of God. To achieve this, the Father-God and Logos-Son imagery had to be carried forward against the background of the Kyrios form of address for God in a manner that would make it possible, despite this differentiation, to conceive of and to express the still greater unity of God. The assimilation of the *Spirit* into this field of imagery—for which Hellenistic Jewish Sophia speculation and ideas about pneuma had already paved the way—made this possible. The Spirit is the effective medium, both divine and personal, through whom the differentiation between Father and Son within the unity of divine fellowship is conveyed. The Spirit plays a leading role in the appointment of Jesus, the one who has been raised, as Son of God (Rom. 1:4; 8:11) and thus in the revelation of God's true nature; but not only this: he also is the one who searches the deep things of God (1 Cor. 2:10) and helps us to call God Father and to understand that we are his children (Rom. 8:14–17). The Spirit thus becomes the integrating element of the imagery by means of which Christians seek to conceive of the differentiated unity of the one God as Father and Son, an imagery that, as such, is basic to the Christian concept of God.

5. In the New Testament this development emerges not only in the preexistence statements and in the story of Jesus's baptism by the Spirit in the Jordan but also in the birth stories. These indicate a transition to another background

76. Cf. Vermes, *Jesus the Jew*, chap. 5.

metaphor that speaks of the Son of God by specific reference to the Spirit of God. Thus the saving presence of God within the person of Jesus, which Jesus himself proclaimed, is shown, in a (quasi-)genealogical interpretation of the Son image, to be the result of his conception by the Spirit of God. Matthew and Luke present this in the form of a narrative interpretation of Isaiah 7:14: "The virgin will conceive and give birth to a son, and will call him Immanuel" (Matt. 1:23 NIV; cf. Luke 1:31). While Matthew presents this story as the fulfillment of Isaiah's prophecy, making reference to the Spirit of God in order to link the confessional images of Jesus as the Son of God and the Son of David, Luke emphasizes first and foremost that these events demonstrate the miraculous sovereign power of God, by placing the virginity of Mary and the divine work of the Spirit at the heart of his interpretation (cf. Luke 1:26–35). Each of these stories is a secondary restructuring of the Son image against the background of a changing field of imagery. Both of them pick up representational devices from the old imagery (promise of salvation, nearness of God, Sonship) to which they give realistic narrative form (virgin birth, conception by the Spirit) by focusing on the role of the Spirit of God within the context of the new field of imagery. Both of them take the first steps down a road on which the background metaphors that guide theological thought and utterance will be pneumatologically transformed so as to integrate the diversity of theological imagery into one fundamental field of Spirit imagery. And both make real contributions to the process of developing this Spirit imagery by providing in narrative form the stimulus and the starting point for further realistic restructuring of the images of Father, Son, and Spirit, thus paving the way for the doctrine of the Trinity (i.e., the formulation of the trinitarian grammar of Spirit imagery).

### 1.3.3. GOD THE FATHER

This brings us to the third issue. The use of the Father image and the correlated Son image has significant consequences not only for our understanding of Jesus but for our understanding of God. Precisely because Jesus originally used the image in relation to God rather than himself, the initial consequences of the post-Easter formulation of the Son image to describe Jesus inevitably also had an impact on the Father image that had always been taken for granted and used to describe God. The deep grammar of the Father image is transformed in a way that corresponds hermeneutically to the dynamic of the restructuring of the Son image and its own deep grammar. Since both developments need to be seen as interrelated, certain interpretations of the Father image for God (perfectly possible in themselves but theologically erroneous when taken in isolation from this concrete relationship) are fundamentally irrelevant or even misleading. Thus the biblical use of the Father image for God goes back to the inheritance background of the (Davidic) covenant promise (2 Sam. 7:14) and, as such, is anchored in the patriarchal form of the Jewish family and its legal and economic structures.[77] Nevertheless, Jesus's use of the Father image in addressing God as "Abba" has nothing to do with two misunderstandings frequently encountered today. First, Jesus is not stressing the dependence or immaturity of the one who addresses God as "Father," and neither is he implying that such a one has the virtually lifeless status of a material possession. Second, this image is neither making a statement about God's gender nor describing God as a Roman-style patriarchal paterfamilias.[78] Since Lactantius, perhaps even earlier, the Father image used by Christians had become associated with the Roman paterfamilias concept, and a misapprehension of the true basis for the perception of God as Father[79] undeniably encouraged this association.[80] But this is testimony only to the interpreters' lack of ability to understand either the usage or the deep grammar of the Father image that Jesus used for God and was picked up by the Christian community. To link such associations with the Father image is just as misguided as it would be to ask about God's eyebrow when confronted with the picture of God's eye,[81] or to infer that Michelangelo thought "that when God created Adam he looked just like" the picture of him he had painted.[82] This proves merely that one neither recognizes nor understands the field of imagery to which the Father form of address for God belongs and the grammar of that governs this figure of speech and its implications. To demand that the Father image be completely avoided when speaking about God, or that it be replaced or supplemented by mother images, is therefore nothing but an attempt to correct one error with another[83]—quite apart from the theological

77. Cf. Hamerton-Kelly, "Gott als Vater in der Bibel," 55–75.
78. Cf. J. Moltmann, "'Ich glaube an Gott den Vater': Patriarchalische oder nichtpatriarchalische Rede von Gott?," in *In der Geschichte des dreieinigen Gottes: Beiträge zur trinitarischen Theologie* (Gütersloh: Gütersloher Verlagshaus Mohn, 1991), 25–44; Moltmann, "Der mütterliche Vater und die Macht seines Erbarmens," in *In der Geschichte des dreieinigen Gottes*, 45–53.
79. As W. Pannenberg rightly emphasizes in his *Systematic Theology*: "Patriarchal forms of the family . . . are not the basis of the concept of God which comes to expression in calling him Father. Instead, we are to seek this basis in the divine election or in God's covenant relation to Israel" (1:261–62).
80. Cf. A. Wlosok, "Vater und Vatervorstellungen in der römischen Kultur," in *Das Vaterbild im Abendland*, ed. H. Tellenbach (Stuttgart: Kohlhammer, 1978), 1:18–54, esp. 48–54.
81. L. Wittgenstein, *Vorlesungen und Gespräche über Ästhetik, Psychologie und Religion* (Göttingen: Vandenhoeck & Ruprecht, ²1971), 109.
82. Ibid., 101.
83. Cf. M. Daly, *Beyond God the Father: Toward a Philosophy of Women's Liberation* (Boston: Beacon Press, 1973); V. R. Mollenkott, *The Divine Feminine: The Biblical Imagery of God*

frivolity of such a projection theory of religious concepts of God (whether the emphasis be on social history, depth psychology, or the hermeneutics of symbols).[84] Theology must insist not on such dubious secondary processes but on careful attention to the underlying field of imagery and its grammar, which can be historically-critically reconstructed and systematically elucidated with the aid of the available texts.

Any attempt to do this will show that, for Jesus, the Father image is no mere time-conditioned, patriarchal idea of God to be dispensed with without detracting from his message. Rather, it is an integral part of his message; indeed, it is *the integral and summary of his entire understanding of God*. It is not one figure of speech among others but the basic image, which—together with its associated field of imagery—encompasses everything that Jesus can say about God. This basic image has two fundamental distinctive features.

First, it finds its place and its function *as a manner of addressing God in prayer*, so it serves not so much as a way of thinking and speaking *about* God as a way of speaking *to* God. Thus it manifests an understanding of God that involves not a cerebral relationship with him but one sustained by prayer and day-to-day living. Jesus does not promulgate a (theoretical) concept of God; rather, he promulgates a (practical) understanding of God that can be realized only from an inner, participatory perspective and cannot be adequately grasped from the external perspective of an observer. By concentrating his entire understanding of God in the Father image, Jesus underlines the fact that God, whose dawning reign he proclaims, cannot be known and experienced in third-person mode but only in second-person mode: God can be truly perceived only when we address him as "you" and live our whole lives as a "child of God," aware of his personal nearness and fatherly presence.

Second, this basic image of God as Father is not used just as a semantically vague formula when addressing God in prayer. On the contrary, because of its associated field of imagery, it has a meaning that can be explained, which Jesus picks up, and to which he gives substance through his life and his message, thereby imbuing the Father image for God with a very specific content. In the aftermath of the crucifixion and resurrection, Jesus's crystallization of the Father image and its metaphoric field then becomes in turn the trigger for the development of a specific (trinitarian) concept of God, which has three distinctive features. First, it evolves from an expansion of the Father image in the light of Easter to become the integral notion of God overall: God is

*as Female* (New York: Crossroads, 1984); E. Godel, "Die Heilige Geistin," *Radius* 3 (1989): 47; E. Tamez, ed., *Through Her Eyes* (Maryknoll, NY: Orbis, 1986).

84. Cf. W. Pannenberg, *Systematic Theology*, 1:262.

conceived of logically and consistently against the background of the Father image to which the eschatological event of Easter has given tangible form; every statement about God has been modified and defined more precisely in the light of the grammar of this image. Second, it explicitly carries forward the practical import of Jesus's use of the Father image to address God in prayer, in that it has a consistently doxological significance. Finally, in the light of the Easter experience, the meaning that Jesus's life and message impart to the custom of addressing God as Father is now defined in such a way that God can no longer be addressed as "Father" without at the same time involving Jesus and the Spirit as well. As a result, the whole of the associated metaphorical field required a trinitarian reformulation and reconstruction—a task that is still engrossing Christian liturgy and theology right up to the present day. None of these three elements means that the trinitarian God is a different God from the one whom Jesus addressed as "Father" and who emphatically acknowledged this form of address at Easter. On the contrary, the trinitarian concept of God is intended to ensure that this very God, whom Jesus addressed as "Father," and his Fatherhood continue to be comprehended in precisely the same sense in which he was revealed in the story of Jesus Christ and in which he may always be approached through the Spirit of Christ. Thus, Jesus's use of the Father image (Luke 11:11–13), and the parables in which he illustrated it (Luke 15:11–32), make clear that his purpose is to highlight God's mercy (Luke 6:36), goodness (Mark 10:18; Luke 11:13), care (Luke 11:3; 12:30), willingness to forgive (Mark 11:25; Luke 11:4), unreserved generosity to those who have alienated themselves from him (Luke 15:11–32), and unbounded joy over everyone who returns to him (Luke 15:4–10). God is close to us as a loving Father who is always and in all circumstances accessible and devoted to his children—not because he finds everything they do equally acceptable or good (in which case he would not be taking them seriously as individuals) but because he will not let anything they do prevent him from staying with them, being there for them, and waiting for an opportunity to demonstrate his deep love for them.

In order to address God as "Father," one must have been enabled to do so by God himself, and one's conduct must be in keeping with that awareness. Anyone who thus addresses God as "Father" does so in and with Jesus Christ; anyone who confesses Jesus Christ as Lord does so by the Holy Spirit (1 Cor. 12:3); and anyone who knows that he believes in Jesus Christ, not by his "own reason or strength" but only by the Holy Spirit,[85] will live his life of faith in wholehearted doxological thanks to God the Father, the Son, and

85. *BSLK* 511–12.

the Spirit. The trinitarian concept of God is rooted in this doxology, which proves its practical relevance and distinguishes it from other purely speculative thought forms. Anyone who addresses God as "Father" in a trinitarian sense and bases his life on a God-given assurance of the direct, unconditional, and beneficent nearness of God will shape his life accordingly. He will not worry about everyday things, nor will his conduct toward others be in direct contrast to God's conduct toward him. He will know that in every sense he is so closely connected to God that he would not rank any other connection, even a family relationship, higher than this bond (Mark 3:32–35; Luke 8:20–21); indeed, he will derive his very identity wholly from his relationship to God and not—as prescribed in Jewish law—from his relationship with his mother,[86] knowing himself to be the child and heir of his Father in heaven. All of this applies outstandingly to Jesus, who is therefore rightly called the Son. Since Jesus perceives himself entirely on the basis of God's relationship with him, and since he experiences and proclaims this relationship as the generosity and nearness of the merciful Father, he lives in the assurance that what he says and does is in accordance with the will of God. Hence, Jesus can also claim that God's relationship with a person is based on that person's relationship to Jesus himself (Matt. 16:27; Luke 12:8–9; 9:26). Just as his claim to authority is rooted in his assurance of God's fatherly generosity to him, so the demand for a decision inherent in his preaching is rooted in his assurance that all his activity is a true and authoritative portrayal of the character of the divine Father and the nature of his nearness.

Christian confession took up Jesus's claim to authority, together with how, in light of Easter, a relationship with him decisively affects God's relationship with us, in such a way that it recognized him not just as the *Son of God* but specifically as the *firstborn* or the *one and only* Son of God. This meant that the identity question "Who is Jesus of Nazareth, whom God raised from the dead?" was answered soteriologically in explicating the implicit Christology of the life of Jesus, and its further implications were explored in trinitarian theology. This is entirely legitimate. For if, in a post-Easter environment, one pursues the logic of the Father image, in whose use and practical activation by Jesus the concept of Son was appropriately applied to him,[87] then the significance of the Son image is not merely to indicate Jesus's differentiation between himself and God but is itself an explicit statement about God. Indeed, it underlines the fact that God is making himself known and accessible, in

86. Cf. Sch. Ben-Chorin, *Mutter Mirjam: Maria in jüdischer Sicht* (Munich: Paul List Verlag, 1971), 99–117.

87. F. Hahn, *Christologische Hoheitstitel: Ihre Geschichte im frühen Christentum* (Göttingen: Vandenhoeck & Ruprecht, ⁴1974), 333.

and through this Jesus, as merciful Father and fatherly mercy—not just for Jesus but, through him, for us. God is present to this Jesus through his Spirit (Mark 1:9–11; Luke 4:14; John 3:34; cf. Acts 10:37–47) in a unique way (Luke 10:21–22) as a merciful Father. In this way he marks out as his "Son" the one in whose actions he himself is at work in his mercy. Through the actions of the Son, God's Spirit is thus made manifest to us as the Spirit of Christ. Through this Spirit, made manifest as the Spirit of Christ, God draws near to us too as a merciful Father and enables us to recognize and acknowledge his presence revealed in Jesus: "For there is one God and one mediator between God and mankind, the man Christ Jesus" (1 Tim. 2:5 NIV).

So he is not a different God, nor a new one, but is always the Father who, in the power of the Spirit through the Son, is confirmed as absolute unconditional mercy and love. Through the power of the same Spirit this Father is confirmed, first of all as the Father of his Son, Jesus Christ, but then, through Jesus Christ's mediation, as our Father too, so that we can and should pray, "Our Father." The question of Jesus's identity is thus answered by reference to God himself: Jesus Christ is the one in whom and through whom God is confirmed as our merciful Father. His identity lies in the fact that in his person he brings God before our eyes as *deus pro nobis* [God for us], because his person and his story make God accessible to us as a gracious Father. So he is who he is through God alone, but also because he is the one through whom God accomplishes our salvation, since God's fatherly love is perfectly revealed in him and achieves its full effect through the Spirit. This brings us to the second fundamental problem of Christology.

## 2. The Salvific Significance of Jesus Christ for Us

Christian theology does not encounter the question of the personal identity of Jesus Christ in isolation; it does so within the context of the question of the *salvific significance of Jesus for us*. If it is true that without explicit reference back to God there can be no theologically satisfactory answer to the former, it is even more true for the latter. But in each case the mode of reference to God is different. Indeed, there is also more than one way of answering the soteriological question "What is Jesus for us?" as is evident from the plethora of christological titles, characterizing confessional statements, and descriptive faith narratives contained in the New Testament.[88]

88. Cf. H. Schlier, "Die Anfänge des christologischen Credo," in *Zur Frühgeschichte der Christologie: Ihre biblischen Anfänge und die Lehrformel von Nikaia*, ed. B. Welte (Freiburg: Herder, 1970), 13–58; K. Wengst, *Christologische Formeln und Lieder des Urchristentums* (Gütersloh:

## 2.1. *Soteriological Diversity and the Grammar of Trinitarian Theology*

The grounding and structure of this variety of answers to the soteriological question, however, are different from those of the identity question. With the identity question there is an intensifying process of concentration, a progress, or rather, a gradual regress toward ever more fundamental answers, which could be described as the concentrated integration of historical, eschatological, and soteriological levels to embrace, ultimately, trinitarian theology. Here, on the other hand, we have open and incomplete processes of cross-referencing between the soteriological fields of imagery to be found in the various christological confessions, narratives, and other texts, showing how the soteriological significance of the way Jesus lived, died, and was raised was interpreted—not only but predominantly[89]—in the light of the Jewish eschatological expectations familiar to his followers. In the course of history, these processes of cross-referencing have led to the construction of the verbal, conceptual, and practical soteriological framework, which, together with its specific institutional structures, characterizes the *Christian tradition*. This has occurred by means of the formation of semantic nodules (the integration and concentration of the meaning of different images relating to the raised crucified one), the preferential theological treatment of particular fields of imagery, and the recurrent necessity of linking new fields of imagery with the existing traditions.

Right from the outset this tradition has been complex, plural, and open. Hermeneutically speaking, it can be likened not so much to a conceptual system as to a network of images that has fairly stable image structures in certain areas but spreads beyond its boundaries in others. And in at least two respects it is still an incomplete process. First, this tradition is in a state of continuous osmosis owing to the ever-changing societal and cultural environments that influence and modify it, as it in turn influences and modifies them. Indeed, a distinctive Christian tradition and way of life stand in a multiple relationship with other traditions and spheres of life—a relationship that can be described, on the hermeneutical level on which we are engaged, as an ongoing exchange of ideas, concepts, evaluations, perceptions, interpretations, and the like. This was barely noticeable at first, although it began with the Christian use of images and ideas from

Gütersloher Verlagshaus Mohn, ²1973); Hahn, *Christologische Hoheitstitel*; Hahn, "Bekenntnisformeln im Neuen Testament," in *Unterwegs zur Einheit: Festschrift für Heinrich Stirnimann zum 60. Geburtstag*, ed. J. Brantschen and P. Selvatico (Freiburg: Herder, 1980), 200–214.

89. Most christological-soteriological titles go back to Jewish Old Testament backgrounds. But it is clear from the use of the title of σωτήρ for Jesus Christ that at a fairly early stage there was already a broadening to adopt Hellenistic concepts.

the Hellenistic Jewish world around the time of the birth of Christ, leading to the emergence of Christianity as a variant of Judaism. But the more
vigorously this differentiation from changing environments progressed, and
the more clearly the Christian tradition organized itself as an independent
sphere with its own identifiable and identity-shaping internal structures, the
more apparent were the problems of its relationship (both regulated and
unregulated) with these environments, and the more urgent was the need
to give particular theological attention to the processes of accommodation
and assimilation of which these contacts and relationships formed a part,
in order to be able to take at least some degree of control of the changes
taking place within the Christian tradition.

Second, however, this tradition was never simply given; it was shaped and
reshaped as it established itself through the process of embracing the faith,
and it was expressed and carried forward within ever-changing contexts as the
soteriological image complexes of faith were individually and communally
received. The complexity and diversity of the images and fields of imagery
linked to this tradition result from the varied experiences, cultural patterns,
and linguistic options available to those who were assured of salvation through
their encounter with the gospel of Jesus Christ, and who articulated this
salvation, each using the means available.[90] It is true that in every case they
are confronting something entirely new, but they can only articulate it using
the limited means provided by their own era and situation. Two particular
aspects of this process should be highlighted.

First, there is an entirely new element in the story. On the principle of *ex
nihilo nihil fit* [nothing comes from nothing], the new element appears in
contexts without which it could not have arisen in the way it has. That applies on the level of what is described as well as on the level of its description:
both what is articulated and how and as what it is articulated bear traces of
their provenance. Even something new that unlocks its own linguistic forms
can only be articulated using predeveloped media. Insofar as it is genuinely
new and not a new instance of something already familiar, it is not in fact
described by these media but only recorded in an explorative and heuristic
way. In that case the media of articulation function not as defining concepts
but as elucidating images.

Second, however, this new usage leaves its mark on these media of articulation and agents of representation. Precisely as a result of the figurative
articulation of the new element, the continuity of the old form is disrupted
by the discontinuity of the intended new content, and its linguistic identity

---

90. Cf. I. U. Dalferth, *Religiöse Rede von Gott* (Munich: Christian Kaiser, 1981), 488–94.

is overlaid and displaced by the functional difference.[91] It is the *soteriological images* of the Christian tradition that are particularly illustrative of this. These representational agents originate from a variety of pre- and non-Christian contexts. At first glance they appear to be connected in most cases by little more than their Christian usage. But through their predicative reference to Jesus Christ and his life story, they are often drastically modified and accentuated. At first glance the common ground between these manifold titles, images, metaphors, and patterns of semantic determination seems to consist principally in the fact that they are all predicated on the risen Jesus.[92] Through liturgical practice (the parallel use of different images in the same worship situation), literary proximity (e.g., in the Gospels or the New Testament Epistles), and theological interpretations (the search for transition points and potential coherences between different images), connections were created between them. This then led to a combining of their fields of imagery and—in the course of history—to the development of a verbal and practical framework that was specifically Christian. In the process, particular images such as "Lord," "Christ," or "Son of God" are given privileged significance because they are held to be especially suitable as *models for preaching and reflection*. They become nodes of a christological designation network, around which the remaining soteriological designations can be organized. These nodes can then in turn be linked together in patterns of soteriological reflection (such as the doctrine of the threefold office of Christ). The complete network of designations is essentially founded on a *grammar of trinitarian theology* that governs the whole of Christian discourse about Jesus Christ, God, ourselves, and our world.[93] This grammar clarifies that Jesus's salvific significance for us is correctly expressed only when it is anchored exclusively in God himself and his activity on behalf of his creation by reference to the Father, the Son, and the Spirit. Only this exclusive and unconditional anchoring in God himself guarantees that the salvation experienced in Jesus Christ is not a way of salvation for a small minority but is *universally inclusive* (i.e., relevant to everyone) and in principle accessible to all. Jesus's salvific significance for us is therefore properly expressed only when it is presented as *a salvation desired and*

91. This process can sometimes—as in the case of sacrifice, for example—be described as metaphorization or spiritualization.

92. It goes without saying that many of the links between these different image complexes predate this predicative reference to Jesus Christ—hardly surprising, given the coexistence of different fields of imagery within one cultural tradition.

93. Cf. B. Studer, *Gott und unsere Erlösung im Glauben der Alten Kirche* (Düsseldorf: Patmos, 1985).

*effected by God himself for the benefit of the whole of creation*: one God, one mediator, one creation (cf. 1 Tim. 2:5).

## 2.2. Soteriological Models

This *soteriological inclusiveness* is a consistent characteristic of all true confessions of Jesus Christ. Since this inclusiveness is the result not of any particular Christian claim to absoluteness but of the exclusive and unconditional saving activity of God himself, it manifests itself in a special way in images that consider Jesus wholly from the divine point of view: in addressing Jesus as *Lord* (κύριος); in the use of the name *Christ*, by which he quickly became known; and in his identification as *Son of God*. In Christian thought and speech all three images are key elements of prayer, doxology, and confession. All three consider Jesus with regard to his fundamental relationship with God and his distinction from God. And all three images have therefore become generally accepted during the critical processes of the formation of christological confessions and of theological reflection,[94] not least because they unequivocally emphasize the link with God as a specific link between God and Jesus, and, through him, between God and us. "God," according to Peter's Pentecost sermon, "has made this Jesus, whom you crucified, both Lord and Messiah" (Acts 2:36 NIV). Each of the three images mentioned accentuates his fundamental relationship with God in a different way.[95] Thus the κύριος title defines his relationship with God from the perspective of the universal reign of God, while the title "Christ" emphasizes the presence of the Spirit, and the title "Son of God" stresses God's fatherly love in his relationship with Jesus and with us. When we combine these images, they explain God's nearness to Jesus and to us all, summarizing and defining it theologically as the presence of universal creative, redeeming, and perfecting love.

### 2.2.1. Lord

"Lord" (κύριος) is the Greek equivalent of the substitute word used in postexilic Judaism in place of the tetragrammaton YHWH (Lord) and, as such, is the dominant form of address for God in the Septuagint: God, whom, out of reverence, one does not dare to address by his name Yahweh, is the real king of Israel and the Lord of all creation (Josh. 3:11–13; Isa. 1:24; 6:1–3; Mal. 3:1). When this title for God was adopted by the Christian community by way of confession and acclamation of Jesus (1 Cor. 2:8; 8:6; 16:22; Phil. 2:11), it

---

94. Cf. Schlier, "Anfänge des christologischen Credo," 36.
95. This does not mean that only the accentuated aspect of the image matters, however.

was expressing two things. On the one hand, by interpreting his life in the light of his message, it was emphasizing that in Jesus the glorious lordship of God was shown to be a universal lordship over life and death, that Jesus had been exalted or taken up into this lordship, and that it is present in him. The presence of the glorious lordship of God in Jesus is fleshed out in the New Testament Gospels by means of numerous images and narratives, from the image of the descent of the Spirit through the miracle narratives and the account of the transfiguration to the conception, birth, and ascension narratives. On the other hand, the use of the title κύριος for Jesus simultaneously applies a specific interpretation to God's lordship as seen in him, defining it through his life and cross so that it is recognized, in the light of the resurrection experience, as the *power of love and faithfulness*. The lordship of God proclaimed by Jesus offers a horizon of understanding and a theological interpretament of his life, which reveals it as the physical presence of the reign of God. By the same token, the life of Jesus, experienced historically and eschatologically, becomes a soteriological interpretament of the reign of God by presenting it as a lordship of salvific love.

### 2.2.2. CHRIST

A similar, essentially hermeneutic circle of interpretation and definition also applies to the title "Christ," which was adopted as a cognomen for Jesus at an early stage. Jesus was crucified by the Romans as a messianic pretender, as the inscription over his cross made plain (Mark 15:26), and he became permanently identified as such.[96] In the Hellenistic Greek–speaking world the Greek translation of the Jewish title of Messiah was understood not as a title but as a cognomen for Jesus. The definition of "Christ" thus acquired its content entirely from Jesus, but it was understood, in the light of his cross and resurrection, in a manner that could not be derived from the Jewish title of Messiah. In Jewish tradition, however, the title of Messiah refers back essentially to God. It is true that it is ascribed to a (single) human being who is expected to be the Davidic redeemer who, in his kingly (and/or priestly and prophetic) role, will establish justice and righteousness in Israel. But this in itself concerns the ultimate fulfillment of God's promises and the establishment of his lordship in Israel and throughout the world. In contrast to the title of Lord, the title of Messiah emphasizes not merely the fact of this lordship but also the form it will take—in other words, that

---

96. Cf. W. Kramer, *Christos Kyrios Gottessohn: Untersuchungen zu Gebrauch und Bedeutung der christologischen Bezeichnungen bei Paulus und den vorpaulinischen Gemeinden* (Zürich: Zwingli, 1963), 15–60. Cf. Pannenberg, *Systematic Theology*, 2:314–15.

it will be shaped and established by one endued with the Spirit of God and acting in God's power. Although the expectations and ideas linked with the hope of the Messiah varied widely,[97] in every case they emphasized that God would establish his reign by means of an eschatological savior, anointed by the Spirit. The use of this title for Jesus underlines that God's reign is made present in him, that the eschatological kingdom *has already* dawned and no longer needs to be merely hoped for and expected. At the same time, however, its use means that this distinguished name, associated as it is with Jewish expectations of salvation,[98] takes its measure from Jesus and not the other way around.[99] That is to say, the content of the title is defined by Jesus's story, in which it joins with other images in a common semantic currency to give soteriological expression to his life, death, and being raised. This process of definition introduces a quite specific understanding not only of the role of the Messiah but also of the nature of the eschatological reign and nearness of God that is ushered in and established by the Messiah. Experienced both historically and experientially, Jesus's life, death, and being raised thus become the soteriological interpretament not only of the reign of God but also of the messianic visualization and realization of the reign of God, thereby correcting and reorienting the Jewish messianic expectation and defining it more precisely in christological terms.[100]

The cognomen Christ thus conveys the fact that Jesus is *not only* the Messiah awaited by the Jews but is *more* than this:[101] he is not the Messiah within the meaning of the Jewish messianic expectation but—as J. Ringleben puts it—the

97. Cf. H. Ringgren, *The Messiah in the Old Testament* (London: SCM, 1956); H. Klausner, *The Messianic Idea in Israel* (New York: Macmillan, 1956); Vermes, *Jesus the Jew*, chap. 6; H. Gese, "Der Messias," in *Zur biblischen Theologie* (Munich: Christian Kaiser, 1977), 128–51; J. Becker, *Messiaserwartung im Alten Testament* (Stuttgart: Katholisches Bibelwerk, 1977); A. Chester, "Jewish Messianic and Mediator Expectations and Pauline Christology," in *Paulus und das antike Judentum*, ed. M. Hengel (Tübingen: Mohr Siebeck, 1991), 17–89.

98. Cf. M. Buber, *Das Kommende: Untersuchungen zur Entstehungsgeschichte des messianischen Glaubens*, vol. 1, *Das Königtums Gottes* (Berlin: Schocken, 1936); and vol. 2, *Der Gesalbte*, in *Werke* (Munich: Kösel, 1964), 2:727–845; S. Mowinckel, *He That Cometh*, trans. G. W. Anderson (Oxford: Blackwell, 1956); W. Dieterich, "Gott als König: Zur Frage nach der theologischen und politischen Legitimität religiöser Begriffsbildung," *ZThK* 77 (1980): 251–68.

99. Cf. F. J. Schierse, "Die neutestamentliche Trinitätsoffenbarung," in *Die Heilsgeschichte vor Christus*, ed. H. U. von Balthasar et al. (Einsiedeln: Benziger, 1967), 2:85–131, esp. 2:104.

100. Cf. J. Moltmann, *The Way of Jesus Christ: Christology in Messianic Dimensions*, trans. M. Kohl (London: SCM, 1990), esp. 28–37; Moltmann, "'Ich glaube an Gott den Vater'"; Moltmann, "Der mütterliche Vater und die Macht seines Erbarmens."

101. The claim made in Jesus's preaching and in the testimony of his life was more than a messianic claim, since the "kingdom of God of which Jesus spoke is not the earthly messianic kingdom of peace, but the heavenly kingdom of the 'Son of Man'" (cf. Mark 8:38; Matt. 24:27 // Luke 17:24; Matt. 24:37–39 // Luke 17:26–27; Matt. 24:43–44 // Luke 12:39–40; Luke 12:8–9 // Matt. 10:32–33; Niederwimmer, *Jesus*, 41). Cf. also Vermes, *Jesus the Jew*, 153–55.

"*superseded* Messiah,"[102] who transforms these expectations by fulfilling the hope of salvation that they express, though in a completely different way. It is in Jesus the Jew that the self-contradiction of Judaism culminates, in that it is in him as a person that the self-explanatory saving will of the living God confronts the fixed will of God as expressed in the Torah, with its constant need of interpretation.[103] But in him this contradiction is overcome, in that when the messianic bearer of the Spirit is redefined by the cross, God himself is *redefined* in the cross and resurrection of Jesus *as the Father of Jesus*. God's exclusive commitment to the Jewish people is replaced by his commitment of himself to Jesus the Jew, and thus by the inclusive universalization of his divine Fatherhood as soteriological openness and accessibility *for all*. As Paul emphasizes, salvation is conditional on nothing other than *God himself* (*sola gratia* [by grace alone]), and it is realized *through faith* in the presence of God in Jesus Christ *and through nothing else* (*sola fide* [through faith alone]).

### 2.2.3. Son of God

Of course, all this applies to the title Son of God as well. In mainstream Jewish tradition (cf. Exod. 4:22; Jer. 3:19) it is used, as we have shown, not biologically but in connection with the covenant of inheritance, and it conveys the idea of the admission of Israel or its Davidic representative into a special legal relationship with God: Israel has been appointed by God from among all the nations to this legal right of inheritance and must therefore call on this God alone from among all gods as its God, Lord, and Father.[104] This reciprocal, though not equal, but unambiguously asymmetrical legal relationship can be described using either the imagery of the father-son relationship or that of the master-servant relationship (Isa. 41:8–9). The Old Testament usage thus already underlines the nonbiological grammar of this image complex, stressing instead its basis in the legal and economic aspects of inheritance: the "son of God" is the one whom God has chosen of his own free will to be his heir. In Israel's messianic tradition the one anointed by God's Spirit as the representative of the people is called son of God (cf. Ps. 2:7). God himself entrusts his rule and the office of king of Israel to this anointed one. Since this office was tied to the Davidic line through God's special promise, sonship of God and

102. Cf. J. Ringleben, "Der Gott des Sohnes: Christologische Überlegungen zum Verhältnis von Judentum und Christentum," *KD* 40 (1994): 20–31, esp. 21 (italics mine). Cf. also O. Hofius, "Ist Jesus der Messias? Thesen," *Jahrbuch für biblische Theologie* 8 (1994): 103–29.

103. Cf. E. Käsemann, "Zum Problem des historischen Jesus," in *Exegetische Versuche und Besinnungen* (Göttingen: Vandenhoeck & Ruprecht, ⁶1970), 1:206.

104. Fr. W. Marquardt, *Das christliche Bekenntnis zu Jesus, dem Juden: Eine Christologie* (Munich: Christian Kaiser, 1991), 2:69–78.

sonship of David became linked by a close association that was still effective during the formation of Christian confessions (Rom. 1:3–4; Luke 1:32–35). The Christian application of the Son of God image to Jesus, who had not designated himself thus, was legitimized through his use of the "Abba" form of address for God, indicating that he had placed himself within the tradition of the representative chosen by God as his legally appointed heir (i.e., Israel), the "Son of God." The use of this image for Jesus sets in motion a process of defining the image complex in the light of the Jesus story, which can be traced through a series of stages in the New Testament texts and culminates in the trinitarian thought processes of the early church. Here then is a recapitulation of the four most important aspects:

1. Right from the start, or at any rate in pre-Pauline and Pauline confessional texts, Jesus is given the title Son of God (1 Thess. 1:10; Rom. 1:3, 9; 8:29; 2 Cor. 1:19; Gal. 1:16; 3:26). This image was readily adopted for Jesus because of the preexisting close association, within the Jewish tradition, between the figures of Son of God, Messiah, and Son of David. The link made in Romans 1:3–4 between Sonship of David and Sonship of God is therefore a key factor where confession of Christ is concerned, while Mark 1:1 highlights the way in which Messiahship and divine Sonship belong together. Matthew 1 combines both elements by presenting a detailed statement, both of the Davidic genealogical record of the Messiah (vv. 1–17) and of the divine lineage of Jesus (vv. 18–25), showing how they are interconnected and explaining the combination of motifs inherent in the Son of God image from a genealogical and a narrative perspective.

2. One reason for the use of this image complex for Jesus is probably the close and familiar way in which he turned to God as "Abba." This manifest intimacy, closeness, and familiarity between Jesus and God lies at the heart not only of the Abba image but also of the Son of God image. The underlying concept here is not of a physical descent of Jesus from God, such as might be, and indeed is, imagined in other traditions in connection with the Son image. Neither, on the other hand, is this a "purely" honorary predication with functional and legal significance, identifying Jesus as the representative of God's sovereign power. What this title highlights is not the aspect of sovereignty but *God's nearness to Jesus himself* and the *nearness of God to us in and through Jesus*, which are mediated through this title and interpreted through the image of the merciful Father. Once the Son of God title is understood from the point of view of Jesus's use of "Father," and not of the Jewish or Hellenistic background to the Son of God motif, this divine nearness brings about intimacy and trust. Ultimately, the question of the male (or female) attributes of this God who is called Father and the issue of the

(incontrovertible) maleness of Jesus are the least important aspects of the title Son of God when attributed to Jesus. The "stress is not on the masculinity of God's son, but on his 'childlike' relationship,"[105] although, here too, only insofar as "child" is an apposite image for the unique and genuine nearness and intimate connection between God and Jesus. This is the emphasis of the Father image just as it is of the Son image. It was and is essential that these points be made clear if there is to be appropriate theological reflection on the use of images in the original christological confessions.

3. As a result, in the New Testament Jesus is already given the title of the "unique" or "one and only Son" (John 1:18; 3:16, 18; 1 John 4:9). This does not mean that only Jesus and no one else can call God Father or himself or herself a child of God. Rather, it means that the mystery of the saving nearness and beneficent presence of God that enables a life of childlike trust in him was opened up, not just anyhow and anywhere, but by Jesus of Nazareth in his life, death, and being raised (John 1:18), because and to the extent that it was precisely here that God decisively defined himself to be as Jesus proclaimed him: the all-transforming and renewing nearness of fatherly mercy and love. Here, in this one specific life, it became clear what God is, always and everywhere; here he willed to be, and will irrevocably and unmistakably continue to be, the loving Father who waits for each of his creatures as for a prodigal son. Hence, the primary import of the image of the one and only Son is God-related, as the christological formulation makes clear: God is the Father, revealed as such through Jesus's self-differentiation from him, and Jesus is the Son, inasmuch as he makes this God, from whom he expressly differentiates himself, accessible to us as Father. "I am in the Father and the Father is in me[.] The words I say to you I do not speak on my own authority. Rather, it is the Father, living in me, who is doing his work" (John 14:10 NIV). Confession of the Son of God is, and is intended to be, a confession of God who is near to us as a loving Father—the loving Father of Jesus Christ.

4. It was not difficult, however, to add another emphasis to the image of the one and only Son. In Matthew 1 the idea of the Spirit of God operating in Mary is used narratively to expand it into the account of the Spirit-effected conception of Jesus. In John 1 the image is deepened in a similar way, but here by means of the Logos concept, which extends what was already said in Philippians 2 into the idea of preexistence.[106] This requires that we

105. Moltmann, *Way of Jesus Christ*, 143.

106. For the background to this, cf. E. Schweizer, "Zur Herkunft der Präexistenzvorstellung bei Paulus," in *Neotestamentica* (Zürich: Zwingli, 1963), 105–9; Schweizer, "Aufnahme und Korrektur jüdischer Sophiatheologie im Neuen Testament," in *Neotestamentica*, 110–21; G. Schneider, "Präexistenz Christi: Der Ursprung einer neutestamentlichen Vorstellung und das

understand the unique revelation of the nature of God's nearness in and through the life of Jesus as an eternal fellowship of the Word with God. If the Son has in truth revealed the mystery of God, then he must know this mystery, and he can know it only if there is no time and no place in which God was without him or he without God, so that he and the Father must be conceived of as always and everywhere together. The main purpose of this interpretation of the image is to give tangible form, within the person of Jesus himself, to the salvific relevance of all that Jesus said and knew, in such a way that its validity for everyone is clear. But it can be relevant for everyone only if it is anchored in God and his eternal life, so that the declaration in Psalm 2:7, "You are my Son, today I have begotten You," is valid always, everywhere, and for eternity. Once this thought is introduced into the scope of the Son image, it points theological reflection toward the concept of preexistence.

These developments set up the preconditions for combining and integrating what christological confessions are affirming when they speak of Jesus as Lord, Christ, and Son of God, an affirmation that is presented in narrative mode in the Gospels and more vigorously in reasoning mode in the New Testament Epistles: God's lordship is just what the story of Jesus confirms it to be, the all-transforming nearness of the loving Father, as it is continuously imparted and mediated in the Spirit of Jesus Christ (the reality of divine love that ordains everything). The question of Jesus's salvific significance for us can therefore be answered *only* with reference to God as Father and as the Spirit of Christ—in other words, from a trinitarian perspective. Thus, in his self-differentiation from God, expressed, for example, in the way he addresses God in prayer, Jesus relates to God wholly as Father and understands himself wholly as Son. Further, on the basis of this differential relationship with God, he regards God in such an essential and comprehensive sense as Father that he can express God's divinity wholly in terms of the image of merciful father: God's divine essence is his merciful fatherly love. By endorsing this understanding with eschatological finality in Jesus's cross and resurrection, God makes it clear that it is no mere outsider's definition of God (objective genitive) but an intrinsic self-definition (subjective genitive): God himself defines and understands himself as Father in the sense proclaimed by Jesus. He acts as God in accordance with this self-definition, and he wants us, accordingly, to call him Father. That this is so (in other words, that God's divine

Problem ihrer Auslegung," in *Neues Testament und Kirche: Für Rudolf Schnackenburg*, ed. J. Gnilka (Freiburg: Herder, 1974), 399–412; Schimanowski, *Weisheit und Messias*; N. Walter, "Geschichte und Mythos in der urchristlichen Präexistenzchristologie," in *Mythos und Rationalität*, ed. H. H. Schmid (Gütersloh: Gütersloher Verlagshaus Mohn, 1988), 224–34.

self-definition is manifest in Jesus's definition of God as Father) is admittedly not plain for all to see but is revealed only in the Spirit, without whom there is no assurance of the raising of the crucified one. Only the Spirit convinces us that what Jesus says of the Father is true because it expresses God's self-definition. For by assuring us of the resurrection of the crucified one, the Spirit convinces us that, through his life and death, Jesus expresses God's nearness as the presence of the unlimited and inexhaustible love of the Father who defines himself as such, and makes his presence, thus defined, effective in the Spirit. Jesus's salvific significance thus consists in the fact that God brings about our salvation through him and his Spirit. God defines himself in him and through him as the one who draws so near to us as love that we are able to live wholly out of his presence and to thank him as the Father of our Lord Jesus Christ.

## 3. The Divine Basis of What Jesus Christ Is for Us

In Christian thought the issues of Jesus's personal identity and his soteriological inclusiveness are inseparable. The questions "Who is Jesus?" and "What is Jesus for us?" can thus receive the same considered soteriological response: our Savior, our Redeemer, the Christ. The Christian faith therefore holds that Jesus Christ *is* the one *as* whom he is *confessed*. But whatever linguistic format the confession takes, he is confessed as the authoritative clarification of God's nearness and the definitive realization of his love. Thus, the questions of the identity and salvific significance of Jesus can ultimately be answered satisfactorily only by reference to God himself. This has consequences for our understanding of God: God proves to be the one who has redefined himself in and through his relationship with Jesus Christ. But this has consequences for our understanding of Jesus Christ, too, since it is solely by reference to God's self-definition that it becomes clear how Jesus can be what he is for us.

### 3.1. God as Reference Point

It is not just by using many key images, such as Lord, Christ, or Son of God, in its christological predications that the New Testament makes God its reference point. It also underlines the necessity of such a reference point in its hymnodic and narrative expositions of these images by means of various complexes of ideas such as preexistence and sending, conception by the Holy Spirit and virgin birth, incarnation and ascension, and the descent and ascent of the heavenly Son. Each in its own way, by recourse to the Wisdom tradition and other Hellenistic Jewish traditions,[107] makes it clear that Jesus's identity and salvific significance can be comprehended only if one takes God himself as one's starting point: Jesus's salvific relationship to us is an integral part of his identity as the Christ, inasmuch as faith discerns him to be the one through whom God's nearness and love are conclusively demonstrated and unambiguously mediated to us within the environment of our reality, governed as it is by sin. His salvific relationship with us is thus the eschatological fulfillment of God's relationship with us and, as such, emanates wholly and exclusively from God's relationship with Jesus Christ. Who he is and what he is for us are rooted in what God is for him and, through him, for us. Every image must express this in order to be christologically workable, and every narrative and theological exposition must affirm this.

This is far from being universally the case. The history of the Christian church teaches us that, right from the outset, the christological images, together with the New Testament's narrative and reasoned attempts to explicate them, were capable of being interpreted in quite different ways. Before long, therefore, theologians of the early church found it necessary to inquire into the grammar of these images at the level of dogmatic reflection and to lay down explicit guidelines for their satisfactory representational exposition. The classical precedent is found in the trinitarian and christological dogmas that were declared binding by most Christian churches. Both dogmas formulate foundational principles for Christian discussion of God and Jesus Christ, thereby establishing the core grammar of the Christian life of faith. Both relate to the central imagery of Christian thought and speech, and furnish its structural rules with descriptive explication and critical legitimization, by deriving their validity from the principles of the God-related constitution of the Christian life of faith as such. Both dogmas formulate these principles as the integrating element of a two-stage theological program of reconstruction. Based on the exemplary texts of the canon of Scripture, this program both establishes the guiding rules for the use of this imagery within the Christian life of faith (the governing rules of the *regula fidei*) and also makes it clear why precisely these rules, and no others, are valid, by rooting them in the principles of the God-related constitution of the Christian life of faith through God the

---

107. Cf. U. B. Müller, *Die Menschwerdung des Gottessohnes: Frühchristliche Inkarnationsvorstellungen und die Anfänge des Doketismus* (Stuttgart: Katholisches Bibelwerk, 1990); H. Merklein, "Zur Entstehung der urchristlichen Aussage vom präexistenten Sohn Gottes," in *Zur Geschichte des Urchristentums*, ed. G. Dautzenberg et al. (Freiburg: Herder, 1979), 33–62; Schneider, "Präexistenz Christi," 399–412; Schneider, "Christologische Präexistenzaussagen im Neuen Testament," *IKaZ* 6 (1977): 22–30; K. J. Kuschel, *Geboren vor aller Zeit? Der Streit um Christi Ursprung* (Munich: Pieper, 1990); H. v. Lips, *Weisheitliche Traditionen im Neuen Testament*, WMANT 64 (Neukirchen-Vluyn: Neukirchener, 1990), 150–90.

Father, the Son, and the Spirit (the constitutive rules of the doctrine of the Trinity, Christology, and pneumatology). This is why both dogmas belong together indissolubly: the trinitarian dogma explicates the implications of the resurrection confession for Christian discourse concerning God, while the christological dogma does the same for Christian discourse concerning Jesus Christ. For if God's saving presence in Jesus Christ owes its existence solely to God himself, then it is realized within our history solely through God himself, and it is only through him that we are able to perceive it, acknowledge it to be true, and recognize it as a certainty. This means that the one God must be conceived of in this threefold respect as differentiated within himself; that is, he must be identified simultaneously as the sole ground of reality (Father), of truth (Son), and of assurance (Spirit) of the raising of the crucified one and of new life. Similarly, as regards christological dogma, God's saving presence in Jesus Christ cannot be satisfactorily conceived of and acknowledged if the presence of God in Jesus Christ, the difference between Jesus Christ and God, and God's saving activity in and through Jesus Christ for us are not all held together in the unity of a single thought. Trinitarian dogma answers the question "Who is God?" with the soteriological response "the one who, in Jesus and through his Spirit, has proved himself to be fatherly love toward us." Similarly, christological dogma answers the question "Who is Jesus Christ?" with the equally soteriological response "the one in and through whom God has proved himself to be fatherly love toward us." Neither instance contains any new statement concerning God or Jesus Christ, nor anything that is different from what is already expressed in the resurrection confession in its numerous versions and variations. Rather, on the basis of this confession, the grammar of Christian discourse about God and about Jesus Christ is explicitly recorded by formulating the manner in which we should speak of them in order that our discourse might be truly of God and of Jesus Christ.

### 3.2. Truth Conditions for Christological Statements

In christological dogma the divine basis of Jesus Christ's being and his salvific significance for us are formulated in a principle emphasizing that each correct theological statement concerning Jesus Christ must take into account the *vere homo* and *vere deus* in such a way that God's free initiative, rooted solely in his self-definition, is always safeguarded for soteriological reasons. This carries the following meanings.

1. No statement about Jesus Christ is accurate unless it gives unqualified credence to the fact that this is the story of a real person in a specific and non-negotiable historical situation. The historical facts of the life, doctrine, cross,

and death of Jesus of Nazareth are part and parcel of the truth conditions of any christological statement: it can be true only if it does not contradict the truths "Jesus lived" and "Jesus died."[108]

2. No statement concerning Jesus Christ is accurate unless it unreservedly affirms that the substance and character of God's nearness, and thereby our salvation, have been uniquely and irreversibly revealed in this particular life story. If God is the God who the story of Jesus proves him to be, then he would not be God if he turned out to be different in some way; therefore, he must be near to us just as he is to Jesus and as he is to us, time and again, through Jesus and his Spirit: the loving Father who keeps faith with his children even through death and beyond. This eschatological content of Jesus's life, death, and being raised from the dead, together with the soteriological relevance of his story for us, are likewise part and parcel of the truth conditions of every christological statement. It can be true only if it does not contradict the truths "The crucified one (i.e., the Jesus who was killed on the cross) is alive" and "God is just as near to us as to the crucified Jesus."

3. The historical and the eschatological-soteriological truth conditions for christological statements are not only paradoxically adjacent; they are interrelated according to a specific order of precedence. According to the confession of faith, the fact that the crucified one lives denotes not just the twofold truth of the statements "Jesus died" and "Jesus lives" but also that Jesus, who died, has been *raised by God from the dead* and *lives at the right hand of God*, where he *intercedes for us* (Rom. 8:34). Both groups of truth

---

108. At this level—and only at this level—do empirical and historical facts (e.g., that Jesus was male, unmarried, and a Jew) have any theological significance. Taken on their own, none of these facts is soteriologically relevant, and any attempt to derive special theological consequences from them is misguided. It is important to stress this when confronted with any christological model that seeks to interpret Jesus's earthly life as a participatory representation of God, analogizing or allegorizing it as an earthly illustration of the life of God. The confused and inappropriate debate over whether Jesus's Jewishness and his maleness should be considered soteriologically decisive indicates the logical contradictions to which such an approach leads. On the other hand, it must be emphasized that, while all empirical and historical statements concerning Jesus only have theological significance in conjunction with the other truth conditions for christological statements, in this context their force is attributable to the fact that they point *to God* and underline the *reality of his saving activity*. It is not the historical, empirical, or even biological details of Jesus's life that are soteriologically decisive but the eschatological fact that God recognized this life as the place where his all-transforming love is mediated and revealed. Jesus's life, death, and being raised from the dead demonstrate what God is, desires, and does, in the sense that all that Jesus is, does, and endures, both actively and passively, focuses wholly on allowing God himself to be revealed as all-transforming love. The soteriologically relevant aspects of Jesus's life, death, and being raised from the dead are those, and only those, that serve this purpose; a proper representation of Jesus Christ must treat as relevant everything that affirms this soteriological import of his life, death, and being raised from the dead, and nothing else.

conditions are thus held together by a reference back to God's activity, which means that the crucified one lives—through and with God as the eschatological self-revelation of God's conclusive self-definition. This reference must involve God's activity as more than a purely functional category to legitimate the resurrection confession if it is to refer back to God himself and not just to a concept of God; it must conceive of this activity strictly as the *realization of God's self-determination to accomplish our salvation specifically in and through Jesus*, thus allowing it to unfold in a trinitarian sense as the self-determination of the Father, the Son, and the Holy Spirit as saving action in Jesus Christ. Accordingly, a christological statement can be true only if it does not contradict the truth—rooted in the doctrine of the Trinity—that God acts freely and conclusively in and through Jesus Christ for our salvation. The fact that this is the activity of *God* alone is substantiated by the *soteriological universality* of the salvation that the Christian faith confesses. The fact that God acts *in and through Jesus Christ* is substantiated by the *soteriological uniqueness* of Jesus Christ as the place where the eschatological self-revelation of God's conclusive self-definition takes place. And the fact that God is here acting *freely and conclusively* for our salvation is substantiated by the *eschatological conclusiveness* of this salvation. The universality, uniqueness, and conclusiveness of Jesus Christ's salvific significance for us are therefore implications of the foundational fact that *God himself* acts in him and through him to bring about our salvation.

This reference back to God's activity, and thereby to God himself, is fundamental for Christology. It is only when God himself is viewed as the sole initiator of this revelation of his nearness, so that his presence in and through Jesus is perceived strictly as *self-mediation* and *self-revelation*, that we are able to grasp that the manner in which God is near us has been definitively revealed in the story of Jesus within the tension generated by the juxtaposition of the statements "Jesus is dead" and "The crucified Jesus lives." Only by *reference back to God himself* can the historical and eschatological-soteriological truth conditions of christological statements be held together.

## 4. Patterns of Christological Thought

This reference back to God is never abstract but always occurs within the context of a specific thought pattern that aids the attempt to link together the truth conditions of christological statements: the historical (Jesus died) with the eschatological-soteriological (the crucified Jesus lives) and with the theological—in the narrower sense (the crucified Jesus lives through and with

God as the eschatological self-revelation of God's conclusive self-definition [God's Son]). Christological dogma insists on the necessity of this linkage. However, it does this by means of a particular (ontological) pattern that, while not necessary per se, is just one of several that have played a role—often a combined role—in the history of christological reflection.

### 4.1. The Temporal Pattern

Contradictions between true statements about the same referent can be avoided either by introducing the temporal element or by differentiating between aspects. Both approaches to this problem are found in christological thinking. The *temporal pattern*, the sequential reporting of historical and eschatological-soteriological statements about Jesus, played an important part from the outset. It is to be found in narrative texts such as the Gospels and also in doxological or hymnodic texts with a narrative structure, such as the hymn to Christ in Philippians 2. The second article of the Apostles' Creed adopts this Gospel pattern. There are also numerous examples of its theological use: the Johannine sending and incarnational Christology, the Christology of the two Lukan works with its focus on salvation history, the ascent and descent Christologies of the early church, the early Protestant doctrine of the *statibus Christi* [states of Christ] (i.e., *status exinanitionis* [state of self-emptying] and *status exaltationis* [state of exaltation]), up to and including Pannenberg's historical-theological Christology or the Christology of the Way proposed by Karl Barth and, in their different ways, by van Buren or Moltmann.[109] A detailed analysis of these examples shows widely differing approaches: while one approach traces the story of the earthly Jesus up to his exaltation to eternal fellowship with God, the other describes the journey of the eternal Son into the strangeness of his earthly existence, which was to culminate in the cross and resurrection and lead him back to eternal life at the right hand of the Father. In the one case it is the earthly Jesus who is predicated as the referent of the different groups of temporally organized statements; in the other it is the divine Logos. Both lead into the theological sidelines if—as in adoptionism—the eschatological-soteriological statements are no longer applied in their fullest sense to the earthly Jesus or—as in docetism—the historical statements are no longer applied to the eternal Logos. In order to avoid such shortcomings and to demonstrate the inner unity between the different phases of the story of Jesus Christ, the temporal pattern was therefore evolved as a way of shaping a theological-soteriological pattern. The temporal sequence of historical

---

109. P. van Buren, *Discerning the Way: A Theology of the Jewish-Christian Reality* (New York: Crossroad, 1980); Moltmann, *Way of Jesus Christ*.

and eschatological statements was thus integrated within an overarching set of events encompassing the historical and eschatological dimensions of the story of Jesus Christ as phases of God's realization of his plan for salvation history. The soteriological pattern, which presents the fulfillment of God's salvific purpose, is superimposed on the temporal pattern, which sequences the story of Jesus Christ; this not only gives the arrangement of the story a clear direction and import but also focuses the whole account, in all its phases and dimensions, on its true protagonist: God himself. Depending on the version, the narrative-temporal pattern makes reference to God in one of at least three ways (here again Phil. 2 illustrates this): God is conceived of as the source and origin (Phil. 2:6), as the goal and future (2:11), and as the key protagonist (2:9) of this story. It takes place as God's story, and it is consummated as the story in which God's actions constitute the beginning, the middle, and the end. God alone gives it its unity and the inner frame of reference that allows the divergent statements concerning Jesus to hold together christologically.

### 4.2. The Perspective Pattern

From the beginning of Christian thought, the distinction between different aspects or views of Jesus Christ played their part alongside the temporal pattern in making it possible to hold together the contradictory statements concerning him. The pre-Pauline confession in Romans 1:3–4 organized its statements about Jesus by differentiating between "after the flesh" and "after the Spirit" (cf. 1 Tim. 3:16; 1 Pet. 3:18), and this dual approach is continued by Ignatius (*Eph.* 7.2), *2 Clement*, Hippolytus, and also by Tertullian and Cyprian.[110] From Irenaeus onward,[111] early-church Christology encapsulated these different perspectives on Jesus Christ in the double designation of Jesus as *vere homo* and *vere deus*. The sequential function of two stages or phases

---

110. Cf. J. N. D. Kelly, *Early Christian Doctrines* (London: Continuum, ⁵1980), 142–45, where this approach is summarized under the subject of early Spirit-Christologies. H. J. Kraus ("Eine Christologie des Heiligen Geistes," in *Jesusbekenntnis und Christusnachfolge*, ed. B. Klappert et al. [Gütersloh: Gütersloher Verlagshaus Mohn, 1997], 37–46) sees in this "the early church . . . alternative to the philosophically inspired two-natures doctrine" (45), which represented a "clear sign of a dehellenization of Christianity" and "of the return of theological thinking to its Hebrew roots" (45–46). Cf. Kraus, "Die Geist-Christologie im christlich-jüdischen Dialog," in *Messias-Vorstellungen bei Juden und Christen*, ed. E. Stegemann (Stuttgart: Kohlhammer, 1993), 103–10. Of course, he is here ignoring the fact that the two-natures doctrine of church Christology arose out of this very approach (cf. Kasper, *Jesus the Christ*, 26–28, 163–229), even though, for the avoidance of dynamistic misunderstandings and deficiencies, the Logos concept had been substituted for the Spirit since the end of the second century (cf. Pannenberg, *Systematic Theology*, 2:381–82).

111. Irenaeus, *Haer.* 4.6.7.

in the story of Jesus is thus taken over by the coexistence of two parallel perspectives on his person. But this poses fresh problems. Only insofar as both perspectives are held to be valid, not just for specific phases or parts of Jesus's life but for the entire history of his life, death, and raising from the dead, can we avoid all these shortcomings: the Ebionite (Jesus was only human), the docetic (Jesus was never truly human), the dynamistic (Jesus was a human being who became divine through the Spirit at a specific moment in his life), and the kenotic (Jesus was a divine being who renounced the use or possession of his divine attributes for a specific period). The systematic focus of christological interest thus shifts from Jesus's death and resurrection to his conception and birth, where the coexistent divinity and humanity of the person of Jesus Christ is first constituted.[112] Early-church Christology turned

112. If, as happened in early-church Christology, one understands Jesus's conception and birth to bring about not only the initial but also the completed constitution of Jesus as a person, then the incarnation is reduced to the act in which the Logos took on human nature. But, as is shown by W. Pannenberg, this inevitably leads to a dilemma (*Jesus–God and Man*, 291–93). Either—like the Antiochians—one postulates a complete human being but can then only conceive of the incarnation as the paradoxical union of an independent divine with an independent human being, although—as Apollinaris of Laodicea had already emphasized— two beings, each perfect in itself, cannot be one (cf. Pseudo-Athanasius, *Contra Apollinarem* 1.2 [*Patrologia Graeca* 26, 1096 B]). Or—like the Alexandrians—one postulates a nature that is merely human in a general way that "was formed into an individual man only through the incarnation itself," but can then no longer ascribe "specifically human individuality" to Jesus (Pannenberg, *Jesus–God and Man*, 291). In contrast, Pannenberg tries to avoid the dilemma with the proposition "that the constitution of the person of Jesus takes place in the whole process of this history" (*Systematic Theology*, 2:385). It is thus only possible to rule out a "prejudice to the creaturely independence of Jesus in his history" if his relationship with God is included in the concept of his human nature from the outset, so that the latter is identified as a work of creation. For insofar as the Logos, "as the generative principle of otherness," is the basis of its "creaturely independence," it is possible to say that "human nature as such is ordained for the incarnation of the eternal Son in it," since in it the Logos encounters, not something alien, but only what it has itself created (2:385–86). But quite apart from the question of how the Logos can be identical with what it has created—as Pannenberg emphasizes with regard to the concept of "self-actualization" that he uses for this idea, the thought is a "paradox" and, for precisely this reason, is appropriate "for theological use"—the *vere homo* is therefore only affirmed at the cost of diminishing the *vere deus* (2:393). For if the import of the history of Jesus Christ is that he has fulfilled human destiny, in that "the eternal Son takes human form in such acceptance of creatureliness before God," then this history is just what Pannenberg argues that it is not: one instance among others (2:386). It is true that Pannenberg insists, "We do not have here one example of this basic relationship among many others. Only here does the basic relationship find actualization in such a way that we then *perceive* it in other human examples, albeit in what is in many ways a broken and distorted form" (2:316–17, italics mine). Here, in particular, he makes it plain that he understands the difference between Jesus Christ and ourselves in terms of the clarity with which we are able to perceive his acceptance of his creatureliness as compared with our own. But this is an inadequate exposition of the *vere deus*, the import of which is not just epistemic but above all soteriological, namely, that the history of Jesus Christ, and *it alone*, has an integral, irreplaceable, and incomparable significance *for*

back to the then-current ontological thought form of substance metaphysics so that it would be able not merely to confess this constitution, together with the indissoluble coexistence of the two perspectives *vere homo* and *vere deus* in respect of Jesus Christ, in hymnodic form as the incarnation of the Son of God (John 1:14) but also to think through this incarnation and its consequences. Admittedly, it had to revise this radically for the purpose.[113] The outcome of this revision and its application to Jesus Christ has been handed down to us in the two-natures doctrine of Chalcedonian Christology. The significance of this doctrine for historical theology requires us to discuss it in more detail.

### 4.2.1. Two-Natures Christology

Under the perspective pattern the two-natures doctrine starts from the premise that Jesus Christ, "the only begotten Son, our Lord," can be correctly understood only when equal emphasis is placed on his humanity, which he shares with us, and his divinity, which he holds in common with God the Father. These facets were described as the two "substances [*substantiae*]" of Jesus (from Tertullian on), and as his two "natures [φύσει]" (from Origen on); they are the reason for his being equally, though differently, consubstantial with us and with God. According to the christological doctrinal statement formulated in AD 451 by the Council of Chalcedon, in Jesus Christ both natures are interrelated in such a way that "the properties of each nature are preserved and concur in one person and one hypostasis [*salva proprietate utriusque naturae, et in unam personam atque subsistentiam concurrente*]."[114] Jesus Christ is thus defined as a *persona synthetos*, one person in two natures that interrelate in him ἀσυγχύτως, ἀτρέπτως, ἀδιαιρέτως, ἀχωρίστως [without confusion, without change, without division, without separation]. The positive implications of this view, which was formulated in negatives at Chalcedon, were developed, in terms of the relationship between the natures, in the doctrine of the communication of attributes and also, in terms of their basis, in the "*unum eundemque Christum Filium Dominum unigenitum* [one and the same Christ, Son, Lord, only-begotten],"[115] in the doctrine of the Logos as the single hypostasis that gives personhood to the two natures (an- and enhypostasia). The second of these led to the development of the principle of the

---

*our salvation.* In order to grasp this, one must interpret the history of Jesus Christ strictly as a *salvific act of God*, which will not be the case if one removes the creation-theological limits from the concept of human nature while still retaining the two-natures doctrine.

113. Cf. I. U. Dalferth, *Jenseits von Mythos und Logos: Die christologische Transformation der Theologie* (Freiburg: Herder, 1993), 91–101.

114. DS 302.

115. Ibid.

unity of Jesus Christ in the form of a concept of the person differentiated in itself. From Boethius to Leontius of Byzantium, Richard of St. Victor, Hegel, and Pannenberg, attempts have been made to state this ever more precisely—with the prevailing version in each case as the crucial factor in determining the doctrinal formulation of the *unitio* (the event of the incarnation) and the *unio personalis* (the hypostatic union resulting from the incarnation). The initial attempts to work this out in the early church and the medieval period were continued by the early Protestant doctrine of the *communio naturarum* [communion of natures] and the *communicatio idiomatum* [communication of attributes] in particular. These sought to represent the actual communion between the two natures (i.e., the divine-human unity of the person of Jesus Christ) as being constituted by God himself.

Within the scope of the two-natures Christology, this initiative and prerogative on God's part was expressed principally in the form of two doctrinal statements. One emphasized that the agent who gave personhood to the man Jesus was the Logos, the Second Person of the Godhead, who incorporated the nonpersonal human nature in Mary into himself and thereby into communion with the divine nature. The other worked out, in the doctrine of the anhypostasia of human nature and its enhypostasia in the divine Logos, the implications of this view for the two-natures Christology. The first anchored Christology in the doctrine of the Trinity; the second, in the form of the doctrine of the communication of attributes, prepared the ground for a whole series of further christological doctrinal statements. Thus the belief that Jesus Christ is *worthy of worship* is founded on the conviction that, although human, as the mediator of the salvation effected by God himself he is a divine person; thus the reverence and worship due to God alone are also due to him, in the sense that to worship him is not to deify a human being but rather to give thanks to God that in this human person he has revealed himself conclusively to us all and made himself accessible to us. The affirmation of Jesus's *virgin birth*, too, expresses in narrative form that the agent who creates the personhood of Jesus Christ is not a human person deriving from a human father but the eternal Logos, who took human nature in Mary.[116] If our salvation is accomplished through God alone, then Jesus Christ mediates and reveals God's saving presence and nearness insofar as God himself is present in and with him as a person. If Jesus Christ, the mediator of the salvation that God alone has brought about for us, does not proceed from a human father (and therefore his human nature must be conceived of as anhypostatic), then Jesus

116. Cf. R. E. Brown, *The Birth of the Messiah: A Commentary on the Infancy Narratives in Matthew and Luke* (Garden City, NY: Doubleday, 1977).

is unaffected by original sin, his human nature is intact as before the fall, and he himself is unable or unwilling to commit sin and is therefore also free from death and immortal. However, if the human Jesus Christ is free from sin and from death, which is the wages of sin, but nonetheless dies on the cross, then it must be said of his *death* that he suffered the death others deserved because of their sins. Further, if the divine Jesus is fully self-determining, then his acceptance of death and of the consequences of others' sin rests wholly on his free decision and the *voluntary obedience* of the Son to the will of the Father, who desires that sinful human beings be saved from the death they have deserved. This in turn presupposes that Jesus Christ possessed not only two natures but also *two wills and two modes of action* that concurred in obedience, so that Jesus's human will was fully subordinated to the divine will.[117] This doctrine in turn gave rise to the misunderstanding that the duality of wills in Jesus Christ also made it necessary to assume a duality of subjects, so that his divine and human natures must be distinguished not just as *aliud et aliud* [this and that thing] but as *alius et alius* [this and that one]. The rejection of this misunderstanding at Nicaea (AD 787) and Frankfurt (AD 794) made it necessary to explain how Jesus's humanity (his human nature and human will) could logically be considered subject to his divinity (his divine nature and divine will) without diminishing his humanity. Medieval Scholastic theologies sought to resolve this by means of the *habitus* theory (the Logos clothed himself in Jesus's body and soul), the *assumptus* theory (the Logos assumed not merely a complete human natures but a complete human being), and finally, the theory favored by Thomas Aquinas[118]—although not only by him—the subsistence theory (Jesus's human nature had no hypostasis of its own but subsisted in the hypostasis of the Logos). None of these solutions proved fully convincing, however.[119] The doctrines of Jesus's *sinlessness, immortality*, and *voluntary obedience* thus have consequences, not just for the theological understanding of his death but also for the theological definition of the humanity of this "true man," consequences that extend to the doctrines of the excellence and beauty of his soul and his body. Finally, they also have consequences for the theological understanding of his mother, Mary, which led to the gradual development of the Roman Catholic mariological dogmas of the immaculate conception and the bodily assumption into heaven.

The chief problem with these secondary and tertiary approaches to constructing a Christology is that the methods they use for explaining and

---

117. DS 556–57.
118. Thomas Aquinas, *Summa theologiae*, III, Q. 96, Art. 5.
119. Cf. Pannenberg, *Jesus–God and Man*, 304–5.

interpreting christological images and texts realistically within the context
of an ontological thought pattern are uncritical from a hermeneutical point
of view. They take the images to be descriptions of the subject, equate the
representation with the subject matter, and treat pictorial statements as terminological premises from which logical inferences can be drawn. But this
is hermeneutically erroneous and theologically absurd. Modern dogmatic
criticism has rightly targeted these doctrinal statements. It also became plain,
however, that such doctrinal statements result principally from an interpretation of the perspective pattern of the two-natures doctrine based on substance ontology, combined with questionable realistic semantics. They are
not, however, essential implications of the fundamental christological task of
thinking through what it means to confess Jesus Christ in the light of the three
groups of truth conditions for christological statements outlined above. The
critique of the two-natures doctrine[120] and its associated semantics render the
doctrinal statements themselves problematic. But this critique calls neither
the perspective pattern nor christological thinking as a whole in question.

### 4.2.2. Communicatio Idiomatum

A concrete illustration of this is found at the very heart of the two-natures
doctrine, in the doctrine of the *communicatio idiomatum*. This doctrine
sought to think through the consequences of the union of the divine and the
human natures in one person by systematically developing rules governing
the communication of attributes between the two natures and the person
of Jesus Christ.[121] Early Protestant theology distinguished three classes, or
genera, of the communication of attributes. The *genus idiomaticum* [genus
of attributes] states that all attributes of both natures are also to be affirmed
of the person of Jesus Christ. This follows directly from the Chalcedonian
statements and was already being taught explicitly in early-church Christology.
The distinction between the two natures also implies a distinction between
Jesus Christ's two wills and modes of action, as stated by the Lateran Synod
of 649 and the Third Council of Constantinople (AD 680/81), following Pope
Leo's Tome[122] in contrast to the Monothelite and Monergistic derivative forms

120. Cf. ibid., 283–323; Moltmann, *Way of Jesus Christ*, 51–54.
121. The foundations for the development of the doctrine were laid in the Eastern Church
by John of Damascus (*De fide orthodoxa II*, 3 and 4 [*Patrologia Graeca* 94, 993–1000]), in the
Western Church by Thomas Aquinas (*Summa theologiae*, III, Q. 16, Arts. 1–12), and in the
Lutheran tradition by the Formula of Concord, Solid Declaration VIII (*BSLK* 1017–49).
122. In his letter of 449 to Patriarch Flavian, Pope Leo had not only accentuated the continuing distinction between the two natures within the unity of the person; he had also emphasized
that each of the two natures in communion with the other does what is proper to it: "Agit enim
utraque forma cum alterius communione quod proprium est" (DS 294).

of the Monophysitism rejected at Chalcedon;[123] and therefore the inferences of the *genus idiomaticum* are to be drawn not only for the being of Jesus Christ but also for his action or work. This was adopted by Reformed theology in the doctrine of the *communicatio operationum* [communication of operations] and by the Lutheran doctrine of the *genus apotelesmaticum* [genus of official acts], both of which asserted that it is necessary to define the elements proper not only to the being but also to the activities of each of Jesus Christ's two natures. Thus everything that Jesus Christ does and accomplishes can be traced back not just to one of Jesus's wills or one of his two natures but to the concerted activity of both natures.[124] The *genus maiestaticum* [genus of majesty], on the other hand (by virtue of which one must also, on the basis of the *unio personalis* or *hypostatica* [union of the person or hypostasis], attribute the communication of the attributes of divine majesty, omniscience, omnipotence, omnipresence, etc., to the human nature of Jesus Christ), was regarded as contentious and a "dangerous innovation," introduced by Lutheran theology.[125] Lutheran theology insisted on this, since it was otherwise impossible to speak of a unity of person where Jesus Christ was concerned. Reformed theology, on the other hand, held to the teaching of a reciprocal communion between the two natures, so that there was a communication not only of the divine attributes to Jesus Christ's human nature but also of the human attributes to his divine nature. This inference, as a way of expressing the lowliness of God in Jesus Christ, which P. Althaus,[126] following D. F. Strauß[127] and G. Thomasius,[128] designated the *genus tapeinoticon* [genus of humility], was not drawn by Lutheran dogmatics because of the axiomatic premise of the immutability of the divine nature. The divine nature, it was argued, is perfect and therefore fundamentally immutable, so that it can be neither elevated nor diminished, or, as the Formula of Concord emphasized: "because there is 'no alteration' in God . . . his divine nature has neither lost nor gained any of its substance or attributes through his incarnation."[129] It should be said that Luther had addressed this concept of the immutability of

123. DS 500–22, 556–57.

124. *BSLK* 1031, lines 32–45.

125. "Consensus Bremensis," in *Die Bekenntnisschriften der reformierten Kirche*, ed. E. F. K. Müller (Leipzig: A. Deichert, 1903), 746, line 1.

126. P. Althaus, *Die christliche Wahrheit* (Gütersloh: Gütersloher Verlagshaus Mohn, [8]1969), 451–55, 459.

127. D. F. Strauß, *Die christliche Glaubenslehre in ihrer geschichtlichen Entwicklung und im Kampf mit der modernen Wissenschaft* (Tübingen: Osiander, 1841), 2:134.

128. G. Thomasius, *Christi Person und Werk: Darstellung der evangelisch-lutherischen Dogmatik vom Mittelpunkte der Christologie aus* (Erlangen: 1853–61), vol. 2, §43.

129. *BSLK* 1032, lines 10–13.

God as an abstract premise, not yet transformed by Christology itself, in his text "Of the Lord's Supper, a Confession" (1528), quoted in the Formula of Concord,[130] and had affirmed it for soteriological reasons: "If I believed that a human being alone had suffered for me, then Christ must be a bad redeemer who himself requires a redeemer."[131] For if "the divine and the human are one person in Christ," then "for the sake of the unity of that person, everything that pertains to his divinity must pertain also to his humanity and conversely." Even if therefore "the Godhead . . . does not suffer, nevertheless the person who God is suffers," so that it must be said that "God's Son suffers."[132] Thus Luther does not reject the intention of the *genus tapeinoticon* but makes clear that the underlying concept of God needs to be formulated more precisely. The whole doctrine of the *communicatio* in all its genera makes sense only if it employs an understanding of God that is trinitarian from the outset. But this means that we cannot speak of God in isolation from the Christ event, only in relation to it. From a theological point of view, the essence of this "divine nature" or "divinity," which is conjoined with human nature in Jesus Christ without confusion and without division,[133] can be stated only in relation to this historical story. Lutheran theology expressed this by defining the Logos that was active in the *unio personalis* not, as did the early-church tradition, the Reformed Church, and the *extra-Calvinisticum*, as λόγος ἄσαρκος but as λόγος ἔνσαρκος, thus comprehending the Son of God wholly and exclusively from the point of view of his incarnation.[134] Given this premise it could also

130. *BSLK* 1029, line 17–1030, line 35.
131. *BSLK* 1029, lines 30–34; WA 26:319, lines 37–39.
132. *BSLK* 1029, line 40–1030, line 11; WA 26:321, lines 4–7, 11, 26.
133. The same applies to "human nature" or "humanity": one can only say what human nature is when one makes God a central consideration, as W. Pannenberg correctly maintains in his *Systematic Theology*, 2:385–89. The only question is whether one can work out this reference to God from a creation-theological point of view, as he does, or whether one should not instead interpret it directly from a christological point of view in relation to the history of Jesus Christ. For Pannenberg there is no doubt that christological thinking must always presuppose and draw on a religious-metaphysical understanding of God ("infinity") and an empirical-metaphysical understanding of humanity ("creaturely independence"). However, on both counts he goes from the indisputable particular to the general in a manner altogether questionable: just because every christological statement draws on specific ways of understanding God and humanity, it does not follow that all of them draw, or should draw, on the same one. Assuredly there could have been no confession of Christ without Israel's experiences of God. But this does not mean that either a metaphysical understanding of God or an understanding of what it is to be human is essential to any such confession.
134. This is evident from the Lutheran interpretation of the central statements of the Philippian hymn. According to J. Gerhard, *Loci theologici* (1610–22), loc. 4, cap. XIV: *De statu exinanitionis et exaltationis*, ed. E. Preuss (Berlin: Schlawitz, 1863–85), 592–60, the subject of the kenosis is the Logos *incarnatus* [incarnate] not the Logos *incarnandus* [to be incarnate], since the latter was acquainted with neither human form nor death (592). In contrast to the

draw the conclusion, in its theology of the cross, that God himself had undergone death on the cross,[135] although of course it was not God but death that came to an end. Both take the view that the story of Jesus Christ can be understood from a theological point of view only when it is understood wholly as an *act of God* and when *God* is simultaneously understood in an entirely new way in light of this act.

It is no accident that the doctrine of the *communicatio idiomatum* and its implications have been the subject of christological controversies right up to the present day.[136] But the doctrine formulates the conditions necessary for true communication concerning Jesus Christ, the Lord and redeemer of the world. This becomes outwardly apparent in the Christology of classic Lutheran dogmatics, in that within the doctrinal context of the *unio naturarum personalis* [personal union of natures] a clear distinction was made between the particular doctrines of the *communicatio naturarum* [communication of natures], the *propositiones personales* [personal propositions], and the *communicatio idiomatum*.

The first of these doctrines clarifies that christological statements fail to make Jesus Christ their true referent unless they adopt from the outset the double perspective of the mutually interpenetrating perichoresis that constitutes the intercommunication between his divine and his human nature: a "Christology" that deals only with the earthly Jesus is just as wide of the mark as a "Christology" that acknowledges only the divine Logos. The referent of every christological statement is the *persona synthetos* [composite person] of the incarnate Logos, which can be identified and considered only from this double perspective.

The second doctrine explains how, given this premise, one should speak of Jesus Christ in order to witness to him truly: only concrete statements such as "The Son of God suffered" can be true, not abstract statements such as "The

---

early-church interpretative tradition, which conceived of the *status exinanitionis* in terms of a *humiliatio incarnationis* [humiliation of the incarnation] (ibid.), and the *status exaltationis* correspondingly in terms of an *exaltatio incarnationis* [exaltation of the incarnation], in other words, an *assumptio humanae naturae* [assumption of human nature] (598), Lutheran theology defined both positions as *humiliatio incarnati* [humiliation of the incarnate one] (592), that is, as the *exaltatio glorificationis* [exaltation of glorification], the *exaltatio ad Dei dextram* [exaltation to the right hand of God] (598).

135. Cf. E. Jüngel, *God as the Mystery of the World: On the Foundation of the Theology of the Crucified One in the Dispute between Theism and Atheism*, trans. D. L. Guder (Grand Rapids: Eerdmans, 1983), 55–104.

136. The reflections of J. Moltmann, *The Crucified God* (London: SCM, 2001), have made a clear contribution to this debate, latterly generating their own controversy. Cf. M. Welker, ed., *Diskussion über Jürgen Moltmanns Buch "Der gekreuzigte Gott"* (Munich: Christian Kaiser, 1979).

Godhead suffered." The double perspective thus results in true statements only when it is directed wholly and exclusively toward the referent himself, not when it is applied to just one of the two partial perspectives.

Finally, the third doctrine sets forth the general conditions under which concrete statements concerning Jesus Christ can be true from this double perspective: the doctrine of the *communicatio idiomatum* explicates the truth conditions of true communication concerning Jesus Christ.

But this takes the form of a descriptive exposition of the divine-human "facts" that must be the case in order for a christological statement to be true. This is based on a questionable realistic semantic, whereby the truth of statements does not consist merely in the *adaequatio intellectus ad rem* [conformity of the understanding to the thing itself], but where statements as a whole are capable of being true only because and to the extent that their *verba* [words] actually represent the *res* [thing] in its particularity. In order to be true, the subject and predicate components of statements must have an actual and appropriate correlate that they represent verbally, and they must furthermore correctly portray, through the linguistic association of their *verba*, the way in which these correlates are ontologically linked at the level of the *res significatae* [things signified].

Within the context of an interpretation of the perspective pattern of the two-natures doctrine based on substance ontology, this inevitably leads to difficulties. It is true that, on the basis of our experience of the world and of ourselves, we can make moderately reliable statements concerning ourselves as humans. But how, given our sinful condition, can we form an idea of the *perfect* human nature that, according to the Chalcedonian Statement,[137] must be ascribed to Jesus Christ? Moreover, how can we adequately convey facts about God using the linguistic means available to us? Is it possible for us to form any idea at all of the divine nature when, as Anselm and others emphasize, it exceeds all our thinking and knowledge? The normal theological response to this has been that, although we can have no actual concept of God, we can arguably form a nominal idea of "God." But if we can indicate what we mean by "God" only in words, how can we know whether our statements concerning God are true, or whether it is at all possible for them to be true? Can we in fact speak of divine and human "nature" in one and the same way, or is the concept of nature inevitably used ambiguously when applied to God and to ourselves? Even if one believes this can all be resolved with the aid of the classical doctrine of analogy, a central problem remains: surely the predicate components of christological statements express irreconcilable facts from

137. DS 301.

the "human" and the "divine" realms, which are as different as the finite and the infinite. And how they can possibly have a common referent inevitably remains shrouded in obscurity.

In response to this question, the *genus idiomaticum* merely affirms that both groups of facts must be assigned to the same referent, namely, the person of Jesus Christ. It formulates the task but offers no solution. The *genus maiestaticum*, on the other hand, goes a step further. It asserts that one cannot speak of fundamental incompatibility between what is "divine" and what is "human," since human nature at least is in a position to participate in the majestic attributes of the divine nature: *finitum capax infiniti* [the finite can hold the infinite], although—as Lutherans would add—*non per se, sed per infinitum* [not by itself, but with the aid of the infinite]. This makes it clear that the teaching of the *genus maiestaticum* on the coexistence of natures is precisely the same as the teaching of the doctrine of the incarnation on the subject of the christological statements: all activity has its source in God alone. The prerogative of the divine Logos toward the earthly Jesus in the doctrine of the *unitio personalis* [act of uniting the persons] corresponds exactly to the prerogative of the divine nature toward the human in the doctrine of the *unio personalis*. The coexistence of the infinitely distinct human and divine natures in Jesus Christ is thus perceived just as wholly and exclusively as an *actio divina* [divine act] as is the incarnation, in which—understood as *assumptio naturae humanae*—the divine Logos assumed a human nature. Just as human nature possesses no hypostasis of its own in Jesus Christ but subsists enhypostatically in the divine Logos, so the divine and human natures only coexist in Jesus Christ because and to the degree that they are held together by God himself. The *genus maiestaticum* thus takes the doctrine of the incarnation, as it relates to the mutual relationship of the two natures, a logical stage further. If the identity of the referent of christological statements is determined by an exclusive action on the part of God himself, then both the compatibility of the divine and human natures and, therefore, the extent to which christological statements are true and capable of being true must also be traceable exclusively to God himself.

The doctrine of the *communicatio idiomatum* understood the point that both the subject component of christological statements (Jesus Christ) and the predicate component (divinity and humanity) as well as their link (Jesus Christ is *vere homo et vere deus*) are dependent on one *actio divina* [divine act]. *God* is the referent of christological statements, and *God's action* is what inspires them, given that they present, from a faith perspective, God's interpretation of himself for us in the story of Jesus Christ: succinctly stated,

- that it is God himself who here interprets for us who and what he is;
- that it is God himself who is interpreted here for us; and
- that it is God himself who ensures that his self-interpretation is also truly perceived by us in faith.

In contrast to what the representational semantics of the classical doctrine of the communication of attributes suggests, the truth conditions of christological statements do not consist of a dual ontology of human-divine facts. Rather, they exist as a unity within the differentiated *saving activity of God*. Neither is the difference of perspective rooted in a dual structure made up of two distinct spheres of reality, the human and the divine, miraculously unified in Jesus Christ, but rather in the unsurpassable unity and complexity of the reality of God's saving activity and, simultaneously, in the inescapability of the difference between us and God. Accordingly, a doctrine of the person of Jesus Christ is not required to show that and how the incompatible facts of the *natura divina* and the *natura humana* can be held together in relation to Jesus Christ ἀσυγχύτως, ἀτρέπτως, ἀδιαιρέτως, ἀχωρίστως [without confusion, without change, without division, without separation]. On the contrary, it is required to link all that is said and thought about Jesus Christ, in connection with our human world and with God, to the one comprehensive saving action of God himself, and on that basis to assess how God reveals himself in Jesus Christ and through his Spirit and what he thereby reveals about us and our reality.

So the doctrine of the *communicatio idiomatum* does indeed explicate the truth conditions of true communication concerning Jesus Christ, by tracing its content and realization back to God's self-communication. It is *God himself*, as he makes himself understood in the story of Jesus Christ and through his Spirit, prompting us to communicate with him and about him, who is the referent of christological statements. Hence christological statements are not true because they accurately describe God and his saving activity; rather, they are true because they give verbal affirmation to God's self-communication by clarifying that God is understood (if he is understood at all) only in the way he has made himself understood in Jesus Christ and through his Spirit: all true communication about God is rooted in communication with God, which, in turn, is the result of God's self-communication with us.

### 4.2.3. Personhood

This theologically fundamental fact of God's self-communication is developed in the doctrine of the Trinity, which explicates the foundation of

Christology and regulates every aspect of it. The classic two-natures doctrine encapsulated this fundamental reference back to God himself by identifying the Logos, the eternal Son of God who forms the personhood of Jesus Christ, as the point of reference for christological statements. A long period of development was required, however, before the concept of the *person*, thus advanced to the position of central christological concept, was understood from the point of view of God's self-communication and was worked out relationally in a systematic way. I will briefly recall some of the key phases of this development.

In the christological symbolism of Chalcedon the concept of person (πρόσωπον, ὑπόστασις, i.e., *persona, subsistentia*) has a different function from the concept of nature (φύσις, *natura*): it refers to the single concrete reality that is Jesus Christ.[138] Not only is there a distinction between person and nature, but the meaning of "person" is expressed by the concept of hypostasis, which had itself been crystallized in the trinitarian debates with the aid of Platonic criticism.[139] Originally, ὑπόστασις was largely used to mean the same as οὐσία or φύσις, so that there was no differentiation between *hypostasis* (actual realization), *ousia* (substance), and *physis* (nature). While the Stoics used the term *hypostasis* for the realization of an indeterminate primary substance (*ousia*) in individual concrete objects, Neoplatonism no longer used this term for matter but instead transferred it to the intelligible world, applying it to the hierarchical manifestation of the One (*Hēn*) on the different levels of being, so that it was widely treated as a synonym for *ousia*.[140] Christian thought corrected this in two ways. First, debates within the field of trinitarian theology, in contradistinction to Neoplatonist thought with its ontology of hypostatic hierarchies, placed a fresh emphasis on the difference between *ousia* and *hypostasis*; second, there was a correlated redefinition of the concept of *hypostasis*. *Ousia* thus came no longer to denote the numerical unity of an individual being; instead, it denoted a substance that is realized in different hypostases in various ways. At the same time, the Father, the Son, and the Spirit are recognized as realizations of the one divine substance, not subordinate but of equal rank. The hypostatic hierarchy is thus replaced by a hypostatic plurality, while the concept of hypostasis itself is given a *relational*

138. DS 302.
139. Cf. Dalferth, *Jenseits von Mythos und Logos*, 80–101; H. Dörrie, "'*Hypostasis*': Wort- und Bedeutungsgeschichte," in *Platonica minora* (Munich: Wilhelm Fink, 1976), 13–69. Although the πρόσωπον concept was used in the Chalcedonian dogmatic definition, its meaning was not clarified; this was one of the central problems that the council left open, and it subsequently gave rise to further christological debates and attempts at resolution.
140. Cf. H. Köster,"ὑπόστασις," *TWNT* 8:571–88, esp. 8:574–76.

form. But the relationship between the Father, the Son, and the Spirit is to be apprehended not as an external interrelatedness of three substances in the Aristotelian sense but rather as a relational coherence of differences that constitutes the perichoretic unity of God in a diversity of hypostases. Each hypostasis is what it is only in connection with and in differentiation from the others; each is therefore the actual realization of God—not, however, in isolation, but only in perichoretic coherence with the others. This actualization made it possible to revive the concept of the πρόσωπον, or person, in a trinitarian context without imputing modalistic implications to it: God is *tres personae in una substantia* [three persons in one substance], as it had been possible to say since Tertullian.[141]

In the christological frame of reference, the concept of the person, which had thus been defined more precisely, now required a clearer differentiation between ὑπόστασις/*persona* and φύσις/*natura*, in order to surmount the misleading dichotomy between Monophysitism (as one person, Jesus Christ can have only one nature, namely, divine) and Dyophysite Nestorianism (because of his divine and human nature, always thought of in concrete terms, Jesus Christ must ultimately be two persons). The two-natures formula put forward by Leo I,[142] following Theodore of Mopsuestia, and adopted at Chalcedon on October 22, 451, refers to εἰς ἕν πρόσωπον καὶ μίαν ὑπόστασιν συντρεχούσης (*in unam personam atque subsistentiam concurrente*) [concurring in one person and one subsistence],[143] but although this decisive distinction had now been articulated, it had not yet been thought through. The attempt to do this led Boethius to his momentous definition of the person as *naturae rationalis individua substantia*:[144] a person is an individual substance of a rational nature.

But this definition of a person as an individual endowed with reason took no account of the very factor that had constituted the decisive theological gain in the trinitarian development of the hypostasis concept: the insight into the essentially relational quality of the hypostasis. Richard of St. Victor also pointed out that the Boethian concept of the person is unsatisfactory from the point of view of trinitarian theology and replaced it with his definition of a person as *naturae intellectualis incommunicabilis existentia*:[145] a person is a single irreplaceable form of rational existence, but not as an independent substance based in himself, but as an ek-sistence originating in another and

141. Tertullian, *Prax.*, chaps. 2 and 4.
142. DS 293.
143. DS 302.
144. Boethius, *Liber de persona et duabus naturis contra Eutychen et Nestorium ad Ioannum diaconum Ecclesiae Romanae*, chap. 3 (*Patrologia Latina* 64, 1343C).
145. Richard of St. Victor, *De Trinitate*, 4.21, 24.

oriented toward another. This to some extent restored the essential relational quality to the understanding of personhood. But although Scotistic theology in particular continued and deepened this line of thought,[146] there was an initial failure, even in modern times, to recognize the far-reaching implications of this understanding. It is true that, in modern times, substance thinking was criticized, although not for its lack of the relational element but for the absence of the subjectivity and self-consciousness that defines itself autonomously and uses its free self-definition as the basis for a fundamental distinction between itself and the world of objects, subject as this is to external laws. Hegel was the first to succeed in reaffirming the fundamental relational element in the understanding of personhood on the basis of the modern emphasis on autonomy: "It is the character of the person, of the subject, to *relinquish its isolation, its separateness*" and "to win it through immersion, through being immersed in the other."[147] It is in the other that the person becomes himself or herself. A person's being is thus regarded, from its genesis, as an interpersonal process, and Hegel seeks to understand the structure of the process by reference to the concepts of love and spirit: a human being is not a person, but one becomes a person in the course of his or her history. Since Hegel consistently adhered to the modern approach that holds autonomy to be the normative principle of personhood, to a large extent he replaced the concept of person with that of personality. This person, conceived of as personality, may be described as follows: given that it finds itself only through and within its relationship to others, personhood is well suited not only to its nontransferable uniqueness, fundamental relatedness, and active self-determination but also to an essential openness requiring the person to comprehend the process of self-determination as his or her own story, so that personhood is consistently thought of as the *set of events* within which personality is formed.

But how can this set of events be identified more precisely? It is difficult, within the scope of modern thought, to answer this question satisfactorily. It cannot be adequately comprehended, either as a process of *individualization* (as with Schleiermacher) or as a process of *subjectification* (as with Fichte and Hegel), since every such attempt leads to the logical contradiction of always having to require as a presupposition the very factor that cannot be comprehended as the result of this process: the person who, in his or her story, becomes a subject and an individual. In order to be able to think this through, two processes must be differentiated and interlinked: the process of *developing*

146. Cf. H. Mühlen, *Sein und Person nach Johannes Duns Scotus: Beiträge zur Metaphysik der Person* (Werl: Dietrich-Coelde, 1954).

147. G. W. F. Hegel, "Vorlesungen über die Philosophie der Religion, Teil II," in *Werke* (Frankfurt: Suhrkamp, 1969), 17:233.

*into a person* and the process of *developing as a person*,[148] or in other words, the process by which human beings become persons, and the process by which human beings as persons become—or fail to become—human. In the first process human beings become human in the sense of personal counterparts to God; it is a process that must be expounded theologically as the story of God the creator, reconciler, and perfecter, in relationship with whom human beings are formed as persons from outside themselves. This story, to which human beings owe their inalienable dignity as persons, is the prerequisite and foundation of the processes by which they *as* persons become (or fail to become) subjects, individuals, and personalities—more or less identical with themselves. We cannot therefore lose or squander our personhood even if—for whatever reason—we are not in a position to become subjects, individuals, or personalities. If, however, our development as a person is rooted in our development into a person (a development that emanates from God alone) and not from ourselves, then what is true of Jesus Christ is true of every human being: without personhood there can be no humanness, but our personhood emanates wholly and exclusively from God himself. This is not to deny the difference between Jesus Christ and us. This difference consists instead in the fact that we are created beings and therefore persons distinct from God, while Jesus Christ, on the other hand—from the perspective of the classical two-natures doctrine and its crystallization in the doctrine of an- and enhypostasia—is not, as a person, distinct from God but is indeed the Second Person of the Godhead himself. Together with the Father and the Spirit, he participates in God's internal communication with himself, while, on the other hand, we participate in God's communication with those who are other than himself. If, however, the relationship of communication between God and us, to which we owe our personhood, is supported and governed by the trinitarian relationship of communication between God and himself, then our personhood is rooted not in the abstract idea of a relationship with God but in the concrete relationship of the Father, the Son, and the Spirit with us. *Anthropologically* this means that Jesus Christ and the Spirit are already playing a crucial role in our development into persons without waiting until we begin our development as persons. The rug is thus pulled out from under the abstract (modern) antithesis between human autonomy and human relationship with God, since the process by which we achieve autonomy always includes Jesus Christ and the Spirit, so that our autonomy and our creatureliness are to be regarded, without confusion and without division, as

148. Cf. I. U. Dalferth and E. Jüngel, "Person und Gottebenbildlichkeit," in *Christlicher Glaube in moderner Gesellschaft*, ed. Fr. Böckle et al. (Freiburg: Herder, 1981), 24:57–99.

two sides of the same circumstance—namely, that God, in his freely available love, allows us to live in and through his presence.[149] And *christologically* it means that the creation-theological and soteriological connection between Jesus Christ and ourselves is the theme of our reflection on the very person of Jesus Christ, not just on his work. Thus our salvation is in fact present in the very person of Jesus Christ, not merely in what he achieved as a person. Thus the distinction between person and work, which we regard as such an essential element, is a misleading one where Jesus Christ is concerned: he is our salvation because of who he is, not because of what he does; it is in his being that he accomplishes our salvation, even before he begins to act. For, in his very being, he is the one who is so near to us that he, in conjunction with the Father and the Spirit, constitutes us as a person (from a creation-theological perspective) and, in view of the failure of our creaturely personhood, enables us (soteriologically) to become aware of our personhood. In summary: not until the development of the idea of the person within the context of trinitarian theology was the central concept of the relational element of personhood sufficiently well recognized that the modern polarization between autonomy and relationship with God was circumvented and the christological and anthropological constraints of the (Western) tradition were overcome.[150]

### 4.3. The Rhetorical Pattern

With the emergence of historical consciousness in the modern era, the traditional temporal or ontological thought patterns were subjected to a radical historical and epistemic critique. Following Kierkegaard in particular, these patterns were frequently replaced in the new theology by the *rhetorical existential dialectic* of paradox Christology. There is no longer any attempt to hand down the historical and eschatological-soteriological statements concerning Jesus; instead, they are simply placed alongside and in opposition to each other, since—so it is said—given the impossibility of adequately telling the "eschatological story" in terms shaped by our human story, "paradox is

149. Unless our autonomy and creatureliness are held together like this, referring back to God himself, it is almost impossible to avoid the logical contradiction of conceptualizing our need for freedom as the self-justification for our freedom, and to misunderstand the fragmentary and incomplete realization of our freedom as its problematical result. Cf. T. Rendtorff, "Der Freiheitsbegriff als Ortsbestimmung neuzeitlicher Theologie am Beispiel der *Kirchlichen Dogmatik* Karl Barths," in *Gottes Zukunft—Zukunft der Welt: Jürgen Moltmann zum 60. Geburtstag*, ed. H. Deuser (Munich: Christian Kaiser, 1986), 559–77.

150. Cf. also in this regard the studies by J. D. Zizioulas, *Being as Communion: Studies in Personhood and the Church* (New York: St. Vladimir's Seminary Press, 1973); Chr. Schwöbel and C. E. Gunton, eds., *Persons, Divine and Human* (Edinburgh: T&T Clark, 1991).

the only proper mode of expression."[151] Heinrich Vogel defined this paradox as a "double statement with the character of a contradictory antithesis. Two statements that cancel each other out are derived from one idea."[152] If this definition were to be applied to the two statements "Jesus died" and "The crucified Jesus lives," they would negate each other. Nothing at all would then be stated, and neither would the idea acquire any sense of mystery that it could use existentially to salvific effect, although this is what Vogel attempts to show, when, in connection with Kierkegaard's Anti-Climacus and his observations on the "unity between God and an individual human being," he identifies this as the ultimate paradox in the face of which human reason must keep silence: "The God-Man is the paradox, absolutely the paradox. Therefore it is altogether certain that the understanding must come to a standstill on it."[153]

The Christian resurrection confession did not rest content with the mere affirmation of this paradox but sought to communicate it by connecting it with God's re-creating act of resurrection, emphasizing, both implicitly and explicitly: the crucified Jesus lives *through and with God* as the eschatological self-revelation of God's conclusive self-definition. By neglecting to think this through, the rhetorical pattern of paradox Christology not only fails to make a contribution to the task of christological reflection; it does not even represent the task adequately. Christologies of this type remain unsatisfactory when, like Vogel, they attempt to conceive of the "unity of the truth in the reconciliation of contradiction."[154] They relate this to God by attributing to him the ability to reveal himself in contradiction, seeing precisely herein the expression of his lordship over contradiction;[155] they consider this contradiction insoluble for us in the age of *theologia viatorum* [theology of wayfarers],[156] believing that it will not be resolved until the "hereafter" of the eschatological vision "of the contradiction-free unity of his glory."[157] If they are right, then surely it is not the paradox that constitutes the topic of theological reflection

151. O. Weber, *Grundlagen der Dogmatik* (Neukirchen-Vluyn: Neukirchener, ²1972), 2:136; cf. Althaus, *Christliche Wahrheit*, 445–46.

152. H. Vogel, *Christologie*, in *Gesammelte Werke* (Stuttgart: Radius, 1983), 5:170. This definition most certainly does not capture Kierkegaard's position and project. Cf. H. Deuser, *Sören Kierkegaard: Die paradoxale Dialektik des politischen Christen* (Munich: Kaiser, 1974), 27–107.

153. S. Kierkegaard, "Einübung im Christentum," in *Gesammelte Werke* (Düsseldorf: Eugen Diederichs, 1951), 26:77–78. Cf. H. Garelinck, "Gegenvernunft und Übervernunft in Kierkegaards Paradox," in *Materialien zur Philosophie Søren Kierkegaards*, ed. M. Theunissen and W. Greve (Frankfurt: Suhrkamp, 1979), 369–84; Vogel, *Christologie*, 5:186.

154. Vogel, *Christologie*, 5:192.

155. Ibid., 5:197.

156. Ibid., 5:215.

157. Ibid., 5:217–18.

and the christological theme but rather the saving activity of God to which the paradox gives expression and therefore God himself.

### 4.4. *The Trinitarian Pattern*

This is precisely what we find in those approaches that apply a *trinitarian pattern* to christological reflection. Whatever form it takes, the task of christological reflection is to think through the fundamental soteriological reality, namely, that we owe our salvation wholly and exclusively to *God himself* and that *God alone* is the necessary and sufficient prerequisite for our salvation and for Jesus Christ's salvific significance for us. It is thus *God's activity*, not the temporal or ontological categories of classical or neoclassical metaphysics, and not even the rhetorical figures used in the discourse of paradox, that constitutes the context and the cognitive horizon within which the fundamental christological problems should be thought through theologically. In view of the divergent truth conditions of christological statements, God's activity needs to be expounded in such a way that it enables us to consider the truth of Jesus's cross and death in the same way as we consider the truth of his resurrection and the certainty with which, in the Spirit, we are made aware of his eschatological salvific significance. If Jesus's cross and death are to be considered from the outset within the horizon of God's activity, in the same way as we consider his resurrection to a new and eternal life with God and our own awareness of the raising of the crucified one as the eschatological self-revelation of God's ultimate self-definition, then we must regard God's activity, and thus God himself, as differentiated. In order that our consideration of Jesus's cross and resurrection may enable us to perceive God himself as the origin, realization, and fulfillment of our salvation, we must differentiate not only between God's work of creation and his work of reconciliation but also between both of these and his work of consummation; for it is only the latter that identifies and illuminates them all as the work of one and the same God, Father, Son, and Holy Spirit. Trinitarian thinking is therefore essential to christological thinking: in order to perceive the divine basis of Jesus Christ's being for us, God must be apprehended from a trinitarian perspective.

# 4

# Trinity

*The Theological Relevance of the Cross for the Idea of God*

## 1. Confession of Christ and the Idea of God

All theological reflection that wants to do justice to the inherent logic of the Christian confession of faith in Jesus Christ must not only think through the resurrection with the cross in mind; it must also think through both cross and resurrection with God in mind. This is impossible unless one can refer back to a preexisting understanding of "God." Without this, the focus of our reflection on the cross and resurrection of Jesus will remain obscure, and we will not comprehend the extent to which God acts in the cross and resurrection to redefine and identify himself, and reshape our understanding of him.

That God does this, however, is a central affirmation of the Christian confession of faith: only in and through Jesus Christ and his Spirit is there a full and definitive disclosure of who and what God truly is. This alone assures us that God is *unconditional love*, the one who not only desires our salvation but has brought it about in the same way as he has defined himself, namely, as an unconditional love that does not seek to assert its infinite importance to us by demonstrating that it can exist without us, whereas we cannot exist without it. Quite the opposite, this love finds our finite life to be so infinitely important for itself that it binds its own being to our free acceptance of it. God has risked his very self with each of us, because by raising the crucified one he has undertaken to realize his very being, not independently of us, or at our expense, but solely via the path of our free acceptance, by recognizing our otherness and by taking account of our finiteness.

Where our consideration of this divine self-definition is concerned, there is no question of making an arbitrary choice of an understanding of God as the focus of our reflection on the cross and resurrection, or of indiscriminately substituting a (metaphysical or religious) idea of God. The actualization and redefinition of the idea of God by God himself is carried out within a quite specific horizon: faith in the one God and his covenantal history with Israel, which Jesus lived out and to which he gave eschatological crystallization by the testimony of his life. It was in this context that the resurrection of the crucified Jesus by God was originally acknowledged and proclaimed, and it was in this context that a specific redefinition of the traditional understanding of God was achieved. The Christian understanding of God is permanently linked to this context by continuity and contrast. For it owes its specific nature to this context, and only in this context does it become apparent that this new understanding of God is not just a better insight into the God who was already known but rather the *eschatological self-identification and re-definition of this God by God himself* and is therefore the *disclosure of his ultimate self-definition.*

Israel's understanding of God in general, together with its adoption, continuation, and reorientation in Jesus's preaching and way of life in particular, is what needs to be the starting point, though not necessarily the final port of call, for any theological explication of the confession of faith. Jesus's proclamation of God and the testimony of his life constitute the context within which the Easter message was first revealed. So theological thinking must refer back to this context in order to interpret the Easter confession and to shed light on its meaning. But nowhere are we given any direct access to Jesus's proclamation of God and the testimony of his life as such. It is possible to gain access to the original understanding of Easter only by way of the Christian testimony itself, and then only as it was defined and handed down in the light of Easter. For the Christian faith, to which the meaning and truth of the cross and resurrection of Jesus was disclosed in the light of his proclamation of God, took Easter as its hermeneutical starting point. It understood Jesus's death on the cross in the light of his proclamation of God because it gained a new perception of that proclamation in the light of his resurrection; it understood the new life of the crucified one in terms of his being raised by God because it perceived the experiences of Jesus's death and ongoing activity in the light of his proclamation of God; and it understood that it owed both these perceptions to God himself since they sprang not from its own efforts but from the work of the Spirit of God. In the Christian confession of faith and in its testimony, therefore, Jesus's proclamation of God was not simply being extended and continued to provide a horizon of understanding for the cross and resurrection; it was being redefined in the light of the eschatological Easter discontinuity. The result of this redefinition is the transformation of Jesus's understanding of God into the *Christian understanding of God*.

Accordingly, theological reflection furnishes a methodological explication of the Christian confession of faith by applying the implicit confessional horizon of understanding explicitly to the confession itself; the message thus becomes both the source and the goal of its interpretation. In this process theological reflection is able to clarify how what is articulated in the confession redefines the horizon of understanding within which it is articulated: Christian discourse concerning God does not simply continue Jesus's and Israel's discourse concerning God; it redefines it and understands it afresh in the light of Easter. Just as the confession of faith understands Jesus's cross and resurrection within the horizon of the testimony of his life, so theology, too, seeks to understand his life better than it could be understood in its own terms.

This method of deepening the understanding by means of hermeneutical self-application is a standard instrument of theological reflection and argumentation: by interpreting an interpretative relationship ("Jesus is the Christ") *afresh* within its own interpretative horizon, the theological interpreter moves hermeneutically between the two interpretative instances, from Jesus to Christ and from Christ to Jesus, so that the resulting intensification of the original interpretation makes it possible to understand what was originally stated better than it understood itself. Thus the figurative language of the raising of the crucified one shows that the experiences of Jesus's death on the cross and of his living and active presence as the one who had been crucified, in themselves incompatible, are in fact coherently linked and can be perceived as the eschatological manifestation of God's faithfulness and love when they are understood against the background of Jesus's proclamation of God. What is not yet evident, however, is that this is not only a possible new understanding opened up by Jesus's proclamation (itself unaffected by it) but a transformation of the original message by the hermeneutical reference to Good Friday and Easter. For this to become clear, Jesus's proclamation of God must first be given substance by the cross and the resurrection; second, the affirmation of the raising of the crucified one must be reinterpreted in theological terms expressly against the background of Jesus's (now substantiated) proclamation of God. Only then does it become apparent that Christian discourse concerning God is not just an idiosyncratic form and extension of the Jewish understanding of God—possible, superfluous, or distorted, depending on one's standpoint—but that, in spite of its continuity, it seeks to think and articulate something new: the eschatological self-actualization and redefinition of God as unconditional, inexhaustible, and unfettered love. It is impossible to conceive of this, however, unless the existing idea of God is given a fresh definition.

Both these aspects must therefore be borne in mind. In order to understand Jesus's cross and resurrection from a theological point of view, they must be interpreted within the context of his proclamation of God (i.e., they must be thought through while focusing on the God who was known and confessed by Israel in the *shema' yisrael* as the one God on whom Jesus called as Father, the dawn of whose kingdom he proclaimed through his words and actions, and whom he exhorted his disciples to call on as their Father). If, however, we reflect on this God of Israel, whom Jesus addressed as "Father," against the background of Jesus's cross and resurrection, then he is perceived with inner consistency *in trinitarian terms*, since this is the only way in which it is possible for us to gain a real understanding of this God's actual *eschatological redefinition of himself through the cross and resurrection of Jesus Christ*. For in this eschatological event God ineluctably defines *his purpose to be love* and consequently *himself as love*. He thus enters into a commitment that only in, with, and through all that is different and separate from himself will he be who and what he is: our God. As the Christian faith confesses, God's own being as God is love, because through the cross and resurrection of Jesus Christ, God has set himself a new and ultimate eschatological objective: without our free acceptance of him as God, he will not be our God. He binds his divine selfhood to our free assent to him as God, determining that in his identity as our God, Lord, and creator he will only ever exist through and with us, never against us. This means—and precisely herein lies the essential significance, for the idea of God, of the cross and resurrection of Jesus Christ—that God refuses to define himself directly apart from us and, of his own free will, bases the freedom and power of his divine selfhood on our free acceptance of his deity. God exposes his selfhood to the risk of our free acceptance because he is wholly love and is trusting and hoping that his love will be requited, even though he neither wants nor is able to compel this in any way. Jesus Christ's cross and resurrection are the expression of the eschatological redefinition of God because they interpret God's final self-definition as unqualified and ineluctable love. For the idea of God, this means that it is not we who make ourselves dependent on an infinite being whom we have devised for ourselves out of existential dread or insecurity, or in an attempt to overcome our mortality; rather, it is the creator who binds himself to his creation by making his very being as God and creator dependent on his creation's free acceptance of him, allowing it the independence and freedom not only to determine itself but also to codetermine his divine being, while safeguarding its own otherness. God gives himself into our hands, thus making our finite life infinitely important. This "Christian revolutionizing of the concept of God," which shows, as Falk Wagner rightly emphasizes, not merely that the "logic of unmediated self-definition is doomed to fail" but that freedom can endure only within "self-definition mediated through relationship,"[1] is fundamentally dependent on references to Jesus and to the Spirit, who teaches us to confess God as the Father of Jesus and Jesus as God's Son. These are not incidental or superficial to the Christian idea of God but essential, since they are integral elements of God's eschatological redefinition of himself as the God who is God only through our free acceptance of his divine otherness: only when these reference points are taken into account can God be defined as love and identified and perceived as God in the light of the cross and resurrection of Jesus Christ.

But these reference points are crucial, not only from an epistemic point of view for our knowledge of God but also factually for God himself, if, as the Christian faith confesses, it is really true that in raising the crucified one God has proved himself to be love and has redefined himself as God. It is not purely how and as what we can know God but also who and what God actually is that is decided at the cross and resurrection and therefore with reference to Jesus and the Spirit, since it is here that God has identified himself definitively as love. By raising the crucified Jesus from the dead and by making it possible through his Spirit for us to recognize and confess his resurrection activity and to perceive his eschatological saving presence in our own life, he proves himself to be simultaneously the *creator* who calls into being things that are not (Rom. 4:17), the *reconciler* who makes the ungodly righteous (Rom. 4:5), and the *consummator* who will raise the dead and bring about a new world (Rom. 4:17). All three elements are part and parcel of God's self-definition as God in the cross and resurrection of Jesus Christ. A grammar of Christian thought and discourse concerning God must therefore regard all three elements as central to its idea of God. Accordingly, all three elements have normative significance for the interpretation of the images we use for speaking to and about God.

It is therefore not sufficient to speak of God in the same way as Jesus himself spoke of him, simply by continuing his intensification of Israel's discourse concerning God. In the light of his cross and his resurrection, even Jesus's

---

1. Cf. F. Wagner, "Die christliche Revolutionierung des Gottesgedankens als Ende und Aufhebung menschlicher Opfer," in *Zur Theorie des Opfers: Ein interdisziplinäres Gespräch*, ed. R. Schenk (Stuttgart-Bad Cannstatt: Frommann-Holzboog, 1995), 251–85, esp. 251 and 275.

understanding of God must be defined more precisely, and the images and similes he used for God must be fleshed out. After Easter, whatever Jesus himself said must be said differently, and clarifying which amendments are needed and appropriate calls for theological reflection. So when Christians speak of God using, as Jesus did, the term *Father*, it is appropriate that they not only continue the Father image used by Jesus, but that they *perceive God's Fatherhood in the light of the cross and the resurrection* and also *understand God's deity from the perspective of the Fatherhood that received more precise definition through these events*, thus articulating the grammar of this image more exactly in *christological* and consequently in *trinitarian* terms.

This sets in motion a theological process of defining the idea of God that has the following distinctive features. The concept of the Fatherhood of God receives a more precise soteriological definition by reference to the crucified Jesus as his Son, and its content can then be interpreted as inexhaustible love that cannot be constrained, even by death. Further, Jesus's Sonship receives a more precise theological definition through the resurrection activity of his divine Father and can be interpreted as a state of being eternally loved; this is applicable initially and primarily to Jesus himself, but through him to us all. Finally, through the cross and resurrection God's nature as Spirit is revealed as his fundamental life process, in which the differential relationship between Father and Son is perfected as love. This revelation of God's nature as Spirit results in a more precise eschatological definition of Sonship and Fatherhood that can then be interpreted as self-clarifying creative love, the love that re-creates and makes new everything that is other than God, just as Jesus was made anew through the resurrection.

In the light of these definitions, God's divine being is understood to be perfect love—a love without limits—that is universally realized and given substance through the Father, the Son, and the Holy Spirit. But it is only to the extent that these elements are included in our idea of God, so that it is understood *in trinitarian terms*, that we are really considering the God

1. whose dawning reign of love was proclaimed by Jesus, whom he addressed as Father and from whom he unequivocally distinguished himself as a human being and as the herald of this reign of God;
2. whom Christians confess as the one who raised Jesus from the dead, thus identifying him as his beloved Son and himself as the Father of this Son; and
3. concerning whom Christians recognize that they are able to confess him as such only by his Spirit.

. *Of whom* Christians are speaking when they say "God" (the referent of Christian discourse concerning God) and *what* they think and say about God (the content of Christian discourse concerning God) are similarly covered by the trinitarian principle of God's self-definition as Father, Son, and Holy Spirit. So it is only when Christians include the Son and Spirit images along with the Father image, considering God not just as creator but simultaneously as reconciler and consummator, that they are calling the same God Father as Jesus did: God is not just the God proclaimed by Jesus, who wants to be, and indeed is, close to us as a merciful Father. He is at one and the same time the God from whom Jesus differentiated himself entirely by placing himself wholly in the service of this Father and his merciful love, and who, for our sakes, stayed close to this very Jesus as his loving Father in a specific way, even in death, thus marking him out as his beloved Son. And he is the God who is close to us in the same way, as the Spirit through whom he discloses himself to us as Jesus's loving Father. This God, considered as creator, reconciler, and consummator, Father, Son, and Holy Spirit, is only identical with the God Jesus called Father when these different elements are predicatively attributed to him, not just at different times or in different respects, so that he is defined first in one sense as God and then in another sense, according to the context, but when there is a reciprocal interpretation of these three elements, resulting in their united actualization of God's divine being. Then there will be no possibility of considering God as creator unless we also focus on him, at least implicitly, as reconciler and consummator (and vice versa). Nor will there then be any possibility of calling him Father unless we also address him, at least implicitly, as "Son" and "Spirit."

The trinitarian idea of God resulting from the christological clarification of the Father image Jesus used for God thus in no way nullifies the unity, uniqueness, and simplicity of God, as confessed in the Jewish *shema' yisrael* and taken for granted by Jesus when he addressed God as "Father." There is only one God, and this God is essentially simple. To be able to conceive of God in his unity, uniqueness, and simplicity, we must simultaneously hold in mind the conditions for his conceivability; and to be able to conceive of God himself, and not just one of our ideas of God, we must do this in such a way that both God and the conditions for God's conceivability are regarded as being wholly and solely governed by God. But this requires that we make both the *structure of the experiential situation*, in which God discloses himself as God, and the *structure of the thought situation*, in which God is considered on the basis of his self-revelation, central to our idea of God in such a way that both are perceived and affirmed as key elements of God's self-identification and self-definition as love. Now God can be experienced only to the extent that he reveals himself, and he can be thought as God only when and to the extent that he allows us insight into his revelation. The Christian faith holds the first to be indissolubly linked with Jesus Christ and the second to be inseparably connected with the experience of the Spirit of Christ. God, as the Christian faith confesses him, is thus to be conceived of theologically in such a way that the idea of God is defined equally in *christological* and *pneumatological* terms. The content of God's revelation of himself is considered as unconditional love in the face of its contradiction in Jesus's cross and resurrection (christological precision of the idea of God), and formally God's self-definition is considered through our perception of his self-revelation *sub contrario* (pneumatological realization of the idea of God).[2] The first occurs because the content of the idea of God is defined by the differential relationship between *Father* and *Son*, the second because the idea of God thus defined is held to be the specific self-definition of God as love and therefore formally as *Spirit*. For, by defining himself through the distinction between Father and Son as unbounded *love*, God makes his selfhood or his deity dependent not on the preservation of his being in contradistinction to the other but on the free acceptance of his self by the other. That other that is distinct from himself must therefore, in its own particular otherness, accept and affirm, in respect to the divine being of God, the very same freedom it allows itself as distinct from God. One characteristic of the *Spirit*, the consummation of love, is that it acquires its own selfhood from the free acceptance of those whose otherness it freely accepts and affirms. When God is perceived in this way as defined by himself alone from the point of view of both content and form, binding his own being as unconditional and unbounded love to that which is other than himself, and basing his divine being on the free acceptance of him by that which is other than himself, then he is being perceived from a trinitarian perspective as Father, Son, and Holy Spirit: to think in specific terms of God, that is, to think of him as the one who defines himself as unconditional love, and consequently as God for us, means thinking of him in trinitarian terms.

2. Just as the Father image for God must be stated more precisely *in christological terms* in the light of the cross and resurrection of Jesus Christ, so the idea of God must be stated more precisely in *christological and pneumatological terms* in the light of this more precise Father image. For if the conditions for the conceivability of God are taken into account in the idea of God, then God's Fatherhood after Good Friday and Easter cannot be conceived of without taking Jesus Christ into account. Similarly, in the light of this more precise concept of Fatherhood, God's divinity cannot be conceived of unless we take into account the Spirit who gives us the sure revelation both of Jesus Christ as the Son of this Father and of the Father as the divine Father of Jesus the Son.

## 2. Thinking God

To summarize what has been said above: God must be thought of either in specific terms or not at all. This specificity is not due simply to the reference to images and ideas of God from a particular tradition. Such a specificity would be the merely external one of historical particularity and positivity, from which indeed the idea of God cannot escape, but by which it cannot be confined if its precision is to be more than the arbitrariness of an idea perceived in different ways in different traditions. But how is such arbitrariness to be avoided? Stubborn insistence on one's own viewpoint is clearly as unsatisfactory a solution as is indecisive hesitation among the multiplicity of positive ideas of God or an emphatic claim that one's own ideas of God are a God-given revelation. None of these approaches solves the problem, but rather they serve to highlight it. Neither does an appeal to an experience or revelation of God take us any further forward, since, from an intersubjective point of view, such an appeal appears to be merely a claim to revelation or experience. There must be some other method for deciding whether such a claim is valid, a method that is not just convincing for me but allows the claim to be scrutinized and confirmed by others: in other words, a thought process.

If by the term *thought process* one understands the totality of procedures by which thinking persons can decide on the validity of a thought, concept, or idea, then the validity of the idea of God should also be established using a thought process.[3] The actual process of thinking about God must show that the extent to which, in beginning from particular images of God and positive ideas of God, it is beginning from God himself and is not just a surrogate for God. A mere indication of the source and origin of an idea of God does not achieve this. If, however, the thought process itself is able to establish consistently and completely that it is thinking of God and is not merely a surrogate for God, then it should be easy to observe this distinction. As the various ontological arguments seek to demonstrate, the idea of God would not then be reliant on the multiplicity of images and ideas of God at all, as if one could wholly disregard the positive, a posteriori origin of the idea of God.

3. Here thinking is clearly understood not just as something undertaken at the individual level but as an essentially *social* and *communicative activity*: even when it is carried out by individuals, thinking is a communal activity because of the importance of the validity of the thoughts *for others as well* and—within the horizon of the truth question—potentially *for everyone*. The thought process therefore includes *communication, with oneself* in relation both to earlier thoughts and to thoughts still in the future, but also *with others* in relation to what they have thought, are thinking, and may yet think. In summary: the thought process involves advocating the validity of a thought before the universal forum of thinkers who communicate their thoughts to one another.

But God is not just that than which nothing greater can be conceived; he is also greater than anything we can think about him (thus Anselm of Canterbury). The thought process itself therefore has no clear competence to decide that in any given instance it is thinking of God and not something else, or indeed that it is thinking accurately about God at all. It can provide negative criteria at best. So God is certainly not being thought of unless the idea of God satisfies at least two conditions. First, the *distinction between God and the idea of God* must be preserved (i.e., the idea of God must make clear that it is different from God himself, and in what way). Second, there must be clarity about the extent to which God must be perceived in this way and no other, since *God's self-definition* allows for no arbitrariness in the *precision of the idea of God*. Unless an idea of God satisfies these two conditions, it cannot result in true thoughts about God: there is no instance against which it can be measured, because there is no instance to which it relates in any specific way. An idea of God can satisfy these conditions only if God himself is regarded as the determining ground for the (mental) representations of God on which its design is based. This is only the case if what is represented acts as the point of reference for its representations and the method by which it is represented, so that God himself is perceived as the basis, ground, and criterion for the content and the enactment of the representations, idea, and knowledge of God. But this means that, in order for God to be conceived of, and not just superficially in our tentative terms but in terms of who and what God truly is in himself, the *idea of God must itself include the conditions for the possibility of conceiving of and knowing God*. In other words, *both God and the conditions for his conceivability and knowability must be thought of as something that is determined wholly and solely by God himself,* for unless God is perceived as the one who determines himself entirely and solely by himself, and who therefore also determines the manner by which and the conditions under which he is perceived, thought of, and known as God, we are thinking not of God but merely of a surrogate for God.[4]

4. The fact that God is to be conceived of as the one who defines himself entirely and solely by himself tells us nothing, however, about the *manner* of God's self-definition. It is essential to the (properly understood) Christian idea of God that his self-definition be conceived of, not in terms of direct self-definition as self-empowered self-preservation but as self-definition communicated by what is other than God as a result of a free acknowledgment of God. The cross and resurrection of Jesus show that God defines himself entirely by binding his selfhood so fundamentally to the otherness of his creation that it is only through his creatures' free acknowledgment—in the active as well as in the passive sense—that he is who he is: inexhaustible creative love. God's self-definition thus manifests itself through his acknowledgment of the free otherness of created beings and through their free acknowledgment of their creator, not as self-empowered self-preservation but as the process of free love.

The Christian idea of God seeks to conceive of God in precisely this manner and under precisely these conditions. Thus it consistently presupposes that the object of its thoughts was not originally brought into being through its thoughts of it. And it thinks of what it presupposes in such a way that the subject of its thought is given substance and determined through itself alone. This becomes apparent, for example, in that the one whom the Christian faith addresses and identifies as Father, Son, and Holy Spirit is conceived of as *simple in essence*. Only as a wholly simple being can God be wholly near to all of us and to each of us.[5] But God is wholly near to the other only because his relationship to that other is more fundamental than any causal interaction could be.[6] As a wholly simple being, God is not determined by anything different from himself, and as a simple being, God has no internal properties or attributes that determine or constitute his being. God's essence (i.e., what distinguishes God as God and constitutes his identity and individuality)[7] therefore cannot be known by knowing his attributes. We can know God's nature only to the extent that we know how God relates to those who are other than himself; we will know this (as far as it is possible for us to know it) when we understand the totality of God's potential relations with those who are other than himself.

From this alone, however, it does not necessarily follow that God's essence is to be equated with the sum total of his potential relations to the other, such that his essence consists of the totality of his associations and combinations with what is other than himself. The totality of God's potential relations to the other could still be differentiated from God's essence and determined by it, even if we are unable to recognize it independently of those relations. This is the epistemic norm. For example, if one thing relates to another in a manner that may be described as "is annoyed about," then we know that

5. Cf. I. U. Dalferth, *Gott: Philosophisch-theologische Denkversuche* (Tübingen: Mohr Siebeck, 1993), 8–9. For a treatment of the problems inherent in the attempt by classical metaphysics to conceive of God's simplicity in the antithesis of the simple and the compound, cf. E. Stump and N. Kretzman, "Absolute Simplicity," *Faith and Philosophy* 2 (1985): 353–82; J. Ross, "Comments on 'Absolute Simplicity,'" *Faith and Philosophy* 2 (1985): 383–91; E. Stump and N. Kretzman, "Simplicity Made Plainer: A Reply to Ross," *Faith and Philosophy* 4 (1987): 198–201.

6. God's relationship to the world cannot be conceptualized in terms of causality. If it were a causal relationship, God would be defined no longer as creator but as one creature among many. God's nearness must be conceived of instead in pneumatological terms, and it is vital that the presence of the Spirit of God not become entangled with the concept of causality. This is correctly expressed by K. Ward: "The doctrine of the Spirit confirms that one must not think of God and the world as in external causal interaction; such a view would in any case transmute God into a creature among others" (*The Concept of God* [Oxford: Basil Blackwell, 1974], 218).

7. On the concept of existence, cf. I. U. Dalferth, *Existenz Gottes und christlicher Glaube: Skizzen zu einer eschatologischen Ontologie* (Munich: Christian Kaiser, 1984), 85–169.

we are talking about an intelligent living being and not a stone. Similarly, it could be assumed that we can infer from God's potential relations with what is other than himself that his essence is distinct and separate from these relations. After all, every relation that can exist between one thing and another presupposes correlative attributes or properties shared by the members of the relationship. For example, only a human being can laugh at someone, whereas only a substance such as sugar can dissolve in coffee.

Yet with God it is different. God is simple. He does not belong to a generic class or category that defines which relations can be attributed to God and which cannot. The most that can be said is that God exists in relationship to what is other than himself. But this relation is not based in any correlative attribute of God: the relationship between the one and the many is not founded in a divine essence that determines this relationship. Hence God's essence cannot be distinguished from his relationship to others; it is identical with the sum total of his potential relationships with what is other than himself: God really is what and how he is in his actual and potential relations with what is other than God. If, however, God has no essential properties or attributes beyond the totality of his relationship with the other, then there is only one relation between him and the other: relationship, copresence, or *nearness.*

God's nearness to one who is other than himself is not the kind of simultaneity or proximity that can be ascribed to things or events, such that they can be said to be near each other temporally or spatially. Rather, it is that relationship to which all that is different from God owes its very existence, in other words, *God's creative nearness*, which does not stand in an external temporal or spatial relationship to the other, since, as Anselm says, "*quidquid aliud est, ne in nihilum cadat, ab ea* [i.e., of the *summa substantia*] *praesente sustinetur*" [whatever else exists is sustained by its presence—that is, of the supreme Substance—lest it lapse into nothingness].[8] Thus God's creative nearness is not of a kind that can be spatially or temporally determined or localized, since in that case God would be spatially and temporally *distanced* from the other. So one condition of God's ability to be nearer to the other than the other is to itself is that his nearness to all that is spatial or temporal is not, in itself, spatial or temporal. Anselm proposed the *usus loquendi* [ordinary use of language] for God's with-ness: "*convenientius dici videretur esse cum loco vel tempore quam in loco vel tempore*" [it would seem to be more fittingly said that it exists with place or time than that it exists in place

---

8. Anselm of Canterbury, *Monologion*, chap. 22, in *S. Anselmi Opera Omnia*, ed. Fr. S. Schmitt (Stuttgart-Bad Cannstatt: Frommann-Holzboog, 1968), 1:41, lines 6–7.

or time].[9] If one follows this use of language not just in relation to God's creative nearness but also in relation to all other types of God's nearness that faith acknowledges and confesses, then God is *with* all that is different from him as creator, he is *for* all that is different from him as reconciler, and he is *there for* all that is different from him as consummator. Accordingly, God's nearness should be perceived as his creative *with-ness*, his reconciling *for-ness*, and his consummating *there-ness* in relation to all that is different from him.

Given that not all to which God stands in relationship exists simultaneously, the concept of God's creative, reconciling, and consummating nearness and hence also that of his essence need to be differentiated. God is actually near to what really exists and potentially near to what may conceivably exist.[10] If his *essence* is identical with the totality of his potential relationships with the other, then we can call whatever is identical with the totality of his actual relationships with the other his *reality*. However, God's actual relationships are only ever a part of his potential relationships with the other, and different parts can be actual at different times. Thus God's reality changes according to the other to which he is near. But his essence necessarily remains true to himself and marks him out as God in all his realities. God has only one essence, which defines who and what he is, but he has different realities, in which he realizes his essence. Inasmuch as God realizes his essence in different realities, God has a *divine life*. This divine life enacts itself as a succession of God's realities (i.e., the realizations of his essence), but it is not identical either with any one of these realizations or with their totality. The enactment of the divine life should be differentiated from its ground; this ground, without which there neither would nor could be any enactment of the divine life is, as the ground of God's commitment to the realizations of his essence, none other than *God himself*, Father, Son, and Holy Spirit, who actualizes his essence in ever-new forms.

If this is correct, then God has no essence, no essential attributes, and no realities independent of his relationship and nearness to the other, yet without himself being absorbed in this relationship with the other. God's nearness to the other is not a permanent configuration of like with like; it is a relationship between disparates. So God is indeed near to everything that is, but

9. Ibid., 1:41, lines 1–2.
10. The various ways in which God can be near can be summarized by stating that God desires to be near as reconciler to all to whom he is actually near as creator, and that it is certain that he remains near as consummator to all to whom he is near as reconciler. Only what really exists can alienate itself from God so that it is in need of reconciliation; and nothing that really exists, and that alienates itself from God, can be perfected unless God reconciles himself with it and it with him.

not everything that he is near to is simultaneous with everything else that is not God. God's nearness is thus his relationship with each and every reality that owes its existence solely to God and not to itself. But if God is near to every reality precisely because he relates to it, and if he is potentially related to everything to which he is near when it comes into actual existence, then God gives himself an essence by his nearness to what is other than himself: God has no attributes that underlie and are independent of his relationship to the other, but *he gives himself* attributes by drawing near to what is other than himself in successive realities. God determines himself as God through a sequence of contingent configurations with reality to which he draws near creatively, by differentiating himself from it as creator, and by allowing it, as creature, space and time for its own development and self-determination. But by defining himself as God in differentiation from his creation, God does not constitute himself as God (as some confused readings of "*causa sui*" have suggested) but lives as God; thus he presupposes himself to be the one who, as Father, Son, and Holy Spirit, lives this divine life. What God is, and how God is real in concrete terms, is the outcome of his self-determination and the consequence of the fact that God is. For God is the one who determines himself through and through by enacting his Godhead in coming near to what is different from him.

## 3. Knowing God

This has direct implications for our *knowledge of God*. In negative terms this means that God cannot be recognized by us in isolation and in independence of specific realities by which he gives himself certain attributes; the path of the ontological argument cannot be a path to knowledge of God. God is never just given as such; he is only ever given along with an other and can accordingly be perceived and recognized as God only with the aid of that other. In positive terms, however, this means that God can be recognized only where he identifies and defines himself in such a way that he can be recognized as the one whom he has determined himself to be. So there can be knowledge of God only provided that there are those to whom God reveals his nearness under the realities in which he draws near to what is other than himself. Put more precisely, if knowledge consists in knowing that what we know is true, and if what we know is true when we know something to be what it is, then there can be knowledge of God only under two conditions: (1) with the aid of specific experiences we must discern a reality, in and through which God interprets his relationship with his creation for us in a manner that we can understand; and (2) God must allow us to recognize him as our God by means of the cognitive processing of this discernment, assuring us that through these experiences we have discerned his own interpretation of his reality. To put it more succinctly, knowledge of God is the assurance, given by God himself, that our discernment of God's reality with the aid of specific experiences is true.

It has to be said, however, that only God's prevailing reality is recognized, and this is subject to constant change. God's unchanging essence could be recognized as such only if God were to express the totality of his conceivable relationships with the other—and thereby his essence—as the specific character of one of his particular realities, so that through this reality it might be possible to discern what is true for all of God's realities. That this was precisely the case where the cross and resurrection of Jesus were concerned is what the Christian faith confesses when it identifies God as Father, Son, and Spirit and describes him as love: God is confessed as love because the cross and resurrection of Jesus are discerned through the Spirit as the eschatological manifestation of God's essence and thus as the self-disclosure of God's ultimate (re)definition of himself in and through Jesus Christ. Out of all of God's realities it is the reality with which the name Jesus Christ is identified to which he is not just *near* (as he is to all of them), or to which he is so near that his nearness *can be experienced* (as it can with many of them), but to which he is so uniquely near that the *manner* of his nearness discloses the fundamental feature of his essence: his perfect love.

God cannot therefore be either identified or known in himself as such. He can be *discerned* only in the disclosure of his nearness to a given reality with which he is in a specific relationship. But he is discerned and recognized *as God* only where he discloses himself *as himself* in this way—in other words, with the aid of the specific reality in and through which he reveals his divine essence. According to the confession of faith, this is the eschatological reality of Jesus Christ. We can speak of God's different relationships (activities or actions) only to the extent that God is creatively near to different realities in different ways. It is not God as such but the succession of different configurations of God and the other (realities of God) that makes it possible to differentiate

- between *God* and the entirety of all that is different from God and is made real by him, as *creation*;
- between *different ways* in which God actually relates to creation (creation, reconciliation, consummation);
- between the different *realities* and the one *essence* of God; and

- between the different definitions of God's realities, or ways of experiencing his nearness (anger, mercy, help, judgment, etc.), and the nature of his essence, which is always consistently realized as love throughout the succession of his realities.

### 3.1. The Paths to Knowledge of God: Experience of the World and Experience of Self

Taking this as the starting point for our attempt to describe human knowledge of God more precisely, we can affirm the following. Our knowledge of God always manifests itself as a two-stage process, during which what we discern and experience as part of our dealings with our world and ourselves becomes transparent to God, because and to the extent that God allows himself to be discerned and experienced in and through them. The object of our knowledge of God is thus not God as such but the discernment of God on the basis of our experiences, and the path to knowledge is our constantly improving apprehension of the distinctions between God and our experiences, and between our experiences and God. Two conditions must therefore be fulfilled for there to be knowledge of God: God's movement of disclosure toward us, and our movement of experience and thought toward God—a movement that never ends, partly because God is inexhaustible, but also because our experience is limitless.

This applies also to our knowledge of revelation, which reflects God's self-disclosure of his self-definition in specific experiential contexts. It too is based on specific experiences, which it apprehends as experiences through which God makes his self-definition accessible to us. It captures the revelation received in figures of thought and speech (e.g., "love"), which safeguard God's free prerogative in terms of their content and experiential enactment and the cognitive processes based on them. And it manifests itself as a process by which our feelings, thoughts, and actions are drawn into the inexhaustibility of this love, which thus becomes the source of our life. This needs further elucidation.

Knowledge of God is not the direct comprehension of God in himself, and experience of God is not the direct awareness of God himself. Because of the simplicity and uniqueness of God, this comprehension and awareness come about only insofar as our experience of the world and of ourselves becomes transparent to God. But this occurs in markedly different ways in each of these two avenues. As we follow the *path of our experience of the world*—and by this I mean the entire field of our personal and impersonal environments, to which we relate both receptively and actively—the process of knowing God usually begins with our own perceptions or with those communicated to us by others, as a result of which we understand what is perceived, not merely as an instance of what we have previously experienced and already know but as a deepening, a reorientation, a breakthrough, or a transcendence to what is new and unknown, to something we had thus far not discerned and experienced. Specific perceptions and impressions from our realm of experience provoke feelings, sensations, astonishment, terror, gratitude, questions, and the like, so that in seeking to understand them we are led further along the path toward knowledge of God. It is not that we discern God himself; rather, in each case we discern a specific aspect of our realm of experience, which—even by simply intensifying the everyday—differs from the everyday and allows our thought process to discern more than just itself precisely to the degree that it points to something distinct from itself and thus points to God's presence by becoming transparent to it. So we do not discern God himself directly or experience him as such; instead, we experience him with the aid of and in the context of something other than himself. By discerning what is new and different, and by reflecting on these elements of differentiation in the light of the idea of God,[11] we comprehend God's distinctness from the reality we have discerned as his specific relationship to this reality.

This is also the case where God discloses himself in a special way, in, with, and as part of a specific experience, to be distinct from it and the source of

11. The idea of God must therefore always be involved if perception and experience are to be interpreted this way. (One therefore must *have heard of God* at some point during one's life in order to be able to *experience and know God*.) But this does not form or produce the perceptions and experiences that are interpreted in this way. Instead, their differential structure becomes a pellucid pointer to the presence of God as distinct from the perceptions and experiences themselves. This presence is differentiated from everything else that can be included as a theme of such experiential processes, in that it never in itself is given in the form of perceptions and experiences but rather accompanies all that is discerned, perceived, and experienced as the basis of its possibility and reality. In contrast to our experience of the world and of ourselves, experience *of God* as a rule comes only a posteriori, i.e., as part of a process of retrospective interpretation of our perceptions and experiences as we focus on God. The fact that the idea of God *must be explicitly involved* so that we can have the appropriate retrospective experiences on no account means, however, that the involvement of this concept produces something that did not exist before: neither the experiences thus interpreted nor the nearness and presence of God, in the context of which they have been interpreted, become what they are through this interpretation—this fundamental realism is the conviction of the Christian faith, which claims to find reality, not to fabricate it. It means, rather, that this nearness and presence are only disclosed to us as part of the process of interpretation itself, since it is only thus that we can address as *God* that which is distinct from what we perceive and experience and that to which it becomes transparent. *God can only be experienced, and knowledge of God can only be attained, within the context of the idea of God.* This is the proper basic insight, which the ontological argument takes as its starting point but which it also subverts, by seeking to prove, through the a priori positing of the idea of God, that this essential condition of knowledge of God is also a sufficient condition.

it—in other words, where he *reveals himself*. Revelation is not fundamentally distinct from retrospective experience of God. Rather, it makes explicit what is true of such experience: that it is an experience of difference, within which God uses something other than himself to allow himself to be experienced as God. However, in this instance God is at work, not only in what is experienced but also in the interpretation of the experience as a divine action, in such a way that both elements interpret and illuminate each other. God not only renders our experience of the other transparent to himself so that it can be interpreted from God's viewpoint in the light of the idea of God (making the experience of God possible). What is more, by the interpretative work of his Spirit, he renders this interpretation so convincing that he is unequivocally affirmed as God (making the experience of God real). In this respect God's revelation is the experiential process in which he allows us to experience himself as he is, both in, with, and as part of what is other than himself, with the result that we are able to perceive and recognize God in truth as we reflect on this experiential process.

This can happen not only on the path of our experience of the world but also on the path of our experience of the self. On the *path of experience of the self* as well, our experience can become transparent to God. However, we need to distinguish between two possibilities here. In the first, the path of experience of the self is simply a special instance of the path of experience of the world, albeit one that begins within a specific class of experience, namely, experiences of ourselves. If so, then there is nothing more to be said of the experience of the self than has already been said of the experience of the world. Alternatively, this path begins not from specific experiences (of ourselves) but from what is always involved in all our experience and thought about anything (ourselves or something else): the conditions and the structure of experience and thought as a whole. Then it is not in any specific experiences that more is disclosed to our feelings and thoughts than meets the eye but in the structure of our experience overall, which points our thoughts beyond what this structure itself can comprise. We may summarize the decisive issue as follows: we can experience, think, perceive, or—in the wider sense—act at all only because we ourselves are always presupposed in every such activity. By our experiencing, thinking, and perceiving we do not constitute ourselves, but we modify ourselves into something specific: we make ourselves *into something*, but we do not *make our selves*. Inasmuch as, in all our experiences, thoughts, perceptions, and actions, our own self is already posited or given, all our activities are rooted in a fundamental "passivity": the inescapable fact that, when all is said and done, it is not we who have brought ourselves into existence. From Schleiermacher on, this fundamental givenness or absolute dependence was consistently defined as the structure of the idea of God: anyone who thinks "God" is considering the "whence" of this fundamental dependence or givenness, however this idea of God is more precisely defined and whatever content it is given.

Just because we have not brought ourselves into existence, however, need not necessarily mean that another has done so. The fact that we do not generate our selves through our experiences, thoughts, perceptions, and actions but are always conscious of our selves as already there or "given," need not necessarily be indicated using figures of thought such as "passivity," "givenness," or "dependence," the inversion of which leads back to the question of their underlying and correlative "activity," "positing," or "causality." We could simply discover our selves—without any further need of or opportunity for explanation. This is not in any way to dispute the empirical reality that each of us owes our existence to others. But it certainly does not mean that each of us owes our existence to the same others, and neither that there is one other to whom all of us owe our existence, nor that what is true of each of us individually must be true of us en masse: even if each of us originates from an other, it does not follow that all of us originate from a single other.

Thus the path of the experience of the self leads not to God but, at best, to a structural element of the idea of God. For if our perception of God is only adequate when the conditions of his conceivability and recognizability are simultaneously held in mind, then the basic structure, both of the situation in which God is experienced as himself and also of the situation in which God is conceived of as God, must be included in our idea of God. The idea of God would thus not only be defined in terms of its content by the cross and resurrection of Jesus, in which, according to the Christian confession of faith, God has revealed not just one of his specific realities but his true essence, which defines all his realities. It would also be defined in terms of its form by the fact that what we understand as "God" is that on which we know ourselves and all else to be similarly and fundamentally dependent. And just as this form-related definitiveness marks out the Christian idea of God as an *idea of God*, so the other, content-related definitiveness marks it out as a *Christian* idea of God.

However, this argument is unsatisfactory for several reasons. It leads us to conceive of the self-disclosure of God's self-definition in Jesus Christ as a *differentia specifica* [specific difference] that makes purely superficial Christian modifications to an idea of God that has an entirely different basis and can therefore, in principle, be detached from this specific modification and used as a generic term. Admittedly—and from Schleiermacher on, this has always been counted as a plus factor—the reference range for the idea of

God can in that case be extended to cover the sum total of human experience, thought, knowledge, and action. However, this gives the idea of God no really positive specificity but merely the negative specificity assigned to a compensation figure: God is other than our finiteness. To conceive of God in this way does not mean, however, that we should conceive of him in specific terms, because this idea of God owes its definitiveness solely to our thought processes, not to God himself. It is an idea posited by our thought process or our religious consciousness, which does not satisfy the fundamental condition for thought about God (viz., to conceive of God in such a way that even the conditions of his conceivability are perceived as something defined wholly and solely by God himself). However, this means we need to affirm the objection brought by Hegel against the Schleiermacher tradition: the idea of God we have constructed in our thought (consciousness) must itself be perceived to be God's self-definition if it is really God whom we are to perceive. The crux of this objection—independent of Hegel's own expansion of it—lies in the idea that the formal determinacy of the idea of God cannot be established independently of and via a different route from its content-related determination but is to be developed from it. God is only truly conceptualized when the structure of the idea of God is determined by the reality through which, according to the Christian faith, God has revealed not just one of his specific realities but his essence, which defines all his realities. If, however, the determinacy of the idea of God is developed, in terms of its form and its content, out of the self-disclosure of God's self-definition in Jesus Christ, then God is conceptualized with inner consistency *in trinitarian terms.*

## 3.2. On the Structure of the Knowledge of God

This is true not only for the idea of God but also for the knowledge of God: if it is really God who is to be known, this knowledge must originate in its entirety from God's self-determination; in other words, each aspect of it must be attributable wholly to God himself. Since we speak of knowledge when we know that what we know is true, although it is only true if we know it as it truly is, this implies the following.

1. To know God means to know God as he is. But God is as he knows himself to be. Knowing God therefore means *knowing God as God knows himself.* It follows from the self-disclosure of God's self-definition in Jesus Christ that God calls into being things that are not and, through his unconditional nearness, holds them in being. Whatever is is what it is only because it is; and it only is because God is near to it exactly as that which it is. Thus

God differentiates himself not only comprehensively from all that is other but specifically from each and every other. This implies that he can also distinguish each individual other from all else, so that he knows what each is as distinguished from all else, and what it is not. Accordingly, there is nothing that God does not know in its entirety, meaning that there is nothing concerning which he does not know what it can be (the possible), what it must be (the necessary), what it is (the actual), and in what relationships it stands, or could stand, with what is other. But if God knows everything that exists in all its aspects, then he also knows that he knows it, that only he knows it, and that he is therefore the only one who truly knows all that is as it is and as it can be. Inasmuch as God knows anything, he also knows himself; and because he knows himself to be the only one who knows everything, not only does he differentiate himself fundamentally from all else that is and that can be, but he also is the only one who is completely transparent to himself and who therefore knows himself fully. Knowing God, therefore, means knowing God as God knows himself. Knowledge of God finds its object and its scope in God's self-knowledge.

2. This has a series of implications, first of all with regard to God himself. If what has been said above is true, God must manifest a structure identifiable as "self-knowledge" by which he is able to recognize himself as God. The theological tradition has used the term *spirit* to express this: *God is spirit*. This has a double meaning.

First, God is spirit to the extent that he is *wholly transparent to himself* and thus knows himself fully. God knows himself fully because he knows himself to be what he is, and is what he knows himself to be; *and because he knows* that he knows himself as what he is, he therefore knows who and what he is. To use the trinitarian images of Father, Son, and Spirit: God knows himself, to the extent that he knows himself as the Spirit, who recognizes what the Father knows the Son to be, and what the Son knows the Father to be: that is, as the overflowing of love. Accordingly, God is fully transparent to himself because he knows (1) who he is (Father, Son, and Spirit), (2) what he is (love), and (3) that as Father he is the origin and source of love, as Son he is the object and communication of love, and as Spirit he is the realization and recognition of this love that is his being.

The second meaning follows from this: God is spirit inasmuch as he *opens himself up to us in a way that we can understand* by revealing to us his transparency. God's self-knowledge as spirit is therefore an open process in two respects. First, God identifies the truth of his essence against the background of all the possible, successive realities in which he defines himself as the overflowing love that he is. He therefore identifies himself, on the one hand, *definitively as love*, inasmuch as he knows, in principle, that he has destined himself to be love and to act only as love in all his potential and real actualizations; and he knows himself, on the other hand, as the totality of the forms in which he has his essence at any given time and thus as the *dynamic process of the configurations of love* in which he realizes his self-definition. We are required to speak, in the first instance, of the immutability of his saving and loving purpose and, in the second, of the endlessly new forms taken by his love within the process of the divine life. As the totality of these forms, God is *the Absolute*, and given that we are concerned with the totality of configurations of love, he is *absolute love*. Accordingly, the divine life may be described as God's endlessly new self-determination to love in the actualizations of all potential configurations of love and as the *open process from definitive to absolute love*.

Second, God's self-disclosure of himself to us in a way that we can understand is itself part of this process. There are various aspects to this. First, we comprehend specific actualizations of his love as we participate in the realities by means of which he accomplishes them. This (creation-theological) aspect leads us to a variety of perceptions (by no means purely cognitive) of the divine realities, without these being transparently perceptions *of God*. Second, this occurs only when God makes himself comprehensible to us as himself, disclosing himself to be just as he defines himself: as love. The Christian faith holds the conviction that this took place in Jesus Christ, in whom God has revealed his heart, allowing us to perceive that love is his meaning and purpose. In this sense all revelation of God is—in trinitarian terms—revelation of the Son. But to perceive that love is God's meaning and purpose does not mean that we already know this love in its entirety. Third, it is therefore necessary to speak, in a pneumatological sense, of a dynamic that generates an ever-better, ever-deeper comprehension of the love that God is. This does not exceed or replace the revelation of the Son but deepens it and realizes it afresh again and again in both an intensive and an extensive sense, bringing about an ever-clearer comprehension of God's love by more and more people. The process by which God discloses himself to us in a way that we can understand is therefore both precisely defined by the definitive revelation of his essence in Jesus Christ as his self-determination to love, while also at the same time being open in two respects: as the constantly fresh participation, which may be described in creation-theological terms, in God's realities; and also as the ever-deeper comprehension of the love as which God has revealed himself to us in Jesus Christ. These two processes are distinct in that, in the first, the christological definition of God and, consequently, of his manifestation as love are not understood as such, while, in the second, it is precisely this understanding that forms the prerequisite and the basis for all comprehension of God. Common to all these processes, however, is that they are spiritual processes, in which God discloses himself to us in a creation-theological sense in one of his realities: either, in the christological sense, in his essence, or, in the pneumatological sense, in the abundance of the actualizations of his essence.

3. What has been described above, however, also has implications for us. If God is to be able to disclose himself to us in a way that we can understand, we must be in a position to receive such a revelation. We must therefore give theological consideration not only to the fact that we exist at all but also to our capacity to receive God's disclosure of his self-determination in a way that we can understand. The theological tradition therefore regards us humans not merely as *created beings* (which is how it regards everything else that is distinct from God) but as *beings created in the image of God*. Just like everything else that is distinct from God, we are created by God, which means that we exist only because he created us and only to the extent that he allows us to exist. In contrast to everything else, however, we alone are in a position to recognize our createdness and to acknowledge God as our creator. This is because God has enabled us to perceive[12] his nearness to us and presence with us in numerous different ways, to come to a knowledge of the self-disclosure of his self-definition in Jesus Christ and to experience the richness of his creative presence in new ways. Perception, knowledge, and experience of God are thus, in a double sense, due to God alone, as God makes himself perceptible to us and capable of being known and experienced by us, both "objectively" and "subjectively": both *what* we (can) perceive, know, and experience and *that* we (can) perceive, know, and experience it are due in equal measure to God. This is why the Christian faith confesses God simultaneously as *creator* and *revealer*: as *our creator*, God creates the conditions in which *we* can perceive, know, and apprehend him, and experience him more clearly; as the *revealer of himself*, that is, *of his divine self-determination as love*, God creates the conditions in which we can know *God*.

4. If knowing God means knowing him as he knows himself, and if we can know God only insofar as, in the double sense stated above, he creates the conditions for this, then we can know God only on the basis of his *revelation*. This includes the *object* of our knowledge of God (*what* we know),

12. This is in the broad sense of becoming cognitively aware of (the intelligibility of) God's presence as something that is not due to our cognitive processes but is in principle prior to them. Just as God's intelligibility precedes all our knowledge of God, so our capability of coming to know a reality beyond us through perception, experience, and reflection precedes all our actual perceiving, experiencing, and knowing.

the *basis* of our knowledge of God (to what we *owe* our knowledge of God), the *medium* by which we know God (*how* we know God), and the *fulfillment* of our knowledge of God (*what* we know God to be).

The *object* of our knowledge of God is not simply God but *God's revelation*: in other words, what God discloses of himself to us. Hence, "revelation" means God's self-disclosure of his reality to us.[13] Since God's realities change and at any given time God is disclosing his reality to specific recipients, it is to be expected that there will be numerous revelations; in fact, in principle every perception of God has the quality of a revelation. But given that God reveals not just one of his realities but his essence, we must speak not merely of revelation but of *self-revelation*.[14] God's self-revelation is the self-disclosure of his self-definition to us. Because God remains faithful to his nature, God's self-revelation, in contrast to the revelation of one of his realities, is incomparable and occurs, if it occurs at all, irrevocably and conclusively. This does not mean that it is unrepeatable. God's revelation of himself is recipient related: it is a revelation *for us*. If it occurred just once, others could know it only through its onward transmission—secondhand at best. Then what was known would not be God's self-revelation but a human testimony to God's self-revelation. Insofar as God's self-revelation takes place at all, however, it can take place time and again, albeit in such a way that, as the revelation of God's essence for different recipients, it is always the same revelation that is repeated. Hence, God's self-revelation is not unrepeatable but is final; in its finality, however, it can always be repeated by God himself. According to the Christian faith, this final self-revelation of God's essence occurred for the first time in Jesus Christ and occurs over and over again through the Spirit of Jesus Christ in the lives of believers. Christians therefore describe knowledge of God's revelation of himself as *knowledge of Jesus Christ*, that is, as the knowledge of God as he has disclosed and continues to disclose his saving will for his creation and his eternal self-determination to love in Jesus Christ and through the Spirit. They

13. Concerning the concept of revelation, cf. I. U. Dalferth, *Theology and Philosophy* (Eugene, OR: Wipf & Stock, 2002), 40–44.

14. This is not a biblical concept but a doctrinal concept used as a summarizing description of the position to which the New Testament bears witness in so many and various ways, namely, that, on the one hand, God has acted in and through Jesus Christ with eschatological finality to bring about our salvation and has disclosed himself as love working on our behalf, *and* that, on the other hand, God is also the one who, as Spirit, gives us the assurance of faith that in Jesus Christ he has acted definitively to procure our salvation. It is only God's Word that opens up God's activity in Jesus Christ as God's self-revelation in this way; the classical expression of this is found in Ignatius: "εἷς θεός ἐστιν, ὁ φανερώσας ἑαυτὸν διὰ Ἰησοῦ Χριστοῦ τοῦ υἱοῦ αὐτοῦ, ὅς ἐστιν αὐτοῦ λόγος [one God who manifested himself through Jesus Christ his Son, who is his Word]" (*Magn.* 8.2).

trace this knowledge of Jesus Christ back to God himself by understanding it as a *Spirit-effected* knowledge in which, through the medium of the testimony of Jesus Christ, God imparts his self-knowledge to us convincingly in a way that can be understood. Thus God's self-revelation does not open up to us everything God knows, and neither does it exclude the possibility that God will reveal further aspects of his realities. Rather, it discloses the nucleus of God's self-knowledge as it pertains to his relationship with us: his irreversible self-determination to love where one who is distinct from him is concerned. Hence the one who knows God on the basis of his self-revelation knows God's nature, or in other words, what makes him God—in himself and for us.

The *ground* of this knowledge of God is *God himself*, who is perceived, known, and experienced by us only because and to the extent that he discloses himself to us as capable of being perceived, known, and experienced. A true knowledge of God therefore includes the understanding that one owes this knowledge not to oneself but to God alone: to know God means to acknowledge God as the ground of one's own and indeed of all knowledge of God.

The *medium* for all knowledge of God is the *Spirit*—in other words, God himself as he discloses his self-determination to love where we are concerned. The Spirit of God is the enactment of the life of God,[15] transparent to himself, and as such he is the medium for all our perception and knowledge of God. As the *Spirit of Christ*, God's Spirit may be more precisely defined as the one who gives us an understanding and assurance of the self-disclosure of God in Jesus Christ and who thus makes it possible for us to understand not just one of God's realities but his very essence.

The *way in which* this knowledge of God's essence *is fulfilled* is *faith*, which is to say, our appropriation of God's saving will as disclosed in Jesus Christ and by the Spirit. In faith we conform to God's will to the extent that we accept his saving will as applicable to us and therefore direct our lives as God would direct us. Hence it is only in faith that there can be true knowledge of God—in other words, a knowledge of God in which we know God in accordance with his disclosure of his self-knowledge to us in Jesus Christ and through the Spirit.

5. If God's essence can be known only by faith, then one cannot know God's essence unless one knows oneself, and vice versa; the *cognitio Dei et hominis* [knowledge of God and man] are two sides of one coin. Hence, in order to shed theological light on the issue of our knowledge of God, we now need to consider the theme of faith. Where God is concerned, this means that he enters our field of vision in the guise in which he is perceived by us, because

---

15. Cf. I. U. Dalferth, *Kombinatorische Theologie: Probleme theologischer Rationalität* (Freiburg: Herder, 1991), 131–48.

and to the extent that he allows us to perceive him as such: as *Deus iustificans vel salvator* [God the justifier and Savior]—in other words, as love. Where we are concerned, this means that we are regarded not simply as human beings, or as subjects who are known or acted on, but as those to whom God discloses his heart in Jesus Christ and through the Spirit, and whom he thus singles out as those who are destined to be loved by God. But we cannot acknowledge this destiny without simultaneously recognizing that we do not measure up to it. On the basis of faith, therefore, the *cognitio hominis* consists in our knowledge of ourselves as created beings, who, although destined for knowledge of God, fail to fulfill this destiny but nonetheless are rescued from this failure through God's love. Luther puts it as follows: the *cognitio hominis* is the insight of the *homo reus et perditus* [the human being who is guilty of sin and is lost] that he or she is *hominem iustificari fide* [a human being who is justified by faith], and this insight brings us, each according to our own self-knowledge, to the realization that "As a creature [*creatura*] I am a justified sinner [*simul iustus et peccator*]."[16]

The faith on which the *cognitio Dei et hominis* is based is not simply a given fact, and neither is it an intersubjective, readily accessible fact. Faith is accessible only through the medium of the confessions in which it is articulated. Articulations of faith represent it using time- and situation-related symbols and thus vary with the context and the contextual variables.[17] As representations of faith, faith confessions are conditioned on their time and their symbols. As such, on the level of what is being represented, they constitute a combination of self-knowledge and knowledge of God specific to their context and, on the level of the representation, are always colored by their cultural situation.[18] In order to interpret knowledge of God on the basis of faith, we therefore need to strike out on the path of epistemic reconstruction, which ascends from *confession* of the faith via *knowledge* of the faith and *faith* itself to knowledge *of God*.

---

16. Cf. M. Luther, *Ennarratio Psalmi LI* [1532], WA 40:2, 327 line 11–328 line 5:
Cognitio dei et hominis est sapientia divina et proprie theologica. Et ita cognitio dei et hominis, ut referatur tandem ad deum iustificantem et hominem peccatorem, ut proprie sit subiectum Theologiae homo reus et perditus et deus iustificans vel salvator. quidquid extra istum argumentum vel subjectum quaeritur, hoc plane est error et vanitas in Theologie, quia non expectamus in sacris literis possessions, sanites corporum vel politicarum rerum, quae Omnia traditia sunt in manus nostras create.

17. Cf. the analysis of the contexts in I. U. Dalferth, *Religiöse Rede von Gott* (Munich: Christian Kaiser, 1981), 161–268.

18. Cf. I. U. Dalferth, "Über Einheit und Vielfalt des christlichen Glaubens: Eine Problemskizze," in *Glaube*, ed. W. Härle and R. Preul, Marburger Jahrbuch Theologie 4 (Marburg: Elwert, 1992), 99–137.

6. Provided we take this path when opening up and reconstructing knowledge of God, it proves to be essentially *a posteriori knowledge*. The philosophical-theological tradition has understood this, in the context of the Aristotelian doctrine of causality, as that knowledge of God that infers from visible results their invisible first cause. But this problematic cosmological thought form is not what is meant here. What is envisaged is rather the biblical term *posteriora dei* [God's back] (Exod. 33:23), meaning that we do not see God face to face but only gaze after him when he has passed by: to know God, we must seek him in the place where he has allowed us to know him. The significance of this is threefold. First, God can be known only *in the manner in which*, and *as what*, he has made himself knowable to us. Second, we can know God only because and to the extent that he makes himself knowable *to us*. Third, we know God only where he has *made himself knowable* to us. Hence, God can be known by us either on an instance-by-instance basis or else not at all. And he is known by us only at the point where we acknowledge how—for a long time—he has been making himself knowable in our lives, even though we had hitherto been unaware of this because we were blinded by sin.

If we can know God only a posteriori, and consequently retrospectively, in the specific manner in which he has made himself knowable to us, then this points us, on the one hand, toward our own individual life processes, which are only ever accessible to us in a fragmented way, and, on the other hand, toward the context and interwovenness of our different life processes, which are never entirely transparent to us. Often it is only after the event that we recognize that God was at work in our life; indeed, sometimes it is not recognized by us at all but only by others whose life story intersects with ours. A posteriori, retrospective knowledge of God is therefore always a *process of working with one's own life story and with the life stories of others that are interwoven with it, in the awareness that these stories are God's field of action*. E. Jüngel and G. Ebeling have described this process as "experience with experience."[19] But if this "meta-experience" is not to be interpreted purely arbitrarily and subjectively, then it must be presupposed that God's actions in certain contexts have been opened up to us in an intelligible way, so that from now on we have a new understanding of our life.

According to the Christian faith, this self-disclosure of God's self-definition took place with eschatological finality in Jesus Christ. In his life story God has disclosed his essence to us as love. For what Jesus actively displayed of the

19. Cf. also G. Bader, "Erfahrung mit der Erfahrung," in *Wirkungen hermeneutischer Theologie*, ed. H. F. Geisser and W. Mostert (Zurich: Theologischer Verlag Zürich, 1983), 137–53; Bader, *Melancholie und Metapher* (Tübingen: Mohr Siebeck, 1990), 45–50.

nearness of God's love in his life was effective passively in the cross and the resurrection of Jesus, as was disclosed by God's Spirit in retrospectively survey-ing this life a posteriori and in giving constant assurance of its truth through the medium of the gospel. Since Jesus Christ's life story, with its active and passive dimensions, belongs to the overall context of human life stories, all others are factually interwoven with it. But only in those life stories in which this interwovenness is perceived through the work of the Spirit, and in which God's self-disclosure in Jesus's life story is appropriated in faith, can God be perceived and experienced in the same way as he disclosed himself in Jesus Christ, with the result that there is a further revelation of God in Jesus Christ through God's Spirit in that life. Where this occurs, former habits and practices that one had taken for granted are shattered, and the whole life is reoriented so that one's own life experience becomes transparent as a field of God's action.[20]

7. Since God's essence can be known a posteriori only by reference to the story of Jesus Christ and its God-effected realization in each individual life, such knowledge of God is essentially *trinitarian*. Conviction of the truth of the Christian faith is followed by knowledge of God's essence only insofar as God has disclosed his self-determination to love in Jesus Christ for us in a recognizable way and has done this through his Spirit in the lives of more and more people. It therefore is possible to know God only by reference to those *aposteriora* [things known from experience] in which God makes it possible for us to know his self-knowledge as unconditional love. This happened his-torically in the eschatological event of Jesus Christ's cross and resurrection; within the individual's life it happens time and again in the acceptance of the divine love revealed therein through the Spirit by faith, which acceptance is no less an eschatological event. Both are conditions for knowledge of God; as conditions put in place and carried out by God himself, they belong intrinsi-cally to that knowledge and, as such, must be taken into account within the idea of God itself if it is really God we are considering. Where this takes place, it is with an inner inevitability that God is *conceived of in trinitarian terms*.

## 4. Antitheism and Christocentricity

One of the most striking characteristics of early twentieth-century theology was the rediscovery of the eschatological dimension of the Christian faith. And one of the most noteworthy elements of late twentieth-century theology was the renaissance of the doctrine of the Trinity. As late as 1983 it was possible

20. Dalferth, *Theology and Philosophy*, 188–223.

to lament the "relative neglect of the doctrine of the Trinity"[21] and to support Schleiermacher's view that this doctrine was still waiting to be reshaped in a manner intelligible for our times. Today, after dozens of books and a host of articles, it is admittedly still legitimate to ask whether the doctrine of the Trinity is any better understood, but it is no longer possible to say that the topic is neglected. On the contrary, the conviction that "the doctrine of the Trinity simply *is* the Christian doctrine of God"[22] is probably one of the least controversial convictions of Christian theologians in all confessional camps. Not a few would maintain, with Nicholas Lash, that "any doctrine of God which has ceased to be trinitarian in character has thereby ceased to be Christian."[23] Lash gives no reasons for this (correct) conviction. But this is imperative if the doctrine is to be truly comprehensible to the present generation. If Lash's thesis is tenable, it must be demonstrated that only a trinitarian view of God can do justice to the fundamental experience of the Christian faith, the eschatological experience of the resurrection of the crucified Jesus. Only if the Christian resurrection confession makes it necessary to conceive of God in the way the doctrine of the Trinity seeks to conceive of him can it be said that an idea of God ceases to be Christian if it is no longer trinitarian.

According to Lash, it was "primarily in German thought that what might be called the 'post-history' of the doctrine of the trinity was worked out," while "in the English-speaking world . . . , with renewed vigour in recent years, the underlying assumptions of eighteenth-century theism have dictated the terms of debate concerning the question of God."[24] It is true that most of the more recent studies relate to the reflections of Karl Barth and Karl Rahner, both of whom were reacting to the widespread marginalization of the doctrine of the Trinity in the theology of their time. Admittedly, very few denied that this doctrine is one of the central mysteries of the Christian faith, but for the church and for individuals this played hardly any practical role in the life of faith. In the wake of Augustine and Augustinian theology, the doctrine of the Trinity had become an increasingly abstract statement of dogmatic theology, and this trend had been further reinforced since the Enlightenment, with its leaning toward a unitarian view of God. Particularly where there was no continuing support for the doctrine of the Trinity for traditional reasons, it was dismissed or speculatively remodeled.

According to Rahner, the first decisive step on the path to the isolation and gradual sterilization of the doctrine of the Trinity was the separation of the

21. J. Mackey, *The Christian Experience of God as Trinity* (London: SCM, 1983), 3.
22. N. Lash, "Considering the Trinity," *Modern Theology* 2 (1986): 183–96, esp. 183.
23. Ibid.
24. Ibid., 185.

tractates *De deo uno* [On the One God] and *De deo trino* [On the Triune God] in the High Middle Ages. The doctrine of the Trinity thus became just one doctrinal statement among others instead of providing the frame of reference or the grammar for all other doctrinal statements. The Reformation did little to counter this development, and at the beginning of the nineteenth century, Schleiermacher noted, not without reason, that a reshaping of the doctrine of the Trinity by the Reformation remained an unfulfilled desideratum of Protestant theology.[25] But this was by no means an issue only for Protestant theology. Since the Enlightenment, theological interest had engaged more with consideration of God's being and essence than with the doctrine of the Trinity, and the approach of philosophical theism, with its view of God as an all-powerful, all-wise, and all-gracious being, had been adopted to a large extent within Christian theology as well. Nineteenth-century attempts to overcome the theism of the Enlightenment and its critique admittedly led to a fresh engagement with trinitarian thought, but they did so by transforming it into a speculative exposition of the Absolute. This alienated the doctrine of the Trinity still further from the practical life of the Christian community, left the imagery of faith without adequate control from conceptual theological reflection, and deepened the gulf between the practical life of faith of the church and the intellectual engagement with the question of God.

Philosophers such as Feuerbach, Marx, Nietzsche, and Freud were the first to apply their religious criticism to this speculative reshaping of the doctrine of the Trinity, subjecting it to a stringent critique. As a result of the close association between speculative and Christian thought in the nineteenth century, their objections inevitably had an effect on Christian theology as well, so that for a long time Christian theologians were unable to appreciate them. Not until the first half of the twentieth century, when theology gradually began to detach itself from the theism of the Enlightenment and its speculative, religious-critical, and atheist aftereffects, could it establish a positive relationship, both with the speculative tradition and with its philosophical critique, by developing a strictly trinitarian and explicitly antitheistic view of God.

One of the principal motives for this revival of trinitarian theological debate in past decades, therefore, is the fundamentally antitheistic orientation of the new theology (i.e., its abandonment of the theism of the Enlightenment, with its philosophical consequences and counterproposals, in the aftermath of the cultural upheavals of the twentieth century).[26] *Antitheism* is the com-

25. F. D. E. Schleiermacher, *The Christian Faith*, ed. H. R. Mackintosh and J. S. Stewart (Edinburgh: T&T Clark, 1989), 747–51.

26. Cf. I. U. Dalferth, "The Historical Roots of Theism," in *Traditional Theism and Its Modern Alternative*, ed. S. Andersen (Aarhus: Aarhus University Press, 1994), 15–43.

mon denominator of such diverse theological studies as those of Moltmann, Jüngel, Pannenberg, or Wagner. They all agree that Christian theology can overcome the sterile alternatives of theism and atheism only if it models itself in consistently trinitarian terms. But they follow different and often irreconcilable paths as they develop and substantiate their trinitarian approaches and design models. I will limit myself to a few comments.

1. For Eberhard Jüngel, and for Barth in his later years, the doctrine of the Trinity has a christological basis: "A consequent interpretation of the New Testament tradition about Jesus as the Christ leads necessarily to the recognition of the triune God."[27] In the prolegomena to his *Church Dogmatics*, Barth developed his doctrine of the Trinity directly from the concept of God's self-revelation as Lord, which he understood as the reiteration of God's trinitarian self-unfolding. Thus, the immanent Trinity formed the basis for his understanding of the independence of God in his revelation.[28] This provoked the critique that, in his unfolding of God's identity as the revealer, the revealed one, and the revelation event, Barth was closer to the speculative tradition of Hegel and Doerner than he himself realized, since, like them, he had developed his concept of the Trinity from the idea of God as absolute subject,[29] and this "construal of the Trinity as the self-unfolding of a divine subject . . . inevitably does damage to the co-eternity of the divine persons, diminishing their plurality to mere modes of being subordinate to the divine subject."[30] But the further Barth's *Church Dogmatics* developed, the more clearly its trinitarian emphasis shifted away from the inner structure of revelation toward the history of Jesus and, above all, the cross. And the primary emphasis here is on the distinction and difference between Father and Son, so that, to an increasing degree, God's inner plurality is highlighted as compared with his unity.[31]

Jüngel criticizes Barth for not having taken this process further. Jüngel himself starts with God's self-identification with the crucified Jesus and understands the doctrine of the Trinity as the development of the identity

27. E. Jüngel, *God as the Mystery of the World: On the Foundation of the Theology of the Crucified One in the Dispute between Theism and Atheism*, trans. D. L. Guder (Grand Rapids: Eerdmans, 1983), 350.

28. Cf. W. Pannenberg, "Die Subjektivität Gottes und die Trinitätslehre: Ein Beitrag zur Beziehung zwischen Karl Barth und der Philosophie Hegels," in *Grundfragen systematischer Theologie: Gesammelte Aufsätze* (Göttingen: Vandenhoeck & Ruprecht, 1980), 2:96–111, esp. 2:98.

29. Ibid., 2:98–111.

30. W. Pannenberg, "Der Gott der Geschichte: Der trinitarische Gott und die Wahrheit der Geschichte," in *Grundfragen systematischer Theologie*, 2:112–28, esp. 2:124.

31. Cf. J. B. Webster, *Eberhard Jüngel: An Introduction to His Theology* (Cambridge: Cambridge University Press, 1986), 75.

of God's being in itself and of God's being for us in the person of Jesus Christ. God's identification with the crucified one compels a "distinction between God and God," which is to say, a "distinction between 'God, the Father' and 'God, the Son.'"[32] But the unavoidable differentiation between Father and Son at the cross can "never be understood as a contradiction in God."[33] In this differentiation God still remains related to himself as Spirit: "The noncontradictory differentiation of God from God implies the event of God as the Holy Spirit."[34] Hence our idea of God must be not merely binitarian but trinitarian. Jüngel follows an old Western tradition when he defines the Spirit as the one "who lets Father and Son be one in the death of Jesus, in true distinction, in this encounter."[35] But in so doing he inherits the difficulty this tradition has in conceiving of the Spirit clearly as a personal center of action.[36] Thus, instead of conceiving of God from the point of view of the cross event as an irreducible plural communion of persons, he concentrates on developing the *unity* of the self-differentiating God, using the concept of love. Because God is love, and because love is to be understood "as the event of a still greater selflessness within a great, and justifiably very great self-relatedness,"[37] God is essentially being-in-relation, both in relation to himself and in relation to what is different from him. For God, being and being-in-relation are one and the same, and the being of God's ontological relatedness is love, that is, "the unity of life and death for the sake of life."[38] This is why God remains true to his nature, even in the self-abasement of the cross. In offering himself, he does not lose himself but becomes what he is: a God who not only loves but who *is* love in essence. There is therefore no cause, or even any possible ground, for seeking some distinct essence of God behind his loving disclosure *pro nobis*: God's aseity manifests itself as the selflessness of love.[39]

2. Jüngel uses the concepts of love and relationship to conceive of God's unity and coherence in view of the distinction between God and God that is inscribed in God's being through the cross. Moltmann takes the same Barthian legacy as his starting point, but he develops it further in another direction by asking, "What do the suffering and death of Christ mean for God?" His

---

32. E. Jüngel, "Thesen zur Grundlegung der Christologie," in *Unterwegs zur Sache: Theologische Bemerkungen* (Munich: Christian Kaiser, 1972), 274–95, esp. 293.

33. Jüngel, *God as the Mystery of the World*, 346.

34. Ibid., 351.

35. Ibid., 368.

36. Cf. Webster, *Eberhard Jüngel*, 77.

37. Jüngel, *God as the Mystery of the World*, 317.

38. Ibid.

39. Cf. Webster, *Eberhard Jüngel*, 72.

answer, "the pain of the Father at the death of the Son,"[40] makes it clear that he sees the necessity of speaking of God in trinitarian terms as rooted in God's real participation in human pain and suffering, most clearly expressed in the cross. On the cross God was forsaken by God.[41] In contrast to Jüngel, Moltmann not only sees the cross as the basis for the distinction between God and God, but he also understands the separation of Father and Son in the forsakenness of the cross in a wholly mythological sense as "'enmity' between God and God," calling for a "revolution in the concept of God": "*Nemo contra deum nisi deus ipse* [No one can be against God except God himself]."[42] He is able to do this because he understands the self-antithesis of God and God on the cross from the point of view of the fundamental priority of persons over their relationships, basing this on the strict rejection of every attempt to trace the three persons of the Godhead back to God as absolute subject or highest substance. For Moltmann, God's original reality is the plurality of persons, so that what Pannenberg says of Hegel is also true of him: "Here the plurality of persons is not derived but original, and *only in this is the unity of God* real."[43]

Using this approach, Moltmann develops his social doctrine of the Trinity of Father, Son, and Spirit, whose perichoretic unity is "the eternal history that the triune God experiences in himself."[44] This means that the Trinity itself is perceived as the history of God, enacted in the history of Father, Son, and Spirit within the eschatological process of salvation history. Moltmann goes so far as to argue against any specific order among the persons, "in favor of a trinity that can be taken 'in any order.'"[45] But "he nevertheless relates it to our progressive ordering towards a free, creative, relationship of 'friendship' to God in the Holy Spirit."[46] Of course this ensures that God is thought of not as an enclosed monad but as a community of mutual love open to others beyond itself.[47] But Moltmann emphasizes the plurality and the personal

40. J. Moltmann, *In der Geschichte des dreieinigen Gottes: Beiträge zur trinitarischen Theologie* (Gütersloh: Gütersloher Verlagshaus Mohn, 1991), 17.

41. Cf. J. Moltmann, *Der gekreuzigte Gott: Das Kreuz Christi als Grund und Kritik christlicher Theologie* (Gütersloh: Gütersloher Verlagshaus Mohn, ³1976), 138–46.

42. Ibid., 144–45.

43. Pannenberg, "Die Subjektivität Gottes," 108–9.

44. J. Moltmann, *The Trinity and the Kingdom: The Doctrine of God* (Minneapolis: Fortress, 1993), 190; cf. also 178–88.

45. J. Milbank, "The Second Difference: For a Trinitarianism without Reserve," *Modern Theology* 2 (1986): 213–34, esp. 223.

46. Ibid.

47. This is where Moltmann's "trinitarian doctrine of creation" fits in. See *God in Creation: A New Theology of Creation and the Spirit of God*, trans. M. Kohl (Minneapolis: Fortress, 1999), 94–98.

activity of Father, Son, and Spirit to such a degree that it becomes difficult to understand how they can be addressed together as one and the same God. Apart from this, in his trinitarian theology of the cross, as he himself admits, he got "no further than seeing a binity of God the Father and Jesus the Son of God," without really taking the activity and person of the Holy Spirit in his relationship to Father and Son into account.[48] Following the work of L. Dabney, he tried to correct this by developing, in addition to the doctrine of the kenosis of the Son, a doctrine of the kenosis of the Spirit.[49] But this only increased the difficulty of differentiating clearly between the activities of the person of the Spirit and those of the Son. Furthermore, it becomes impossible not only to invoke the Spirit as the basis for the openness of the trinitarian communion of persons but also to ascribe to him the function—as Jüngel does—of constituting the unity of God in the differentiation of Father, Son, and Spirit. As a result, the question of the unity of God remains unresolved.

3. Moltmann's difficulties in thinking through the unity of God are a significant reason for Wolfhart Pannenberg's efforts to find another solution to the problem.[50] He agrees with Jüngel and Moltmann on the unsatisfactory nature of Barth's initial attempt to develop a doctrine of the Trinity out of the formal concept of revelation, guided by the statement "God reveals Himself as the Lord." Instead of the concept of revelation, we must take the content of God's revelation in Jesus Christ as our starting point.[51] However, for Pannenberg, this content is to be found less in the cross and in the relationships between Father, Son, and Spirit that allow us to understand the cross as a salvation and revelation event, than in the particular relationship of the historical Jesus to God, and above all in the fact that "Jesus expressly differentiated God the Father from himself"[52] and, through this self-differentiation from God and subjection to the Father, opened the way for the Father's saving activity and the coming of his kingdom. Precisely this is what Pannenberg understands as God's self-revelation. Accordingly, in the historical fact of

48. Moltmann, *In der Geschichte*, 231.

49. D. L. Dabney, *Die Kenosis des Geistes: Kontinuität zwischen Schöpfung und Erlösung im Werk des Heiligen Geistes* (Neukirchen Vluyn: Neukirchener Verlag, 1997); H. H. Lin, "Die Person des Heiligen Geistes als Thema der Pneumatologie in der reformierten Theologie" (Diss. theol. masch., Tübingen, 1990); J. Moltmann, *Der Geist des Lebens: Eine ganzheitliche Pneumatologie* (Gütersloh: Gütersloher Verlagshaus Mohn, 1991), 64 and 77.

50. For the following, cf. Christoph Schwöbel, "Wolfhart Pannenberg," in *The Modern Theologians: An Introduction to Christian Theology in the Twentieth Century*, ed. D. F. Ford (Oxford: Blackwell, [2]1997), 180–208.

51. W. Pannenberg, *Systematic Theology*, trans. G. W. Bromiley (Grand Rapids: Eerdmans, 1991), 1:304–5.

52. Ibid., 1:263.

Jesus's self-differentiation from God, he sees the expression of the eternal self-differentiation of the Son from the Father, which corresponds to the self-differentiation of the Father from the Son.[53] And for him, this mutual self-differentiation is the key to the correct interpretation of the cross.

But even if we concur with him in proceeding from the historical fact of Jesus's obedient self-differentiation from God, whom Jesus called Father, to the eternal mutuality of the self-differentiation between Father and Son, the result is a concept of God that is binitarian, not trinitarian. Not until we turn from the cross to the resurrection do the contours of the third person become clear. For it is not the cross but the resurrection that demonstrates that the Spirit is "constitutive for the fellowship of the Son with the Father."[54] Similarly, Pannenberg describes the three persons as three mutually related activity centers, not as three modes of being of one absolute subject.

This approach by Pannenberg, in which he understands the "story of Jesus as the Son in self-distinction from the Father on the one side and the Spirit on the other" to be the "starting point for an establishment of the trinitarian distinctions,"[55] has a series of highly significant consequences. The traditional Western distinction between the immanent and the economic Trinity is thus in fact withdrawn, inasmuch as "the mutual self-differentiation of Father, Son, and Spirit in the divine economy must be seen as the concrete form of the immanent trinitarian relations."[56] Furthermore, Pannenberg understands the mutuality of the active relationships among the three persons to mean that the "monarchy of the Father is not the presupposition but the result of the common operation of the three persons"[57] in salvation history. From this point of view the world as a whole can be defined and understood as the history of God, in which the unity of the triune God will ultimately be confirmed and verified.[58]

But when Pannenberg declares that the "eschatological consummation is . . . the locus of the decision that the trinitarian God is always the true God from eternity to eternity,"[59] he is caught in an unresolved dilemma. If the full realization of the monarchy of the Father is the kingdom of God, and if, as the outcome of the cooperative action of Father, Son, and Spirit, this is fully realized only at the end of the whole course of world history, then the

53. Ibid., 1:310.
54. Ibid., 1:268.
55. Ibid., 1:273.
56. Cf. Schwöbel, "Wolfhart Pannenberg," 191.
57. Pannenberg, *Systematic Theology*, 1:325.
58. Ibid., 1:327–36.
59. Ibid., 1:331.

divine unity of the three persons remains hidden, obscure, and unrecognizable throughout the entire process of history. Pannenberg emphasizes that the tension between the differentiation of Father, Son, and Spirit is already evident and the hidden unity of God in the world will only be resolved eschatologically. But, as Schwöbel has rightly observed, the question is "how the three persons of the Trinity can be understood as presenting one divine essence without reducing them to moments or aspects of the one essential Godhead and without positing the divine essence as a fourth subject lurking behind the persons of Father, Son, and Spirit."[60] Herein lies the central weakness of Pannenberg's trinitarian concept. He fails to put forward a theological trinitarian solution to the question of the unity of God that is more than an eschatological consolation reserved for a time in the future. Instead, he is trapped in a dualistic cul-de-sac. On the one hand, he develops the distinction between Father, Son, and Spirit on the basis of his doctrine of revelation as Jesus's self-differentiation from the God whom he calls Father and from his Spirit. On the other hand, he bases the unity of God on a metaphysical concept of God's essence independent of his revelation: the concept of God as the truly infinite.[61] This idea of God, which we can adopt before and regardless of all specific revelation, as Pannenberg tries to show,[62] is the normative "framework concept" of God that governs all our thinking and speaking about God, even the doctrine of the Trinity.[63] For whatever we want to say about Father, Son, and Spirit on the basis of revelation must concur with this basic metaphysical concept of God as the truly infinite.

4. Falk Wagner is clear in his criticism of this as inadequate halfheartedness. He seeks to deal with the remnants of revelation theology in Pannenberg's doctrine of the Trinity by developing the trinitarian concept of God within the context of a theo-logical theory of the Absolute, following Hegel and Wolfgang Cramer.[64] According to him, a convincing and tenable concept of God must start from the concept of the Absolute, not from a particular revelation event in history or from a factual understanding of God held in the religious consciousness. A religion taken purely as a set of data is no better than a superstition, while a theology restricted to the explication of *the* self-understanding of a religion finds itself targeted by the objections of religious

60. Schwöbel, "Wolfhart Pannenberg," 192.

61. Pannenberg, *Systematic Theology*, 1:68–73, 397–422, 446.

62. Ibid., 1:63–118.

63. Ibid., 1:106–7.

64. F. Wagner, *Was ist Religion? Studien zu ihrem Begriff und Thema in Geschichte und Gegenwart* (Gütersloh: Gütersloher Verlagshaus Mohn, 1986), 570–89; Wagner, "Theo-Logie: Die Theorie des Absoluten und der christliche Gottesgedanke," in *Rationale Metaphysik: Die Philosophie von Wolfgang Cramer*, ed. H. Radermacher (Stuttgart: Klett-Cotta, 1989), 2:216–55.

criticism. However, it also is not sufficient, along the lines of the frequent attempts made since Schleiermacher, to base the idea of God and the validity of religion on a religious consciousness that seeks to verify its relationship to its ground by "defining its own dependency as the starting point for its elevation to the position of absolute ground."[65] For all versions of this route lead to a logical contradiction, namely, that the absolute ground of grace supporting the reasoning of the religious consciousness is the consciousness that envisages it: inasmuch as it ever expresses this ground only in dependence on its dependent existence, it can indeed comprehend the idea of the absolute ground but not the ground itself. This can succeed only through theo-logical argumentation that seeks to argue from an unfolding of the religious content conceived of for itself to the religious consciousness of it, and not the other way around: "God must be conceived of in such a way that the human qualification of God as the Absolute appears to have been established by God himself."[66] Of course the Absolute can be conceived of only as the concept of the Absolute. But this concept is to be apprehended as the process of the self-interpretation of the Absolute in conceptual form, so that the concept of the Absolute is apprehended as the manifestation of the Absolute itself.

Wagner attempts to show how this can happen by means of a trinitarian extension of Cramer's theory of the Absolute, in which he conceives of God as a process of absolute self-determination—in other words, as a self-determination that determines itself to be self-determination: "God as absolute self-determination can be grasped only because of his internal self-differentiation. This self-differentiation is governed by a self-determination that not only is differentiated from itself, but the interpretation of which as difference is also fundamental."[67] This means that "the only valid self-representation of God is a trinitarian one" and thus that "the Trinity is the only reasonable theo-logy."[68] Trinitarian speculation and a theory of the Absolute in terms of a logic of self-determination therefore find their place in a proper coalition on which religion and theology ought to be based: God is conceived of as a self-determination that distinguishes among its three elements: that which determines itself, that which is capable of being determined by itself, and that which realizes itself as the self-determination of that which can be self-determined by the one who self-determines. Wagner understands this threefold distinction as a terminological reference to the difference between Father, Son, and Spirit; he therefore claims to have shown

---

65. Wagner, *Was ist Religion?*, 573.
66. Ibid., 572.
67. Ibid., 580.
68. Ibid., 585.

that we are able to use purely rational or conceptual methods to develop a theory of the Absolute that has a fundamentally trinitarian structure without needing to take a historical revelation or any other contingent fact of religious consciousness as our starting point: the Trinity may be a fundamental mystery of faith, but it is a mystery that is rationally penetrable by a process of philosophical reasoning.

Even without a detailed critique, it is obvious that this proposal raises fundamental questions concerning the use of the concepts of reason, argumentation, rationality, and conceptual structure, and concerning its handling of the issue of language and the translatability of the figurative images and symbolic language of faith into the conceptual language of a theory of the Absolute in terms of a logic of self-determination.[69] All of this has provoked the series of critical inquiries with which we have been familiar since Wittgenstein. Nevertheless, it should be noted that Wagner is seeking to solve a central problem. Only when the doctrine of the Trinity claims to be more than a mere expression of the Christian view of God does it present a correct understanding of God. It must be clear that it seeks to present a correct idea *of God* and that this idea is not just of a *Christian* God, and neither does it represent various supplementary, idiosyncratic Christian views of Father, Son, and Spirit held by Christians, although not by Jews and Muslims, over and above their common monotheistic faith. The God of the Christian faith is not a special Christian God; he is the one and only God, who is experienced, believed in, confessed, and worshiped by Christians in their encounter with the good news of Jesus Christ through the Spirit. A doctrine of the Trinity that does not make this clear is inadequate from the start.

Above I have highlighted the *antitheistic* position as a common motif of recent trinitarian theological models. This brief overview of the thought of Jüngel, Moltmann, Pannenberg, and Wagner makes it possible to identify a second motif as well: their *fundamental christocentric orientation* (i.e., their concentration on the story of Jesus Christ, and in particular on the consequences of his death on the cross for the being and understanding of God). This certainly applies also to Wagner, inasmuch as he seeks to show that what Christians confess concerning God in the light of Jesus's cross and resurrection is not simply their particular individual opinion; rather, it expresses a universally valid truth concerning God, one that can be apprehended not just by faith but also by reason.[70]

---

69. Cf. my review of Wagner in *Philosophische Rundschau* 36 (1989): 155–59.
70. F. Wagner, *Was ist Theologie?* (Gütersloh: Gütersloher Verlagshaus Mohn, 1989), 298–308, esp. 304–8; cf. 309–42.

Both of these central trinitarian motifs, the antitheistic position and the fundamental christocentric orientation, stand side by side and are interconnected. They can be shown to be consequences of the eschatological reorientation of theology in the twentieth century. I will now move on to demonstrate this.

## 5. From the Eschata to the Eschatos

The rediscovery of the eschatological dimension of the Christian faith within modern (Protestant) theology has not only produced a degree of clarification but has also made for a fundamental "linguistic confusion within current eschatological discussion."[71] Not a few have therefore leveled the criticism that the expressions "eschatological" and "eschatology" "can make their appearance in every conceivable kind of context and be applied in a bewildering variety of senses,"[72] until they assume a meaning that has nothing to do with the end of history and consequently nothing to do with the original meaning of these terms.[73] It is emphasized that eschatology, correctly understood, has to do with the last things, with the ἔσχατα (i.e., with what will take place shortly before the end of this world and the beginning of the next), and that this has been largely obscured in recent discussion.

The criticism is correct, in that the term *eschatology* was originally coined within the context of seventeenth-century Lutheran dogmatics.[74] There it functioned as a title for the final section of dogmatics, also headed *De novissimis*, which discusses the doctrinal fields of death, the resurrection of the dead, the day of judgment, the end of the world, eternal life, and eternal damnation. But it was a creative polysemy that was decisive for the continuing theological use of the term *eschatology*: "The 'last' things are . . . simultaneously the things 'of ultimate significance' and thus possess a *doubly* superlative quality."[75] Their conclusiveness makes clear what is of significance for everyone, not only in the future but here and now. The eschata are therefore not simply the last things in the chronological sense; they are also the most important things with regard to one's present life orientation. Second, however, eschatology is not

71. S. Hjelde, *Das Eschaton und die Eschata: Eine Studie über Sprachgebrauch und Sprachverwirrung in protestantischer Theologie von der Orthodoxie bis zur Gegenwart* (Munich: Christian Kaiser, 1987), 15.

72. G. W. H. Lampe, "Early Patristic Eschatology," in W. Manson et al., *Eschatology: Four Papers Read to the Society of the Study of Theology* (1953; repr., Edinburgh: Oliver & Boyd, 1957), 17–35, esp. 17.

73. A. W. Argyle, "Does 'Realized Eschatology' Make Sense?," *The Hibbert Journal* 51 (1953): 385–87, esp. 386.

74. Cf. Hjelde, *Das Eschaton und die Eschata*, 36–68.

75. Ibid., 49.

just an appendix to dogmatics, one that deals with future events that radically transcend our current life and knowledge. Rather, it deals with the fundamental, normative orientation of our life by pointing to its eventual purpose and ultimate parameters. In this sense it is of fundamental significance for the whole of dogmatics, for by viewing human life as a process of existence destined to find its fulfillment and completion in communion with God, it highlights an essential feature of the Christian understanding of reality that relates to every area of Christian living and theological thought.

It has to be said that, for the most part, the dogmatics of baroque Protestant orthodoxy regarded the eschata in the chronological sense as the last, and not in a practical sense as the ultimate, things. But it required only a slight shift of emphasis to bring about a fundamental reevaluation of the significance of eschatology within the sphere of Christian dogmatics. As far as the history of theology was concerned, this began to happen toward the end of the nineteenth century in the context of historical theology through the work of Johannes Weiß, Franz Overbeck, and Albert Schweitzer, who came to a new recognition of the fundamentally eschatological character of Jesus's teaching and of the deep gulf that separated the essentially eschatological orientation of Jesus and the early Christian community from later Christendom.[76] Weiß, Overbeck, and Schweitzer gave the concept of eschatology an essentially historical significance by limiting it to the description of certain early Christian convictions that could no longer be adhered to, but Karl Barth, under the influence of the First World War and following on from Overbeck and the two Blumhardts, drew precisely the opposite conclusion, emphasizing that a "Christianity that is not wholly and utterly and irreducibly eschatology has absolutely nothing to do with *Christ*."[77] Theologically therefore, *everything*, not just the traditional eschata, must be treated from an eschatological perspective.

In the course of the twentieth century, there was thus a shift of meaning within the understanding of eschatology. Its key characteristic can be summed up in the formula taken from the study by Hjelde titled *From the Eschata to the Eschaton and from the Eschaton to the Eschatos*.

The first stage is illustrated by Tillich's statements on eschatology in the 1920s, where he systematically replaced the traditional term *eschata* with the term *eschaton*.[78] The basis for this is "that eschato-logy is not about

76. Cf. ibid., 217–346.

77. K. Barth, *The Epistle to the Romans* (1922; repr., Zurich: TVZ, [10]1967), 298. Cf. I. U. Dalferth, "Theologischer Realismus und realistische Theologie bei Karl Barth," *EvTh* 46 (1986): 402–22.

78. P. Tillich, "Eschatologie und Geschichte (1927)," in *Hauptwerke, Theologische Schriften*, ed. G. Hummel (Berlin: de Gruyter, 1992), 6:107–25.

things [i.e., events] that will unfold one day at the end of time, but about the overall meaning of the event, insofar as it is pointing toward something. However, the thing to which the event points, 'the ultimate,' is not in itself another event but the transcendent meaning of the event."[79] This ultimate meaning is equally close to each historical event and manifests itself at the point where there is a question of *"fulfillment* and *decision"*:[80] "The end of each event is its position in the eschaton. For this is where it reaches its goal."[81] But if *"there is nothing in the eschaton . . . that is not in history,"*[82] then the basic eschatological images of the Christian faith (e.g., the resurrection of the dead, the day of judgment, or eternal life) must be interpreted existentially and not chronologically or cosmologically. Only thus can its universal meaning be apprehended, and only by connecting history with the eschaton in this way can theology assert the unity of history and salvation history.

Tillich's attempt at an existential reshaping of eschatology was not only imitated by many but also criticized from various points of view. *"To eschaton* (neuter) is not actually a New Testament phrase," objected John A. T. Robinson. "Loyalty to the Christocentric nature of all New Testament theology would require us to speak always of ho eschatos—not the last Thing, but the last Man [i.e., Jesus Christ]."[83] Jesus Christ is the *Eschatos* and Fulfiller of the eschaton. For this reason, Tillich's existential reshaping must be converted into a new christological model of eschatology. Tillich's teacher, Martin Kähler, had already begun to explore this path. Karl Barth followed it to its logical conclusion. But if eschatology engages primarily with the eschatos, its scope becomes identical with that of Christology so that it governs the whole of theology. It then deals no longer with individual eschata but with one subject only: Jesus Christ, his life and teaching, his cross and resurrection, and the soteriological consequences of all of these for the human race and the whole of creation. Hence theology must engage not with a series of eschatological fields of doctrine but with the single eschatological reality of the one who has been raised—Jesus Christ. This will inevitably have its effect on the doctrine of God, which, when developed from this starting point, becomes necessarily *trinitarian*. But to what extent?

79. P. Tillich, *Religiöse Verwirklichung* (Berlin: Furche, 1930), 291n4.
80. Tillich, "Eschatologie," 114 (italics in original).
81. Ibid., 115.
82. Ibid., 114 (italics in original).
83. J. A. T. Robinson, *In the End God: A Study of the Christian Doctrine of the Last Things* (London: James Clark & Co., 1958), 56.

## 6. The Doctrine of the Trinity and Christian Salvation Experience

According to C. H. Dodd, Jesus's death and resurrection are "eschatological events in the full sense; that is to say, they are not simply important events, not even the most important events in the series, but unique and final events, in which the God beyond history intervened conclusively to reveal His Kingdom on earth."[84] What is expressed here is neither factually self-evident and plain for all to see, nor a readily accessible truth that anyone can verify, provided one complies with certain conditions or follows certain steps, and certainly not a necessary reality that is disclosed to each one who embarks on the quest to understand what "God" means. Under these circumstances it might be an everyday, empirical, or ontological reality. But it would not be an eschatological reality, a reality that not only owes its existence and its recognition solely to God himself but also communicates a unique and ultimate truth concerning God and his relationship to his creation. Ontologically, epistemically, and in terms of their content, eschatological realities are unique; this means that they cannot be subsumed under general concepts or structures, and they bypass our practice of classifying our knowledge of the world according to systems of the general and the particular or the contingent and the necessary. They concern God, and God is not an element of the world as we know it.

But the Christian confession of Jesus as the Christ concerns eschatological realities. Thus Christians confess that Jesus is the Christ, the Lord, or the Son of God, who has revealed and mediated to us, once and for all, God's loving nearness to his creatures. They are convinced that in this confession they are affirming a true and universally valid insight into God's being and the nature of his nearness to us. But they are not claiming that it articulates a reality universally accessible and comprehensible to anyone. On the contrary: a significant aspect of their confession is that God alone is the originator not merely of the content but also of the existence and the declaration of their faith conviction, so that they can confess that Jesus is the Christ whom God raised from the dead only because and to the extent that the Spirit of God has opened their eyes to this divine eschatological reality and activity. God (Rom. 10:9), specifically God the Father (Gal. 1:1), raised Jesus from the dead—this has been the fundamental confession of Christians from the very beginning. At the same time, however, they also emphasize that "no one can say, 'Jesus is Lord,' except by the Holy Spirit" (1 Cor. 12:3). Their testimony is not simply that God raised Jesus but that this Jesus, "exalted to the right hand of God," has received the Spirit from the Father and has poured him out on those who

---

84. C. H. Dodd, *History and the Gospel* (New York: Charles Scribner's Sons, 1938), 35.

are witnesses to him (cf. Acts 2:32–33). Only through the power of the Spirit can we acknowledge and confess Jesus's life, death, and resurrection as the true expression of our situation before God and of God's loving nearness to us. Without the Spirit this eschatological perspective, the sole perspective in which the events associated with the name of Jesus of Nazareth are disclosed as the unique and ultimate revelation of God's kingdom, remains closed to us.

Where the Spirit does bring about the recognition of this eschatological truth, however, practical consequences are inevitable. The Christian tradition uses the terms *repentance* and *conversion* for this fundamentally new orientation and—in a manner not without its problems—attempts to describe it systematically by devising an *ordo salutis* [order of salvation].[85] In so doing, it perceives (entirely correctly) that a recognition of eschatological truth is never purely theoretical but always practical; in other words, it is a recognition of truth that involves the whole person. It is the unanimous testimony of Christians that the insight into the truth of the confession of Christ brought about by the Spirit leads not simply to an expansion of our theoretical knowledge but also to our understanding of ourselves, of God, and of the world being reshaped and created anew in the light of the fundamental eschatological distinction between the old and the new. We learn to distinguish between our old life, with its God-forsakenness and its blindness to creation, its past lifestyles and circumstances, and the damage these incur and mete out, and the new life in a community of mutual love and reciprocal service. This is a life that is focused on the whole of humanity and is therefore universal, and in which human beings become what they can and should be, according to the will of God: created beings who, in their own day-to-day living and within the scope of the opportunities available to them, freely and fully affirm the goodness and love of God, from whose creative nearness they exist. From the viewpoint of the Christian faith, true (i.e., saving) knowledge of God, Jesus Christ, our human situation before God, and the divinely willed ordering of creation is rooted in God's raising of Jesus, into which we are drawn through the power of the Spirit of God, who makes us open and sensitive to the nearness and saving presence of God's love.

This self-revelatory and self-mediating nearness of God's creative and renewing love is the complex eschatological reality from which the Christian faith lives and that is the point of reference for Christian theology. It manifested itself in the resurrection of Jesus in such a way that it confirmed his

85. Cf. M. Marquardt, "Die Vorstellung des 'Ordo Salutis' in ihrer Funktion für die Lebensführung der Glaubenden," in *Lebenserfahrung*, ed. W. Härle and R. Preul, Marburger Jahrbuch Theologie 3 (Marburg: Elwert, 1990), 29–53.

proclamation of God's nearness and of the dawn of God's kingdom as the true expression, the valid announcement, and the correct interpretation of this nearness, demonstrating it to be the authentic proof of the eschatological presence of God. This presence is eschatological inasmuch as it is the final and ultimate reality in and through which we all exist. Its eschatological quality can be summed up in three central characteristics revealed by Jesus's resurrection: It is produced *by God alone*. Its content is determined by *reference to Jesus Christ*. And it is experienced as the unanticipated invasion of our life and our world by *something entirely new and radical*. These three characteristics of eschatological reality are determinative for the Christian understanding of Jesus Christ, of ourselves, of our world, and of God. When they are worked out and thought through theologically in relation to God, the result is the doctrine of the Trinity.

## 6.1. The Eschatological Roots of the Doctrine of the Trinity

1. From an ontological and epistemic point of view, the eschatological reality, which faith acknowledges as the final and ultimate reality, originates *from God alone*. It cannot exist unless it is brought about by God himself; it cannot be recognized unless God himself brings about this recognition; and it is recognized only when it is recognized that from an ontological and epistemic point of view it originates from God alone. What is conditioned and determined so fundamentally by God alone, without necessarily following from God or being taken for granted as already present with God as such, emanates solely from God's self-determination that it should be conditioned and determined just so.

To be conditioned in this manner solely through self-determination is a characteristic of freedom of action. In theological terms, eschatological reality is therefore to be conceived of as a complex action by God, rooted in his self-definition, that unveils the true nature of God and of created reality, and that we can perceive only if God himself discloses it to us. Since it is brought about *solely* by God, it owes all its aspects wholly and solely to God himself. From a theological point of view, *that* it is (its reality), *what* it is (its nature), and *that we (can) perceive its reality and its nature* (its intelligibility) must all be accounted for by reference to God's activity. But if God's activity is determined solely by God himself, so that his being is no more and no less than his actions (*esse est operari* [to be is to act]), then God himself is not something beyond or behind his activity; rather, he is the one who he is in his activity and at the same time the one as whom he allows himself to be perceived in his activity.

Precisely this is what makes it necessary for theology to present the idea of God in trinitarian terms. For if the reality, the nature, and the intelligibility of the eschatological reality emanate from God alone, then that reality is rooted in a complex activity of God that includes three fundamental and irreducible subactivities. Depending on whether its emphasis was soteriological, christological, or epistemological, the dogmatic tradition has identified these as *creation, reconciliation,* and *redemption;* as *creation, incarnation,* and *consummation;* or as *creation, revelation,* and *inspiration.*[86] Thus, formulating it in epistemological terms:

- everything that is distinct from God owes its possibility and reality to God himself alone (creation);
- God discloses to us in and through Jesus Christ that the unfettered realization of his love is the intention guiding his creative activity (revelation); and
- God opens our eyes so that we perceive and are willing to accept that what he discloses to us in his revelation concerning his loving nearness to his creation is absolutely true and reliable (inspiration).

Thus God's creative action constitutes all reality, God's revelatory action discloses the truth of this reality, and God's inspiring action brings about the assurance of the truth of this reality. Just as without creation there is no revelation and without revelation there is no inspiration, so without inspiration there is no recognition of the revelation, and without this there is no recognition of one's own creatureliness. Creation, revelation, and inspiration are therefore aspects of God's activity that are neither wholly separate nor wholly fused. They are differentiated from each other through the manner of their relatedness: while inspiration presupposes revelation and creation (protology), the creation achieves its goal and its consummation through revelation and inspiration (eschatology), and both creation and consummation are differentiated from each other and related to each other through revelation (Christology) and inspiration (pneumatology). Creation, revelation, and inspiration are therefore interconnected through the specific manner of their differentiation, and indeed in such a way that created reality is thereby given time and space to realize its potentialities and to fulfill its destiny

86. Cf. Chr. Schwöbel, "Divine Agency and Providence," *Modern Theology* 3 (1987): 225–44; Schwöbel, "Die Rede vom Handeln Gottes im christlichen Glauben: Beiträge zu einem systematisch-theologischen Rekonstruktionsversuch," in *Vom Handeln Gottes,* ed. W. Härle and R. Preul, Marburger Jahrbuch Theologie 1 (Marburg: Elwert, 1987), 56–81; Schwöbel, *God: Action and Revelation* (Kampen: Peeters, 1992).

autonomously. This well-ordered relationship among creation, revelation, and inspiration is a key feature of eschatological reality. Together these three types of divine action constitute the one, all-encompassing activity of God that allows all that is distinct from God in time and space to become what it should and will ultimately be.

These three basic types of divine action are primary and fundamental. They cannot be reduced to anything more basic without fragmenting the idea of God's *activity*, and they cannot be attributed to three different acting subjects without destroying the unity and uniqueness of *God's* activity. If therefore the eschatological reality that the Christian faith confesses in relation to the one who has been crucified and raised is to be accurately conceived of, then God's unfathomable activity must be explicated within the context of trinitarian theology—for example, as an internally differentiated activity field with three activity centers: the center of creativity and reality (Father), the center of intelligibility and truth (Son), and the center of newness and assurance (Spirit). These activity centers are not different acting subjects; they are "three distinctive though internally related *types of action*"[87] belonging to the one divine action. They are constituted by their differential relationships to each other, and they give structure to God's action as an internally differentiated process of divine self-constitution, self-organization, and self-communication, the grammar of which theology attempts to formulate in the doctrine of the immanent Trinity.

2. The second central characteristic of eschatological reality is its intrinsic reference to *Jesus Christ*, whose life, cross, and resurrection unveil to us the character and import of the divine creative activity. According to the New Testament, Jesus lived in an unreservedly trusting relationship with the God of Israel, whom he called Father and whose dawning reign he announced to his contemporaries in word and deed. Thus the whole conduct of his life made it plain that God's nearness signified not annihilation but rescue for sinners. Not even human rebuff and rejection can prevent God from coming as near to them as a loving father comes to his lost son, or from pursuing them into the remotest corners of life like a good shepherd. This unswervingly beneficent, loving, and life-giving nearness of God, especially to the sinner, which Jesus announced in his parables and underlined with his death and his resurrection, demonstrates God's creative activity as the activity of a radical, tireless love that never abandons anyone. For the first Christians, the fact that the Jesus, who proclaimed this, was raised by God from the dead was clear proof that Jesus's message of the loving nearness of God was not negated by the cross but had in fact been confirmed by means of this antithesis (*sub contrario*) as

87. Schwöbel, "Divine Agency," 240.

valid right into the dimension of death. By raising the crucified Jesus into his eternal life, the Father reinforced and confirmed Jesus's proclamation of the creative nearness of God's loving, saving presence as the authentic portrayal of his divine being and his will for the whole of creation. And by assuring human beings through his Spirit that Jesus's message is true and that God himself has reinforced it, he brings about the faith in which we too can live our lives in reliance on the nearness of his love. With the name "Jesus Christ," therefore, Christians point to the fundamental eschatological experience in which God himself broke into the context of human life and experience, generated faith in his nearness, disclosed his nature as love, and demonstrated that it is possible for human life to reflect that which became manifest in Jesus's life, cross, and resurrection: eternal life in communion with God.

This, too, is included in the trinitarian idea of God, which speaks not only of the Father but also of the Son. It is integral to the Christian understanding of God that its Father image relates not purely to an absolute and original creative activity but simultaneously to Jesus Christ. There are two decisive reasons for this. First, by differentiating himself as a human being from God, whom he called Father, Jesus Christ revealed this God as the divine Father. Second, in the light of this understanding of God, the cross and resurrection revealed him as the Son who gave definitive expression not just to the Fatherhood of this God but also simultaneously to the Godhead of this Father. Through Jesus's cross and resurrection, however, the creative activity of this Father becomes evident as the effective power of saving and life-giving love that even in death does not reach its limit but remains true to itself under all circumstances. In the face of the unfathomable implications of the cross for God, the resurrection of Jesus Christ makes it manifest that God committed himself to be the love that was expressed in Jesus's message as the unconditionally faithful love of the heavenly Father. Theological tradition has formulated it thus: God does not simply love; he *is* love. The objective basis for this formula is found in the cross and resurrection of Jesus Christ, understood in the light of Jesus's message of God's nearness and unconditional fatherly love. The cross and resurrection of Jesus Christ show that love is the normative principle of God's being and is thus the ultimate overall reality. For this love is not simply factually omnipotent, all-encompassing, infinite, and dependable. It is all this because it owes its existence to God's irreversible self-determination to love; in other words, it has no other origin than God himself. It could therefore be called in question only by God himself, and the cross and resurrection of Jesus Christ have proved once and for all that this is the one thing that will never happen. Through Jesus Christ, therefore, Christians know that they are right to turn to God as their Father too, just as Jesus taught them in the

Lord's Prayer; and his confirmation as the Christ in the resurrection is the basis of their assurance by the Spirit that the essence of the activity of this divine Father is his creative love and life-giving nearness to his creation.

The Christian idea of God is therefore indissolubly linked with Jesus Christ in the double sense that, on the one hand, it picks up Jesus's proclamation of God and, on the other hand, it extends this in its own distinctive way in the light of the cross and resurrection of Jesus. Furthermore, in comparison with Jesus's proclamation of God, the idea of God is redefined in Christian thought because God has redefined himself eschatologically in the cross and the resurrection of Jesus. The Christian idea of God must therefore be understood with reference to the message of Jesus, but not purely on the basis of this message. Rather, it is Christian precisely because it continues Jesus's proclamation of God by giving it substance through the cross and resurrection: if this eschatological distinction is not taken into account in our idea of God, we are not conceiving of the God whom Jesus proclaimed.

Now, the unavoidable Christocentrism of all Christian discussion and thought concerning God does not promulgate a special Christian God, and neither does it have anything to do with limitation to a particular religious community's individual way of speaking of God. The "Christian community has a focus for its identity in Jesus, yet the 'limits' set by Jesus are as wide as the human race itself. The Christian 'community' is potentially the whole world."[88] Jesus proclaimed God's nearness in such a way that it opened up a new direction and orientation for the life of each human being, not merely a special identity for a specific group or community. He was not proclaiming a new God but was revealing and interpreting, in a new and definitive manner, the nature of the one and only existing God. For he made two things plain, both actively through what he proclaimed and did and passively through what God did to him and allows to be said of him. First, God determines and limits himself in his creative activity in such a way[89] that he grants his creatures time and space to react freely in their lives and actions to God's activity as creator. Second, in the face of our denial and hardness of heart, God went to extreme

88. R. Williams, "Trinity and Revelation," *Modern Theology* 2 (1986): 197–212, esp. 202.
89. The idea of God's self-limitation is belittled and misunderstood (in a moralizing way) if we construe it as constraint and loss, and not as *gain* and as an *increase* in the divine opportunities for action or for life. By allowing a created being, distinct from him, space and time, God gains opportunities for relationship that would not have existed, and of which he could not have taken advantage, without the creation: only as creator, and therefore because of the creation, can God determine himself to be reconciler and consummator and live as the God he is. In the same way as self-abasement, God's self-limitation is an increase and not a curtailment of his Godhead. Only through it does God live as the God he is: the creator, reconciler, and consummator of his creation.

lengths to pave the way for us to respond freely to his creative love, not by forcing us in his infinite otherness and power to recognize him as our creator but by involving himself with us so closely that his love is present with us, even in death, as the power, the beginning, and the environment for new life.

It is important to give theological emphasis to the fact that this self-determination, self-limitation, and self-abasement on God's part is not some extra or alien element of his divine creative activity; as the expression of God's love, it belongs to his being and is therefore universally applicable. From a theological point of view it was thus not inappropriate to express it in the form of the metaphor of the Word (Logos) or of the Son as the eternal answer and the eternal obedience of the Son toward the Father. The Son not only participates in the divine creative activity of the Father; he determines how, by the Spirit, he clarifies and communicates, through his self-differentiation from the Father, the nature of this creative activity as unlimited and inexhaustible love. And since, like all love, this love looks for a free counterpart, the point of creaturely existence is defined as the free answer to the love of the creator.

3. The third central characteristic is that, in the (inspirational) operation of the *Holy Spirit*, God's eschatological reality radically breaks through our normal continuities and all that is self-evident about our life and removes every trace of "self-evidentness." Where this takes place, it breaks through the experience and language structures of our existing world orientation; disrupts the patterns of our habitual perception of our world and ourselves, the conduct of our lives and our relationships with the world; and establishes a fundamental distinction between the old and the new: the old, self-centered life, which contradicts our human destiny as God's creatures, and the new, God-centered life, which conforms with it.

This new life is not merely a vision of what is to come or a purely theoretical future possibility. Indeed, the requirements of our active day-to-day living, which carry on even after the event of God's eschatological self-mediation, compel us here and now to reorganize and reorient ourselves and our whole worldview in the light of the eschatological disruption we have experienced. The life of the individual Christian and of the whole Christian community finds not disorientation but reorientation in place of our shattered orientation when we begin to perceive in Jesus Christ and through the Holy Spirit that the free grace, radical creativity, and inexhaustible renewing power of God's love are the bedrock and the ultimate goal of every created being.

This radical, fresh orientation and reshaping of our life is given appropriate theological expression in images such as "new birth," "new creation," or "new life": we do not initiate it or bring it about of ourselves, but once it happens, it affects and governs everything that we are and do. So we cannot become aware of the divine constitution and the salvific nature of this eschatological disruption we have experienced unless we apprehend it as a gift of God (i.e., as the enlightenment of our spirit by God's Spirit), enabling and motivating us to recognize and confess Jesus Christ as God's beneficent nearness and creative love for us. As the recognition of God's work in us, this recognition is never purely theoretical but always essentially practical. As is shown by Paul and by many others, it cannot take place without repentance (i.e., without a complete reorientation of the whole of our life in the light of the eschatological contrast between old and new), that is, between the way our life actually looks at present and the way it could and should look once we react and respond to God's nearness and love.

This experience too is reflected in the trinitarian idea of God. The reference to the radical, eschatological shattering of our living environment, which is effected by God alone and defies all attempts at assimilation into existing structures of experience and language, is an essential element of this idea. It is contained within the basic idea that God the Father is not derived from anything (*nec genitum nec procedens* [neither begotten nor proceeding]) but is the generator and author of everything, the final and ultimately unfathomable source of all that is and can be. Since it speaks not only of the Father but simultaneously also of the Son, the trinitarian idea of God reflects the fact not just that God is the radical Other who breaks into our lives in an inexplicable and indescribable way, but that the creative, eschatological shattering of every previous experience leads to a specific reordering of the world and a new orientation in the world, to a new life in which our thoughts, our desires, and our actions are a response to God's fatherly love and nearness as disclosed in Jesus Christ. Hence both the impossibility of fathoming God's creative power and the possibility of experiencing God's love are essential characteristics of the Christian understanding of God.

But it reflects another essential feature of Christian experience. In that our life is given a fresh orientation and a new structure in the light of the eschatological breakthrough experience, God's creative power and love are experienced not as opposites that cancel each other out but as elements of the divine life that shed light on each other: love is seen as *the* characteristic of God's creative power, and creative power as *the* characteristic of God's love. God is creator, inasmuch as he creates what he loves and creates it in order to love it, and God is love, inasmuch as he loves what he creates and creates because he loves. The third central characteristic of the Christian understanding of God is therefore the attempt to do justice to the experience of the constant appearance from nowhere of something new and unexpected, an experience that owes its existence to the unfathomable creative power of the love within which God's comprehensibility and incomprehensibility are linked in such a way that God is identified as the origin, advent, and future of all life-giving newness in the life both of human beings and of the creation as a whole. This is why the Christian idea of God speaks not only of Father and Son but also of the Spirit: the eschatological experience of unfathomable divine creativity and the possibility of experiencing God's love and his radical nearness and newness, thanks to the inexhaustible creativity of his love, are thus integrated in a complex pattern of divine activity. The Spirit takes priority over the Father and the Son in ordering the experience and recognition of eschatological reality, inasmuch as he enables us to confess Jesus as the Christ and God as love. As the divine Spirit, however, he can be identified only as a result of his relationship with the Son, who reveals the Godhead of the Father as his delivering and saving nearness and love. And just as the doctrine of the procession of the Son from the Father is necessary to guarantee the clear identification of God as Father and as love, so the *filioque* is indispensable to guarantee the clear identification of the Spirit as *God's* presence and hence the recognizability of the Spirit as God's Spirit.

### 6.2. God and the Trinitarian Idea of God

The trinitarian idea of God clearly reflects the three central characteristics of eschatological reality set out above. It seeks to do justice to the eschatological point of reference, the christological specificity and the radical openness for the new, that characterize all Christian thought and discourse concerning God. So the doctrine of the Trinity does not systematically befog our understanding of God; and neither does the trinitarian idea of God turn him into an incomprehensible and impenetrable mystery. Rather, this idea of God serves to refer us constantly back to the place where this God, who surpasses all our understanding, made himself understandable for us: the eschatological breakthrough experience of the raising of the crucified Jesus of Nazareth by the God whose all-transforming nearness he had proclaimed. At the same time, however, this idea of God requires us to take constant care not to confuse our ideas of God with the living God himself, whom we can comprehend, grasp, and focus on only to the extent that he makes it possible for us to comprehend, grasp, and focus on him as Father, Son, and Spirit.

In prayer, confession of faith, preaching, and theological reflection we really focus on *God* only if in the process we take into account the eschatological breakthrough experience, which resists any complete assimilation or absorption into the symbolic and linguistic structures available to us. Where symbols are concerned, we achieve this by using negative terminology ("God is *not* . . .") and qualifications ("God is *like* . . . , *but* . . ."). In other words, when we think and speak of God, we qualify and define the images and models we use for thinking and speaking of God in such a way that we preserve and pay heed to the irrevocable difference between God and our realm of experience ("almighty Lord," "heavenly Father," etc.). The methodological principle underlying this process, which involves focusing on what is beyond comprehension with the aid of the comprehensible, was formulated as a rule by Anselm of Canterbury: the conditions for using every model we employ to think and speak of God must include the principle that what we are thus seeking to consider ultimately goes beyond anything we can comprehensibly think or say, since God is greater than all that we can say or grasp. This means that we must qualify our thinking and speaking of God in such a way that we also explicitly affirm, on the level of symbolization, the irrevocable difference between our limited symbolic ideas of God and God himself, of whom we seek to think in this way.

As we think and speak of God, Anselm's rule helps us to pay heed to the dialectic between comprehensibility and beyond-comprehensibility. However, it obviously overemphasizes the element of the beyond-comprehensibility, or even incomprehensibility, of God, since it fails to take account of the specific origin of this dialectic of Christian thinking and speaking of God: the eschatological breakthrough experience of the resurrection of Jesus Christ, on which all Christian discourse concerning God ultimately depends. This does not eliminate or dispute the element of God's beyond-comprehensibility, but it also leaves us with a clearly articulated idea of who or what God is. It means, rather, that God's beyond-comprehensibility is defined and can be defined in christological terms; in other words, it can be expressed by reference to Jesus Christ's life and teachings, his death, and the fact that he was raised from the dead. We can accurately grasp and confess what God really is if we hold onto what God makes clear to us and allows us to recognize in Jesus Christ and through his Spirit concerning himself as primordial creative love and concerning us as his creatures.

One can fall back on the rule of analogy, which states that, despite the similarity between God and the creation, there exists a still greater dissimilarity, but this is an inadequate means to a theological doctrine of God if we wish to do justice to the dialectic between the comprehensibility and the beyond-comprehensibility of God. This applies both to the analogy of attribution and to the analogy of proportionality, as well as to their combination.[90] If we take into account the specific origin of the dialectic of comprehensibility and

90. Cf. Dalferth, *Religiöse Rede von Gott*, 626–47.

beyond-comprehensibility, theological light may be shed on the meaning of Christian discourse concerning God, not by means of the semantic resources of analogy but by the provision of rules that clarify how the different figurative, metaphorical, and pictorial (as well as conceptual or near-conceptual) terms used for God in theological thought relate to, or can be back-translated into, the diversity of Christian faith discourse concerning the eschatological reality of the risen Jesus Christ. Only thus can there be any theological guarantee that in our thought and speech God's comprehensibility will not be dominated by his incomprehensibility. Theological ideas of God and doctrines of God are not shown to be meaningful by being reformulated in the context of an abstract theistic conception of God and then put back into concrete terms by means of a theory of analogous predication in respect to our experience of the world. Rather, they are meaningful precisely to the extent that they are interpretatively back-translated into the story of Jesus Christ or the faith discourse of the Christian community or are back-related to them or interpreted in the light of them.

To enable this is the methodological point of the doctrine of the Trinity, which Nicholas Lash has rightly described as "'the summary grammar' of the Christian account of the mystery of salvation and creation."[91] In this doctrine Christian theology emphasizes that every Christian use of "God" must be defined by the eschatological breakthrough experience that bears witness to the good news of Jesus Christ, which is accepted and confessed as true through the power of the Spirit. The doctrine of the Trinity thus insists on the fundamental *specificity* of all Christian discourse concerning God—a specificity that cannot be transmuted into any kind of abstract concept and defies all attempts to generalize the idea of God as a conceptual principle, no matter how well defined. Within the context of trinitarian theology, this is typically reflected in the fact that no universal pronouncements can be made concerning Father, Son, and Spirit, so that no generic term can be applied to them. Not even the concept of personhood (or one of its equivalents) can be used of Father, Son, and Spirit in an identical way.[92] The ground rule of trinitarian theology (i.e., that all Christian discourse concerning God must be related back to the basic eschatological experience of the raised crucified one) therefore leaves unresolved the dialectic of comprehensibility and non- or beyond-comprehensibility in our efforts to understand God. But the accent is now on God's comprehensibility, so that God's saving activity, made manifest

91. Lash, "Considering the Trinity," 183.
92. Cf. B. Lonergan, *Divinarum Personarum Conceptionem analogicam* (Rome: Università Gregoriana, ²1959), 236.

in the story of Jesus Christ, which is proclaimed to us in the gospel, and which we confess to be true by the operation of the Spirit, makes possible a specific Christian orientation, with a demonstrable content, toward life in the world.

So the doctrine of the Trinity is not merely the "summary grammar" of Christian speech and thought concerning God. It is the *basic framework governing the whole of the Christian life*. Since, as the doctrine of the immanent Trinity, it both distinguishes Father, Son, and Spirit from one another and relates them to one another in a specific way on the basis of the eschatological experience of the one who was crucified and raised, it offers a basic integrating model for all aspects and dimensions of Christian life, experience, thought, and activity. So it is not just the historical relationship of Jesus to the God whom he addressed as "Father" that is represented and concisely brought into focus in the intratrinitarian *Father-Son relationship*. In that the God thus described as "Father" is the God of Israel, the remembrance of the irreplaceable importance of Israel's experience of God for the Christian understanding of God is thereby kept alive; and in that this Father is also described as our Father, the soteriological importance of the story of Jesus as the eschatological paradigm of our story too is highlighted. In a similar way, through the *Son-Spirit relationship*, it is not just the factual experiential basis of the Christian confession of Jesus as the Christ that is represented and concisely brought into focus. This relationship makes it clear that the identity of this Spirit as the Spirit of God is decisively characterized and defined through his relationship to Jesus Christ: if God had not been identified and interpreted to us in and through Jesus Christ in a way that we can understand, and if he were not directly copresent with us as Spirit, we could neither know nor address nor confess him as God. After all, this relationship is a constant reminder that the Christian community, or the church, is justified in claiming to be the place in which God is confessed and worshiped as he truly is, only because and to the extent that it is intrinsically defined and characterized both by the story of Jesus and by the work of the Spirit. And finally, through the *Father-Spirit relationship*, not only the ultimate ground of our confession of Jesus as the Christ is represented and concisely brought into focus. It recalls that God is at work, not just in Israel and in the church but everywhere, in the whole of creation, albeit in a manner that often seems indeterminate and nonspecific to us: the triune God is not a special God belonging to Christians; he is the one Lord of the whole of creation. This is true regardless of whether it is confessed and acknowledged, and without disputing whether it is only in and through Jesus Christ that his lordship can be recognized and confessed as the saving power of love.

In summary, as the working-out of the grammar of the combined fields of imagery of Father, Son, and Spirit, the doctrine of the Trinity is the concentrated symbolic summary of the structures of Christian perspectives on God, the world, human existence, and history within the horizon of the basic images of the Christian faith. Consequently, it is the grammar of a perspective expressed in specific images, rooted in the eschatological experience of the Jesus Christ who has been raised, and extending to everything actual and potential, so that its range of reference is universal. By constantly pointing Christian thought and speech back to these eschatological roots, the doctrine of the Trinity safeguards the concreteness, historical contingency, christological definitiveness, universal inclusiveness, and radical openness for the new that characterize the Christian perspective and are a feature of its life.

The function of this doctrinal field of Christian theology is therefore first and foremost *regulatory* and *critical*. It does not describe a mysterious, transcendent reality but summarizes the structure of an understanding of God, the world, and human existence that is rooted in the experience of faith in Jesus Christ, who has been raised, an experience in which God's creative activity is disclosed conclusively as the saving and life-giving work of divine love. The creative, effective power of this love is the fundamental eschatological reality that is articulated in the confession of Christ and on which all other theological statements are founded. Only with this as its starting point can the doctrine of the Trinity be established theologically as the effective regulator governing the idea of God, and every statement of this type must therefore take the form of an eschatological ontology of the creative, saving, and consummating activity of God.[93] This ontology is not a descriptive conceptual interpretation of divine action as such—just as the resurrection confession does not claim to describe the resurrection of Jesus from the dead. It is the attempt to explicate the terms and conditions that must be fulfilled if the eschatological experience of the one who was crucified and raised is to be true. And the concentrated summary of these conditions and their fulfillment in the idea of God is itself the trinitarian idea of God.

## 7. The Trinitarian Grammar of "God"

In its function as a combined grammar of the fields of imagery of Father, Son, and Spirit, the doctrine of the Trinity works out the implications of the eschatological salvation experience of the resurrection of the crucified Jesus Christ for the idea of God. More than this, however, it has a fundamental

93. Dalferth, *Existenz Gottes und christlicher Glaube*, 193–237.

regulatory function for the whole Christian understanding of the self and of reality: it is the fundamental grammar of the Christian life of faith.

If one understands the doctrine of the Trinity in this way, then it is not a speculative theory concerning the inner life of God but an eminently practical doctrinal statement. It seeks to do justice to the salvific nature and the person-involving power—which we call faith—of the eschatological experience of God's saving activity in Jesus Christ by speaking of God not from the theoretical (external) perspective of an observer, but by adopting the basic linguistic images of the Christian faith into the practical (internal) perspective of believers. Christian believers do not affirm God to be just the one to whom they owe their very being, and indeed everything else, so that it is impossible to conceive of anything actual or potential that can be excluded "from origination by God."[94] They first and foremost affirm God to be the one from whom everyone can expect all that is good, because he has revealed himself once and for all in Jesus Christ and through the Holy Spirit as the one whose entire meaning and purpose is love and is thus always and everywhere at work as love. Hence, in their confession of faith, believers express their certainty that they and all other created beings owe themselves, in their entirety, to God's creative love and life-renewing nearness, which constitute the source of all life, even when they are ignored or impugned.

This certainty, affirmed from the participatory perspective of faith, opens up the doctrine of the Trinity, taking this very perspective as its starting point. To that extent, it takes the form of a critical reflection of faith itself. It opens up this certainty in such a way as to give insight into its origin: it goes beyond the confession of faith by going back to its origin and basing its legitimization of the certainty of the confessors on the truth of what is confessed. And it accomplishes this by making clear, in the form of a regulatory system, that believers are right to confess God in this way, since this allows the idea of God to be defined in the way God defined and disclosed himself in Jesus Christ and through the Holy Spirit: as inexhaustible creative love.

### 7.1. On the Linguistic Form of the Doctrine of the Trinity

The linguistic form of the third person, in which this doctrinal statement is commonly formulated, can easily lead us astray. When the doctrine of the Trinity speaks of Father, Son, and Spirit, it is not describing God as such; it is reminding us that God himself (as distinct from our ideas and conceptions of God) is either known in the second-person mode of those who address God in

---

94. Schleiermacher, *Christian Faith*, 149.

response to his self-communicating presence in the first-person mode ("I am your God") as "*our* Father" and "*my* Lord" or is not known at all. There is no knowledge of God worthy of the name that does not go back to the fact that God makes himself present to us in such a way that the object of our knowledge of God is simultaneously discernible to us as its sole origin. This active and effective presence of God cannot be communicated directly but only in signs, if we are to be able to survive it and perceive it as the presence and nearness of God. But neither its intelligible communication as such nor the presence of God on its own constitutes knowledge of God. We arrive at such knowledge only when we experience both at once: the communication of God's presence in signs and the explanation that this is what is being communicated.

All three elements of genuine (i.e., saving) knowledge of God—the initiative of God alone; the direct presence, in the course of a human person's life, of God with a human person who acknowledges him; and the intelligible communication of God's presence to the human person who acknowledges him—are combined in the Christian understanding of God as Father (God's initiative), Son (God's intelligible communication), and Spirit (God's direct presence with us) in a fundamental manner. For as Christians confess, the God who has always been near to us in his creative capacity has made himself present to us in Jesus Christ and through the Holy Spirit in a way we can understand; time and again he makes his presence intelligible to us anew through the good news of Jesus Christ and the affirming witness of the Spirit. But in the process of God's making himself clearly present to us as love, the second-person mode is never dispensed with: God is only ever known as *my* or *our* God by those who respond to the presence of God in first-person discourse (I, we) by addressing God in a second-person mode (You). It is therefore impossible for us to perceive God's saving presence in Jesus Christ and his presence with us in the Spirit without responding with doxology, prayer, a confession of faith, and repentance. True knowledge of God (i.e., knowledge of the creative nearness of God, the God whose saving and redemptive character is disclosed and communicated to us through Jesus Christ) is to be found only where people are enabled through the Spirit to lead a life oriented to God's presence in Jesus Christ, by experiencing their acceptance through the Spirit into the presence of God as interpreted by Jesus, and where they express this by confessing their faith in God's unmerited love. In formulating this internal doxological perspective on God, the doctrine of the Trinity speaks of God in the second-person mode, even, in fact, where it uses third-person language to interpret the combined images of Father, Son, and Spirit.

So the doctrine of the Trinity offers no definitive concept of God, but it gives particular emphasis to the fundamental and irrevocable distinction

between God and all our images, models, ideas, and concepts of God; between
the primordial creative reality of love that we call "God" and our many and
various figurative, pictorial, and conceptual attempts to consider this divine
reality. When Christians describe Jesus Christ as God's revelation of himself,
it is not because he finally gave clear expression to our vague natural understanding of God, but because he takes the inherent understanding of God
we somehow or other had always seemed to possess, calls it critically into
question, and exposes it as a problematic idol. But in his person and story
he shows us that God is present with us and that the creative power of his
love within our world exceeds all that we can grasp and all our attempts to
comprehend it using symbols that hold it at arm's length.[95] This is because
God comes nearer to us than we ever can to him, or to ourselves, through the
use of symbols to aid our thought, imagination, and apprehension.[96] God's
nearness, so much greater than any idea of God of which we are capable,
is what is emphasized by the doctrine of the Trinity. Hence it insists that
to really be about God, all Christian discourse concerning God must relate
to the eschatological reality of the self-mediating presence of God in Jesus
Christ and through the Spirit. In doing this, it has a regulatory rather than
a descriptive function. In the form of a rule complex, it expresses that the
Christian understanding considers our thought of God to be adequate when,
and only when, we observe the following:

- there is a fundamental difference between God and our ideas of God;
- in Jesus Christ God disclosed himself as love, so that here—and only
  here—despite all of God's beyond-comprehensibility, it is possible to
  speak of an even greater comprehensibility;
- without the presence of God in the Spirit and his self-mediation in Jesus
  Christ, we cannot truly know God and thus cannot reorient and reshape
  our lives accordingly in the light of God's love; and
- we can never fully apprehend or take conceptual control of the creative power of God's love as disclosed in Jesus Christ, but must remain
  perpetually open to new and unexpected aspects of this love.

God is thus not a completely incomprehensible and dark mystery; he
can be experienced and understood as love. But the creativity of this love is
greater than anything we can think or imagine. Hence we cannot formulate
an adequate concept of God's love or domesticate it conceptually to some

95. Cf. Williams, "Trinity and Revelation," 203.
96. Dalferth, *Gott*, 8–15.

degree for our human use. It evades all our attempts to bring it under control with our symbols, models, images, ideas, or attitudes. It is the inexhaustible mystery, the unfathomable source, and the unsurpassable future of the whole of creation and its creative progress toward the ever more complete realization of this love. We can recognize an outline of what this encompasses only by adhering to the eschatological pattern of Jesus's life, death, and resurrection. But—and this is the basis of the Christian hope—we believe that his story is the paradigm of all our stories and that the manifestation of God's life-giving love in his life is the promise and confirmation of what will prove, in our life and in each life, to be the ultimate reality. What this means in detail and how it will be realized in concrete terms, we do not know, because it is interpreted and demonstrated not *coram mundo* [before the world] but *coram deo* [before God] and thus only from the inner perspective of each life. God's love works underground most of the time and likes to operate in secret, so much so that we can often barely perceive it even in our own life. It is not in view of our own life experience, however, but with Jesus Christ in view that we can have the certain hope that God's creative love, which manifested itself eschatologically in the resurrection of Jesus Christ, will complete its silent work of change in each life and will thus achieve its objective of transforming the whole creation into a free and perfect mirror of God's goodness and love.

### 7.2. The Doctrine of the Trinity as a Regulatory System for "God"

The doctrine of the Trinity provides us with a grammar for accurate speech and thought concerning God on the basis of the Christian salvation experience of the raising of the crucified one and the love of God disclosed therein. It does this in the form of a system of rules that set out the elements to which we should give attention, in our thought and speech concerning God, so as to preserve the specificity of the Christian experience of God, the precision of Christian thought about God, and the universality of the Christian claim to truth and validity: nothing deserves to be called God that cannot be addressed as "*my* God." I cannot *justifiably* address anything as "God" unless—under appropriate conditions—it could be addressed as "God" by *everyone else as well*. Nothing can justifiably be addressed as "God" by anyone unless it is *itself the basis* on which it can be and is addressed as God. Nothing could be this basis unless it determines itself through and through; that is to say, it not only determines *that* it is and *what* it is and that it determines *itself* to be what it is, but it also determines *that* it can be determined by something other than itself, *how* it is determined by the other, and *as what* it is thereby determined.

This has two important implications: the *uniqueness* and the irrevocably *specific nature* of God. On the one hand, nothing else could be considered as God in the manner described above, if indeed anything at all can justifiably be considered as such. For if it is at all possible to consider a being who determines itself with absolute freedom, then there can be no other that can with equal justification be considered as such, since the totality of God's self-determination otherwise would be negated, and the idea of such a being would be invalidated as self-contradictory. On the other hand, however, nothing could with good reason be considered to be such a being if it were not clear that something, at any rate, can be considered as such. But this clarity cannot be achieved merely by analyzing the idea of such a being. For even if it were clear that it is possible to consider such a being (i.e., the idea is not meaningless), it would still be far from clear that there must be, or actually is, something that can be considered as such (i.e., the idea is justified). If this is the case, then it cannot be deduced from this idea itself and as such. Rather, the converse is true: if this idea is meaningful and justified, it is only because God has revealed himself thus. Precisely this is what the Christian confession of faith in God takes as its starting point. Christian thought and speech use the term *God* to refer to the one whose meaning and purpose is love through and through and who is therefore at work always and everywhere as the one who he disclosed himself to be in Jesus Christ and continually discloses himself to be through the Holy Spirit: as inexhaustible creative love. It is only where this christological precision and this pneumatological self-determination by God are taken into account that God is perceived specifically as love; accordingly, it is only there that we can properly speak of God. And since it is only where God is perceived in specific terms that God is perceived at all, the doctrine of the Trinity insists on this christological and pneumatological specificity of all speech and thought of God.

The historical development of the trinitarian regulatory system involving specific, definitive, and universal thought and speech concerning God followed a somewhat tortuous route that we will not trace here.[97] Augustine's theology of the Trinity became definitive in the West and was concisely summarized in the *Quicunque*, the so-called *Symbolum Athanasianum* [Athanasian Creed].[98] The Athanasian Creed's central affirmations concerning the God whom the Christian faith confesses and worships are as follows:

97. For the historical aspect, see G. Kretschmar, *Studien zur frühchristlichen Trinitätstheologie* (Tübingen: Mohr Siebeck, 1956); Pannenberg, *Systematic Theology*, 1:259–336; A. M. Ritter, "Dogma und Lehre in der Alten Kirche," in *Handbuch der Dogmen- und Theologiegeschichte*, ed. C. Andresen and A. M. Ritter (Göttingen: Vandenhoeck & Ruprecht, 1982–88), 1:99–283.
98. *BSLK* 28–29.

1. The *fides catholica* [catholic faith] worships *unum Deum in trinitate et trinitatem in unitate* [one God in Trinity and Trinity in unity]. The unity is thought of under the concept of the substance (*substantia*), the Trinity under that of the three persons (*personae*). The rule established is that one is thinking and speaking of God correctly only if, on the one hand, the distinction among the persons is preserved so that they are not confounded and, on the other hand, the divine substance is neither divided nor separated but is held to be one and the same in respect to all three persons. If this rule is not observed, the result is either an undifferentiated (mono-)theism or an untenable tritheism, resulting in a use of "God" that is other than Christian.

2. The unity of the divine substance is presented in the form of a system of divine attributes—indicated by means of examples and without any claim to completeness. These attributes are properties of all three persons alike and together constitute God's divinity (*divinitas*) in its glory (*gloria*) and eternal majesty (*maiestas*). Accordingly, the rule is that nothing deserves to be called God unless the terms *divinitas* and, therefore, also *gloria* and *aeterna maiestas* can truly be applied to it, and that these terms can legitimately be applied only to the one defined (at the very least) by the attributes *increatus*, *immensus, aeternus*, and *omnipotens* [uncreated, incomprehensible, eternal, and omnipotent] and thus rightly be addressed as *Deus* and *Dominus*.

3. The distinction among the persons, under their descriptive titles of Father, Son, and Holy Spirit, serves to indicate that the one divine substance is manifest in the Father, the Son, and the Spirit alike. Accordingly, each of them is defined alike through the divine attributes and can accurately be addressed as "God" and "Lord" without thereby giving rise to a plural form that would convey the idea of *tres Dei* [three Gods] or *tres Domini* [three Lords]. Hence, the relationship of Father, Son, and Spirit to the divine substance is not the same as the relationship of particular individuals (human beings) to their species and genus (the human race). For one thing, a species or genus can be defined only in comparison with and in distinction from other species and genera. But it is impossible to define the divine substance by means of comparison and differentiation in this way, because God cannot be identified and characterized within the system of what can be perceived and conceptually defined: God is not a particular instance of a general class, and God's divinity is not something general that can be illustrated by means of particular instances, even if there is only one such instance. For another, this conceptual relationship between the general and the particular, which is acquired from and appropriate to our realm of experience, cannot be applied to the relationship of the divine substance to Father, Son, and Spirit; this derives from the fact that God is not just one but unique and singular (*unus*). Nothing is therefore

rightly called God unless it is absolutely specific and is so unique in every respect that no meaningful distinction can be made between the general and the particular. How then is this relationship of Father, Son, and Spirit to the divine substance to be defined?

4. The *Quicunque*'s answer is by seeking to explicate the specific singularity of God by describing the unique relations between Father, Son, and Spirit. Only in and through these relations, which cannot be generalized but are unique and specific, do the Father, Son, and Spirit realize the divine substance in such a way that each of them can rightly be called *Deus* and *Dominus* without it being possible or necessary to speak of *tres Dei* or *Domini*. Hence, the following is true of the Father: "*a nullo est factus, nec creatus, nec genitus* [is made of none, neither created nor begotten]"; of the Son: "*a patre solo est, non factus nec creatus, sed genitus* [is of the Father alone; not made nor created, but begotten]"; and of the Spirit: "*a patre et filio, non factus nec creatus nec genitus, sed procedens* [is of the Father and of the Son; neither made nor created nor begotten, but proceeding]."[99] With the aid of a limited number of descriptive images (make, create, beget, begotten, proceed), Father, Son, and Spirit are portrayed in such a way that the sum of these differential definitions gives equal expression to both their characteristic relatedness and their distinctions. A system of comparison perspectives is therefore set out, under which it is possible to state what distinguishes Father, Son, and Spirit from one another without turning them into special instances subsumed under these comparative perspectives. The later doctrine of the Trinity therefore sought to systematize this statement in the form of four basic rules.

- Father, Son, and Spirit may be characterized in their unique relationship to one another by five *notiones personales* [personal notions]: The identifying characteristic of the Father in relation to himself is *innascabilitas* [innascability]; in relation to the Son, *generatio activa* [active generation] (or *paternitas* [paternity]); and, in relation to the Spirit, *spiratio activa* [active spiration]. Similarly, the identifying characteristic of the Son in relation to the Father is *generatio passiva* [passive generation] (or *filiatio* [filiation]) and, in relation to the Spirit, *spiratio activa* [active spiration]—the latter being rejected in the East. And finally, the identifying characteristic of the Spirit in relation to the Father (and the Son) is *spiratio passiva* [passive spiration].
- Accordingly, among Father, Son, and Spirit there are four relations: *generatio activa* and *passiva* and *spiratio activa* and *passiva*.

99. *BSLK* 29, lines 20–22.

- Father, Son, and Spirit are thus each characterized by one of three *pro-prietates personales* [personal properties]: the Father by *innascabilitas* [innascability], the Son by *filiatio* [filiation], and the Spirit by *spiratio passiva* [passive spiration] (i.e., *processio* [procession]).
- The relationship of Father, Son, and Spirit is thus ultimately character-ized by two *processiones* [processions]: the generation of the Son by the Father and the *spiratio* of the Spirit by the Father and the Son.

Despite its quasi-conceptual wording, the point of these rules is missed if they are construed as an attempt at a conceptual systematization of the relationship of Father, Son, and Spirit. The opposite is true: their objective is precisely not that these concepts should be subsumed under universal concepts but that the specific uniqueness of God should be preserved. They seek to do this by describing the unique relationships of Father, Son, and Spirit to one another in such a way that the description itself makes clear that these relationships cannot be unfolded conceptually and collected into a discursive system of thought operating with the concept of the difference between the general and the particular and the conceptual relationships of judgment and conclusion. Hence, the description of the relationships of Father, Son, and Spirit does use *images* instead of *concepts*: the images of making, creating, begetting, being born, and proceeding. The use of these images protects them from being understood as conceptual analogies, since interpreting them as concepts results in absurd, meaningless statements. This is what results from the use of negation, paradox, and empty semantic formulas that state, with regard to the Father, that all these images do *not* apply to him; with regard to the Son, that he was *born from the Father alone*; or, with regard to the Spirit, that he proceeds from the Father and the Son, *without* being something made, created, or born from them. Conceptual reading of all these assertions tells us *nothing*; neither the character of the Father, Son, and Spirit, nor indeed the nature of the relationship between them, is determined. When these descriptions are understood as images, everything changes. Images do not function according to the logic of a comprehension involving subsump-tion. They do not define the Father, Son, and Spirit as instances of what they express; instead, they open up a specific context of meaning within which it is possible to speak intelligibly of Father, Son, and Spirit. Images help us to localize something within contexts of meaning in which it can be understood, even if the concepts involved have not yet been opened up or are impossible to open up. In contrast to opposing concepts, opposing images can be used together without a problem, without preventing each other from fulfilling their function of aiding understanding and without canceling each other out.

They open up perspectives on something by delineating, inferring, or localizing it in the context of a specific field of imagery, and they bring about (the
possibility of) understanding, because they do not fix the attention on what
they say but, instead, steer it toward what they are seeking to bring into the
foreground with the aid of what they say. Images differ from concepts therefore
in that, in order to understand images, it is not enough to understand their
internal structure of meaning. Instead, one must allow them to draw one into
an independent acceptance of what they seek to illuminate with the aid of the
context of meaning they embody. Images do not apprehend or represent the
subject on which they focus; instead, they indicate ways in which the subject
may be understood and made one's own: they are signposts to the subject
under discussion, not disguised judgments on it. In order to grasp the point
of the trinitarian rules for correct speech concerning God that are offered
by the *Quicunque*, therefore, we must pay attention to two things: they use
*images rather than concepts* to speak of Father, Son, and Spirit; and these
images must be understood and interpreted in a *nonanalogous* way. Both of
these principles are rooted in the uniqueness of what they seek to express in
specific terms: the Godhead of Father, Son, and Spirit.[100]

They mark two boundary points that were crossed time and again during the
later development of the doctrine of the Trinity, so that it continually became
an example of theological self-misunderstandings. Hence, every attempt to
encompass the doctrine of the Trinity in the thought forms of concept, judgment, and conclusion is misleading and doomed to failure from the outset
since the doctrine itself thinks in images, not conceptually. Any attempt to
interpret the trinitarian images analogously, based on the relationships and
experiences familiar from our own lives, however, is equally wide of the mark.
While the traditions of speculative theology are an example of the first of these
attempts, the second is found principally in the approaches currently taken by
experience-oriented feminist and (deep) psychological theology. In both cases
the approach is, in its different ways, generalizing instead of specific, in that
the trinitarian theological images are misunderstood as extendable concepts or
as copies of our life experience. But they are images that are trying to express
something unique and specific that cannot be generalized: namely, what the

---

100. Both are always overlooked when—as, for example, in W. Joest, *Dogmatik*, vol. 1.1,
*Die Wirklichkeit Gottes* (Göttingen: Vandenhoeck & Ruprecht, 1984), 326—reference is made
to the "development of concepts" by which "the doctrine of the Trinity . . . reaches the margins
of what can comprehensibly be said," because its "concepts such as 'beget' or 'breathe' . . .
bear no further relation to the real content of these human words," so that "every analogous
context" for this way of talking about God using our normal speech breaks down and we have
to ask whether "anything is still actually being said" here.

Christian faith speaks of when it says "God." It is true that these images are expressed in terminology used elsewhere; however, their sense is to be deduced not from the semantics of the terms used but from the unique history of divine activity that is summarized and encapsulated with their help: God's saving activity, which reached its eschatological pinnacle in the raising of the crucified one and is affirmed time and again, through the work of the Spirit, in faith in the manifest saving presence of God. The fundamental statements of trinitarian theology are thus understood not as a result of these images either being further developed in their semantic structure by applying term logic within the context of a philosophical theory, or being interpreted, illustrated, or criticized from the point of view of (social) history or (deep) psychology on the basis of ordinarily accessible life experiences. Both choose a generalizing approach, albeit a different one in each case, rather than a specific one. In order to understand the specific meaning of these images, we should not start from the images as such, with their consistently philosophical or anthropological sense, open as it is to generalization; instead, we should consider their *usage and its specific context*. The significance of this usage becomes clear if, and only if, these images are related back to the stories and confessions that faith initially used and still uses to express God's saving activity.[101] Accordingly, the trinitarian rules for the use of "God" are to be understood as a grammar *of the Christian use* of the basic images with which the Christian faith speaks of God in specific terms.

This grammar is tied not to the images of the *Quicunque* in themselves but to their peculiar usage and, hence, to the story they encapsulate and summarize. It seeks to formulate the rules of this usage, not the semantic implications of the images, which is why it can be transferred to other image sequences and explicated with their help. The following section will show how this can happen with reference to three sets of images and ideas: love, life, and activity.

### 7.3. God's Love, Life, and Activity

Every such reshaping of the doctrine of the Trinity must keep two tasks in mind. First, the grammar regulating the use of "God" must be set forth. Second, the scope of "God" must be described; in other words, one must indicate the subject area to which this regulated use of "God" relates.

In the dogmatic tradition both tasks are in fact dealt with under the key concepts of the *immanent* Trinity (i.e., the Trinity within the Godhead) and the *economic* Trinity (i.e., the Trinity in salvation history). Admittedly,

---

101. Cf. Dalferth, *Religiöse Rede von Gott*, 668–78.

for the most part these doctrines were understood differently. The doctrine of the immanent Trinity was conceived of as the portrayal of the inner life of God, which "was understood as the quasi-ontological premise of the trinitarian revelation of salvation."[102] Similarly, the doctrine of the economic Trinity was presented as a speculation, from the point of view of salvation history or historical theology, concerning the three ages or kingdoms of the Father, the Son, and the Spirit. Both of the above are examples of an overly hasty, realistic reading of the trinitarian doctrinal statements as descriptions of the nature and work of the Trinity. This approach leads to fundamental methodological and factual difficulties when we observe that the "doctrine of the Trinity . . . does not belong directly to the content of the revelation, nor is it a direct expression of faith."[103] But the real content of the trinitarian doctrine does not consist in using the word *Trinity* to name a being whose characteristic structure and modes of action are described in the doctrine of the immanent and economic Trinity. The word *Trinity* does not denote the subject matter dealt with by the doctrine of the Trinity; it summarizes the complex of rules that aid this doctrine in explicating the grammar of the Christian use of "God." When it is understood thus, the "immanent Trinity" does not describe the hidden inner life of God but rather summarizes the rules governing the use of "God." Similarly, the "economic Trinity" does not describe the work of Father, Son, and Spirit in salvation history; it sets out the (universal) range of reference covering this regulated use of "God" in Christian speech and thought.

Once this is taken into account, the basic structure of this grammar can be summarized as follows, using the sets of images and ideas associated with love, life, and activity:

1. *God's love.* The *God* confessed by the Christian faith is to be conceived of as the original and inexhaustible creative love, which has manifested itself with eschatological finality in the raising of the crucified one and finds its practical outworking in the faith, hope, and love of Christians produced by the Christian community's experience of the Spirit. The image of *love* proffers itself from the Johannine and Pauline writings because this basic image of the Christian faith gives equally appropriate expression both to the practical, normative principle of the life of the Christian community and also to its divine basis in the light of the raising of the crucified one, while disclosing what holds the world together at its core: the fact that true being-with-oneself, and hence the highest degree of freedom and joy, is realized in

---

102. Joest, *Wirklichkeit Gottes*, 324.
103. Ibid., 332.

loving being-with-others, given its tangible forms in eros, philia, and agape.[104] This image provides us with an accurate perception of *God* because the cross and resurrection of Jesus Christ have made it clear that God himself, in his being and actions, has freely determined not only to allow what is other than himself to exist but also to conduct his relationship with that other in such a way that the life, freedom, and free independence of the other are enabled and fostered, while safeguarding and respecting its otherness. This love characterizes *God's being*: not only does God love; he *is love* (i.e., he is fully defined as love), so that nothing can truly be said about God unless it characterizes him as a lover, whereas all other lovers except God can truly be defined and characterized, from other perspectives and viewpoints, in other ways.[105] This divine love must be called *original* because there can be nothing apart from itself from which it emanates. It is *inexhaustible* because there neither is nor could be anything that can nullify, limit, or restrict it. It is *creative* because everything other than it that is or can be must emanate from it, thus bearing out the final theological thesis of the Heidelberg Disputation of 1518: "*Amor Dei non invenit sed creat suum diligibile* [The love of God does not find but creates that which is pleasing to it]."[106] It has *eschatological finality* because there neither is nor can be anything that could induce or move God to define himself as other than that which is expressed in the raising of the crucified one. And it is *specific* because it is God's self-definition, which is not limited to God himself but has an effect on creation and is recognizably experienced in the life of the Christian community.

2. *God's life*. The dynamic and efficacy of this love as which God is defined and perceived require and entitle us to speak of the *life of God* against the background of this basic image. This life manifests itself as the primordial self-perpetuating process of divine self-differentiation and self-relationship that gives specificity to the love of God.[107] In this process the love of God is crystallized through the establishment of internal and external distinctions in endlessly new forms in the following manner.

First, in this process by which his love is crystallized, God constitutes himself as himself, independently of any contradistinction vis-à-vis the other,

---

104. Cf. G. Meckenstock, "Liebe," in *Gute Werke*, ed. W. Härle and R. Preul, Marburger Jahrbuch Theologie 5 (Marburg: Elwert, 1993), 63–93, esp. 76 and 81–93.

105. Dalferth, *Existenz Gottes und christlicher Glaube*, 212–26.

106. WA 1:365, line 2.

107. I use "self-differentiation" in the same sense as W. Pannenberg uses "self-distinction" to mean "that the one who distinguishes himself from another defines himself as also dependent on that other" (*Systematic Theology*, 1:313). The element of self-relationship is therefore already given within the concept of self-differentiation, and the same applies conversely to the concept of self-relationship.

in the sense that he lives in permanent perichoretic self-differentiation and self-relationship as the one God, Father, Son, and Spirit.[108] Thus nothing deserves to be called God if it emanates from something other than itself; nothing emanates wholly and exclusively from itself unless it can be understood as an original and inexhaustible act of trinitarian self-differentiation; and nothing can properly be understood thus unless it is defined as the self-actualization of love.

Second, because of this self-constitution through internal self-differentiation, God is in a position to determine freely that what is other than himself may exist, by differentiating himself from it and it from himself, in order to manifest his love specifically in, through, and for what is other than himself. Thus nothing deserves to be called God unless it functions as a creator on the basis of free self-determination and not through inner necessity.

Finally, by means of this internal and external process of differentiation, God profiles himself vis-à-vis all that is other than himself and that he has enabled and brought forth, as the one and only God; and the greater the independence with which the creation develops and expands its own complexity, the clearer the affirmation of this difference. Thus nothing deserves to be called God unless, as the creation develops, it differentiates itself more and more clearly from the creation as its creator. The consummation of the creation is thus to be conceived of not as the elimination of the distinction between creator and creation in a panentheistic absorption of the creation in God but as the unequivocal and comprehensive affirmation of this distinction in the universal acknowledgment of God the creator by his creatures—in other words (as Luther would have put it), in the universal fulfillment of the first commandment.

3. *God's activity.* The self-differentiation and self-relationship that gives specificity to the love of God is not something that happens to God; it is the manner in which God is and lives. God's life can therefore be conceived of as *original self-activity* or *original action.*[109] This original self-activity cannot be ascribed to a subject that may be distinguished from it in such a way that it would be possible to distinguish between God's being and God's activity: God's being is his activity,[110] God himself is the original activity of love, and his actions are constantly and consistently the acts of love, both where he himself is concerned and, equally, where an other is concerned. It is therefore not possible to refer accurately to anything as God unless it has defined itself

---

108. Dalferth, *Existenz Gottes und christlicher Glaube*, 199–205.

109. Ibid., 203–26.

110. Cf. Dalferth, *Gott*, 95–127; G. Ebeling, *Dogmatik des christlichen Glaubens*, vol. 1, part 1, *Der Glaube an Gott den Schöpfer der Welt* (Tübingen: Mohr Siebeck, 1979), 230–35.

as the self-actualization of inexhaustible love. And nothing can be accurately said about God unless it is shown to be a qualification of his acts of love: God's "attributes" or "perfections" are therefore to be explicated as *characteristics of his loving activity*,[111] and all God's activities or actions as *manifestations of his loving activity*.

If God is conceived of as the original activity of love, then the structural elements of the concept of action used in the image of *God's activity* are accentuated in a specific way. Four points make this particularly clear.

1. *Distinguishability of action and actor*. Even if the originality of God's activity makes it impossible to attribute it to a subject that may be distinguished from it, the question "Who is acting?" can still be meaningfully asked and answered, because and to the extent that God's activity is always real and specific. The answer to this question is found by reference to the particular manifestation of the action that makes it transparent and recognizable for us: the eschatological self-identification of God in Jesus Christ, which Christians pick up and retain by identifying God as *Father*, *Son*, and *Spirit*. Accordingly, God's activity is always, everywhere, and in every respect to be conceived of as the activity of Father, Son, and Spirit, and God himself is to be conceived of as the one who acts as Father, Son, and Spirit, thus manifesting the love that he is.

2. *Connection and recognition*. Activity, as Schleiermacher showed in a paradigmatic way,[112] cannot be thought of as universally solipsistic. Rather, every activity takes place in the context of other activities, and to that extent it always connects with other activities and is intended to be continued in further activities. In other words, all actions are interactions. They have a social, deep structure and presuppose a community that is continually regenerated through every action. This is possible only to the extent that every action is accessible to some other activity (i.e., can be identified and understood as action in and through some other, epistemic action). This in turn presupposes that in every case it is possible to distinguish between action and actor, and that there is a recognizable actor manifesting himself in the activity—both the activity that does the connecting, and the activity with which it connects. Since (social) actions always connect with other actions, there must always be recognition of the one who acts.

It is essential to bear in mind these structural elements of the concept of action where the image of God's original activity of love is concerned as

111. Dalferth, *Gott*, 214–25.
112. Cf. M. Moxter, *Güterbegriff und Handlungstheorie: Eine Studie zur Ethik Friedrich Schleiermachers* (Kampen: Peeters, 1992), esp. chap. 4.

well. Given that God's activity is original activity (i.e., it cannot be attributed to anything other than God himself), any of his activities can connect only either with another of God's own activities or with an activity by one other than God that, for its part, is attributable to God's activity; similarly, it can be continued only in another activity by God or in an activity that is other than God's. In the first instance, God's activity of love connects with God's activity of love, presupposing an internal differentiation between these occasions of God's activity or actions. This is in fact what the dogmatic tradition meant by the key concept of the *opera trinitatis ad intra* [internal operations of the Trinity]. In the second instance, God's activity of love connects with something that was enabled and brought forth by this activity in the first place, thus presupposing an external difference between God and what is other than God: This is what the dogmatic tradition meant by the key concept of the *opera trinitatis ad extra* [external operations of the Trinity].

a. *Opera ad intra* [internal operations]. God's activity of love, as the *original* activity of love, cannot connect with anything distinct from itself. But it can connect only with itself insofar as there is a difference between God and God that can be perceived and defined as the self-differentiation of God's activity of love. If this were not possible, the image of God's activity would be useless as a model for conceiving of God. The Christian idea of God conceived of this self-differentiation of God's activity of love (with its link to Jesus's proclamation of God, its extension in the cross and resurrection of Jesus Christ, and the associated experience of the Spirit) by differentiating between *Father*, *Son*, and *Spirit*. God's activity of love is self-connected and self-differentiating inasmuch as God's love manifests itself in concrete terms as the unified activity of Father, Son, and Spirit, jointly but differently enacted by Father, Son, and Spirit. The following integral and inseparable enactments of God's love may therefore be distinguished:

- Father and Son: the love of the Father for the Son
- Son and Father: the love of the Son for the Father
- Father and Spirit: the love of the Father through the Spirit
- Spirit and Father: the love of the Spirit as the extension of the love of the Father for the Son
- Son and Spirit: the love of the Son through the Spirit
- Spirit and Son: the love of the Spirit as the extension of the love of the Son for the Father

These enactments are separate and distinctive in that they are characterized in each case by different relationships of connection and recognition. Hence the love of the Father, in its primordial freedom, brings forth the Son, in the sense that the Father distinguishes between himself and the Son; acknowledges him as a distinctive Other, the object of his love; and appoints him to take up and extend his divine activity of love. Conversely, the love of the Son for the Father connects with the love of the Father, in the sense that the Son acknowledges him as the Father to whom he owes himself entirely, purposing that, in his self-differentiation from the Father, he will reciprocate this love to which he owes his very self. But the love of the Father for the Son would not be accessible as such to the Son, and hence something to which he could connect, were it not enacted through the Spirit; and the love of the Son for the Father could not acknowledge him as Father were it not enacted through the Spirit. Consequently, the Spirit proceeds in equal measure from, and originates equally in, the love of the Father for the Son and the love of the Son for the Father (*filioque*). He is not this love, as was held by the Augustinian tradition, but he is the one in and through whom this love is enacted, who makes it transparent, and in whom therefore—inasmuch as he is acknowledged as such by Father and Son—the acknowledgment of the Son by the Father and the Father by the Son is rooted. Hence, as the complete self-transparency of God's activity, the Spirit is not just the condition for the link between the love of the Son and that of the Father; he is also the ground and medium for the acknowledgment of the Son by the Father and the Father by the Son. The love of the Spirit in turn is ultimately, on the one hand (formulated from the point of view of the Father), the extension of the Father's love for the Son onto another object, and on the other hand (formulated from the point of view of the Son), the extension of the Son's love for the Father from another subject. Just as with the Father it is the basic principle of the love of God, and with the Son it is the principle of the otherness and specificity of this love that is conceived of,[113] so too with the Spirit it is the principle of the extension of God's love to what is other than God and simultaneously the principle of the gathering in of all love for God into the love of the Son for the Father. The Spirit is thus not just the one through whom the love between Father and Son is enacted; he is also the one who extends this love beyond Father and Son to what is other than God and who draws this other into the love between Father and Son.

113. Cf. Pannenberg, *Systematic Theology*, 2:22 and passim.

In the *Father*, therefore, the process of the self-actualization of God's love finds its inexhaustible ground; in the *Son* it finds the principle of its specificity; and in the *Spirit* it finds the principle of its openness and unity. In that God is conceived of as Father, Son, and Spirit, he is conceived of as unique, actual, and universal at one and the same time: only he (as Father) owes his existence solely to himself; only he (as Son) manifests himself in concrete terms entirely as love, which is his meaning and purpose; and only he (as Spirit) draws everything into the process of this love while safeguarding its otherness and freedom.

    b. *Opera ad extra* [external operations]. As the original *activity of love*, God's activity is not confined to himself but is designed to be continued in other loving activity and in the loving activity of others. The activity of others can connect with this divine loving activity, provided that three conditions are fulfilled. (1) There are those who are other than God whom God, in his loving activity as Father, Son, and Spirit, acknowledges as different from himself and from whom he expects and hopes for a reciprocal acknowledgment of himself as God. (2) The activity of Father and Son is identified as free love and as such is revealed as love both for himself and for others in the activity of the Spirit. (3) As the activity of the Spirit, this divine activity of love is intended from the outset to widen the love between Father and Son to that which is other than God and to draw those who are other than God into the love between Son and Father. The fulfillment of these three conditions is what the Christian idea of God has in mind when it identifies God as *creator*, *reconciler*, and *consummator*. All that is, was, will be, and can be is thus marked out as God's sphere of action and as the reference range of Christian discourse concerning "God," so that the specificity and the universality of Christian discourse concerning God are honored in equal measure.

Creation, reconciliation, and consummation are aspects of God's action and, as such, actualizations of the love that God is. The different interactions between Father, Son, and Spirit, which in their diversity are essential elements of the divine activity of love, are also essential to the extension of this activity to that which is other than God. But Father, Son, and Spirit participate jointly, each in his own way, in creation, reconciliation, and consummation, since it is only in their cooperative action that God's activity is accomplished as the creative, loving activity that enables the connection and recognition of others.

    Given that God's activity of love is intended to connect with activity other than God's (or does indeed connect with such activity), it organizes itself in terms of a structure that expresses the relationship among creation, reconciliation, and consummation. On this basis, creation is God's positing, freely undertaken out of love, of that which is other than God and of its acceptance as other than God (*creatio ex nihilo*), which means that everything that is different from God owes its possible and actual existence to God. It would not exist if God had not desired it for its own sake, and it exists for a double reason: not only did God not *not* desire it, but he positively *did* desire it. But then the creation is the prerequisite, on the basis of which God's activity of love can connect with activity other than God's in reconciliation and consummation. At the same time, God cannot connect with any such activity without simultaneously connecting with his creation activity. In this respect reconciliation and consummation may also always be understood as extensions of God's creation activity: Reconciliation is the mode of God's creative activity of love by which he confirms himself to us in creation as our creator. Consummation, in contrast, is the mode by which individual and ultimately all created beings come to acknowledge God as their creator on the basis of God's reconciling activity. In this respect God's creation activity establishes the preconditions for acknowledging him as the loving creator; within the environment of creation his reconciling activity affirms the truth and justice of this creation activity, so that within the context of creation itself God is shown to be its loving creator, who acknowledges his creatures as independent counterparts, and of whose own acknowledgment he too is worthy; and his consummating activity brings about the reality that is the aim of his creative and reconciling activity: his creatures' free acknowledgment of God as their creator.

3. *Intentionality*. Actions are different from events or occurrences, in that an intention—which under certain circumstances is standardized in a social convention—or a specific desire underlies their enactment. If there is no suggestion of this, the term *action* cannot be used meaningfully. Actions can therefore always be the subject of meaningful questions about their purpose and their aim: they have a meaning that can be understood, they present problems of understanding, and they permit us to inquire seriously into their meaning. All of this also applies to God's activity. If creation, reconciliation, and consummation are conceived of as the activity of Father, Son, and Spirit, it must be possible to inquire into the meaning, purpose, and aim of this activity. The answer to these questions unfolds from the identification of creation, reconciliation, and consummation as actualizations of the love that God is. Their meaning, purpose, and aim consist in the actualization of this love in different ways: as creation, in the creation, for the creation, and with the creation. And what this love comprises can be inferred precisely from the way in which it is given substance in God's creative, reconciling, and

consummating activity. It is in the confession of the Christian faith in Jesus
Christ through the Holy Spirit that love is revealed as the fundamental intent
of this entire context of divine activity. But just as an action can be perceived
and understood as such only when its underlying intention is perceived and
understood, so too God's activity is perceived and understood only by the one
who perceives and understands God's love as the fundamental intention of
creation, reconciliation, and consummation. But that can be perceived only
if and to the extent that God himself opens one's eyes to it. Christians call
this occurrence *faith*, and they explain this faith itself, to themselves and to
others, as an instance of God's loving activity: the particular instance that
convincingly reveals to us God's love as the fundamental intention of all his
activity. This brings us to the final point.

4. *Mediality*. Actions consist not just of an intention but of their realization by means of an outward enactment that affects another (or others) and
can be perceived by him or her (or them). This outward enactment requires
a medium, with the aid of which the underlying intention is implemented.
Where human activities are concerned, this medium is the body. All our activities are carried out physically: we can convert our intentions into actions
only by physical activities that change our environment.

We cannot disregard the mediality of activity where God's activity is concerned, either. But, in analogy to ourselves, if we conceive of this in terms of
the physical or the corporeal, there would seem to be an unavoidable dilemma
that threatens to dismantle the idea of God. For either God is essentially different from the world, in which case he is noncorporeal and cannot act, or
God can act and must consequently possess a body, so that he can no longer
be clearly distinguished from the world. In either case he can no longer be
conceived of as the one whom the Christian faith addresses and confesses as
God. For if, in common with the majority of the Christian tradition, we deny
God any kind of corporeality, then it would seem to be impossible to conceive
of God's relationship to the world as activity, or even, strictly speaking, as
causality, so that it no longer would be possible to conceive of the relationship
between God and the world at all. If, on the other hand, in common with
pantheistic schemes of thought, we identify God with the world (be it wholly,
in part, or in some respect), it not only is no longer necessary to conceive of
any relationship between God and the world; it also becomes impossible to
preserve the distinction between them. Time and again attempts are made to
bypass this dilemma either by seeking to conceive of God's activity excluding
any mediality or by defining the world in its entirety as the medium. Hence,
on the one hand, it is disputed that God's activity is structured medially, and
an attempt is made to show that a concept of noncorporeal or disembodied

action is reasonable and realizable and—in God's case—actually realized.[114] Given that the concept is only negatively defined (as *non*corporeal activity), we are left in doubt about how it should be understood in positive terms, what relevance such noncorporeal activity by God can have for our factual realm of experience, and how a being who acts in this way can be identified at all. As a result, others hold onto the mediality of God's activity and, on the premise of the distinction between the world and God, seek to conceive of the world as God's body while God himself is the soul of this body and hence to be conceived of as distinct from his world-body.[115] This ensures God's identifiability through the medium of the world as a whole. But such attempts tend to break down, not just because they generalize the conceptual model of soul and body in a questionable way and transfer that of living beings in the world onto the world as a whole.[116] They can preserve the distinction between God and the world only by making either the world into God's environment or God into the world's environment, and as a result they oscillate between pantheism and panentheism. Above all, however, they are too quick to make the assumption that the essential mediality of all activity, even God's, is to be perceived as corporeality, although, on the basis of the universality of God's activity, they equate it not simply with specific enactments in the world but with the world as a whole. But to take this assumption for granted creates a problem. If the world is understood as God's body, then it cannot be God's creation, which contradicts the Christian understanding of God and of the world. But if it is his creation and if God is the original activity of love, then the medium of his activity cannot be something different from God, since otherwise God would be dependent on something other than himself and would not be defined as the one who loves in creative freedom.[117] The

114. Cf. T. Penelhum, *Survival and Disembodied Existence* (London: Routledge and Kegan Paul, 1970), 37–44; R. H. King, *The Meaning of God* (Philadelphia: Fortress, 1974), 49–99; L. van den Brom, *Divine Presence in the World* (Kampen: Peeters, 1993), 34–70.

115. Cf. G. M. Jantzen, *God's World, God's Body* (London: Westminster John Knox Press, 1984); Ch. Taliaferro, "The Incorporeality of God," *Modern Theology* 3 (1987): 179–88; G. M. Jantzen, "Reply to Taliaferro," *Modern Theology* 3 (1987): 189–92; Th. T. Tracy, *God, Action, and Embodiment* (Grand Rapids: Eerdmans, 1984); W. D. Hudson, "Could the World Embody God?," in *Logical Foundations*, ed. I. Mahalingham and B. Carr (London: Macmillan, 1991), 172; M. Sarot, *God, Passibility and Corporeality* (Kampen: Peeters, 1992).

116. Most attempts of this type take place either against the background of the conceptions of Plato and Aristotle (cf. Dalferth, *Theology and Philosophy*, 21–34) or within the Cartesian tradition of a dualism of self and body (cf. R. Swinburne, *The Evolution of the Soul* [Oxford: Oxford University Press, 1986]; A. Peacocke, "God's Action in the Real World," *Zygon* 26 [1991]: 455–76, esp. 471; Peacocke, *Theology for a Scientific Age: Being and Becoming—Natural and Divine* [Oxford: Oxford University Press, 1990]).

117. This is true even if one seeks to understand God's dependence on what is other than God himself as his freely chosen self-determination to dependence.

world as the totality of all that is different from God can therefore not be conceived of, in an analogy to our body, as the medium through which God acts, without either the world being defined in some way as a dimension of God or God being defined as a dimension of the world. But this does not mean that there is no such medium or that God cannot act through what is of the world. Indeed, in the realm of the *opera trinitatis ad intra*, in which God's activity of love connects with nothing but itself, we have already seen that the medium by and through which the love between Father and Son is enacted is the *Spirit*: as Spirit, God himself constitutes the medium through which he realizes, spells out, and gives substance to his love. Exactly the same applies in the realm of the *opera ad extra*: given that the Spirit is not only the principle of the opening up and extension of God to that which is other than God but also the inclusion of that which is other than God in the love between Father and Son, he is the creative medium through which God acts. To put it in a nutshell, the "corporeality" of God's activity is the Spirit. It is through him that God realizes his intentions, including in relation to what is other than himself, in such a way that those intentions become real and discernible to the other(s). Thus it is through the Spirit that God acts in the creation as creator and as reconciler and consummator. So the Spirit is the source of the *materiality* of the creation, which is itself the medium of activity with which God connects in the realm of that which is different from him. But the Spirit is also the source of our *perception* of the creation; he is the insight into our creatureliness and the assurance of the truth of what God enables us to discern and understand about himself in and through Jesus Christ and his Spirit: that he is original and inexhaustible love.

The attempt to conceive of God as the original activity of love and so at one and the same time both to regulate the use of "God" and to describe the scope of "God" therefore requires us to unfold the concept of God's activity consistently in pneumatological terms: God's original activity of love is enacted in all his dimensions—in the perichoretic differentiation in God himself as well as in creation, reconciliation, and consummation—as the *work of the Spirit*. God is made actual in the work of the Spirit, in that he enacts his life as a process of self-actualization through the perichoretic differentiation between Father, Son, and Spirit.[118] Each is what it is only in and from within the others. God lives and makes his divine life eternally real through the continuous

118. In this respect *perichoresis* can be defined as the process, intrinsic to God's being, of the formation of personal differences in which God's life is actualized as love. This takes place in such a way that, as living love, it renders the finite (i.e., that which is other than God) as possible and actual, while binding it, as creation, to the creator in a manner distinct from all purely external relatedness. Thus, on the basis of his perichoretic differentiation as the ground

self-differentiation and self-relating of Father, Son, and Spirit. But this life is not a self-sufficient event. Rather, the point of God's self-actualization through the perichoretic differentiation and mutual indwelling of Father, Son, and Spirit is the realization of the love that God is. This love reaches far beyond itself and extends to what is other than itself: it is precisely as God's self-love that it is his love for the other. Hence it is fully realized only because, in his perichoretic self-relating, God simultaneously places himself in relationship to what is other than himself and opens his eternal life up to this other. His eternal life not only makes it possible for him to relate to the world; it implies that this relationship is the manner in which God freely conducts his life, since, in the work of the Spirit, he brings the world into being as its creator, relates to it as its reconciler, and, as its consummator, draws it into his perichoretic life as a creation distinct from himself. As Spirit, in the Spirit, and through the Spirit, God is therefore not just real and alive in himself; he draws nearer to all that is different from him than it can to itself by differentiating himself fundamentally as the One from the Many and by relating to them, thus including all the Many in his perichoretic being in such a way that this inclusion and integration become discernible to us created beings.[119] We live as creatures distinct from God because and to the extent that through God's Spirit we are caught up, time and again and further and further, into the perichoresis and the trinitarian being of God. To live as if this were not the case is sin. To discern and affirm it is faith.

---

of creation, God is at once both operative and at work in creation without thereby removing the difference between himself and it.

119. Cf. I. U. Dalferth, "Der Eine und das Viele," in *Pluralismus und Identität*, ed. J. Mehl-hausen (Gütersloh: Gütersloher Verlagshaus Mohn, 1995), 141–52.

# 5

# Atoning Sacrifice

## The Salvific Significance of the Death of Jesus

In the preceding chapters the resurrection has been interpreted with respect to the cross, the cross with respect to God, and the idea of God in the light of the cross and resurrection of Jesus; this has been done to outline the starting points and main features of Christology and the doctrine of God. This explicit reference back to God is vital because it is only from the point of view of God—understood in trinitarian terms in light of the cross and resurrection of Jesus—and not directly from the viewpoint of the cross event or of the life and death of Jesus himself that the salvific significance of this event is highlighted for us and the soteriological implications of the confession of Christ are unfolded. It is only at this point that the fundamental question can and must be asked: *What does God's activity in the cross and resurrection of Jesus mean for us and our world, and hence also for our correct understanding of ourselves and our world?*

---

Some of the material in this chapter appears in a slightly different form in I. U. Dalferth, "Christ Died for Us: Reflections on the Sacrificial Language of Salvation," in *Sacrifice and Redemption: Durham Essays in Theology*, ed. S. W. Sykes (Cambridge: Cambridge University Press, 1991), 299–325; Dalferth, "Die soteriologische Relevanz der Kategorie des Opfers: Dogmatische Erwägungen im Anschluß an die gegenwärtige exegetische Diskussion," *Jahrbuch für biblische Theologie* 6 (1991): 173–94.

## 1. Christ Died for Us

The answer to this question, too, is contained within the Christian community's confession of Christ and must be unfolded from it. However, it is often only to be found implicitly and indirectly within what is explicitly stated there concerning Jesus's life and death. The Apostles' Creed, for instance, declares, "born of the Virgin Mary, suffered under Pontius Pilate, was crucified, dead, and buried."[1] There is an entirely matter-of-fact naming of the events that led up to the death of Jesus, but not a word is spent on the salvific significance that Christians attach to the life and death of this Jesus. The events listed simply speak for themselves. It is only the overall setting of the creed and the contextualization of these events in a (quasi-)narrative sequence covering not just Jesus's life and death but also God's actions in his conception, resurrection, and ascension that give an indication of the soteriological relevance of these events and allow us to recognize why Christians confess this Jesus as Christ and as their Lord. And it is only when all of this is confessed, jointly or individually, by Christians in the settings of baptism, Eucharist, and services of worship that it becomes crystal clear that confession of faith in Jesus the Christ is concerned not with an event receding further and further into the past but with the salvation of us all. In order to consider the salvific significance of Jesus Christ from a theological point of view, it is thus not enough to go into the events and details of Jesus's life and call them to mind. We must bear in mind their overall context as it is unfolded in the three basic articles of the creed and understand this context from the point of view of the setting in which this confession was and continues to be uttered.

The Nicene-Constantinopolitan Creed, in contrast, is not content with these indirect, contextual indications. It states expressly that Jesus "*for us men and for our salvation* came down from heaven" and was "crucified *for us.*"[2] The salvific significance of the events of Jesus's life as a whole and of his crucifixion in particular is clearly highlighted: all this took place for us and for our salvation. Jesus did not just die; it was *for us* he died. It is therefore plain that the matter-of-fact presentation of his life in the creed is intended from the outset to be something more than a biographical sketch of the Jew Jesus, a figure from the distant past. In stating that Jesus was crucified *for us*, the creed focuses on an all-encompassing salvation event, in which not just Jesus but also confessing believers and all other human beings and creatures

1. *BSLK* 21, lines 11–14.
2. *BSLK* 26, lines 13–15 and 17 (italics mine).

are involved in different ways.[3] Thus the creed speaks not just of the story of Jesus but, simultaneously, of the story of each one of us.

This was the precise point of Christian confessions from the outset. Whether they consist of exclamatory prayers such as "Jesus is Lord" (e.g., 1 Cor. 12:3; Rom. 10:9; and Phil. 2:11; cf. Acts 16:31), of declarations such as "Jesus is the Son of God" (cf., for example, Mark 15:39) or "Jesus is the Christ" (cf., for example, Matt. 1:16; 27:17, 22), of songs (e.g., 1 Tim. 3:16; Phil. 2:6–11; or John 1:1–5), or of narrative-doxological accounts (such as the Gospels): they always speak of Jesus Christ in such a way that the salvation of us all is involved as well. If, for instance, we compare examples of early Christian confessions such as Romans 1:3–4; Philippians 2:6–11; John 1:1–5; 1 Timothy 3:16; 2 Clement 9.5; 14.2; or Justin, 1 Apology 63.10, then we cannot help but notice that, in spite of all their differences as regards language, the images used, and the detail of what is being articulated, four obvious, basic structures are common to them all:

1. They all speak of an *event* that took place in the life, death, and resurrection of Jesus Christ. This is clear from the event or action predicates they use (John 1:14; 2 Clem. 9.5: ἐγένετο; 1 Tim. 3:16; 2 Clem. 14.2: ἐφανερώθη; Phil. 2:7–8: ἐκένωσεν, ἐταπείνωσεν).

2. This is an *eschatological* event ἐπ' ἐσχάτων τῶν ἡμερῶν, at the end of time (2 Clem. 14.2). *Now* (νῦν δέ: Justin, 1 Apol. 63.10), in this event, by the will of God, the turning point from the old to the new aeon, from the time of calamity to the time of salvation, is accomplished; the eschatological call has gone out to us (2 Clem. 1.8; 2.7; 9.5: ἐκάλεσεν ... ἡμᾶς, etc.), drawing us into the new era of salvation (2 Clem. 9.5).

3. This eschatological event is thus, additionally and essentially, a *salvation* event. It took place *for us* (Justin, 1 Apol. 63.1: ὑπέρ), or *because of us* (2 Clem. 1.1–2: ἕνεκα ἡμῶν), in order that we might be saved (2 Clem. 14.2) and called from nonbeing into being (2 Clem. 1.8).

3. Believers confess their faith that God desires and is bringing about salvation *for all* his creatures. Since they see salvation as grounded wholly and exclusively in *God's own will and work*, it is a misunderstanding of the import of the Christian confession of faith—frequent among Christians themselves—to see it as "group salvation," in other words, as what God has done for the confessing community (or believers or baptized believers, etc.). God's saving activity concerns everyone, even if only some gratefully confess and acknowledge it. Paul makes the position clear in 2 Cor. 5:18–21 since it is certain from God's point of view that *he has* reconciled us with himself through Christ, the *whole cosmos* is reconciled with him. And because of this, Christians can and must confront everyone, without exception, with the call to accept God's reconciliation and to assent to the Christian confession of faith—not because it is a *Christian* confession but because it confesses *God's saving activity for all humankind.* Cf. O. Hofius, *Paulusstudien* (Tübingen: Mohr Siebeck, 1989), 1–14, 15–32, 36–49, 148–74.

4. That, however, is something that can be pronounced only by God. The eschatological salvation event is therefore accomplished *through God* (i.e., *by God*). He has made Jesus Christ to be salvation for us by appointing him the Son of God (Rom. 1:4), declaring him righteous (1 Tim. 3:16), and exalting him to the highest place (Phil. 2:9).

In speaking of Jesus Christ, therefore, these confessions describe, in their different ways, the definitive, eschatological saving event that is of ultimate significance for the whole world, since it decides on the being or nonbeing of each of us, and to that extent it is effected and accomplished wholly and exclusively by God himself alone. Hence, when Christian confessions speak of *Jesus Christ*, they are dealing—at varying levels of detail and with differing emphases—with *our salvation* and with *God's saving activity for us*.[4]

This also applies to the Apostles' and Nicene-Constantinopolitan Creeds, the two authoritative early-church summaries of Christian salvation experience: Jesus Christ died for us that we might live. Both are remarkably matter-of-fact and soteriologically restrained. They cite the relevant facts, making it clear that they have to do with our salvation, but by and large they refrain from interpreting these facts of salvation. Yet without interpretation they can be neither understood nor communicated to others. From the beginning, therefore, Christians have attempted to achieve a deeper understanding of the salvation event and to explain it to themselves and others by means of interpretative reflection on what is summarized and recited in the creeds and expressed in greater detail in Scripture. This interpretation, explication, and communication of the creeds always takes place under particular historical conditions and in specific cultural and semantic contexts, which from the outset has led to fundamentally different (and even, to some extent, contradictory) interpretations of the salvation event. This has resulted in the development of differing soteriological doctrines, which in turn have affected the wording and content of new confessions of faith.[5]

The Reformation confessions of faith provide examples that illustrate this particular issue. The third article of the Augsburg Confession, for example,

---

4. The emphasis can vary considerably according to the situation within which the confession originated. While in the Corinth of Paul's day it was still sufficient and unambiguous to confess one's faith in Jesus Christ with the cry "Jesus is Lord!" (1 Cor. 12:3), by the time of the Johannine community it was essential to add explicitly that this Jesus had come *in the flesh* (John 1:14). To that extent, the accentuated statements concerning the humanity of Jesus Christ contained in most of the confessions and the detailed, stylized summary of Jesus's life in the Apostles' Creed ("born, suffered, crucified, died, buried") as such are *soteriologically motivated*.

5. Cf. A. Grillmeier, *Jesus der Christus im Glauben der Kirche*, vol. 2, part 1, *Das Konzil von Chalcedon (451): Rezeption und Widerspruch (451–518)* (Freiburg: Herder, 1986).

contains the wording that Jesus Christ was "truly born, suffered, was crucified, died, and was buried, in order to be a sacrifice not only for original sin
but also for all other sins and to appease God's wrath."[6] With this allusion to
sacrifice and appeasement, the article goes well beyond the statements of the
early church creeds concerning Jesus's death. Was that justified? Are Christians distinguished by the fact that they confess God's saving activity in Jesus
Christ, or must they go beyond this to hold a particular interpretation of this
saving activity? It is the core of the Christian confession that, in Jesus's death
on the cross and his resurrection, God acted *for us* and *for our benefit*. But
is it therefore also imperative to understand this redemptive activity by God
as appeasement of his wrath, and to understand Jesus's death as atonement
and sacrifice, in order to comprehend its salvific significance?

## 2. The Tübingen Antithesis

This view has been advocated with renewed vigor in recent times. The peculiar
dialectic of theological reflection in recent years has produced the Tübingen
Antithesis about a theme regarded as virtually obsolete: the relevance of the
category of sacrifice to our evaluation of the salvific significance of the death
of Jesus Christ.[7] The thesis that the antithesis opposes here[8]—admittedly not
always by name but nevertheless quite unmistakably—is the assertion made
in 1941 by Rudolf Bultmann (though he was by no means either its first or
its only proponent), for instance, that today it is no longer possible to take
seriously the set of ideas associated with a vicarious, atoning sacrifice offered
by Jesus Christ as the punishment for our sin so that we might be freed from
death: "We can no longer accept this mythological interpretation [of the cross
of Christ] in which notions of sacrifice are mixed together with a juristic
theory of satisfaction."[9]

6. *BSLK* 54, lines 8–12.
7. The word *category* in what follows is used quite generally to denote a type of predicative
determination or statement, while the expression *category of sacrifice* denotes a specific type
of soteriological statement about the nature of salvation.
8. H. Gese, "Die Sühne," in *Zur biblischen Theologie: Alttestamentliche Vorträge* (Munich:
Christian Kaiser, 1977), 85–106, esp. 85–86; M. Hengel, *The Atonement: A Study of the Origins
of the Doctrine in the New Testament* (Philadelphia: Fortress, 1981), 74–75. Cf. also U. Wilckens,
*Der Brief an die Römer*, EKKNT 6 (Zürich: Neukirchener/Patmos, 1978), 1:233–43; Hofius,
*Paulusstudien*, 1–49.
9. R. Bultmann, "Neues Testament und Mythologie," in *Kerygma und Mythos*, vol. 1, *Ein
theologisches Gespräch*, ed. H. W. Bartsch (Hamburg: Herbert Reich-Evangelischer Verlag,
⁵1967), 42; cf. I. Henderson, *Myth in the New Testament* (London: SCM, 1952), 11: "The idea of
sacrifice is one which belongs to a bygone era rather than to the essence of the Christian faith."

However, his basis for this thesis is not just anthropological (i.e., the modern person's objection to categories of thought taken from an alien worldview); it is also, indeed primarily, exegetical: the interpretation of "for us" to imply a satisfaction or sacrifice theory *does not mean what it should mean at all, even within the perspective of the New Testament.*[10] According to the witness of the New Testament, the salvific significance of the death of Jesus is by no means limited to the idea that he procured our pardon by taking the penalty for our sins on himself. Christ did not just atone for our sins and their consequences as a sacrifice on the cross: he broke the power of sin. Briefly stated, Bultmann contests the use of the category of sacrifice to express the salvific significance of the cross *because for him it says too little.*

In sharp contrast, the view held in Tübingen appears to allow *only* this category *to capture* its significance. "The salvific significance of the death of Jesus," says Hartmut Gese, "can be captured only by the idea of atonement. This is what we mean when we speak of the blood of Jesus."[11] It is true that the ideas of atonement and sacrifice are not simply identical, as can be shown from the Old Testament, at least where the preexilic period is concerned,[12] but for the postexilic atonement cult this frame of reference is fundamental. For if (1) *salvation* is to be understood as "fellowship with God"[13] and "enduring life-contact"[14] with the Holy One; if (2) *atonement* is "incorporation into the Holy One,"[15] that is, the process by which one is "brought into contact with God himself";[16] if (3) *sacrifice* in the postexilic cult of Israel is no longer a mere penitential rite but is rather the factual enactment of atonement, a vicarious life-offering by means of which "a coming to God that consists of passing through the death sentence"[17] is symbolically realized and enacted; and if (4) at the time of Jesus the rabbinic position was that every sacrifice atones—then, in this situation, the idea of atonement can only be conceived of in concrete historical terms using the category of sacrifice, and the essence of sacrifice, regardless of the factual differentiation between different types of sacrifice, is atonement. But if—and this is the core thesis in summary—the salvific significance of the cross of Jesus Christ can be adequately comprehended only within the horizon of the

10. Bultmann, "Neues Testament und Mythologie," 41.
11. Gese, "Sühne," 104.
12. Ibid., 90.
13. Ibid., 98.
14. Ibid., 99.
15. Ibid., 98.
16. Ibid., 104.
17. Ibid.

idea of atoning sacrifice, then Christian soteriology cannot dispense with the category of sacrifice.[18]

This thesis has provoked protest, not least because it can be misunderstood both hermeneutically and theologically, as is demonstrated by the exegetical controversies surrounding the Tübingen Antithesis.[19] The acrimony of these controversies is an indication that not just exegetical but also dogmatic interests are involved. This is a clear case of exegesis calling for a critical dialogue with dogmatics.[20]

My attempt at dialogue starts with the observation that where the soteriological relevance of the category of sacrifice is concerned, both thesis and antithesis appear to be advocated from almost identical motives.[21] Both Bultmann and Gese are anxious to affirm that Jesus "did not die for himself";[22] in

18. The newly awakened interest in the category of sacrifice is documented by, among others, G. Wenz, "Die Lehre vom Opfer Christi im Herrenmahl als Problem ökumenischer Theologie," *KD* 28 (1982): 7–41; K. Lehmann and E. Schlink, eds., *Das Opfer Christi und seine Gegenwart in der Kirche: Klärungen zum Opfercharakter des Herrenmahls*, Dialog der Kirche 3 (Freiburg: Herder, 1983); K. Lehmann, "Die Gegenwart des Opfers Jesu Christi im Herrenmahl der Kirche: Zur Bedeutung eines neuen ökumenischen Dokuments," *KD* 29 (1983): 139–48. Cf. also J. Blank and J. Werbick, eds., *Sühne und Versöhnung*, Theologie zur Zeit 1 (Düsseldorf: Patmos, 1986).

19. G. Friedrich, *Die Verkündigung des Todes Jesu im Neuen Testament*, Biblisch-Theologische Studien 6 (Neukirchen-Vluyn: Neukirchener, ²1985); P. Stuhlmacher, "Sühne oder Versöhnung? Randbemerkungen zu Gerhard Friedrichs Studie: 'Die Verkündigung des Todes Jesu im Neuen Testament,'" in *Die Mitte des Neuen Testaments: Einheit und Vielfalt neutestamentlicher Theologie; Festschrift für Eduard Schweizer zum 70. Geburtstag* (Göttingen: Vandenhoeck & Ruprecht, 1983), 291–316; C. Breytenbach, *Versöhnung: Eine Studie zur paulinischen Soteriologie*, WMANT 60 (Neukirchen-Vluyn: Neukirchener, 1989); O. Hofius, "Rezension von C. Breytenbach, *Versöhnung*," *ThLZ* 115 (1990): 741–45; C. Breytenbach, "Abgeschlossenes Imperfekt? Einige notwendig gewordene Anmerkungen zum Gebrauch des griechischen Imperfekts in neutestamentlichen Zeiten," *ThLZ* 118 (1993): 85–91; O. Hofius, "2 Kor. 5,19a und das Imperfekt," *ThLZ* 118 (1993): 790–95; P. Stuhlmacher, "Cilliers Breytenbachs Sicht von Sühne und Versöhnung," *Jahrbuch für biblische Theologie* 6 (1991): 339–54.

20. Attempts may be found in A. Gläßer, "Jesus Christus der Erlöser: Anmerkungen zur Soteriologie," in *Der Dienst für den Menschen in Theologie und Verkündigung: Festschrift für Alois Brems, Bischof von Eichstätt, zum 75. Geburtstag*, ed. R. M. Hübner et al. (Regensburg: Friedrich Pustet, 1981), 247–77; K. L. Lehmann, "'Er wurde für uns gekreuzigt': Eine Skizze zur Neubesinnung in der Soteriologie," *TQ* 162 (1982): 298–317; M. Plathow, "Schuldübertragung oder Schuldübernahme: Stellvertretung als dogmatisch-ethisches Thema," *ZThK* 104 (1982): 411–26; N. Hoffmann, *Kreuz und Trinität: Zur Theologie der Sühne* (Einsiedeln: Johannes Verlag, 1982); H. Hübner, "Sühne und Versöhnung: Anmerkungen zu einem umstrittenen Kapitel Biblischer Theologie," *KD* 29 (1983): 284–305; G. Bader, "Jesu Tod als Opfer," *ZThK* 80 (1983): 411–31; J. W. Werbick, "Versöhnung durch Sühne," in *Sühne und Versöhnung*, ed. Blank and Werbick, 92–117.

21. This does not mean that they have the same theological purpose. In spite of the convergence of their individual motifs, their fundamental concerns diverge to an even greater degree.

22. Gese, "Sühne," 106.

other words, the salvation event on the cross is not an "isolated occurrence" at the biographical end of the life of Jesus, or a "past event to which one looks back."[23] Both are concerned to emphasize the *pro nobis* format of this event, "its importance . . . for faith"[24] and of the fact that with "his blood . . . we become partakers of the new reality of salvation."[25] Both of them emphasize that this "importance has a 'cosmic' dimension,"[26] that is, that Jesus's death has "atoned for the cosmos."[27] Both are certain that the salvation procured on the cross "*is constantly present*,"[28] since "atonement has taken place" and we have "life . . . in the cross of Jesus."[29] And finally, both agree that "death and resurrection are meant simultaneously"[30] and that therefore "cross and resurrection . . . [belong] together as one unit."[31]

How can there be such an apparently high level of agreement and yet such widely differing assessments of the soteriological relevance of the category of sacrifice? The answer can only be that *thesis and antithesis have a different understanding of "sacrifice"* and are following *different grammars of this complex of ideas*. Bultmann's concept of sacrifice reflects the understanding of sacrifice held by the dogmatic tradition of the *munus Christi sacerdotale* [Christ's priestly office] and its satisfaction theory, which was specifically not cultic but juridical. In one breath he can speak of "a satisfaction or sacrifice theory,"[32] demonstrating, just as is demonstrated by his critique of the theory alluded to above, that he understands reference to Christ's sacrificial death essentially in terms of "reparation through substitution."[33] Gese, however, argues that this misses the very point of the biblical idea of atoning sacrifice. This must be understood as "existential substitution [*Existenzstellvertretung*]," as "(substitutionary) total self-offering" the effect of which is "the life-saving action that human beings earnestly seek and that God enables."[34] Its purpose is not an external transaction of transmissible obligations, not just a "negative process of the simple removal of sin or mere repentance";[35] it is *incorporation into the Holy One*.

23. Bultmann, "Neues Testament und Mythologie," 42.
24. Ibid., 42.
25. Gese, "Sühne," 106.
26. Bultmann, "Neues Testament und Mythologie," 42.
27. Gese, "Sühne," 106.
28. Bultmann, "Neues Testament und Mythologie," 42.
29. Gese, "Sühne," 106.
30. Ibid.
31. Bultmann, "Neues Testament und Mythologie," 44.
32. Ibid., 43.
33. Gese, "Sühne," 87.
34. Ibid.
35. Ibid., 104.

If this exegetical and historical hypothesis is correct—and there is a great deal in its favor[36]—it is a decisive corrective to the contemporary critique of cult and sacrifice as reflected in Bultmann's thesis: the grammar of the Old Testament idea of sacrifice differs from that suggested by the concept of sacrifice in the soteriological tradition of dogmatics. But the intention of the Tübingen Antithesis appears to go beyond being such a corrective. It is not only the exegetical or historical claim of Gese's assertion that the salvific significance of the death of Jesus can *only* be conceived of under the idea of atonement (given tangible form in the cult of sacrifice) that is surprising; rather, it is the *range of application to which it lays claim*. It appears to be saying that *thus and only thus* can the salvific significance of this death be apprehended, so that Christian soteriology is impossible without recourse to the idea of atoning sacrifice—that it is indeed no more and no less than the interpretation of the New Testament event on the basis of the Old Testament theology of atonement.[37]

However, this misunderstandable and misunderstood claim puts the Tübingen Antithesis in danger of mutating from a necessary exegetical corrective into a dogmatically misleading doctrine. This must be energetically resisted, or else the exegetical gain will be turned into a dogmatic loss.

To elucidate and substantiate this, it is vital that we differentiate between three sets of issues that are not always kept distinct in the controversial discussion surrounding the Tübingen Antithesis:

- the *homiletical* issue of the correct proclamation of the salvation procured by Jesus's death, including its pastoral-theological and diaconal dimensions
- the *exegetical-hermeneutical* issue of the correct understanding of the New Testament witness to the salvific significance of the death of Jesus
- the *dogmatic* issue of the correct assimilation and presentation of this witness in the field of soteriology

There is no doubt that the idea of sacrifice as a soteriological category gives rise to homiletical problems because today we either do not understand it at all or understand it wrongly, namely, according to the religio-historical model "*do ut des* [I give that you might give]" and not according to the

---

36. Cf. F. L. Hossfeld, "Versöhnung als Sühne: Neuere Anstöße zur Wiederaufnahme eines biblischen Themas," *BK* 41 (1986): 54–60, esp. 55–58. From a critical angle, cf. R. Rendtorff, *Leviticus*, BKAT 3 (Neukirchen-Vluyn: Neukirchener, 1985), 1:32–48.

37. H. Gese, "Das biblische Schriftverständnis," in *Zur biblischen Theologie*, 9–30, esp. 26.

(supposed) biblical model "*do quia dedisti* [I give because you have given]."[38] But this gives no indication of its soteriological relevance. One cannot decide soteriological questions (i.e., questions relevant to salvation and truth) on the basis of hypotheses taken from reception theory, since this would make the content that is to be explained dependent on contemporary comprehension or incomprehension. Neither can one put the homiletical cart before the soteriological horse and ask, as G. Friedrich does, whether "it is *justified* today, in view of the situation described, *to speak of the sacrificial death of Jesus.*"[39] If the category of sacrifice is soteriologically relevant, then the only question is how it can be communicated in an unambiguous way; to stop using it avoids misunderstandings, to be sure, but communicates nothing. Under no circumstances should our difficulty with the category of sacrifice lead us to the mistaken exegetical and dogmatic conclusion that, along with the idea of the substitutionary death of an innocent person as a guilt offering (rightly castigated by Nietzsche as "absurd" and "gruesome"), we should also reject the biblical references to the atoning sacrifice of Jesus Christ and dismiss the related texts as dogmatically irrelevant because they are morally offensive and no longer tenable today.[40] The soteriological relevance of the category of sacrifice is not to be decided on the basis of the grammar of our concept of sacrifice; it must be demonstrated first and foremost exegetically from the biblical texts.


## 3. The New Testament Findings

Even if neither explicit allusions to the concepts of the sacrificial cult in the priestly writings nor clear references to sacrifice make a significant quantitative contribution to the New Testament Scriptures,[41] the whole of the New

---

38. Cf. B. Janowski, *Sühne als Heilsgeschehen: Studien zur Sühnetheologie der Priesterschrift und zur Wurzel KPR im Alten Orient und im Alten Testament* (Neukirchen-Vluyn: Neukirchener, 1982), vii. However, even this formula captures only some of the strands of biblical salvific thinking—not, for instance, those of Pauline, Johannine, or Markan soteriology.

39. Friedrich, *Verkündigung des Todes Jesu*, 148 (italics in original).

40. F. Nietzsche, *Antichrist: Fluch auf das Christentum*, §41, in *Sämtliche Werke: Kritische Studienausgabe* (Munich: de Gruyter, 1988), 6:214–15. This applies also, mutatis mutandis, to the sacrificial critique put forward by R. Girard and the resulting requirement for a non-sacrificial interpretation of the Gospel text. Cf. R. Girard, *Das Ende der Gewalt: Analyse des Menschheitsverhängnisses* (Freiburg: Herder, 1983), 187–231; Girard, *Le Bouc émissaire* (Paris: Grasset, 1982); A. Schenker, *Versöhnung und Sühne* (Freiburg: Herder, 1981); R. Schwager, "Versöhnung und Sühne," *ThPh* 58 (1983): 217–25; Schwager, "Der Tod Christi und die Opferkritik," *Theologie der Gegenwart* 29 (1986): 11–20.

41. F. Hahn, "Die alttestamentlichen Motive in der urchristlichen Abendmahlsüberlieferung," *EvTh* 27 (1967): 337–74.

Testament is steeped in the imaginative world of sacrifice and the sacrificial cult. At all levels, from the pre-Pauline to the Johannine literature, the saving event of Jesus's death is defined with varying degrees of clarity as sacrifice or self-sacrifice, and our redemption is described as reconciliation through his blood. This is found in numerous different images and ideas linked in various ways with different forms of the sacrificial cult in the temple and its theological reflection in the Old Testament Scriptures, as well as with images and image complexes that give expression to the salvation event.[42]

The most striking evidence of this is the Epistle to the Hebrews,[43] which understands Jesus's death as the final and "unblemished" self-sacrifice (9:14

---

42. Cf. H. D. Wendland, "Opfer III. Im NT," *RGG*[3] vol. 4, cols. 1647–1651; W. Kraus, "Sacrifice 5. New Testament and Early Christianity," *RGG* vol. 11, cols. 385–87; C. Brown, "Sacrifice," *NIDNTT* 3:418–36; S. W. Sykes, "Sacrifice in the New Testament and Christian Theology," in *Sacrifice*, ed. M. F. C. Bourdillon and M. Fortes (London: Academic Press, 1980), 61–83; F. M. Young, *Sacrifice and the Death of Christ* (London: SPCK, 1975), part 1; M. L. Gübler, *Die frühesten Deutungen des Todes Jesu: Eine motivgeschichtliche Darstellung aufgrund der neueren exegetischen Forschung* (Fribourg, Switzerland: Universitätsverlag, 1977); A. Weiser, "Der Tod Jesu und das Heil der Menschen: Aussageweisen von Erlösung im Neuen Testament," *BK* 41 (1986): 60–67; F. Humphreys, "The Mystery of the Cross," *PRSt* 14 (1987): 47–52; J. B. Green, *The Death of Jesus* (Tübingen: Mohr Siebeck, 1988), 314–23.

The current practice of speaking of the "interpretation" or "interpretations" of the death of Jesus should be used with care in a theological or hermeneutical context. It becomes problematic when it denotes only the subjectivistic results of human interpretative activities (i.e., the human view or interpretation of a particular historical event), without considering it in pneumatological terms within the context of a trinitarian hermeneutic. Cf. I. U. Dalferth, "The Stuff of Revelation: Austin Farrer's Doctrine of Inspired Images," in *Hermeneutics, the Bible and Literary Criticism*, ed. A. Loades and M. McLain (London: Macmillan, 1992), 71–95. After all, the subject of the Christian community's interpretative activity is not simply the death of Jesus as a set of historical facts but the saving activity of God that is enacted in this historical event. (Cf. I. U. Dalferth, *Theology and Philosophy* [Oxford: Oxford University Press, 1988], 53–59.) But God's activity can be correctly understood and interpreted by us only if God himself interprets it and makes it comprehensible to us, revealing it to us in such a way that we can repeat this revelation in our own words. In this sense Christians claim that, when they speak soteriologically of the cross and death of Jesus, they are conveying not merely their own interpretation but God's self-interpretation; in other words, they are using the forms of speech and thought available to them to articulate the truth of this event as God understands it. Unless this is taken into account, any proper insight into the symbolic or metaphorical nature of all soteriological discourse concerning the death of Jesus Christ will be operating hermeneutically with an understanding of metaphor that cannot do justice to the creative truth claim of soteriological metaphors and thus loses its decisive theological point. Cf. G. Röhser, *Metaphorik und Personifikation der Sünde* (Tübingen: Mohr Siebeck, 1987); G. Bader, *Symbolik des Todes Jesu* (Tübingen: Mohr Siebeck, 1988); C. E. Gunton, *The Actuality of Atonement: A Study of Metaphor, Rationality and the Christian Tradition* (Edinburgh: T&T Clark, 1988), esp. chaps. 2 and 5; J. Fischer, *Glaube als Erkenntnis: Zum Wahrnehmungscharakter des christlichen Glaubens* (Munich: Christian Kaiser, 1989), 76–90.

43. A. N. Chester, "Hebrews: The Final Sacrifice," in Sykes, ed., *Sacrifice and Redemption*, 57–72.

NIV): "For by one sacrifice he has made perfect forever those who are being made holy" (10:14 NIV). As high priest, Christ has carried out the priestly service required by God "once for all" (9:12) and perfectly, thereby rendering the sacrificial cult of the temple obsolete and superfluous (10:1–18). The author of the Epistle to the Hebrews expresses this *finality* and *perfection* of Christ's self-sacrifice by means of two interventions in the traditional grammar of the sacrificial image. First, he allows the roles of offerant (i.e., the one bringing the sacrifice), sacrifice, and priest, which were clearly differentiated in the cultic act of sacrifice, to be brought together in Christ: he is the offerant, even though, in contrast to the cultic ritual, he does not enact the slaughter himself; he is both the sacrifice on the cross and the priest who brings his own sacrifice of himself to God by ascending to heaven and appearing before the face of his heavenly Father (9:7, 21–24). And while his self-sacrifice took place once for all on the cross (9:15–17, 25–28), he presents it to God forever in the heavenly sanctuary (8:1–5; 9:11, 24). Second, Christ is described as the perfect and final form, not only of one type of sacrifice but of all types. In Hebrews 9–10 his death is presented as the perfect form of the sin offering on the great Day of Atonement (Lev. 16:21–22; 17), of the covenant sacrifice (Exod. 24), and of the purification offering of the red heifer (Num. 19).

This links the traditions that were clearly differentiated in the Old Testament, although in the rabbinic interpretation they were connected, and that were employed either separately or together in other places in the New Testament to describe Jesus's crucifixion as sin offering (Matt. 26:28b) or as covenant sacrifice (1 Cor. 11:25; Mark 14:24; Luke 22:20; Matt. 26:28a). Similarly, in Ephesians 5:2 the image of the burnt offering is used to describe the self-sacrificial love of Christ. The imaginative world of sacrifice also plays a role in the many passages that speak of the blood of Christ (throughout Hebrews; also Rom. 5:9; Col. 1:20; Eph. 1:7; 2:13; 1 John 1:7; Rev. 5:9) and in which he is represented as the sacrificial lamb (John 1:29; 1 Pet. 1:19; Eph. 5:2; Rev. 5:6–10) or explicitly as the Passover lamb (1 Cor. 5:6–8). Texts like Romans 3:25; Hebrews 2:17; or 1 John 2:2; 4:10, too, where derivations of the root ἱλασκ- are used together with περί, which the Septuagint uses to translate the Hebrew *kipper 'al* (כפר על), express the salvific efficacy of the death of Christ as analogous to the sacrificial act of the temple cult.

It is highly probable that the set of ideas behind the sacrificial act also lies behind the identification of Christ with the suffering servant of Isaiah 52:13–53:12 (esp. Isa. 53:10). The same applies to the tradition of the Last Supper, which speaks of Jesus having poured out his blood "for many" (Mark 14:24) or "for you" (Luke 22:20), even though it is by no means clear or beyond dispute that Jesus himself understood his death as a vicarious self-sacrifice.[44] According to the tradition quoted by Paul, the Lord's Supper "proclaim[s] the Lord's death until he comes" (1 Cor. 11:26 NIV), but this does not mean that the sacrificial death of Jesus was being proclaimed by this or even that it was related to a sacrificial event at all. Similarly, the image of self-giving as used in Mark 10:45 and 1 Timothy 2:5–6 can have theological connotations of sacrifice, though not necessarily in every case.

But although it is possible to argue over the interpretation of specific passages, it can hardly be seriously disputed that in the New Testament the imaginative world of sacrifice is used in numerous different ways to express the salvific significance of the death of Jesus. However, it by no means follows from this that dogmatic reflection, too, must understand the salvific significance of the death of Jesus in terms of a theology of sacrifice, or even that acceptable soteriological thought is possible only within the category of sacrifice. The indisputable fact that the imaginative world of sacrifice plays a substantial role in the New Testament is one thing; to regard it as soteriologically essential or definitive is quite another. Even though the imagery of the sacrificial cult shapes and characterizes certain aspects of Pauline and Markan thinking and is central to the thought of the Epistle to the Hebrews, where the majority of this type of imagery for the salvific significance of the death of

---

44. That Jesus understood his death thus is argued or assumed by J. Jeremias, *Die Abendmahlsworte Jesu* (Göttingen: Vandenhoeck & Ruprecht, [4]1967); Jeremias, *Neutestamentliche Theologie*, part 1, *Die Verkündigung Jesu* (Gütersloh: Gütersloher Verlagshaus Mohn, 1971), 263–84; H. Patsch, *Abendmahl und historischer Jesus* (Stuttgart: Calwer Verlag, 1972); L. Goppelt, *Theologie des Neuen Testaments*, vol. 1, part 1, *Jesu Wirken in seiner theologischen Bedeutung*, ed. J. Roloff (Göttingen: Vandenhoeck & Ruprecht, 1975), 234–37, 241–46, 261–70; R. Pesch, *Das Abendmahl und Jesu Todesverständnis* (Freiburg: Herder, 1978); H. Schürmann, "Jesu ureigenes Todesverständnis," in *Begegnung mit dem Wort: Festschrift für Heinrich Zimmermann*, ed. J. Zmijewski and E. Nellessen (Bonn: Hanstein, 1979), 273–309; Pesch, "Jesu Todesverständnis im Verstehenshorizont seiner Umwelt," *Theologie und Glaube* (1980): 141–60; M. Hengel, "Der stellvertretende Sühnetod Jesu," *IKaZ* 9 (1980): 1–25, 135–47; Hengel, *Atonement*, 72–73; P. Stuhlmacher, "Existenzstellvertretung für die Vielen: Mark 10:45 (Matt. 20:28)," in *Werden und Wirken des Alten Testaments: Festschrift für Claus Westermann zum 70. Geburtstag*, ed. R. Albertz (Göttingen: Vandenhoeck & Ruprecht, 1980), 412–27; J. C. O'Neill, "Did Jesus Teach That His Death Would Be Vicarious as Well as Typical?," in *Suffering and Martyrdom in the New Testament*, ed. W. Horbury and B. McNeil (Cambridge: Cambridge University Press, 1981), 9–27; B. Janowski, "Auslösung des verwirkten Lebens: Zur Geschichte und Struktur der biblischen Lösegeldvorstellung," *ZThK* 79 (1982): 25–59.

This view is criticized by, among others, G. B. Gray, *Sacrifice in the Old Testament: Its Theory and Practice* (1925; repr., New York: Ktav, 1971), 397; W. G. Kümmel, *The Theology of the New Testament* (London: SCM, 1974), 90–95; Kümmel, "Jesusforschung seit 1965, IV," *ThR* 43 (1978): 233–65; Kümmel, "Jesusforschung seit 1965, VI," *ThR* 45 (1980): 293–337; and J. Roloff, *Neues Testament* (Neukirchen-Vluyn: Neukirchener, 1977), 211–27.

Jesus is to be found, this is far from indicating that it must be indispensable, essential, or the sole decisive factor for a proper Christian understanding of salvation. Exegetical observations on the texts of the New Testament do not in themselves amount to theological arguments. For this they must first be interpreted hermeneutically and evaluated theologically. In the above instance this requires that we consider at least three aspects of the New Testament use of the imaginative world of the sacrificial cult: the criticism of the sacrificial cult; the so-called spiritualization of the theme of sacrifice, together with the purely metonymic use of concepts of sacrifice; and the restricted part played by the imagery of the sacrificial cult in Christian attempts to articulate the salvific significance of the death of Jesus.

### 3.1. Criticism of the Sacrificial Cult

The indisputable use of the category of sacrifice in New Testament texts cannot obscure the fact that the New Testament shows a clear and obvious tendency to criticize and devalue the sacrificial cult. "A most obvious feature of the New Testament communities is the way in which the language of the Jewish cult—sacrifice, offering, temple, and priesthood—rapidly came to be redeployed . . . and the reason for this astonishing fact lies not in any direct attack by Jesus on the sacrificial system but in the refocusing of religious attention."[45] Christians—not all, and not all at once, but many even so, and in rapidly increasing numbers—ceased to participate in the sacrificial cult of the temple, announcing instead that the crucified Jesus was the Christ, God's expected Messiah. The salvific significance ascribed to Jesus's death on the cross and his resurrection contributed crucially to the criticism of the sacrificial cult and the rapid devaluation of the significance and imagery of the sacrificial cult in Christian thinking and activity. They (sometimes) made use of these concepts to articulate and communicate the salvation experience of Jesus's cross and resurrection. But the Jerusalem sacrificial cult soon ceased—permanently, after AD 70—to play an active part in the life of the new Christian community, as did the worship of the synagogue. Centered on the crucified Jesus as the risen Christ, the Christian life took place outside the rituals and sacrificial cult of the Jerusalem temple and the worship of the synagogue, and hence beyond the boundaries of the basic religious orientation of contemporary Judaism. Consequently, when Christians described and proclaimed Jesus's death as a sacrifice, it was not because they understood the crucifixion as a ritual slaughter or sacrificial offering, something that, as

---

45. Sykes, "Sacrifice in the New Testament," 68.

"an entirely noncultic event,"[46] it was not, but because they believed that this event, which embodied God's love in giving up Jesus and Jesus's life given up in the love of God, could best be expressed and made comprehensible in the image of sacrifice.

There were a number of reasons for this. First, the use of this familiar imagery could confront the central religious practice of Judaism with the Christian antithesis: Jesus Christ is the true way to salvation, not the temple cult and the worship of the synagogue. Second, sacrifice constituted the universal religious rite not just of Judaism[47] but of the whole of Hellenistic late antiquity, so that anyone in the Greco-Roman world could be expected to understand allusions to the event of sacrifice.[48] On the other hand, it was precisely this hermeneutical accessibility and communicative availability of the imagery of sacrifice that gave rise to difficulties when it was being employed to make clear the soteriological uniqueness and incomparable distinctiveness of Jesus's cross and resurrection. It had to become clear, in the very use of the language and imagery of the cult of sacrifice, that they were to be transcended and how this was to be done. The hermeneutical process of qualifying the category of sacrifice could provide only a partial solution to the problem: even if Jesus's death was described as the "highest sacrifice," the "sacrifice offered once for all," the "perfect sacrifice," or the "end of sacrifice," the ritual context of the sacrificial cult with its reflection in the Pentateuch is still what was being employed typologically as a hermeneutical tool to express the salvific significance of Jesus's death. But for Christians this was and is an essentially backward-looking perspective that understands Jesus wholly in the light of past history. The soteriological use of the category of sacrifice therefore fostered

the misunderstanding that in fact the death of Jesus was only as important as temple worship, and stood alongside it; it could not represent the eschatological superseding and abolition of it. In the last resort this is the reason for the astonishing predominance of the preposition ὑπέρ as an expression of the

46. Cf. F. Hahn, "Das Verständnis des Opfers im Neuen Testament," in *Gesammelte Aufsätze*, vol. 1, *Exegetische Beiträge zum ökumenischen Gespräch* (Göttingen: Vandenhoeck & Ruprecht, 1986), 262–302, esp. 272–76, 284.

47. Even if it is debatable that "ultimately, all sacrifices in the Old Testament depend for their context upon the story of God's deliverance of his people from Egypt at the Exodus" (J. Rogerson, "Sacrifice in the Old Testament: Problems of Method and Approach," in *Sacrifice*, ed. Bourdillon and Fortes, 45–59, esp. 57), these different traditions are already so interconnected in the Old Testament that the imagery of sacrifice could be linked soteriologically with the imagery of liberation and redemption in Christian usage as well.

48. Cf. Young, *Sacrifice and the Death of Christ*, 9–12.

saving efficacy of the death of Jesus in the New Testament texts, as opposed to περί made more familiar through the LXX as a translation of the Hebrew 'al.[49]

The use of the language of sacrifice in the New Testament must therefore be understood in the context of the overall New Testament trend toward a redefinition of the understanding of salvation and a reorientation of one's life so that it was aligned with and focused on Jesus Christ himself wholly and exclusively, rather than the context of meaning associated with sacrifice and cult. For, in the light of Easter, the New Testament writers were convinced that with Jesus Christ something entirely *new* had made a conclusive appearance on the eschatological stage.

This fresh orientation did not just lead to a fresh fundamental (viz., christological) understanding of the imagery and idea of sacrifice; it is also a hallmark of the Lord's Supper, the act of remembrance of the "new covenant in my blood" (1 Cor. 11:25 NIV). Previous covenants, indeed all covenants, have been surpassed, not because they have been dissolved and declared invalid or because a new covenant has been added to them, as the Abrahamic covenant was added to the Noachian covenant, or the Mosaic covenant to the Abrahamic covenant; but rather because everything is now concentrated on the *person of Jesus Christ himself.* Christ is not a second Moses, the mediator or establisher of a new covenant. He *is* the new covenant. It was not that he established a new covenant with God through his shed blood, a covenant that is still valid for us, even though he himself is no longer here. The new covenant is Jesus Christ himself in person, not merely a work that he has accomplished. Consequently it is also true that we cannot participate in this covenant unless we participate in the person of Jesus Christ himself.[50] His death is therefore not to be understood as the sacrifice enacted at the sealing of the covenant and offered on the cross; it must be understood instead as God's covenant faithfulness in action, since in this covenant God makes himself one with Jesus Christ and thereby also with us, even in and beyond death, so that, in enacting his unity with him, he also realizes his oneness with us. In the person of Jesus Christ this "at-one-ment" is reality; it is not merely accomplished by what he did, and it is valid not only for those who are still alive, as Jesus's death and resurrection prove: God's life-giving nearness to us does not reach its limits, even when we die. Participating in Christ means participating in his death, and anyone who participates in his death also participates in his divine life (Rom. 6:8–10). The soteriologically decisive factor is not Jesus's

---

49. Hengel, *Atonement*, 52.
50. Wenz, "Lehre vom Opfer Christi," 7–14.

death as such, after all, but "more than that, [Christ Jesus] who was raised to life" (Rom. 8:34 NIV); in other words, in him God acted definitively and eschatologically. Jesus's death only becomes a salvation event through God's activity of raising him, the very one who through this act becomes God's saving activity. God alone is soteriologically active and effective, which is why the Christian confession of faith applies to the very person of Jesus and not just to one thing he did or accomplished. This in turn means that the Lord's Supper is not the remembrance of a new covenant that Jesus Christ established but the remembrance of Jesus Christ himself (1 Cor. 11:25b). This is clear from the fact that in the Lord's Supper we share in his body and blood, rather than merely recalling, in rite and symbol, the founding sacrifice of a new cult. When we eat the bread and drink the wine in remembrance of him (11:24–25), we are making it clear over and over again, to ourselves and to others, that our assurance that God will stay as near to us in death as he was to him is rooted in the fact that we are attuning our life wholly and exclusively to him and to the nearness of God revealed by him. By eating and drinking together in the name of their Lord (11:26), Christians proclaim that the fact that Christ died for us, that his body was broken and his blood was shed for us, is the center of their lives because through the work of the Spirit it has become evident to them that the presence of God in Jesus Christ is the sole authoritative basis on which true life can be orientated.

### 3.2. "Spiritualization" of the Category of Sacrifice

A second obvious characteristic of the way the New Testament handles the theme of sacrifice could be termed its *spiritualization*. By this we mean not merely the spiritual sacrifice of which the New Testament speaks in various places (1 Pet. 2:5; Heb. 13:15; Rom. 12:1–2) or the occasional allusion to the fact that Christians suffer on account of or for Christ (Phil. 1:29). These are derived uses of the category of sacrifice. Christian life and Christian worship are described in this way only because Jesus Christ himself is understood as a sacrifice: because they proclaim his death as a sacrifice, Christians can also describe their service of God as offering spiritual sacrifices. The Christian "spiritualization" of the theme of sacrifice therefore has its basis and starting point in christological, not ecclesiological or ethical, insights. When the New Testament calls Jesus's death a sacrifice, it is not speaking of a ritual act of killing; instead, it is using the category of sacrifice as an image to communicate the unique salvific significance of his death. It does not use this image to articulate the process of killing involved in crucifixion, which was a legal execution, or a cultic act of killing; rather, the image expresses

Jesus's surrender of himself to the life-giving and saving nearness of his heavenly Father in order to disclose this nearness to others as well. This surrender was enacted in the self-effacement of his person in view of the dawning rule of God's love, and it culminated in his acquiescence in and acceptance of death on the cross. When the category of sacrifice is applied to Jesus Christ, his entire life and death are illuminated as the story of his surrender of himself to God on behalf of others. And because his story forms part of the story of each one of us, through this characterization as self-sacrifice it gives paradigmatic meaning to the life of each of us: Jesus Christ is not just the example for Christian life and death, but he is first and foremost the sacrament of true human life. In his person he is the essence of what a human being should be, *coram Deo*.

However, it would be a mistake to think that, by its metaphorical use of the category of sacrifice as an image for Jesus's life and death, the New Testament is spiritualizing these events or is no longer referring to them as something that really happened. On the contrary, in describing them with the term *sacrifice*, it is in fact emphasizing the reality of what happened. The Christian message of the crucified Son of God must have sounded blasphemous to Jewish ears and aesthetically and ethically repulsive to Hellenistic ears.[51] However, precisely because the salvation event of Jesus's death on the cross and his resurrection represents a wholly exceptional eschatological reality in our world of sin and godlessness, categories like that of sacrifice must be used in a figurative way to express the salvific significance of such a unique reality in a way that can be understood.

So what was spiritualized was not the eschatological event itself but the category of sacrifice that is used to render it comprehensible. The application of this category to the story of Jesus Christ, however, initiated a hermeneutical process that led to a *christological transformation of the imaginative world of the sacrificial cult*. Although the cult initially had served to interpret the story of Jesus Christ, now the story was interpreting the cult. Given the uniqueness of its eschatological character, this story could not be understood as sacrifice unless the nature of a true sacrifice was understood in christological terms in the light of the salvation event of Jesus's death and resurrection. For this reason it was understood, in Christian speaking and thinking, not merely as one sacrifice among others but as the altogether central, conclusive, and perfect sacrifice, as the fulfillment and archetype of all other sacrifices. In concentrating the category of sacrifice exclusively on Jesus Christ, his life,

---

51. Hengel, *Atonement*, 31–40; C. F. D. Moule, *The Origin of Christology* (Cambridge: Cambridge University Press, 1980), 150–51.

death, and being raised from the dead became the focal point of the imaginative world of sacrifice. Christian spiritualization of the category of sacrifice thus began with its figurative use to express the salvific significance of Jesus's death and resurrection and led on to the complete christological redefinition of this category.

With its figurative use of the category of sacrifice, the New Testament was participating in the widespread process of spiritualization prevalent in the religious world of the Roman Empire at the time the Christian faith began.[52] The Christians did not begin this process, but they did participate in it and used it to communicate their own message. Spiritualization is to be formally understood as a metaphorical process in which things or actions (i.e., descriptions of things or actions) from one context are used as interpretive categories in another context and in which the meaning the things or actions have in one context is enlisted and used to uncover, illuminate, articulate, or express the meaning of things or actions in another context. Hence, the spiritualization of the category of sacrifice means that interest is focused on the figurative and imaginative world of sacrifice rather than on the sacrifice itself and its enactment. This is linked to the semantic problem areas of meaning, understanding, and communication, but not to the specific cultic enactments of particular sacrificial offerings and types of sacrifice. This removal of its specific referential relationships with cultic procedures makes it possible to use the category of sacrifice outside the cultic context as well, so that, alongside the meaning it has acquired there, new meanings are disclosed within another, noncultic context. This can happen in a positive way through the disclosure or establishment of partial analogies, as well as in a negative way, which validates new elements in contrast to the sphere of meaning of the category adopted. This implies a shift in emphasis from the purely cultic to the broader religious and ethical implications of the category. To spiritualize the category of sacrifice in this sense means to give it the semantic structure of a symbol, a metaphor, or an image. It is thus used—under specific cultural conditions—as a context of meaning comprehensible in its own right, with the aid of which another context of meaning can be disclosed as comprehensible without implying any relationship of representation or analogy.

This is especially clear where the category of sacrifice is concerned. Sacrifices themselves have a symbolic structure. One integral part of a sacrifice is an act

52. H. Wenschkewitz, *Die Spiritualisierung der Kultusbegriffe Tempel, Priester und Opfer im Neuen Testament* (Leipzig: Pfeiffer, 1932); R. J. McKelvey, *The New Temple* (London: Oxford University Press, 1969).

of consecration, in which something becomes a symbol for something else.[53] Thus the sacrificial animal becomes a symbol for "the person or persons who are making the sacrifice or upon whose behalf the sacrifice is being made."[54] Similarly, in the sacrificial act the offerant is sacrificed symbolically in the form of a part of himself, in that the consecrated animal is killed and its life is offered up before God as a proxy for the life of the offerant. This vicarious function of the sacrifice depends entirely on the consecration of the sacrificial animal, and it requires an entire system of religious rules and cultic conventions that not only specify the effects of the sacrifice but also determine what is to be sacrificed in specific situations, how it can become a symbol, precisely what is symbolized, and how the sacrificial act is to be carried out in a valid manner. So a sacrifice posits a relationship between God and human beings that is regulated by cultic law: a cultic framework for thought and action, one that assigns specific roles and functions to the participants and bestows on their actions an efficacy they would not possess in and of themselves. It is only in such a cultic context that the idea of a vicarious sacrificial death has a comprehensible meaning.

However, in Christian thought and speech it is not the sacrifice but the *category* of sacrifice that is used figuratively. Furthermore, what matters is not primarily the linguistic term (or its substitute) but the *meaning* of this category.[55] Here too, the use of this category depends on a regulatory system that permits it to be used figuratively beyond the boundaries of its primary context of use. These rules are of a semantic and linguistic nature, because they regulate the figurative use of the category of sacrifice and not the enactment of the sacrifice. They highlight the meaning, not the enactment, of the sacrifice, and this meaning is determined not by the cultic act of killing but by the attitude and conduct of the participants and by the rules and conventions that direct their actions within this context. This was already becoming apparent in pre- and non-Christian developments, where the spiritualization of the category of sacrifice led to a shift in emphasis to the broader religious and ethical implications of the concept of sacrifice; and in the christological usage this led to a complete semantic reconstruction of the category of sacrifice, as will be shown below. In spite of their dissimilarity, both instances share

53. J. H. M. Beattie, "On Understanding Sacrifice," in *Sacrifice*, ed. Bourdillon and Fortes, 29–44, esp. 30.

54. Ibid.

55. Where this meaning originates from is a subject of hermeneutical controversy, of course. While Gese traces its derivation through the history of revelation and of tradition, Stuhlmacher deduces it historically, Janowski religio-historically, Bultmann in terms of anthropological existentialism, and Hofius strictly christologically.

the hermeneutical characteristic that the image used is not the ritual act of killing as such but, rather, the overall meaning of this act, determined as it is by the attitude of the participants and by the religious system that regulates and controls their actions.[56]

Therefore, if Jesus's life and death are confessed as self-sacrifice, then something is being said not only about his life but, simultaneously, about the attitudes of those whose actions and judgments contribute to this event, and about the regulatory system that determines this context of action and of judgment. All these premises must be taken into account if this confession is to be correctly understood. If it is not seen or is no longer understood that the cultic use of the category of sacrifice presupposes the regulatory system of cultic law that governs the relationship between God and human beings, then the christological use of the concept of sacrifice can no longer convey any clear understanding of the salvific significance of the death of Jesus. The same would apply for a different reason if, for example, the life, teaching, and death of Jesus offered no kind of reference point that would allow his life to be understood as one of selfless surrender to God for the sake of others. Further, if the category of sacrifice did not help us to express God's saving activity on the cross and in the resurrection of Jesus in a clear and unmistakable way, it would be of no soteriological use. And finally, it also would be of no use if it did not contribute to the clarification and illumination of our own life story. In that case it would not accomplish the very thing it is intended to accomplish: conveying the salvific significance of the eschatological event of Jesus's death on the cross and his resurrection and making it possible for us to understand it. If our individual stories form part of his story, then any interpretation of his story is soteriologically inadequate unless it simultaneously interprets our story as well: for then it does not communicate *for us* what is soteriologically important.

### 3.3. The Limited Function of the Category of Sacrifice in Soteriological Use

Does this mean that where there is little or no understanding of our actual life as sacrifice, our attempt to interpret it in the light of Jesus's life, perceived

56. Thus the process of spiritualization is constantly in danger of becoming a process of secularization. The former takes place within a religious system and broadens the use of the category of sacrifice from its primary cultic context of use to other ethical and religious contexts. The latter transfers the category into an entirely different system, with the result that its metaphorical image structure disintegrates and is gradually lost. After all, in the context of a wider enterprise (such as a war or a commercial operation), any death can be held to be a sacrifice.

as sacrifice, must lead to sadomasochistic consequences? A number of feminist theologians have accused the Christian tradition of encouraging such an antilife attitude, particularly where women are concerned.[57] Even though a number of examples of this can be quoted, any such judgment must bear in mind that the imaginative world of sacrifice is just one figurative context among a variety of complexes of images and ideas the New Testament uses to express the Christian salvation experience. To isolate this particular mindscape, therefore, is inevitably misleading, and to consider it in isolation can hardly avoid giving a one-sided and oversimplified representation of a complex situation. Indeed, the New Testament texts demonstrate this. In his detailed but far from exhaustive study of the central ideas the New Testament uses to express the salvation experienced in Jesus Christ, E. Schillebeeckx has examined the semantic structure and historical background of sixteen "key concepts that occur repeatedly in all parts of the New Testament."[58] Taken together, they are an impressive demonstration of the astonishing and frequently far from compatible ways in which the New Testament authors express their understanding of salvation.[59]

This diversity and dissimilarity are significant in themselves, since they defy all attempts to reduce them to a few central ideas. No single idea is so comprehensive that it can integrate all or even most of the New Testament conceptions of salvation. As John Knox has shown,[60] at the very least we need the categories of victory and sacrifice in order to do justice to the material,[61] and even then we would have to subsume such widely differing conceptions under the heading of "sacrifice" that the category would have to be broadened beyond recognition and would lose any specific meaning.[62] But there is no

57. D. Sölle, *Suffering*, trans. E. R. Kalin (Philadelphia: Fortress, 1975), 22–28; M. Daly, *Beyond God the Father: Toward a Philosophy of Women's Liberation* (Boston: Beacon Press, 1973); E. Sorge, *Religion und Frau: Weibliche Spiritualität im Christentum* (Stuttgart: Kohlhammer, 1985), 42; Sorge, "Das Kreuz mit dem Kreuz," *Fama: Feministisch-theologische Zeitschrift* 1, no. 4 (1988): 1–3; R. Strobel, "Das Kreuz im Kontext feministischer Theologie: Versuch einer Standortbestimmung," in *Vom Verlangen nach Heilwerden: Christologie in feministisch-theologischer Sicht*, ed. D. Strahm and R. Strobel (Fribourg, Switzerland: Exodus Verlag, 1991), 182–93.

58. E. Schillebeeckx, *Christus und die Christen: Die Geschichte einer neuen Lebenspraxis* (Freiburg: Herder, 1977), 461.

59. Cf. also G. Barth, *Der Tod Jesu Christi im Verständnis des Neuen Testaments* (Neukirchen-Vluyn: Neukirchener, 1992).

60. J. Knox, *The Death of Christ: The Cross in New Testament History and Faith* (London: Abingdon, 1959), 146–48.

61. Cf. J. P. M. Sweet, "Maintaining the Testimony of Jesus: The Suffering of Christians in the Revelation of John," in *Suffering and Martyrdom in the New Testament*, ed. W. Horbury and B. McNeil (Cambridge: Cambridge University Press, 1981), 101–17.

62. The work of F. M. Young, for example, bears this out; here, to all intents and purposes, "sacrifice" disintegrates into "service of God" and "prayer" (*Sacrifice and the Death of Christ*, 135–36).

interpretation of the death of Jesus that provides an authentic expression of salvation on its own in a way that all others do not. It is not just the canonical diversity of the New Testament that contradicts this. Anyone who denied this would be committing the hermeneutical fallacy of "absolute interpretation," of which the quest for the "original understanding" is the most familiar version: even if we knew that Jesus understood and construed his own death as sacrifice, we would still have to ask whether this was a reasonable understanding, or even the only reasonable one.[63] The mere fact that an interpretation is of earlier historical provenance does not necessarily make it objectively more reasonable; the fact that the interpretation of Jesus's death as sacrifice can be traced back to the beginnings of the Christian faith does not prevent other interpretations from being just as accurate or even more satisfactory.

Hence, attempts to reduce the diversity of soteriological interpretations of Jesus's death and resurrection to a single normative basic understanding fail for exegetical and hermeneutical reasons. However, there is a still deeper theological reason for its irreducibility. These interpretations would lose their crucial point if we sought to reduce them to an overall basic soteriological model, a uniformly structured salvation experience, or a stereotypical interpretation of Jesus Christ. Despite all its identical determinacy of content, provided by the story of Jesus Christ, the Christian salvation experience, as an experience *of my* (and your) salvation and of the life desired and brought about by God precisely *for me* (and for you), is marked out decisively by its specific detail and its unrepeatable individuality—but not by any kind of overall abstract structural element;[64] and the same is true of the complexes of ideas, images, and categories used to represent it in words. This salvation experience is available only in specific forms and can be represented only in specific terms. But since it always belongs simultaneously to Jesus's story, to God's story, and to the story of each one of us, its manner of representation can only ever be drawn from these stories. But this means that even Jesus's story and God's story, with which each specific Christian salvation experience corresponds, can only ever be expressed within the scope and under the conditions of each of our own stories, in other words, not in a quasi-objective, external manner, but in different inward or autobiographical perspectives. It is therefore integral to their essence

63. Cf. N. Lash, "What Might Martyrdom Mean?," in *Suffering and Martyrdom*, ed. Horbury and McNeil, 183–98.

64. What Christians experience as *salvation* can be expressed in a manner that can readily be generalized by reference to the story of Jesus Christ. But the *experience* of this salvation, and hence its decisive personal actualization, is only ever given in the perspective of the participants (i.e., those affected), not that of those who are observing and describing. To speak of salvation is one thing, but to live in salvation is quite another.

that theological reflection encounters them only in an irreducible diversity of expressive forms. To focus theologically on only some or a few of them cannot be justified in principle, but only from a pragmatic point of view (e.g., in the light of the question of how far these different *expressive forms* of the faith can really constitute expressive forms *of the same faith*). This equivalence of faith is admittedly always assumed, but it is not given in the same form. It is not identical with any specific formulation, but it always remains to be discovered and constructed; and both the *regula fidei* of the practical consensus of faith and also the canon of authoritative witness handed down are the resources and aids to orientation with which the Christian church has equipped itself for this purpose. Neither frequency, nor length of use, nor any privileged status in the dogmatic tradition are in themselves a sufficient criterion for holding one complex of images or ideas to be a better or more acceptable representation of salvation than another. For certain tasks, in certain situations, and in the context of certain experiences, particular representational and expressive forms may appear more suitable than others, and there is no doubt that some image complexes are in a better position to integrate or associate with other groups of ideas, or to unleash their creativity, and thus to function as soteriological guiding metaphors or basic images. But these are practical, pragmatic, and, for the most part, a posteriori judgments rather than preferential treatment based on principle; one cannot exclude the possibility that any one of them may be ousted and replaced by others in the course of history.

Just such a preferential, principial treatment of particular strands of the figurative and imaginative world of Old and New Testament soteriology was repeatedly attempted by the dogmatic tradition in its endeavors to work out the details of a theological grammar of the Christian faith.[65] Thus attempts were made to unfold the Christian salvation experience within the framework of particular guiding models, each of which gave preference to certain categories of the soteriological figurative material as especially appropriate. The main examples are

- the *political model* of the power struggle, with images such as captivity, ransom, victory, liberation, and annihilation;[66]

65. Cf. the exposition by F. Chr. Baur, *Die christliche Lehre von der Versöhnung in ihrer geschichtlichen Entwicklung von der ältesten Zeit bis auf die neueste* (Tübingen: Osiander, 1838); A. Ritschl, *Die christliche Lehre von der Rechtfertigung und Versöhnung*, 3 vols. (Bonn: Adolph Marcus, ⁴1895–1902); G. Aulen, *Christus Victor: An Historical Study of the Three Main Types of the Idea of the Atonement* (London: SPCK, 1931); G. Wenz, *Geschichte der Versöhnungslehre in der evangelischen Theologie der Neuzeit*, 2 vols. (Munich: Christian Kaiser, 1984–85).
66. Cf. J. S. Whale, *Victor and Victim: The Christian Doctrine of Redemption* (Cambridge: Cambridge University Press, 1960).

- the *cultic model*, with images such as sacrifice, suffering, surrender, substitution, atonement, renewal of life, acceptance, and rejection;
- the *juristic model*, with images such as contract, covenant, rights and obligations, breach of law, reparation, guilt, penalty, satisfaction, retribution, forgiveness, compensation, repentance, and vindication; and
- the *personal model*, with images such as fellowship, friendship, freedom, responsibility, disappointment, injury, betrayal of confidence, deception, forgiveness, and love.

Each of these models offered the option of a different or—as can be recognized from the differing conceptions of atonement and reconciliation—even conflicting theological interpretation of God's saving activity on behalf of his creation in Jesus Christ and through the Holy Spirit. It is no accident, however, that the church neither promulgated any of these dogmatic reflection models as the definitive interpretation of salvation nor codified them as the doctrine of salvation. The New Testament reminder that Christians can and must testify to and describe salvation in Jesus Christ in many and varied ways, not just in one, is too emphatic for that. For it is never merely a question of Jesus's own story, or just of God's story in this story, but rather, within and through these, the story of each one of us, with the distinguishing qualities, heights and depths, hopes and disappointments, successes and failures, and joys and fears that make up our individual and incommutable life stories. Salvation must constantly be affirmed *in* these stories, because only in them can it be conceived of and apprehended autobiographically. But there is never just one way of telling these stories. None of them has only one accurate or true representational form. Each is so complex that it has numerous possible inner autobiographical and outward biographical perspectives, which enable this story, in all its uniqueness, to be captured with varying degrees of success. None of these perspectives can claim to be the only true one, or even to give an overview of the complete truth of this story: that could only be said of the abstract ideal represented by the integral of all possible perspectives on it, which none of us is capable of realizing.

All of this applies not just to the story of each one of us but also to the story of Jesus Christ. It too can only ever be considered in perspective and, indeed, not just from various perspectives, both soteriological and nonsoteriological, but also in various ways within the soteriological perspective. The dogmatic tradition in fact acknowledged this by seeking to understand the soteriological meaning of this story consistently against

the background of the Old Testament story of God and Israel and to sum
it up in the model of the *munus triplex* [threefold office]: in order to be told
in a way that is soteriologically accurate, the story of Jesus Christ must be
told against an Old Testament backdrop in at least three different ways,
none of which can be curtailed in favor of another. In other words, it must
be told as the story of the divine prophet, priest, and king. Yet even this is
far from being the whole story. This story is just as diverse as our stories,
as is the accurate portrayal of the salvation it accomplishes. Each attempt
at systematization must therefore be aware that it is just one possibility
among others. Dogmatic reflection that remains self-critically conscious of
its relative and limited nature will refrain from trying to assert or stipulate
that either one particular complex of images or ideas or one particular
guiding soteriological metaphor is the only authoritative one: a different
and better way of imagining and expressing it will always be possible. This
is not a plea for a doctrinal free-for-all but rather a description of the doctrinal task. Instead of tying itself to specific normative image complexes
or to a particular guiding soteriological model, doctrinal thinking must
concentrate on explicating the contextual and structural conditions for
soteriological thought and speech in Christian theology: it must unfold the
grammar of the soteriological imagery of faith, the main features of which
it has outlined in the christological and trinitarian doctrines. Hence, the
diversity of soteriological images that is a characteristic of the Christian
faith is properly understood and interpreted from a theological point of
view only when these images are presented in trinitarian terms and given
a christological emphasis.

    That said, one thing is undeniable at any rate: the imagery of sacrifice is
not the only hermeneutical tool for expressing the salvific significance of Jesus
Christ's death on the cross and resurrection, and not every use of the idea of
sacrifice is necessarily an appropriate representation of the salvation confessed
by Christians. The appropriateness of each use will be decided, in context and
in comparison with other ways of expressing salvation, by its observance of
the christological and trinitarian grammar of Christian soteriology; and by
whether and how it can make the life story specific to each of the confessing
persons intelligible to themselves, and can render God's saving activity visible
in that story. This does not necessarily have to result from the successful use
(or, for that matter, from any use) of the imaginative world of sacrifice. But
if under certain circumstances the latter is indeed an appropriate medium
for soteriological thought and speech, then salvation experiences that make
use of other media of articulation must either be capable of being translated
into it or at least remain consistent with it.

## 4. Versions of the Tübingen Antithesis

The considerations of the preceding section have highlighted two virtually indisputable facts:

1. In the New Testament the salvific significance of Jesus's cross and resurrection is expressed through the category of sacrifice not just in one way but in different ways—by Paul, Mark, John, in the General Epistles and in the Epistle to the Hebrews.
2. In the New Testament the salvific significance of Jesus's cross and resurrection is also expressed using other categories and image complexes in numerous different forms that are not always neatly partitioned or in complete agreement.

From a hermeneutical point of view, the question of the soteriological relevance of the category of sacrifice is decided on the basis of the relationship between these two exegetical positions. But it comes down to two alternatives: Is the soteriological polyphony of the New Testament to be understood as a many-sided interpretation of the sacrificial death of Jesus Christ, or, when we speak of the sacrificial death of Jesus Christ, are we alluding to one of the principal interpretations of the salvific significance of his death, albeit not the only soteriologically acceptable one? To rephrase the question, does the sacrificial death of Jesus Christ refer to the *interpretandum* of every soteriological statement, or does it express one soteriological *interpretament* among, alongside, or beyond others?

The Tübingen Antithesis appears to favor the first alternative. To speak of the salvific significance of the death of Jesus in this way means ipso facto to speak of him as an atoning sacrifice or a sacrifice for sin. It is impossible to capture the *pro nobis* of his death unless it is presented as an atoning, sacrificial death. Karl Barth—to name just one—saw the issue differently. For him it is a matter of a particular "*variation* . . . in which the New Testament speaks of this *pro nobis* and in which the church too has repeatedly spoken of it."[67] Who is right?

It is too soon to pose this question. Barth's position is clear, whereas the Tübingen Antithesis is ambiguous. How else could it provoke the objection that it was "wrong to restrict the statements concerning the meaning of Jesus's death to specific New Testament images and terms, and to canonize and

---

67. K. Barth, *Die kirchliche Dogmatik*, IV/1:301 (italics in original). Cf. also K. Rahner, *Grundkurs des Glaubens* (Freiburg: Herder, 1976), 260–79.

dogmatize them in the belief that they alone are correct and appropriate"?[68] This is the precise misunderstanding that needs to be removed or, if it is applicable, corrected. After all, what can it logically mean to say that the salvific significance of Jesus's death can be captured only by the idea of atoning sacrifice? At least five different interpretations are available, all of which could but need not be advocated. Let us consider these different possibilities with a brevity that unfortunately is inevitable here.

1. First of all, the Tübingen Antithesis can be treated as an *exegetical thesis* where certain texts are concerned. In that case, it is asserting that *in a given text* the salvific significance of the death of Jesus can be understood only by reference to the idea of atoning sacrifice. Otfried Hofius, for example, argues that in 2 Corinthians 5:21 "reconciliation and atonement . . . are two sides of *one and the same* coin—that of the cross event."[69] Admittedly, this could be—incorrectly—disputed (e.g., based on the absence of cultic terminology),[70] but this would then constitute an exegetical dispute concerning the text, a restriction that would deprive the Tübingen Antithesis of its normative application and hence of its doctrinal point.

2. Second, it can be presented as a *historical genetic thesis*, which means that the salvific significance of Jesus's death derived from the idea of vicarious atoning sacrifice and has become integrally linked to this origin; as a result, the soteriological character of his death can be conceived of only in the light of that original understanding. Here, by amalgamating historical and theological questions, an attempt is made—by Martin Hengel, for instance—to highlight the *originality* of the concept of atoning sacrifice by tracing it back to its earliest Jerusalem origins or even (on the basis of the presumed historical authenticity of Mark 10:45 and 14:24) to Jesus's own understanding of his death.[71] Yet even if the originality of the concept of atoning sacrifice could

68. Friedrich, *Verkündigung des Todes Jesu*, 146. It should simply be noted here that it requires more "to canonize and to dogmatize" a theological concept than Friedrich appears to imply.

69. O. Hofius, "Erwägungen zur Gestalt und Herkunft des paulinischen Versöhnungsgedankens," in *Paulusstudien*, 1–14; Hofius, "Gott hat unter uns aufgerichtet das Wort von der Versöhnung," in *Paulusstudien*, 15–32; cf. Hofius, "Sühne und Versöhnung: Zum paulinischen Verständnis des Kreuzestodes Jesu," in *Paulusstudien*, 33–41; Hofius, "Wort Gottes und Glaube bei Paulus," in *Paulusstudien*, 148–74.

70. Friedrich, *Verkündigung des Todes Jesu*, 70–71.

71. Cf. only H. Patsch, *Abendmahl und historischer Jesus*; H. Schürmann, *Jesu ureigener Tod* (Freiburg: Herder, 1975); Schürmann, "Jesu ureigenes Todesverständnis," 273–309; Schürmann, "Jesu Todesverständnis im Verstehenshorizont seiner Umwelt," 141–60; R. Pesch, *Abendmahl und Jesu Todesverständnis*; W. Grimm, *Die Verkündigung Jesu und Deuterojesaja* (Frankfurt: Peter Lang, ²1981), 231–58 (and further to 277); Hengel, *Atonement*; V. Hampel, *Menschensohn und historischer Jesus: Ein Rätselwort als Schlüssel zum messianischen Selbstverständnis Jesu* (Neukirchen-Vluyn: Neukirchener, 1990), 302–42.

be proved within the bounds of historical probability, at most this would have implications for the understanding of the *verus sensus historicus* [true historical meaning] but not for that of the *veritas rei* [truth of the thing itself]. Age in itself is not an argument either for truth or for adequacy. Even if we knew that Jesus himself had understood his death as a sacrificial death, we still—as N. Lash rightly emphasizes—would have to ask whether he was right and whether this self-understanding was appropriate or the only appropriate understanding of the salvific significance of his death.[72] Here, too, historical verification does not excuse us from the duty of theological argumentation. The idea of atoning sacrifice may belong to the original strata of soteriological thought, but this alone does not make it the foundation stone of Christian soteriology.

3. Closely linked with the genetic thesis, though distinguished from it by another perspective, is the *traditio-historical thesis*. According to Peter Stuhlmacher, the many and diverse soteriological representations in the New Testament constitute "*historical milestones on the path of the gospel of reconciliation as it presses on toward a perfected linguistic form*";[73] these can be traced back to the idea of the vicarious atoning sacrificial death of Jesus as the original understanding of salvation.

Of course there are notable historical, systematic, methodological, and doctrinal obstacles standing in the way of this position.

*Historically*, it is true that analogies do not constitute genealogies and that the wide range of soteriological terminology in the New Testament (apart from the exceptions in Mark 10:45 and 1 Tim. 2:6) can hardly be reduced to "unanimous positions of the New Testament message of salvation"[74] proceeding one from the other in a direct evolutionary manner.[75]

*Systematically*—as has already been emphasized—at least two circles of ideas, "victory" and "sacrifice,"[76] are required (or, as the dogmatic tradition of the threefold office emphasized, the categories of prophet, priest, and

72. Lash, "What Might Martyrdom Mean?"
73. P. Stuhlmacher, "Das Evangelium von der Versöhnung in Christus: Grundlinien und Grundprobleme einer biblischen Theologie des Neuen Testaments," in *Das Evangelium von der Versöhnung in Christus*, ed. P. Stuhlmacher and H. Claß (Stuttgart: Calwer, 1979), 13–54, esp. 48 (italics in orginal); cf. Stuhlmacher, *Vom Verstehen des Neuen Testaments: Eine Hermeneutik* (Göttingen: Vandenhoeck & Ruprecht, 1979), 245; Stuhlmacher, *Biblische Theologie des Neuen Testaments*, vol. 1, *Grundlegung: Von Jesus zu Paulus* (Göttingen: Vandenhoeck & Ruprecht, 1992).
74. Stuhlmacher, *Vom Verstehen*, 227.
75. Cf. the critique by M. Oeming, *Gesamtbiblische Theologien der Gegenwart* (Stuttgart: Kohlhammer, 1985), 104–35; Hossfeld, "Versöhne als Sühne," 59–60.
76. Cf. Knox, *Death of Christ*.

king) in order to do even partial justice to the diversity of New Testament references to salvation.

*Methodologically*, although the application of the traditio-historical principle is fully appropriate within the horizon of a Christian reading of the Old Testament, it is nonetheless problematic when applied to the diversity of soteriological language in the New Testament, because then it is no longer teleologically but archaeologically oriented. In Jesus Christ the apocalyptic historical Telos *was there*. To that extent, the polyphony of Christian utterances concerning salvation is not a process of the gradual unfolding of truth and the perfecting of linguistic form.[77] Traditional New Testament formulas show, as do early church standardizations of tradition (dogmas), that time and again the issue was to identify the cross of Jesus Christ as the point of reference and thereby to ensure the specificity and continuity of the Christian statements concerning salvation in new situations and under altered circumstances.[78]

And *doctrinally*, we must then ask whether the many and varied forms in which the New Testament speaks of salvation are to be apprehended only as "historical milestones on the path . . . to the perfect linguistic form" of the gospel. The gospel accomplishes its purpose, however, when it awakens faith in the effective presence and nearness of God and when the proclamation of Jesus Christ is apprehended as a message concerning *our* salvation and, to be precise, concerning our salvation as individuals, not merely in the abstract as specimens of the human race.

This sharp focus on the individual is part and parcel of the message that salvation proclaimed as good news possesses, not fortuitously and temporarily but intrinsically, the quality of πολλαχῶς λέγεσθαι [multiplicity of meaning]. Individuals live their lives in specific circumstances; they have a unique story characterized by their experience and activity, and they articulate this story in their own language. Linguistic diversity belongs to the essence of the Christian salvation experience, and the irreducible multiplicity of soteriological images and ideas is a direct consequence of this. As has been said, in the course of the history of theology there have been a number of systematic and dogmatic

77. It is important to emphasize this in view of the entirely different, obscure attempt by Bader. He organizes the New Testament symbols of Jesus's death in such a way that they reach their pinnacle in the symbol of sacrifice and wants us to understand this progress from one symbol to another as the correct way to experience the death of Jesus. According to him, sacrifice is the "most nonlinguistic, intensive intensity of reality, the thinging of the things before and outside of any language," in which the "progressive reification and simultaneous removal from linguistic consciousness" of the symbols of Jesus's death reach their "root." "Once the sacrifice is complete, it is time to speak again"—in prayer (*Symbolik des Todes Jesu*, 215).

78. Cf. P. G. Müller, *Der Traditionsprozeß im Neuen Testament: Kommunikationsanalytische Studien zur Versprachlichung des Jesusphänomens* (Freiburg: Herder, 1982).

attempts to grant special status to one or another complex of New Testament soteriological images and categories. Thus the Christian salvation experience has been interpreted principally or exclusively in the context of law and repentance using the categories of substitution, satisfaction by merit, or vicarious penal suffering; or in the context of a power struggle between God and evil using the categories of captivity, victory, and liberation; or in the cultic context using the categories of sacrifice, suffering, and self-giving; or in a personal context using the categories of love, mercy, obedience, fatherhood, and filiation. There is a good reason, however, that none of these soteriological sets of ideas was adopted by the church as the only adequate and legitimate doctrine of the salvific significance of Jesus's death: the Christian faith has too great and irreducible a multiplicity of ways of expressing the salvific significance of Jesus Christ, as the New Testament reminds us. In fact, the universal soteriological relevance of the story of Jesus Christ consists precisely in the fact that it is the story of each and every human being in his or her own distinctive individuality, because it is the story of how God, who wants us to live in his presence, mediates and interprets his nearness to us. But only within the realm of each life story is it possible to say with certainty that this is the case. The history of God's salvific involvement with us humans, culminating as it does in the cross and resurrection of Jesus, demonstrates its universality in the fact that it can only be recognized and confessed as it pertains specifically to the life story of each of us. Within each story, God's saving activity is enacted in such a way that the reaction to his self-mediating nearness is one of thanks and adoration. It is *salvation* history because God does not wait until we stumble on him and notice him (something that experience tells us would never happen); rather, he uses it to affirm himself in such a way that, as Paul puts it, he cannot be recognized unless he is also glorified and thanked as God (cf. Rom. 1:21). Given that it is an event of an eschatological nature, it cannot be described to us in any objective, external way; it can only ever be articulated inwardly from various autobiographical perspectives. Whenever the salvific significance of the death of Jesus is expressed in a way that is more than a mere human report of it, the speaker gives an insight into his understanding of his own involvement in the salvation event.

This applies to the New Testament texts as well. Their unanimous soteriological stance is not a linguistic form that develops along traditio-historical lines. Rather, this personal involvement and thus—hermeneutically speaking—the practical usage of these texts and—doctrinally speaking—the trinitarian grammar are what underlie their practical understanding of salvation from an inner perspective and are the result of the christological specificity and pneumatological enactment of what is expressed in and through these texts. From a hermeneutical point of view, this means that theological reflection entails a constant reference back, from what is said to what is spoken of, from the confession to what is confessed, from the text to Christ himself. This applies to the soteriological use of the category of sacrifice as well. What is soteriologically relevant and must be kept in our doctrinal sights is not this category as such but the salvation event it articulates. This event is never presented to us without interpretation, but it also is not presented with a preferred principal interpretation. For those affected, the interpretation preferred at any given time is the one that makes present and comprehensible in their lives God's saving nearness, as it is realized in Jesus Christ and interpreted through the Spirit. For the observer, on the other hand—and hence for the theologian too—there is only ever a polyphony of interpretations expressing the different interpretations of this salvation event. These interpretations cannot be detached from what they express without causing the latter to disappear. But conversely, they themselves are not what they articulate and interpret. This is the dogmatic trigger both for the question of the traditio-historical context of these linguistic forms and also for the primary and recurring question of the *equivalence* of the salvation thus diversely confessed by the Christian faith. A traditio-historical development model that is only oriented to the linguistic form breaks down here unless, within the framework of a diachronically restricted communication model, there is an ongoing development of fresh answers to the same, continually recurring appeal of the gospel.[79] This is the only type of approach that can reconstruct both of the soteriologically relevant dimensions of Christian discourse: (1) the consistency of its discourse concerning *salvation* and (2) the variability of its *discourse* concerning salvation (i.e., the *christological focusing* of soteriological perspectives of different provenance on Jesus Christ and the liturgical and theological *integration* of these Christ-focused soteriological perspectives by means of their parallel use in worship and successive semantic cross-linking of the predicates, images, models, and stories used to articulate the salvation experienced in Jesus Christ). At any rate, a grammar of Christian salvific language is soteriologically adequate only if it does justice to both dimensions (to its consistency of reference to Jesus Christ and to the variability of the salvific statements it makes concerning him) and to their relationship to each other.

4. A fourth possibility would be to take the Tübingen Antithesis as a *theologically normative thesis*, which would make it the category of atoning sacrifice that best captures the salvific significance of the death of Jesus. This is the argument put forward by Frances Young (uninfluenced by Tübingen

---

79. Cf. I. U. Dalferth, *Religiöse Rede von Gott* (Munich: Christian Kaiser, 1981), 376–91.

considerations), namely, that "in the concept of sacrifice are enshrined the deepest experiences of the Christian religion and the most far reaching challenges, both to the individual believers and to the Church as a community as a whole. It covers the basic gospel of forgiveness in Christ, and its outworking in worship and service. Can any other image or symbol claim so much?"[80] It is of course significant that the basis for this theological thesis is not exegetical but systematic, in that reference is made to the integrating power of the symbol of sacrifice for the different areas of Christian life. Yet just as the soteriological relevance of the category of sacrifice cannot be called into question because of homiletical difficulties, it also cannot be substantiated on the basis of its ecclesiological and ethical productiveness. This cannot be the ground but is at best the consequence of its soteriological relevance.

From a purely exegetical point of view, the claim that the salvific significance of Jesus Christ is best captured by the category of sacrifice cannot be sustained.[81] In view of the other New Testament references to salvation, on the one hand, and, on the other hand, of the christologically engendered loss of relevance of the cult of sacrifice[82] and ultimately the (similarly) christologically triggered "spiritualization" of the concept of sacrifice, which was indispensable to the recognition of the eschatological uniqueness of the Christ event and made it "necessary to bring the anti-Jewish element in Christianity into evidence under the Jewish form itself"[83]—in view of these, any absolutizing of the category of sacrifice rules itself out, so that any such claim is seen to be asserting more than can be demonstrated exegetically or theologically.

5. The fifth possibility, advocated below, avoids this exaggerated claim. It is a *theological-hermeneutical thesis* that regards the salvific significance of Jesus's death as being captured in the idea of atoning sacrifice; it does not do this in an ideal way, but it nonetheless does it *sufficiently appropriately* that this idea can serve as a hermeneutical key to the exegetical appraisal and systematic integration of the many facets of New Testament soteriology. If we apprehend "atonement as salvation event," and if the biblical understanding of sacrifice is demonstrated to be a concrete historical realization of this atonement event and is thus freed from the erroneous understanding of it as a transaction between

80. Young, *Sacrifice and the Death of Christ*, 138; cf. Young, *Can These Dry Bones Live?* (London: SCM, 1982); M. Walker, "The Atonement and Justice," *Theol* 91 (1988): 180–86, esp. 183.

81. Cf. M. Anderson and Ph. Culbertson, "The Inadequacy of the Christian Doctrine of Atonement in Light of Levitical Sin Offering," *ATR* 68 (1986): 303–28; Weiser, "Tod Jesu."

82. Cf. Sykes, "Sacrifice in the New Testament," 68; H. Merklein, "Der Tod Jesu als stellvertretender Sühnetod: Entwicklung und Gehalt einer zentralen neutestamentlichen Aussage," *BK* 41 (1986): 68–75, esp. 74.

83. F. D. E. Schleiermacher, *The Christian Faith*, ed. H. R. Mackintosh and J. S. Stewart (Edinburgh: T&T Clark, 1989), 439.

human beings and God, then the *claritas externa* [external clarity] of Scripture would seem to make it impossible to deny that the salvation realized in Jesus's death is adequately realized, in the soteriological conceptual horizon of the first Christians (judged *per analogiam fidei* [by the analogy of faith]), through the application of the idea of sacrifice to the cross of Jesus and the fundamental staurological (cross-based) modification and correction of that idea resulting from that application. By adopting a preferential treatment of the category of sacrifice that is methodological rather than purely a matter of principle, the adequacy of other soteriological models can thus be assessed according to the extent to which they can be converted to the corrected staurological model of atoning sacrifice and can function pragmatically as its theological equivalent. It is a hermeneutical-criteriological thesis; it neither claims theological exclusivity for the idea of atoning sacrifice, nor does it necessarily postulate historical originality for it or make all other soteriological conceptions historically and traditionally dependent on it. It does just one thing: it lays claim to soteriological appropriateness for the biblical category of atoning sacrifice in its staurologically corrected form and attributes criteriological meaning to this understanding of it from a hermeneutical point of view. Understood in this way, however, it has doctrinal relevance as well. For an understanding of sacrifice such as that of the third article of the Augsburg Confession or of Calvin's *Institutes*,[84] for example, is then at the very least highly problematical, while the images of the liberator or leader are theologically equivalent to the idea of sacrifice without necessarily being linguistically or historically derivable from the conceptual field of sacrifice.

This interpretation seems to me to offer the best match for the authentic import of the Tübingen Antithesis. Correctly understood, the question of the soteriological relevance of the category of sacrifice cannot be answered by a genetic, by a traditio-historical, or by an exclusively systematic thesis, but only by a theological-hermeneutical thesis. Such a thesis does not assert that

> to speak of the salvific significance of the death of Jesus means ipso facto to speak of him as an atoning sacrifice.

Rather, it claims that

> to speak of the salvific significance of the death of Jesus means to speak of his death in such a way that what is expressed is what the New Testament is seeking to say of him when it describes him as an atoning sacrifice.

84. Cf., e.g., J. Calvin, *Institutio Christianae Religionis* IV, 18.13 (Opera Omnia V) (Munich, ³1974), 429, lines 10–11.

This distinction is far from being a trivial one. For from this point on, what is of theological importance is no longer the category of atoning sacrifice but rather what is intended by the use of this category. It is not the soteriological indispensability of a terminology of atonement or sacrifice that is advocated here, but (1) the theological assertion that such a terminology assists the satisfactory New Testament articulation of the Christian salvation experience, and (2) the associated hermeneutical thesis that this articulation can be allowed the status of one criterion (but not necessarily the only one) for an acceptable soteriology: from the staurological reshaping of the category of atoning sacrifice we may discern how we can give adequate expression to the salvation experienced in and through Jesus Christ. This position differs from that of Bultmann in its exegetical appraisal of the soteriological relevance of the category of sacrifice in the New Testament, but not in respect to the theological intention lying behind the exegetical pros and cons.[85] It differs from that of Barth, on the other hand, in that it affords the terminology of sacrifice the preferential status of a soteriological criterion. This should be perceived as a necessary corrective to the modern understanding of sacrifice and its philosophical and theological critique, which we have yet to examine. From an objective point of view, however, it does not lead to different or fresh theological implications.[86] No excessive dogmatic demands should therefore be made on the antithesis.

## 5. The Christological Revision of the Old Testament Category of Atoning Sacrifice

We have seen that *speaking of the salvific significance of the death of Jesus means speaking of his death in such a way that what is expressed is what the New Testament is seeking to say of him when it describes him as an atoning sacrifice.* This hermeneutical rule is the systematically relevant implication of the Tübingen efforts to achieve a fresh understanding of the biblical language

85. This is true regardless of the fact that Gese, Stuhlmacher, and Hofius, each in his own way, in a countermove against the apparent subjectivistic reduction of the salvation event to individual decision and Bultmann's specific self-understanding, are essentially concerned with emphasizing the *extra nos* of salvation in contrast to the danger of its dissolution into a subjectivistically understood *pro nobis*: in other words, they stress the objective validity of God's saving activity independent of faith. In the light of *Confessio Augustana* 4, however, it is necessary to ask whether the reality of the Christ event can in fact be contrasted with faith in this way. In other words, we must ask whether faith—albeit not necessarily *my* faith and thus a specific condition applicable to certain subjects—does not belong intrinsically to the reality of the salvation event, so that even though it is possible to differentiate between Christ and faith, the two should not be separated.

86. It is no accident that the study by Janowski ends with a quotation from Barth (*Sühne als Heilsgeschichte*, 362).

of atonement and sacrifice. However, the rule is soteriologically sound only if the model of atoning sacrifice bears adequate testimony to the salvific significance of the death of Jesus. And it can function as a rule only if the model of atoning sacrifice, as used in the New Testament, suggests a soteriological structure against which other models of Christian discourse concerning salvation can be measured. It is worth examining both of these issues by taking Romans 3:25–26 as an example; with its aid we can compare the grammar of the Old Testament category of atoning sacrifice with the grammar of its use in its christologically qualified New Testament context.

In order to carry out a comparison that is not just associative but also verifiable, we must first denominate the soteriological point of comparison by answering the question, What is being stated soteriologically by the use of the category of sacrifice in the Old and New Testaments (or, more precisely, in the P school and the Pauline writings)?

Gese pinpoints the decisive soteriological element as "incorporation into the holy,"[87] which leads to enduring "life contact"[88] and to "fellowship with God."[89] According to him, this is the issue at the heart of Israel's sacrificial cult and, equally, of the salvation event of the cross and resurrection. Atonement is the incorporation event, sacrifice the symbolic act of incorporation; the cross event is the eschatological incorporation into fellowship with God, accomplished once and for all.[90] Both the New Testament references to the sacrificial death of Jesus and all other soteriological statements are to be systematically interpreted in the light of this soteriological point of reference.[91]

87. Gese, "Sühne," 98. In the same year Gese's study of the idea of atonement appeared, Moule similarly focused on the concept of "inclusion" or "incorporation" (*Origin of Christology*, 86) as the central soteriological term by providing evidence that all New Testament Christologies, above all the Pauline, do not just speak of Christ as an individual; they present him as the "corporate Christ," with whom we are externally related and who also incorporates us into his person, so that it can truly be said, "What Christ is, all others are potentially involved in becoming" (ibid.). The meaning of this statement is supported by the fact that such a committed critic of the position as Friedrich compares the Pauline "message of the cross" with the "proclamation of the sacrificial death of Jesus," preferring the former because it does not require that an imperative follow the indicative but clarifies that anyone who follows the crucified one "is gathered into the cross event" (*Verkündigung des Todes Jesu*, 141). Here again the incorporation event is highlighted, although this time in critical opposition to the category of sacrifice. The fundamental soteriological meaning of the incorporation event corresponds to the English term for reconciliation (which goes as far back as William Tyndale): "atonement" = "to be made at one with God."

88. Gese, "Sühne," 99.

89. Ibid., 98.

90. Ibid., 98–99, 105–6.

91. The idea of incorporation functions as a formula for the key soteriological facts *within the framework of the cultic model*. This does not mean to say that every other thought and speech model must also express it in the same way: the formulation of the soteriological

For what is soteriologically relevant and systematically normative is not the category of sacrifice as such but rather the incorporation event it articulates.[92]

In order to grasp this event, together with the grammar of the Christian use of the category of sacrifice, with doctrinal precision, however, it is important not to overlook the fundamental *about-face* that represents the culmination of the continuity and the contrast between cult and cross. There is continuity inasmuch as in the Old Testament context *"God himself*

---

point of reference, too, is dependent on the image complex, or representational model, that is being used to formulate it. *Each formulation of the Christian understanding of salvation is model specific—including each dogmatic formulation.* Each one does not just use certain images; it uses them against the horizon of a background image or a soteriological guiding metaphor that determines the reality content of the images used and the formulation of the basic soteriological process they describe. The dogmatic attempt to arrive at clear concepts for the latter is doomed to failure unless it makes two things clear. First, it is never completely free from all reference back to the model but is beholden to it, regardless of how abstract it is. Second, for this very reason it cannot convert the creedal salvation statements into absolute concepts and enduring doctrinal formulas; it can only ever lay down relative *rules* that permit a well-ordered and verifiable transition from certain formulations of salvation, together with the guiding metaphors underlying them, to other formulations. For only when the variously formulated soteriological processes are taken into consideration can different soteriological models and image complexes be compared with the understanding of salvation that they represent. And this comparison cannot have the aim of replacing and improving on these differing soteriological imageries with unambiguous concepts; instead, its aim is to enable controlled translation processes between them, so as to point up the biases and shortcomings of the respective image complexes from a critical angle and to assist with their correction. Dogmatic doctrinal statements such as "Jesus Christ is true man and true God" are therefore far from being nonexperiential and abstract. This is not because they describe a mysterious reality realistically and sum it up conclusively, but because, on the basis of the Christian resurrection confession, they state the actualization and truth conditions of Christian discourse concerning Jesus Christ, conditions that ignore any figurative and nonfigurative allusion to Jesus only at the cost of failing to speak of the one who is the topic of the resurrection confession.

92. In the face of the danger of a theology of semantic speculation, it must be strongly emphasized that it is not the *concepts* (Who is *reconciled* with whom? Who is *liberated*, to what extent, from what, and to what end?, etc.) that are decisive. Rather, it is the *issue* that needs to be understood, using these ideas, that matters. The clarity of our apprehension of these ideas is improved not by our treating images as concepts or seeking to transform them into concepts but by our taking them seriously as images and models for the articulation, communication, and reflection of the Christian salvation experience, so that we seek to understand them not by way of their internal semantic structure, but on the basis of the experiential contexts that they express. Treating the figurative language of faith as descriptive language, and hence interpreting it literally, is most certainly not taking it seriously but means, instead, that we are content with its semantic surface level so that we perceive only the linguistic *tool* with the aid of which faith is communicated, and, since it is not recognized *as a tool*, that we miss *what it is communicating*. This type of descriptive reading gets stuck with what is being said, instead of pursuing what is being expressed by what is said and what the speaker is seeking to communicate. It is therefore precisely not what it claims so emphatically to be: a satisfactory understanding of the language of faith.

*is the one who makes atonement possible*,"[93] and even in the New Testament context all the salvific activity is carried out by God alone, albeit in such a way that he not only makes atonement possible but also realizes and enacts it himself.[94] In both cases, therefore, God alone is the subject of the incorporation event and we are his beneficiaries, the ones on the receiving end. But whereas the cultic sacrificial atonement was restricted to Israel and, for this very reason, required constant repetition by priestly intermediaries, Christ's eschatological atonement, as the activity of God himself, is open to the whole world (1 John 2:2) and therefore has taken place once and for all. The incorporation of sinful human beings into fellowship with the holy God, which the New Testament expresses by its use of the category of sacrifice for the cross of Jesus Christ, is distinguished from the Old Testament sacrificial cult by five characteristic elements: exclusive theocentricity, soteriological universality, christological historicity, eschatological finality, and radically noncultic enactment. This volte-face also manifests itself in a characteristic reshaping of the grammar of the Christian use of the category of atoning sacrifice.[95] To what extent?

The Old Testament atoning sacrifice is a symbolic context of action that can be described on three levels:[96] on the level of real enactments, on the level of their symbolic meaning, and on the level of the cultic regulatory system, which the first two levels together communicate. At the first level it is seen as the activity of the offerant and the priest and the slaughter of the sacrificial animal. At the second level it is a symbolic event that endows the actions of the people involved with effects and a significance they do not have in themselves: the symbolic incorporation of the human person into saving fellowship with God. At the third level, which is evident in the Old Testament theology of the Pentateuch and its P school, it is the subject of theological substantiation and cultic regulation.

From this network of aspects the dogmatic tradition for the most part isolated only the element of vicarious *substitution*, making it the starting point for soteriological reflection.[97] But this is abstract in that it extracts one aspect

93. Janowski, *Sühne als Heilsgeschehen*, 353 (italics in original). In the context of the Old Testament, however, it is an understatement to say that God merely makes atonement possible.
94. Cf. Hofius, *Paulusstudien*, 39.
95. Cf. ibid., 48–49.
96. Cf. W. Burkert, *Homo Necans: Interpretation altgriechischer Opferriten und Mythen* (Berlin: de Gruyter, 1972), 31–38.
97. Herein lies the basic problem with substitutionary Christologies. Of course it is possible to take the view that the idea of substitution corresponds to the idea of incorporation, as does H. Vogel, for instance, in his *Christologie* (*Gesammelte Werke* [Stuttgart: Radius, 1983], 5:300–304), in which he seeks to expound the mystery of Christ's substitution in terms

from the symbolic context of sacrificial action and makes it a christological *tertium comparationis* [third element of the comparison], which, it is true, is an implication but not the essence of the sacrificial event.

If we concentrate on the meaning, on the second level of the symbolic event, then we find that the Old Testament atoning sacrifice has two constituent elements: the act of *consecration*, by which a sacrificial animal becomes a symbol for the offerant, and the act of symbolic *incorporation*, in which "through the sacrificial animal's offering of blood the offering of the offerant's own life is symbolically enacted."[98] In the Old Testament cult the consecration takes place when the owner of the sacrificial animal lays (literally, "presses with") his or her hands upon the head of the sacrificial animal, so that there is a "transference of subject," an identification of the offerant with the sacrificial animal. Without this transference of identity, the slaughter of the animal would not constitute a sacrifice. But even with this transference it is only a sacrifice if the priest enacts the blood ritual, the symbolic incorporation into

---

of his existence in our existence. Cf. E. Jüngel, "Das Geheimnis der Stellvertretung: Ein dogmatisches Gespräch mit Heinrich Vogel," *Biblisch-theologische Zeitschrift* 1 (1984): 65–80; J. Fischer, "Vom Geheimnis der Stellvertretung," *Evangelische Kommentare* 21 (1988): 165–67. Fischer interprets the idea of substitution as indicating a "process of recognition," one in which there is no theoretical affirmation or awareness of an existing state of affairs, but in which the act of recognition brings about that which is recognized, as it truly is, for the first time (*Glaube als Erkenntnis*, 82). Hence, the vicarious character of Jesus's death on the cross is understood when it is apprehended as a "hermeneutical instruction" to the effect that "we ought to perceive ourselves in this death in the same way as God perceives us in it" (84). Since only on the basis of revelation, and therefore by faith in Jesus as the Christ, can we attain a self-knowledge in which we perceive ourselves as God perceives us, it would seem that the *extra nos* is as assured as is the fact that without faith the cross can have no soteriological effect. But looks can be deceiving. The transition from the status of sinner to the status of the justified is enacted as a change in the perception God has of us, and this change is grounded in the death of Jesus and triggered by it. With his recognition terminology Fischer has reformulated the Reformation understanding of justification as being *propter Christum per fidem* [on account of Christ through faith] in such a way that justification can be described as our inclusion in the perspective with which God recognizes Jesus Christ. The *propter Christum* and its *extra nos* character are not taken into account in the same way. For Fischer, at the cross God participates "not as one who acts but as one who *recognizes*," who "*through his recognition bestows reality*" on the salvific nature of this event as confessed by faith (82, italics in original). But this has only been thought through in relation to faith, not in relation to Jesus Christ, with the result that the proposed solution is left as a christological understatement. And logically the reference to the change of recognition perspective leads to an interpretation of the idea of substitution that would make it possible to speak intelligibly of the atoning sacrificial death of Jesus without speaking of Jesus himself (78). Fischer's analysis demonstrates that a theological understanding of the salvation event in Jesus Christ is not tied to the idea of substitution, so that Christology need not necessarily be conceived of as substitutional Christology. But how it should be conceived of remains obscure.

98. Gese, "Sühne," 98.

the holy. The sequence of the acts is therefore crucial and cannot be altered: *consecration–slaughter–incorporation*.[99]

None of this seems to apply to the New Testament use of the category of atoning sacrifice for Jesus's death on the cross.[100] The cross is not preceded by any act of consecration, and neither is it followed by any act of incorporation. In itself it is a "wholly noncultic event,"[101] a public execution, not a ritual act of killing or even an atoning sacrifice. It can be identified as such only from the standpoint of the experience of Jesus's resurrection. For the experience of his resurrection alone makes it plain that

- (formulated from the human point of view) an "act of consecration"—to use the imagery of sacrifice—does not precede the cross *but follows it*, and that this act of consecration is not followed *but preceded* by an "act of incorporation"; and that
- (formulated from God's point of view) the cross is not preceded by an "act of consecration" but *is* an act of consecration and that this act of consecration is only followed by an "act of incorporation" because and to the extent that it *is* simultaneously in itself an act of incorporation.

What does this mean?

In the sacrificial context, as we have seen, consecration is transference of identity. Where, in the case of the cross of Christ, do we find a transference of identity? Paul picks out the point precisely when in Romans 3:25 he adds διὰ πίστεως [by faith] to the early Christian confession he is quoting. The cross becomes a saving event by faith, not because faith was what made the cross into a saving event (God, not faith, openly delivered Jesus Christ up as a ἱλαστήριον [atoning sacrifice]!) but because without faith the cross event is realized not as salvation but as judgment: under those circumstances it highlights the absolute absence and remoteness of God, and not his even greater presence and nearness. Considered against the background of the category of sacrifice, the function of *faith* corresponds to the *transference of identity*

99. Here the slaughter has no independent meaning but is significant only in a purely functional way as the means by which blood is procured. Cf. R. J. Daly, *The Origin of the Christian Doctrine of Sacrifice* (Philadelphia: Fortress, 1978), 30; S. J. Schultz, "Sacrifice in the God-Man Relationship in the Pentateuch," in *Interpretation and History: Essays in Honour of Allan A. MacRae* (Singapore: Christian Life, 1986), 109–21; but particularly Janowski, *Sühne als Heilsgeschehen*, 221–65.

100. Schwager ("Tod Christi und die Opferkritik," 18–20) accentuates other interpretational "elements" of "Jesus's self-offering as sacrifice," because he is orienting himself by aspects of the life of Jesus rather than by the structure of the category of sacrifice.

101. Hahn, "Verständnis des Opfers," 284.

that takes place at the moment when the hands are laid upon the sacrificial victim in the Old Testament cult; this transference of identity is what makes Jesus's death a *saving* event for all who believe (Rom. 3:22). By means of this transference of identity by faith, formulated within the context of the category of sacrifice, Jesus's death becomes, for Jesus himself, the enactment of our now unavoidable sinful death; for us, it becomes a salvation event by which we gain access to the enjoyment of God's righteousness (2 Cor. 5:21). Without faith, therefore, the cross is not a salvation event, and neither can it be recognizable as such. Faith is an objective and epistemologically constitutive element of the salvation event of the cross.

However, faith follows the cross and does not precede it. Thus a *double inversion* of the cultic relationship has been effected. For one thing, the order of consecration and death has been reversed: on the cross death precedes faith. For another, from the human point of view, where faith is involved, transference of identity follows the opposite direction from that of the cultic consecration: it is not I who transfer my identity to Christ, but rather I am content to accept that *he has* identified himself with me (1 Cor. 1:30). In this way any remaining possibility of human καύχησις [boasting] is excluded. In contrast to the Old Testament cult, God has not just made atonement possible, leaving it to human beings to avail themselves of this possibility;[102] he has graciously accomplished it for them on the cross and, through the δύναμις [power] of the gospel, has included the whole human race, both Jews and gentiles alike, in the salvation event of Jesus's cross and resurrection. Faith thus proves to be for us not just the transference of identity but more specifically the *attainment of identity*, as πίστις Ἰησοῦ Χριστοῦ [faith in Jesus Christ], a share in the person of Jesus Christ and hence participation in God's life-giving eschatological nearness to him.

This brings us to the second issue. The attainment of identity by faith is only possible at all because of the incorporation event already enacted on the cross in advance, which the resurrection discloses. Whereas in the Old Testament there could be no incorporation without consecration, in the New Testament we find that without our *incorporation, proleptically enacted on the cross by God himself*, there could be neither consecration nor faith. Incorporation is no longer a soteriological objective but a soteriological prerequisite of transference of identity. It is no longer necessary to enact it symbolically: it has already been enacted for real in Jesus Christ. In the cross, therefore, we find precisely that which the cult did not provide: there is fundamentally and universally no "outside" to fellowship with God, because

102. Cf. Gunton, *Actuality of Atonement*, 126–27.

here—as Schleiermacher says—"God sees us, not each of us for himself, but only in Christ."[103]

Here again we see a double inversion of the symbolic incorporation event of the Old Testament blood ritual. On the one hand, the incorporation event of the cross is enacted *before* any transference of identity, inasmuch as, by raising Jesus from death, God himself held Jesus up publicly as the locus of his saving presence and *has* incorporated us, in the person of Jesus Christ, proleptically into his fellowship.[104] On the other hand, this incorporating salvation event is no longer—as Gese says—"a coming to God that consists of passing through the death sentence"[105] symbolically celebrated in the human sacrificial cult by availing oneself of the opportunity for atonement offered by God in the cult. It actually is the other way around: God comes to us in Jesus Christ's death on the cross, which the human person accepts in faith and resists in unbelief.[106] In the cross God really comes to the human person: it is no longer the human person who comes, purely symbolically, to God; and God comes, not vaguely, somewhere or other, but in concrete terms and in human form in the person of Jesus Christ. The incorporation event enacted *before* any human quest for salvation begins is thus intrinsically *personal* and therefore fundamentally desacralized.[107] It is the person on the cross, whom God raises into his life, and no longer the temple cult and the invisible beyond of the "transcendental plane," that highlights the *extra nos* of salvation, and indeed in such a way that the *historia praeveniens* [prevenient history] of the divine action *pro nobis* here becomes *historia praeveniens* for everyone. Accordingly, the salvation that is fellowship with God and achieved by our incorporation is defined more personally and precisely in the New Testament as *being in Christ*, and in fact in the double

103. Schleiermacher, *Christian Faith*, 454.

104. Questions are therefore raised when Friedrich says that "through the death of Jesus the possibility of reconciliation now exists for everyone who has faith" (*Verkündigung des Todes Jesu*, 57). Jesus's death brings about not merely the possibility but the reality of reconciliation; and faith is not just the condition on which reconciliation becomes possible but is its real enactment.

105. Gese, "Sühne," 104.

106. *Tertium non datur!* [There is no third possibility!] There is no *status indifferentiae* [state of indifference], which allows both faith and unbelief to be considered equally eligible options for human existence. The human person with whom God initiates a real relationship in the cross of Jesus Christ in fact finds himself or herself in a state of unbelief, out of which he or she must be enticed and led. Where this occurs (i.e., where faith drives out, replaces, and overcomes unbelief), the person concerned experiences the *attainment of identity*. He becomes something that he previously was not and that, of his own accord, he could never have become: a justified sinner.

107. Cf. J. Blank, "Weißt du, was Versöhnung heißt? Der Kreuzestod Jesu als Sühne und Versöhnung," in *Sühne und Versöhnung*, ed. Blank and Werbick, 21–91, esp. 82–91.

sense: in Christ, God is there for us and we are there for God. It is specifically and solely through this double meaning of his death on the cross that Christ is the effective and, in this sense, sacramental reality and universality of our salvation.

The use of the category of sacrifice allows the soteriological incorporation into the holy to be stated in characteristically different ways in the Old and the New Testaments, especially in the Pauline context. For one thing, the structure of the cultic event *consecration–slaughter–incorporation* is replaced by the structure of the cross event *Christ–cross–faith*. For another, on the cross, in contrast to the cult, no one but *God* appears as the acting subject in incorporation and consecration: the soteriological culmination of *sola fide* and *solus Christus* is *solus Deus*, who establishes faith as πνεῦμα and the person of Jesus Christ as λόγος, and who must therefore be conceived of in trinitarian terms as differentiated: Father, Son, and Spirit. If the laying on of the hands by the offerant and the priest's enactment of the blood ritual were constitutive for the cultic atonement ritual, then for the salvation event of the cross—considered in the light of the category of sacrifice—the sole constitutive elements are *God's* proleptic activity in Jesus Christ and *God's* activity in granting us a new identity by faith. Thus, in the relationship of the human being to God, *Christ* and *faith* fulfill the functional roles that were played in the sacrificial model by *incorporation* and *consecration*. And this reconstruction of the grammar of the sacrificial model is rooted in the eschatological event that takes place, on the cross and in the resurrection, in the relationship of the human person Jesus to God, and can be defined, within the scope of the sacrificial model, as the *concurrence of consecration and incorporation within the performance of a single, self-differentiated action by God.*

For if we regard the cross and resurrection not simply from the perspective of the faith-filled person in general—as we have done thus far—but from the perspective of Jesus in particular, then there emerges a reconstruction of the sacrificial model considerably more profound than what has been said so far. For Jesus, whom faith confesses as the Christ and the Son of God, it is true that—formulated within the scope of the category of sacrifice—the structure of *consecration–slaughter–incorporation* is retained, inasmuch as the *cross* takes on the function of consecration, while the *resurrection* acquires the function of incorporation. But the cross as the integral element in the life of Jesus is an act of consecration and hence of identity transference, not in the sense that Jesus there symbolically transfers his identity to something other than himself, but quite the opposite. In his life, culminating as it does on the cross, he actually *receives a transferred identity*, one that now at last makes him what he in fact is: the *Christ* or *Son of God*.[108] This means that on the cross, at the culmination of his life, Jesus does not identify himself with someone or something. Rather, *God* is there identified as the one who determines to make this very Jesus into the creaturely locus of his nearness and presence, the eschatological, definitive, and perfect ἱλαστήριον (Rom. 3:25). God defines himself by his identification with Jesus, who has identified God for us as the Father who loves us. God's self-identification with Jesus consists in the fact that through his Spirit he has made us partakers in his own divine identity without eliminating Jesus's humanity or surrendering his own divinity.[109] As a result, not only does Jesus gain a *double identity*, but God himself thereby shows his own *identity, distinct in itself*. For God can identify himself with something other than himself only to the extent that there is something other than God (a work of creation that differs from God) and to the extent that God himself differentiates himself from it in such a way that, in identifying with this other, he still remains God in relation to it. Hence, God's self-identification with Jesus implies a self-determination by God in which God differentiates himself from himself in such a way that he becomes one with him who is other than himself, without ceasing to be distinct from him. In this sense, God's self-identification with Jesus means that God redefines himself in relation to the cross of Jesus by differentiating himself from himself in order to be able to draw Jesus into his divine identity without being compelled to negate either Jesus's humanity and createdness or his own being as God and creator. Formulated using the basic trinitarian images, God differentiates himself as Son from himself as Father; he identifies himself as Son with Jesus, who unambiguously differentiated himself as a human being from God and gave God the glory as the heavenly Father; and he identifies himself with Jesus by making this human person, through his Spirit, a partaker in his own divine identity,[110] so that, on the one hand, he himself is present in him in creaturely form without eliminating the distinction between creator and creature, and,

---

108. This circumstance is what trinitarian theology perceives as the *generatio* [generation] of the Son by the Father.

109. From the point of view of trinitarian theology, therefore, it is correct to teach not only the *filioque* in relation to the procession of the Spirit but also the *spirituque* in relation to the *generatio* of the Son. Otherwise it can be almost impossible to avoid temporalizing the asymmetry between the *generatio* of the Son and the *spiratio* [spiration] of the Spirit in a questionable manner, rather than conceiving of both as distinct but mutually dependent constitutive elements of the self-differentiating unity of God.

110. In contrast, we are included in God's life through the Spirit in such a way that we become partakers in Jesus's inclusion in the divine life by faith. We have no direct relationship with God but only ever one mediated by Jesus Christ: the Spirit does not place us in a relationship with God; he places us in Jesus Christ's inclusion in God. This is why, for us, Jesus is the way, the truth, and the life, and no one comes to the Father but by him (John 14:6).

on the other hand, the creation is present, with Jesus Christ, in God himself, since it remains eternally included in the identity of God, without abrogating the distinction between creator and creature.

Precisely this is what enables and entitles Christians to confess Jesus as Christ and as Son of God: when they do so, they are glorifying the crucified Jesus not in himself but in and with this *God* who has identified himself with the crucified Jesus by recognizing him as his beloved Son (Rom. 8:32) and by showing us himself as the loving Father and making himself present to us. Yet this is exactly what cannot be stated in respect of Jesus's death on the cross, taken in isolation. The cross is not an act of consecration on its own, but only when it is linked with the resurrection. Jesus is correctly confessed as the Christ or as God's Son only when he is declared to be not merely the one who died but rather the one who was also raised from the dead (cf. Rom. 8:34). Hence the *resurrection*, viewed from the perspective of Jesus, takes on the function of *incorporation* in the sacrificial model. Here, too, this eschatological act of incorporation is effected not merely symbolically but actually, in that God the Father admits the crucified Jesus into living fellowship with him as his Son. By the power of the Holy Spirit, in other words, he appoints him to a position of authority as the Son of God (Rom. 1:4) who together with the Father constitutes the Spirit (*filioque*) through whom, by the Father, he is constituted as Son (*spirituque*, if you will). Without this resurrection act of incorporation, effected solely by God himself, the cross would not be an act of consecration, and neither could it be recognized and confessed as such. Only when joined with the resurrection in a united act of consecration and incorporation is the cross the eschatological salvation event.

So if we conceive of Jesus's relationship with God in terms of the sacrificial model, it becomes apparent that the cross and the resurrection are inextricably bound together, in that they owe their eschatological salvific quality solely to God's activity in them. So the cross is not preceded by an act of consecration; rather, it *is* just such an act. But it is such an act only because it *is at one and the same time* an act of incorporation by which God raises the crucified one, the one with whom he identifies himself—whom he marks out as his heir and representative by giving him, through the Spirit, a share in his divine identity—and admits him to eternal, living fellowship with him. It is only because, viewed from God's perspective, Jesus's cross and resurrection are both defined *at one and the same time* as consecration *and* as incorporation, so that both are characteristically *overdetermined*,[111] that this event can be the

111. This *overdetermination* is the consequence of a *multiple coding* that results from the recurring use of every significant element of the appropriated sacrificial model to elucidate and

proleptic incorporation of all believers that faith confesses it to be. Hence, just as *Christ* and *faith* take over the function of incorporation and consecration in the sacrificial model, in the relationship of the human person to God, so in the same way, the *cross* and *resurrection* take over this function in the relationship of the human Jesus to God. In each case God alone is the one who acts, who accomplishes salvation, but this very fact demonstrates not only his self-differentiation but also the characteristic differentiation between his activity in each case. So in God's relationship to Jesus, consecration and incorporation coincide at the cross and the resurrection in one single event, marking Jesus Christ out as soteriologically unique. Conversely, in God's relationship to us, they divide into his christological incorporation activity (in Jesus Christ) and his pneumatological consecration activity (through faith in Jesus as the Christ) and thus preserve the soteriological uniqueness of Jesus Christ and the irrevocable distinction between us and Jesus Christ. It is in him and through him alone that salvation comes about—not in our suffering and death;[112] we participate in this salvation only by participating by faith in

articulate the salvation event of the cross and resurrection. This principle of multiple coding can be generally identified as the hermeneutical tool used in Christian speech and thought to break up and remodel the grammar of the images and image complexes that the Christian faith draws on to express and communicate the eschatological saving activity of God experienced in Jesus Christ.

112. It is therefore theologically frivolous to give equal status to the uniqueness of the cross event and the atrocities that occurred in Auschwitz, even if it is done with moral emphasis. The cross is incomparable because there it is God who acts; this is shown by Jesus's resurrection, without which the cross would be neither a salvation event nor a manifestation of God's self-abasement. Viewed from this angle, Auschwitz, in contrast, is far from unique; on the contrary—and this is precisely why it is so dangerous to repress the memory of it or to belittle what happened—it is hideously repeatable, because there it was not God but we humans who acted. So it is wrong to say, "Golgotha is not just a historical parallel to Auschwitz: it takes place in Auschwitz." And it is wrong to support this erroneous characterization of Auschwitz as a "historical, bloody repetition of the sacrifice on the cross" by saying that "not only does the exalted Lord declare his solidarity with the sufferers; he is eternally present, in his earthly form, in the sufferers themselves" (O. Fuchs, "Die Herausforderung Israels an die spirituelle und soziale Praxis der Christen," *Jahrbuch für biblische Theologie* 6 [1991]: 89–113, esp. 108–9). The error committed by this faulty theology of suffering corresponds to that of the faulty nineteenth-century theology of the incarnation: just as the incarnation of the Son of God in Jesus of Nazareth cannot be given a wholesale immanentist interpretation as God's entry into and surrender to world events without abrogating the soteriological specificity of the Christian confession of salvation, so in the same way Jesus's suffering on the cross cannot be given a wholesale immanentist interpretation as God's entry into and surrender to the suffering of the world without abrogating the soteriological specificity of the confession of Christ and hence the ground of the Christian hope of salvation. Either case involves a theological generalization along similar lines, rather than the specific thinking that is called for. Both instances therefore fail to reflect the thinking that leads Christians to proclaim the unique saving activity of God in the resurrection confession: God has come so near to us in Jesus Christ that, as Paul puts it, nothing, "neither death, nor life, nor angels, nor principalities, nor things present, nor things to

Jesus Christ, and we are not transplanted into this faith as a result of our own reasoning, strength, and resolve; it is solely through the Spirit of God himself.

For the ordering of the relationships between God and human beings and between God and Jesus Christ, this implies that *in the Pauline interpretation the sacrificial model is soteriologically demolished from within and the salvation event is radically redefined from the ground up.* For both the inversion of the soteriological order of consecration and incorporation where we are concerned and the coincidence of both enactments where Jesus Christ is concerned, as well as the displacement of this saving activity exclusively to God himself, are evidence that the cross and resurrection event cannot be understood as sacrifice either in terms of a *do ut des* or in terms of a *do quia dedisti*. In the salvific raising of the crucified one, humanity gives nothing at all to God, while God gives humanity everything. Where the cross is concerned, therefore, we can speak of sacrifice at most in a paradoxical sense, by speaking of the self-sacrifice of God, which can be unfolded only in trinitarian terms and to which the only appropriate human response is a λογικὴ λατρεία [spiritual worship], a doxological thanksgiving; the first signals the semantic end of the idea of sacrifice, while the second signals its soteriological end. With the removal of the soteriological relevance of the sacrificial cult, the cross simultaneously marks the cancellation of the soteriological relevance of the category of sacrifice: Christian soteriology is possible without this category, but it is impossible without what is said with the aid of this category in the New Testament about the cross of Christ and hence about us. For this very reason, where it makes use of the sacrificial mindscape, it is essentially a fundamental critique of the sacrificial system.

This would appear to contradict the dogmatic tradition and reality found within the church. For how are we then to understand the central role that the idea of sacrifice has played and still plays in the Christology, soteriology, and ecclesiology of the great confessions? It is no accident that modern religious and theological criticism evolved largely as a *critique of sacrifice*. This will now be considered in greater detail in order to profile and support the thesis put forward.

## 6. Critique of Sacrifice

*What exactly is being censured when sacrifice is critiqued? On what is the critique focused? And what aspect of it is being critiqued?* These questions

---

come, nor powers, nor height, nor depth, nor any other created thing, will be able to separate us from the love of God, which is in Christ Jesus our Lord" (Rom. 8:38–39).

have more than one answer. Sacrifice is not a single phenomenon that can be isolated; it takes a variety of forms. In view of the central significance of sacrifice in most religions and the diverse types of sacrifice, the critique does not focus on a unified phenomenon, a unified use of language, or even a unified concept of sacrifice. Instead of one comprehensive term, most languages and religions (even the Hebrew and Greek of the biblical tradition) are familiar with a plethora of descriptive names for different sacrificial practices and types of sacrifice. These vary with the overall cultural context of the particular religion and its system of cultic rites, so that even within any one religion an attempt to systematize them or subsume them under a common concept of sacrifice is bound to be rudimentary and inadequate. It is true that many such attempts have been made, but in such cases the critique has applied to only one construct. A focus on actual sacrificial practices and specific views of sacrifice has always proved more fruitful than the construction of a universally applicable, and therefore unavoidably abstract, concept of sacrifice and its critique. Such practices or views can be described phenomenologically according to their function in the system of rites and cults pertaining to the tradition, and they can be analyzed as aspects of activity by their symbolic structure and the regulatory system governing them. The structures, regulations, and functions thus exposed can then be examined from a critical angle in order to ascertain which (culture-bound and particularistic or anthropologically generalized) characteristics of human existence and life orientation they manifest, or, in other words, how they give structure to the perception of reality (their epistemic implications) and what understanding of reality and self they imply (their ontological implications).

A phenomenological critique of this kind takes as its starting point the view that sacrifices are not phenomena that can be treated in isolation; they are symbolic actions performed within the context of a religious system whose cultic rules and rites lend a symbolic character to the actions performed, attaching to them a meaning and efficacy they do not have in and of themselves. The presentation of food and living creatures can thus serve as a request to the divinity for help and blessing or as an offering of reverence and thanks. The meal frequently linked with the sacrifice can bring about or restore fellowship both between the cult participants and between them and the divinity. A *sacrificial act* therefore merely makes a particular *type of sacrifice* real. For a sacrifice is not just a certain sequence of actions; it always includes a regulatory system governing the correct enactment of these actions and gives them their symbolic quality.

Where this regulatory system is explicated and established on a theological basis, as it is in the Old Testament, particularly in the Pentateuch and the

P school, the understanding of God and of reality implied in the various forms of sacrifice finds formal expression in a specific *theology of sacrifice*. The latter, in turn, opens up the possibility of searching for functional equivalents for sacrifice (i.e., the replacement of the sacrificial cult by noncultic acts; the sacrifice of atonement, for example, could be replaced by almsgiving, fasting, and prayer). This then initiates a process of "spiritualization,"[113] in which outward acts are replaced by an inner attitude of the heart and sacrificial acts are converted into sacrificial metaphors. It can be shown that this process takes place not only in Judaism, Christianity, and Islam but also in Hinduism and Buddhism.[114] Horkheimer and Adorno have made the following broad claims on this subject: "The history of civilization is the history of the introversion of sacrifice. In other words, the history of renunciation."[115] R. Girard emphasizes that the discontinuation of vicarious sacrifice in modern civilization renders impossible any constructive end to the chain of violence and counterviolence rooted in the aggressive drive; instead, it leads to an increase in society's potential for destruction, which threatens to culminate in civilization destroying itself.[116]

In the face of such generalizations, we must stress the need to examine the process of the "introversion" of sacrifice rather differently. The process can take place on both a moral and a religious level, so that it may contribute to the reduction or the increase of religiosity. Both processes metaphorize sacrifice, but they can quickly veer into secularization if the epistemic and ontological implications of the underlying concept of reality linked with the practice of sacrifice are ignored. Hence, those bringing the sacrifice (the offerant) make the assumption (1) that there is another, more crucial reality than the world of human experience and actions (culture) and its basis and preconditions in the natural and material realm (nature); (2) that the realm of human action is not necessarily just as it should be in the light of that reality; (3) that the consequences of these dysfunctions and tensions between the factual realm of experience and normative reality are life threatening for the individual and the community; (4) that they cannot be corrected and eliminated by human

113. Wenschkewitz, "Spiritualisierung der Kultusbegriffe"; J. Hermisson, *Sprache und Ritus im altisraelitischen Kult: Zur "Spiritualisierung" der Kultbegriffe im Alten Testament* (Neukirchen-Vluyn: Neukirchener, 1965); G. Klinzing, *Die Umdeutung des Kultes in der Qumrangemeinde und im NT* (Göttingen: Vandenhoeck & Ruprecht, 1971).

114. E. Hulmes, "The Semantics of Sacrifice," in *Sacrifice and Redemption*, ed. Sykes, 265–81.

115. M. Horkheimer and Th. W. Adorno, *Dialektik der Aufklärung: Philosophische Fragmente* (Amsterdam: Querido, 1947), 71.

116. R. Girard, *La violence et le sacré* (Paris: Grasset, 1972); Girard, *Des choses cacheés depuis de la fondation du monde* (Paris: Grasset, 1978); Girard, *Ende der Gewalt*; Girard, *Bouc émissaire*.

activity alone, but only in cooperation with this normative reality; and (5) that the correctly performed sacrifice is the means intended by the divinity and established by the institution for the regular removal of these disorders and tensions, or at least for the correction of their life-threatening consequences. Accordingly, the anthropological background to the practice of sacrifice is the yearning for order, salvation, wholeness, and purity as the biblical *creation narratives* describe it;[117] the experience of disorder, calamity, fragmentation, and impurity that finds its expression in the *idea of sin*; and the insight conveyed by the *idea of redemption* that, in the face of the existing disorder and impurity, the longed-for order and purity cannot be achieved and maintained in one's own strength. Viewed in this way, the function of a sacrifice (enabled by the divinity itself) is to restore and maintain people's lives and their relationship to the divinity (i.e., to counter, within the life of the community and the individual, the breakup of the realm of experience and normative reality, a breakup experienced as chaotic, culpable, and essentially threatening). Regardless of their particular special features and purposes, from a theological point of view sacrifices therefore always have a creation-theological, hamartiological, and soteriological dimension. It is particularly important that these be preserved when a cultic system is theologically transformed into a faith system that replaces cultic sacrificial enactments with an inner attitude of the heart, a specific life orientation and its associated way of living, and that substitutes the metaphorical use of sacrificial images for real sacrificial acts.[118] And because this process is constantly at risk of exhausting itself in moralizing and descending into secularization, the transformation of cult into dogmatics (as Luhmann has called it[119]) cannot lead to the full deritualizing of a religion and the complete elimination of any worship practice without dismantling it as a religion: if Christianity were now nothing but a belief system, it would no longer be Christianity.

It is therefore decisive that Christianity has two distinctive features where the issue of sacrifice is concerned: (1) it recognizes no sacrificial practice, yet (2) it does have a worship practice. Both features are communicated theologically, in that both Christianity's eradication of the sacrificial cult and its retention of a specific worship practice have a christological basis

117. W. Burkert, *Anthropologie des religiösen Opfers: Die Sakralisierung der Gewalt* (Munich: Carl Friedrich von Siemens Stiftung, 1984); M. Douglas, *Purity and Danger: An Analysis of Concepts of Pollution and Taboo* (Harmondsworth: Penguin Books, 1970), 41–72; Gunton, *Actuality of Atonement*, 117–20.

118. Cf. G. Scholem, *Die jüdische Mystik in ihren Hauptströmungen* (Frankfurt: Suhrkamp, 1967), 384.

119. "Dogmatics are constructions that succeed rituals on a higher level." N. Luhmann, *Religious Dogmatics and the Evolution of Societies* (New York: Edwin Mellen, 1984), 14.

in being related to Jesus Christ: the cross and resurrection of Jesus Christ
are proclaimed as both the end of all sacrifices and the ground and focus of
Christian worship.

*That Jesus died for us is a central message of the Christian faith.* That his
death on the cross "to be a sacrifice not only for original sin but also for all
other sins, and to propitiate God's wrath"[120] is a controversial and, in modern
times right up to the present day, heavily criticized narrowing down of the
New Testament witness concerning the saving death of Jesus. Criticism is
directed at this narrowly defined confessional statement and its accompany-
ing doctrinal framework of the *munus* or *officium sacerdotale* (priestly office)
because of the problematic way they interpret the saving death of Jesus by
intertwining such widely different soteriological complexes of ideas as sacrifice
and (noncultic) atonement, substitution and satisfaction, and penal suffering and obedient self-giving. In the interpretation of the Christ title and the
christological appropriation of the central Old Testament offices of prophet,
priest, and king, the *pro nobis* of God's saving activity in Jesus Christ has
been developed as the doctrine of the threefold office of Christ. This began
in the Reformed tradition with Calvin,[121] and it continued in the Lutheran
tradition with J. Gerhard,[122] who continued Luther's own initial interpretative approach. The focal point of this development is the doctrine of the
*officium sacerdotale* of Christ, according to which Christ accomplishes our
redemption by bringing about our reconciliation with God, the restoration
of the broken relationship of sinners with God by a double action. On the
one hand, he takes away, once and for all, the guilt toward God with which
we have burdened ourselves: as priest he does not make a vicarious offering of
another's life; rather, on the cross he gives his own self as a vicarious offering
for our sins (*satisfactio*). On the other hand, as the risen and exalted Lord
he intercedes perpetually for us with the Father in order that we may receive
the full benefit of the salvation he purchased for us once for all on the cross
(*intercessio*). Christ's sacrificial death on the cross is thus the *satisfactio* that
met the requirements of God, who was dishonored by our sin and who, because
of his holiness and justice, was compelled to insist on our punishment. For
not only did Christ, as the God-man without sin or guilt, freely, willingly, and
perfectly fulfill God's law, to which he himself was not subject (*oboedientia
activa* [active obedience]); he also voluntarily took on himself the penalty we
ought to have suffered (*oboedientia passiva* [passive obedience]). By virtue of

120. *BSLK* 54, lines 10–12.
121. Calvin, *Institutio Christianae Religionis*, II, 15.16–17 .
122. J. Gerhard, *Loci theologici*, loc. 4, chap. 15 (1610–22; repr., Leipzig: F. Frank, 1885).

the merit earned thereby, he makes perpetual intercession before God for the redemption of human beings, who enter into the enjoyment of this salvation when they appropriate it in faith.

Since the Enlightenment, the critique of this doctrine has been directed toward the problem of fusing irreconcilable cultic, juristic, and moral ideas. Hence the primary focus has been on interpreting Jesus's death as a sacrificial death, his cross as the act that appeases God's wrath, his journey to the cross as vicarious self-giving to liberate us from death as the penalty for our sin, and his suffering and death, taken together, as the vicarious penal suffering willed by God of an innocent person. The following critique highlights various aspects of this.

1. The *historical critique* emphasizes that sacrifices are time-dependent religious behavioral and conceptual forms.[123] These forms were once mandatory but are now wholly incomprehensible, given that in the realm of Christianity there has been no sacrificial practice for centuries. Hence we are left with the question of whether any reference to the sacrificial death of Jesus can still be supported dogmatically and justified homiletically.[124]

2. The *logical critique* answers this question with a firm negative; it objects to any understanding of Jesus's death in terms of a theology of sacrifice as being *for all intents and purposes self-contradictory*. Heraclitus ridiculed the idea: "To reason that one can purify oneself of bloodguilt by shedding more blood is as if one who had stepped in mud were to wash with mud."[125] In Christian thought this argument is formulated in creation-theological terms: Montaigne, for example, stated that the corrupted creation cannot be put right through sacrifices, since every sacrifice itself is a transgression against God's creation.[126] But the argument also occurs (e.g., in Nietzsche) as a charge of self-abolition of the gospel: the fact that God is said to have given "his Son for the forgiveness of sins as a sacrifice" is a declaration of the bankruptcy of the gospel.[127] "Sacrifice for guilt, and indeed in its most repulsive and barbaric form—the sacrifice of the innocent for the sins of the guilty! What appalling

123. Spinoza, *Tractatus theologicus-politicus*, in *Opera*, ed. G. Gawlick and F. Niewöhne (Darmstadt: Wissenschaftliche Buchgesellschaft, 1979), 1:160–86; H. Grotius, "De veritate religionis christianae 5, 7," in *Opera omnia theologica* (1679; repr., Stuttgart-Bad Cannstatt: Frommann-Holzboog, 1972), 3:75–76; cf. I. Henderson, *Myth in the New Testament* (London: SCM, 1952), 42.

124. Friedrich, *Verkündigung des Todes Jesu*, 145–55.

125. Heraclitus, frag. 22 B 5 in *Die Fragmente der Vorsokratiker*, ed. H. Diels and W. Kranz (Berlin–Grundewald: Weidmann, ⁶1951/2), vol. I, 22 B. 5.

126. Montaigne, "Essais II, 12," in *Œuvres complètes*, ed. A. Thibaudet and M. Rat (Paris: Gallimard, 1962), 502.

127. Nietzsche, *Antichrist*, §41; cf. §39.

paganism!"[128] To proclaim the sacrificial death of Jesus amounts, for all intents and purposes, to a self-abolition of the Christian message.

3. Closely linked with this is the *moral critique* that a sacrifice is not merely a self-contradictory tool for solving a real problem but an abstruse attempt to solve a problem defined as self-contradictory and thus impossible to solve. Anyone who sacrifices takes a fundamentally inadequate understanding of relationship with God as a starting point. In the worst scenario it is treated as a relationship between things, one that can be causally manipulated. In the best scenario it is apprehended as a personal relationship but understood according to the inadequate model of a legal or economic relationship. But a relationship with God is neither a legal relationship, in which the relation between God and human beings is governed by mutual attribution of rights and obligations, nor a barter relationship conducted by means of reciprocal give-and-take (whether this be conceived of in terms of *do ut des* or—as Janowski would have it[129]—in terms of *do quia dedisti*). Both these thought models have morally unacceptable consequences. If the sacrifice is understood as the execution of a legal relationship, it is only the correct outward enactment that counts, not the inner attitude of the people making the sacrifice; this evokes the merely external religious practice that was the target of prophetic criticism from Amos (4:4–5; 5:21–24; Hos. 4:4–19; 6:6; 14:2–3) through Isaiah (1:10–20; Jer. 7:7–20; Isa. 43:23–24) to Jesus (Matt. 5–6).[130] On the other hand, if a sacrifice is understood as an exchange of goods between a human person and God, it does not merely reveal the "mercenary devotion" that Hume criticized as unacceptable from a religious and moral standpoint.[131] It implies above all a morally untenable conception of sin, guilt, and atonement, which Kant diagnosed with precision: moral guilt clings to the person and is nontransferable. It cannot "be extirpated, as far as we can see by our rational awareness of right, by anyone else. For it is not a transmissible obligation that—like, say, a monetary debt . . .—can be transferred to someone else; it is the most personal of obligations, namely, a debt of sins, that only the punishable one can bear, not the innocent one, however magnanimous the latter may be in wanting to take it upon himself for the former."[132] If, however, delegation of guilt is a moral impossibility, then a death that takes vicarious responsibility for guilt is also impossible, and "the sacrifice of the innocent

128. Ibid.
129. Janowski, *Sühne als Heilsgeschehen*, vii and 361.
130. Cf. I. Kant, *Die Religion innerhalb der Grenzen der bloßen Vernunft*, AA VI, 72.
131. D. Hume, "The Natural History of Religion," in *The Philosophical Works of David Hume*, ed. Th. H. Green and Th. H. Grose (1882; repr., Aalen: Scientia, 1964), 4:338.
132. Kant, *Religion innerhalb der Grenzen*, AA VI, 72.

for the sins of the guilty" is precisely what Nietzsche accuses Christianity of: repulsive, barbaric, appalling paganism.[133]

4. The *theological critique* is directed against the understanding of God that lies behind sacrifice in general and behind reference to the sacrificial death of Jesus in particular. It takes a number of specific forms.

Following Plato's *Euthyphro*, the view that God could be bribed by sacrifices or induced to change his mind by human gifts and actions was criticized as unfounded anthropomorphism. Sin against God cannot be erased by sacrifices, not even by Christ's sacrificial death. Ever since Herbert of Cherbury,[134] there has been a tendency to dismiss this doctrine as priestly deception on the grounds that, like sacrifice itself, it was only ever introduced "for the benefit of priests."[135] Schopenhauer sees in sacrifice not merely a sign of priestly egoism but, further, an indication that all religions originate with egoism: the "origin and support of the existence of all gods" is to be found in the human impulse, manifest in sacrifice, "to call upon and purchase the assistance of supernatural beings" because one would "rather entrust himself to another's grace than to his own merit."[136] What is to be criticized as unreasonable is thus not the anthropomorphic image of God found in sacrificial practice but the criticism of anthropomorphism.

Schopenhauer does not see anthropomorphism as a subject for criticism, since he regards the idea of God as being anchored in the human will, not in the human intellect, so that it is only possible to conceive of God in anthropomorphic terms. In contrast, it is always when the fundamental incompatibility of material sacrifice with God's supernatural, spiritual essence is being emphasized that the accusation of anthropomorphism is leveled against the idea of a God who requires sacrifice.[137] Augustine had already answered this charge with the distinction he made between the *sacrificium visibile* [visible sacrifice] and the actual *sacrificium invisibile* [invisible sacrifice] consisting of the offering of the soul to God, of which the former is a sign.[138] In the light of this distinction, Augustine could describe Christ as the *victima perfectissima* [perfect victim]. Christ's sinlessness made him outwardly the perfect sacrificial

133. Nietzsche, *Antichrist*, §41.

134. H. v. Cherbury, *A Dialogue between a Tutor and His Pupil* (1768; repr., Stuttgart-Bad Cannstatt: Frommann-Holzboog, 1971), 253–54.

135. Reimarus, *Apologie oder Schutzschrift für die vernünftigen Verehrer Gottes*, ed. G. Alexander (Frankfurt: Insel Verlag, 1972), 1:405–13.

136. A. Schopenhauer, "Parerga und Paralipomena 1," in *Sämtliche Werke*, ed. A. Hübscher (Leipzig: Brockhaus, 1938), 5:126–27.

137. M. Ficino, *Iamblichus de mysteriis*, in *Opera omnia* (1576; repr., Turin: Bottega d'Erasmo, 1962), 2:1895.

138. Augustine, *Civ.* X, 5–6.

offering; his willing surrender to God made him inwardly the perfect sacrifice. Because he was both offering and offerant, he was also the perfect offerer; and because he identified himself with those for whom he sacrificed himself, he was also the perfect realization of the sacrificial purpose.[139]

The modern critique of sacrifice saw the progress of this Augustinian distinction within the concept of sacrifice as having been lost by amalgamating it with the idea of guilt-sacrifice. J. Bodin found the doctrine of Christ as the perfect sacrifice perfectly abhorrent and irreconcilable with a philosophically tenable understanding of God.[140] From Ch. Blount[141] to Nietzsche and psychoanalysis,[142] and right up to present-day feminist theology,[143] we find a repeated declaration that the notion of Christ's sacrificial death requires us to see God as a cruel tyrant, an oriental despot, and a sadistic patriarch; as one who, in his wrath at the infringement of his honor, does not even recoil from demanding the blood of his own Son. The charge "of cannibalism and sadism" is leveled against this "God, who needs a sacrifice in order to be reconciled,"[144] with the demand that this image of a bloodthirsty tyrant, originating in masculine fantasies of violence, be replaced by a "gentle feminine solution"[145] that would conceive of redemption as "empathizing with the rhythm of life and death as the tidal flow of life";[146] that would substitute for the patriarchal "symbol of the redeeming blood-death" the "contrasting symbol" of the life-giving "bloody birth";[147] and that would help to overcome the "repressive sacrificial theology" of the Christian tradition by reviving the liberating feminine experiences of "Lady Wisdom."[148] The objectively justifiable elements of this critique were already expressed by Nietzsche. The element worthy of theological consideration can already be found in Bultmann, who—as already noted—rejected the "mythological interpretation [of Christ's

139. Augustine, *Trin.* IV, 14/19.

140. J. Bodin, *Colloquium heptaplomeres de rerum sublimium arcanis abditis*, ed. L. Noack (1857; repr., Stuttgart-Bad Cannstatt: Frommann-Holzboog, 1966), 292.

141. Ch. Blount, *The Two First Books of Philostatus* (London: Nathaniel Thompson, 1680), 3.

142. Cf. W. Böhme, ed., *Ist Gott grausam? Eine Stellungnahme zu Tilmann Mosers "Gottesvergiftung"* (Stuttgart: de Gruyter, 1977).

143. Daly, *Beyond God the Father*; L. Schottroff, "Kreuz," in *Wörterbuch der feministischen Theologie*, ed. Elisabeth Gössmann et al. (Gütersloh: Gütersloher Verlagshaus Mohn, 1991), 226–31; Schottroff, "Die Crux mit dem Kreuz: Feministische Kritik und Re-Vision der Kreuzestheologie," *Evangelische Kommentare* 25 (1992): 216–18.

144. Schottroff, "Kreuz," 226; cf. Sölle, *Suffering*.

145. M. Kassel, "Tod und Auferstehung," in *Feministische Theologie: Perspektiven zur Orientierung*, ed. M. Kassel (Stuttgart: Kreuz, 1988), 191–226, esp. 220.

146. Ibid., 222.

147. Ibid., 210–11.

148. Schottroff, "Crux mit dem Kreuz," 218.

death on the cross] in which notions of sacrifice are mixed together with a
juristic theory of satisfaction" as "unacceptable for us" because it "does not
[mean] what it should mean at all, even within the perspective of the New
Testament."[149] And the philosophical rejoinder was already voiced by Hegel
when he stated, in opposition to the "fallacious idea . . . that God is a tyrant
who demands sacrifices," that sacrifice could be speculatively interpreted
as the elimination of otherness and as God's "return from alienation . . . to
himself" in which God turned out to be far from an autocratic despot—a
reconciling Spirit, in fact.[150]

5. The *sociohistorical critique* challenges the political-ideological misuse of the category of sacrifice. Hardly any other concept in the history of
Christianity has been so abused as when the "will to sacrifice" and "absolute readiness to sacrifice" have been demanded—in most cases by others
and not (though this is debatable) by the ones making the demand—as the
Christian corollary of Jesus's sacrifice on the cross.[151] This cynical exploitation of suffering meant accepting the theological inconsistency that human
destiny has manifestly not been fulfilled in Jesus's sacrifice on the cross, as
Kodalle rightly asserts.[152] At any rate, the christological-soteriological use of
the category of sacrifice did not prevent its moral-political misuse. Rather, it
promoted the fallacy that Christ's perfect sacrifice had abolished the cultic
institution of sacrifice only to establish a moral requirement for sacrifice. It
would scarcely be possible to more completely miss the soteriological point
of the saving death of Jesus.

6. The *hermeneutical critique* rejects the typological argumentation, which,
on the basis of the doctrine of Jesus Christ's sacrificial death, attributes a
special enduring meaning to the Old Testament sacrifices as typological
references to Christ's sacrificial death. The doctrinal argument that "all sacrifices are instituted by God in the Old Testament to be a type of Christ"[153]
assumes that Christ's death is to be understood as a sacrificial death. But this
is precisely the point at issue.[154] To understand Jesus's death as a sacrificial
death in the light of the Old Testament traditions of atoning sacrifice is one

149. Bultmann, "Neues Testament und Mythologie," 41–42.

150. G. W. F. Hegel, *Philosophie der Religion*, in *Werke*, ed. E. Moldenhauer and K. M.
Michel (Frankfurt: Suhrkamp, 1969), 17:294–95.

151. K. M. Kodalle, *Dietrich Bonhoeffer: Zur Kritik seiner Theologie* (Gütersloh: Gütersloher
Verlagshaus Mohn, 1991), 106–12.

152. Ibid., 104.

153. Reimarus *Apologie*, 1:195, 200.

154. Cf. J. C. Edelmann, *Abgenöthigtes Jedoch Andern nicht wieder aufgenöthigtes Glaubens-
bekenntnis*, in *Sämtliche Schriften*, ed. W. Grossmann (1746; repr., Stuttgart-Bad Cannstatt:
Frommann-Holzboog, 1969), 9:90.

thing, but to give enduring theological status to this tradition of sacrifice is quite another.

7. In those statements about the death of Jesus that are couched in terms of a theology of sacrifice, the *exegetical critique* sees at best a secondary New Testament thread. Such statements are not particularly numerous,[155] and neither are they among the interpretations of the early post-Easter period,[156] and they consistently take it for granted that any type of cultic ritual sacrifice is ruled out. For these reasons, their dogmatic significance should not be exaggerated. As we have shown, the Tübingen exegetes in particular counter this with the comments "The salvific significance of the death of Jesus can be understood only by reference to the idea of atonement"[157] and "There was (and is) no theological barrier . . . to understanding Jesus's death in terms of a theology of sacrifice,"[158] since between the Pauline view of atonement "and the Old Testament understanding of the cultic atonement ritual there is a profound continuity."[159] Even if, in view of the wide range of soteriological statements and ideas to be found in the New Testament, it is energetically disputed by others that this is the only adequate theological understanding of Jesus's death,[160] it nevertheless is repeatedly declared to be the central dogmatic soteriological statement.[161]

## 7. The Fundamental Dogmatic Problem

The argument between critique and countercritique is inconclusive when the theology of the cross is identified with the theology of sacrifice. One can reject the doctrine of the sacrificial death of Jesus Christ without disputing that his death is a saving death, and one can emphasize the salvific significance of Jesus's death on the cross without holding the view that it is to be understood in terms of a theology of sacrifice. The dogmatic problem is not to be found in the question of whether Jesus's death on the cross is a saving death; theological thinking starts from this assumption. Instead, the question is whether this saving death *can, must,* or *should* be understood as a sacrificial death. Is it possible to understand the saving death of Jesus as a sacrificial death?

155. Hahn, "Verständnis des Opfers."
156. F. Hahn, "Opfer," *EKL* 3:884–87, esp. 3:885.
157. Gese, "Sühne," 104.
158. Stuhlmacher, "Sühne oder Versöhnung," 350.
159. Hofius, *Paulusstudien,* 48.
160. Friedrich, *Verkündigung des Todes Jesu*; Breytenbach, "Abgeschlossenes Imperfekt?"
161. Cf. S. W. Sykes, "Outline of a Theology of Sacrifice," in *Sacrifice and Redemption,* ed. Sykes, 282–98.

If it is possible, must it therefore be understood in this way, or can it also be understood differently? And if it can be understood differently, is it better understood as a sacrificial death than in some other way?

The first question can be answered unambiguously: there is no question but that it is *possible* to understand Jesus's saving death as a sacrificial death. After all, we have seen that the whole of the New Testament is steeped in the imaginative world of sacrifice and the sacrificial cult. The saving death of Jesus is defined at all levels as sacrifice or self-sacrifice, and our redemption is described as reconciliation by his blood, most clearly in the Epistle to the Hebrews, but also where mention is made of the blood of Christ, where he is called a sacrificial or Passover lamb, or where there is a reference to his self-offering. The images and ideas are many and varied. They are linked with various forms of the temple cult of sacrifice and its theological reflection in the Scriptures of the Old Testament.[162] Despite differences in detail, they demonstrate beyond dispute not only that it is possible to speak of Jesus's saving death as a sacrificial death but also that it *is* spoken of in this way.

The second question can also be answered unambiguously: it cannot be said that Jesus's death *must* be understood as a sacrificial death. This understanding is not the only possible one, and neither is it unavoidable on the grounds that it is the only adequate understanding. The imaginative world of sacrifice is just one way in which the New Testament expresses the Christian experience of salvation. Whether, in the dogmatic tradition, one speaks of the kingly and the prophetic offices as well as of the priestly office, or whether one has recourse to the far greater number of soteriological ideas to be found in the New Testament, it is beyond dispute that more than one idea is possible and that no one idea is so comprehensive as to incorporate all or even most of the New Testament ideas of salvation.[163] No interpretation of Jesus's death can claim to be the sole authentic expression of salvation, not even one based on the theology of sacrifice. To argue otherwise would be to overplay the distinction between genesis and validity. The fact that the interpretation of Jesus's death as sacrifice can be traced back to the beginnings of the Christian faith does not prevent other interpretations from being just as accurate or even more satisfactory. And the fact that Jesus's death has been said to be a sacrificial death does not mean that it must necessarily be pronounced as such from a doctrinal point of view.

162. Brown, "Sacrifice"; Sykes, "Sacrifice in the New Testament"; Young, *Sacrifice and the Death of Christ*, part 1; Gübler, *Die frühesten Deutungen*; Weiser, *Tod Jesu*, 60–67; Humphreys, "Mystery of the Cross," 47–52; Green, *Death of Jesus*, 314–23.
163. Barth, *Tod Jesu Christi*.

It cannot be demonstrated from the exegetical findings alone that Jesus's saving death is *better* understood as a sacrificial death than otherwise. That can be argued only from a dogmatic point of view. Sykes attempts to do this using the following ecclesiological argumentation:[164] at the heart of the Christian life stands the worship of God, at the heart of the worship of God stands the Eucharist, and at the heart of the Eucharist stands the symbol of sacrifice.[165] What "sacrifice" means in the Christian context is to be defined by the worship of God: the reorientation of the heart toward God, a reorientation that becomes concrete reality in the celebration of the *sola gratia* in word and sacrament within the act of worship. According to Sykes, cultic metaphors have soteriological priority over other salvation images because these alone are what make worship "the central constitutive reality of the divine-human relationship."[166] Whereas the symbol of sacrifice is said to belong indissolubly together with the act of worship, all other Christian symbols of salvation must be understood as further elucidations of the central symbol of sacrifice. Sykes does not deduce the character of Christian worship from Jesus's sacrifice on the cross; instead, he takes worship and its sacrificial symbolism as his starting point by explicating the act of worship as the *definiens* [that which defines] of the dogmatic understanding of sacrifice: the shift of the decisive encounter between God and his people from the external cult to "the inner theatre of the heart."[167] But the fact that worship and the idea of sacrifice do in fact belong together within a great Christian tradition indicates the problem and not the solution. The standard recourse to Jesus's sacrifice on the cross to justify this fact is unavailable to Sykes, since this is precisely where the problem lies. Yet to attach normative importance to the factual connection between Eucharist and sacrificial symbol means that ecclesiology is given priority over Christology instead of being determined by it. Sykes admits the untenability of giving preferential exegetical treatment to a sacrificial soteriology, but he nonetheless wants to retain an understanding of worship based on sacrifice. Hence he reverses the traditional line of argument from the understanding of the cross via the understanding of God to the understanding of worship. Yet the problem is not the line of the argument but its starting premises: that Jesus's saving death was a sacrificial death and that Christian worship is therefore the remembrance and appropriation of a sacrificial event.

164. Sykes, "Outline."
165. Cf. in contrast Luther, *De captivitate*, WA 6:523–26.
166. Sykes, "Outline," 290.
167. Ibid., 289.

The fact that this understanding gained such centrality and dogmatic authority in church tradition finds its hermeneutical basis in the Christian adoption of the Old Testament; and it finds its historical basis in the transformation of Christianity into a *religio licita* [permitted religion] and ultimately into the state religion of the Roman Empire. Its dogmatic basis, however, is found in the way in which greater attention was paid to the *that* than to the *how* in New Testament discussion of Jesus's death as a sacrificial death. A doctrinal engagement with the soteriological complex of ideas of sacrifice must therefore consider two factors: (1) from the very beginning Christianity was not a religion of sacrifice, and (2) from the very beginning Jesus's death on the cross was confessed and declared to be both a sacrifice and the end of the temple cult. The factors are closely connected. Focused on the crucified Jesus as the risen Christ, Christian life developed in contradistinction to the ritual and sacrificial cult of the Jerusalem temple and distanced itself from the religious context of contemporary Judaism on the basis that Jesus's death and resurrection had put an end to the whole sacrificial system.

But to speak of Jesus Christ as the end of sacrifice is ambiguous. On the one hand, it can mean that Jesus Christ is the end of sacrifice because his death on the cross and his resurrection have demonstrated that sacrifice as a means to the restoration of fellowship between God and human beings is ineffectual and unnecessary. But it can also mean that Jesus Christ is the end of sacrifice because he is the ultimate and perfect sacrifice. This is how church tradition has typically understood it, arguing mainly from the Epistle to the Hebrews that Jesus Christ had "offered himself on the cross as a true and real sacrifice to God,"[168] and thus it has sought to develop and legitimize this idea in terms of trinitarian theology.[169]

But this church tradition has only the literal wording, not the import of the New Testament statements, on its side. The references to Jesus's sacrificial death do not mean that the crucifixion is to be understood as a ritual act of killing. Sacrifice here has a figurative function: it gives intelligible expression to the concurrence of God's loving commitment to Jesus and to Jesus's commitment of himself to God's love. Within the universal mindscape of sacrifice, however, this unique eschatological event could only be expressed by adopting the very language and imagery of the cult of sacrifice in order to make clear that, and how, this language and imagery were to be transcended. The sacrificial theological texts of the New Testament substantiate this.

168. L. Ott, *Grundriß der Dogmatik* (Freiburg: Herder, [10]1981), 222.
169. Hoffmann, *Kreuz und Trinität*.

## 8. The Hermeneutics of the Sacrificial Theological Texts

In the New Testament, faith in Jesus Christ manifests itself in numerous images, metaphors, parables, and stories. These images are historically contingent, but they cannot be eliminated without robbing the Christian faith of its speech, and neither can they be replaced without removing its life-orienting depth of focus. These images do not describe the reality we experience but locate it *coram Deo*; in other words, they consider it from the perspective of God's creative nearness, with its capacity for renewing reality. They therefore speak not of the world but of the *creation*, not of failures and guilt but of *sin*, not of Jesus's death but of his *saving death*. In each case more is ascribed to experienced reality than is apparent.

Now, the images believers use originate from a multiplicity of different experiential and interpretative situations. They are attempts to articulate experiences that can be expressed only in images and not in a conceptual, descriptive way, because they are *not an instance of something already familiar but rather the disclosure of something that is as yet unknown, is only inadequately known, or cannot be conclusively grasped*: the perception of our reality in the light of God's creative nearness. In terms of the logic of subsuming description and conceptual definition, this perception can never be satisfactorily formulated, because it remains bound to the perspective of the perceiver and is only granted along with the redefinition of the perceiver's self-understanding. This perception can develop gradually through practice, or it can occur instantaneously and unexpectedly. In either case our normal perception and experience are fundamentally shattered. Yet even what is encountered as a radical invasion by a new element and a fundamental shattering of our received experience and structures of perception can be articulated only with the aid of traditions of experience and language we already possess. Linguistic innovation always builds on linguistic traditions. The attempt is made to articulate the new and the less familiar using images and conceptual material already available in the tradition and the linguistic community. Faith images thus owe their provenance to their original hermeneutical credibility and intelligibility, particularly when the attempt is being made to use them to articulate something new.[170]

The dogmatic purpose of these images lies therefore not simply in the images themselves or in any far-reaching continuity that they suggest, but rather in the *differences* between the context in which they originated and the new context in which they are being used. The question is not "Which images are being used?" but "How are these images *modified and revised* as part of the

---

170. Cf. Dalferth, "Stuff of Revelation," 82–95.

attempt to use them to express the salvation experienced in Jesus Christ?" This is the decisive hermeneutical question from a dogmatic point of view.

Where the complex of images and ideas associated with sacrifice is concerned, the answer must be that *this complex is subjected to a fundamental christological revision that leads to a semantic inversion of the interpretament (sacrifice) and the* interpretandum *(the saving death of Jesus Christ). The result is that it is not the image that interprets and illuminates the subject matter; the subject matter is what interprets and illuminates the image.* In the New Testament this christological revision of the category of sacrifice is accomplished using different methodologies (e.g., through functional recasting, through equivalence of the functionally distinct, or through *intensification*):

1. *Revision through functional recasting.* As we have shown, taking Romans 3:25–26 as an example, Paul transforms the *consecration–slaughter–incorporation* structure of the cultic sacrifice by recasting it functionally into the *Christ–cross–faith* structure of the cross event.[171] Using the image of sacrifice, salvation is thus restated in a characteristically fresh way that is far from justifying the dogmatic statement that Jesus's death was a sacrificial death.

2. *Revision through equivalence of the functionally distinct.* Not only Pauline texts demonstrate the christological revision of the Old Testament category of atoning sacrifice; this kind of revision is just as likely to be found in other New Testament contexts, though it may take a different form. Thus, in the Epistle to the Hebrews, Jesus Christ is described, on the one hand, as the ultimate and perfect sacrifice, in that he is portrayed simultaneously as the offerant, the offering, and the high priest making the sacrifice, who offered himself on the cross once for all and presents this unrepeatable self-sacrifice to God unceasingly in the heavenly sanctuary, so that all the structural elements of sacrifice find their equivalent in him. On the other hand, he is identified as the perfect form of all types of sacrifice, not just one, so that in him it is not merely one particular type of sacrifice but sacrifice as such, and hence the sacrificial cult as a whole, that is surpassed and superseded.[172] From a theological point of view, the significance of this strategy of equivalence is the same as in the Pauline writings: the sacrificial cult is soteriologically superseded, the category of sacrifice is christologically abolished, and salvation is understood strictly as God's eschatological activity. In both cases the category of sacrifice is used to make it plain that sacrifice has served its time as a practical means to, and thought form about, salvation.

171. Gese, "Sühne"; Janowski, *Sühne als Heilsgeschehen.*
172. Cf. O. Hofius, "Opfer," in *Taschenlexikon Religion und Theologie*, ed. Erwin Fahlbusch (Göttingen: Vandenhoeck & Ruprecht, ⁴1983), 54–56, esp. 55.

3. *Revision through intensification.* The hermeneutical process of intensification ultimately makes it clear that Jesus's death is not to be understood
purely as a sacrificial death. Jesus's death is described as the *true and real*
sacrifice, the *perfect* sacrifice, or the *end* of sacrifice. The Old Testament cult
of sacrifice is typologically adopted as a hermeneutical tool to express the
salvific significance of the death of Jesus through intensification. Here again,
however, it is not the tool as such but the way it is used that is dogmatically
critical. But this too is not without its problems. This kind of typological
argumentation remains caught in an *essentially backward-looking perspective.* Inasmuch as Jesus's death was understood typologically wholly in light
of past practice and history, the soteriological use of the idea of sacrifice
encouraged the misunderstanding that Jesus's death was merely the functional equivalent and replacement of the temple cult, instead of perceiving
him to be its eschatological intensification. Here, however, it is not that one
sacrificial cult is being replaced by another sacrifice and its cult; rather, *the
category of sacrifice is being employed to dismiss the use of sacrificial and
cultic categories for soteriological thinking altogether.* Even this intensification expresses the soteriological *shattering* of the category of sacrifice, not
its supreme fulfillment.

On the one hand, it is beyond dispute that Christianity is not a religion of
sacrifice. According to the New Testament witness, Jesus's death on the cross
put an end to every sacrificial system. On the other hand, it is also beyond
dispute that in the New Testament Jesus's death on the cross is recognized as
and declared to be a sacrifice. Theological thinking has typically linked both
realities together and said that Christianity is not a religion of sacrifice, *because*
Jesus Christ is the end of sacrifice. But this argument is inadequate, since it is
ambivalent to speak of Jesus Christ as the end of sacrifice. It might mean, on
the one hand, that *Jesus Christ is the end of sacrifice because he is the ultimate
and perfect sacrifice.* This is how the dogmatic tradition has understood it in
the main, in that it has held as an article of faith that Christ "offered himself
to God on the cross as a true and real sacrifice."[173] On the other hand, it can
also mean that *Jesus Christ is the end of sacrifice because he demonstrates with
his entire being that sacrifice is unnecessary and ineffectual as a means to the
restoration of fellowship between God and humanity.* The first understanding
suggests itself if one is mindful primarily of *continuity* and *heightening* in the
pre- and non-Christian use of the mindscape of sacrifice, on the one hand,
and in its Christian use, on the other. In contrast, the second understanding
comes to mind if—as above—one is primarily emphasizing the *discontinuity*

173. Ott, *Grundriß*, 222.

and *differences* between the non-Christian and Christian usages. To say that
"*in the new covenant atoning sacrifice can no longer exist*," because "Jesus's
death on the cross . . . puts an end to every sacrificial system," implies not that
Jesus is to be understood "as the ultimate atoning sacrifice"[174] but rather that
God's eschatological saving activity in the death and resurrection of Jesus has
rendered sacrifice superfluous and has made the idea of sacrifice unworkable as
a soteriological thought form. The New Testament demonstrates this clearly in
that it only uses the category of sacrifice strictly in its christologically revised
form. For if one is aware, from a hermeneutical point of view, not only *that*
sacrificial thinking plays a role in the New Testament but also *how* it is used,
then it becomes plain that *the category of sacrifice itself is used to express the
fact that sacrifice as a way of enacting and thinking about salvation has been
made obsolete once and for all through God's eschatological saving activity in
Jesus Christ*. The point at issue is not the possibility of basing "the sacrificial
character of Christ's death on the cross upon the fact that all the requirements of a cultic sacrifice were fulfilled," given that Christ "according to his
human nature was at one and the same time sacrificing priest and sacrificial
gift" but according to his "divine nature was also, together with the Father
and the Holy Spirit, the recipient of the sacrifice."[175] It is not Jesus Christ's
fulfillment of all the requirements of a cultic sacrifice but the *replacement of
sacrifice as a cultic practice* and the *termination of the idea of sacrifice as a
soteriological category* that lie at the heart of the paradoxical argumentation
modeled on equivalence and intensification in the Epistle to the Hebrews and
Paul's soteriological recasting. Christ represents the end of sacrifice and the
sacrificial cult because he stands for the purification and reordering of the
disrupted, damaged fellowship between God and humanity, which should have
been restored, purified, and reordered through sacrifice[176] but has now been
restored, purified, and reordered once and for all *in an entirely different way*
that will hold good for all eternity: God's eschatological self-mediation on the
cross and in the resurrection of Jesus Christ. *God himself* has accomplished
salvation through his all-transforming nearness, and this is why sacrifices and
sacrificial cults are no longer needed. He has accomplished it *in and through
Jesus Christ*, and this is why the soteriological use of the idea of sacrifice is no
longer needed. And he has accomplished it *once and for all*, which is why the
Christian community—when its understanding is correct—does not recognize
any soteriological prolongation of this event, neither ecclesiologically in the

174. Hofius, "Opfer," 55 (italics in original).
175. Ott, *Grundriß*, 223.
176. Cf. Gunton, *Actuality of Atonement*, 118–20.

eucharistic activity of the church nor ethically in the actual appropriation of salvation through the self-sacrificial conduct of its life. It knows nothing but the "sacrifice of praise . . . , the fruit of lips" (Heb. 13:15) and the thank offering of faith (i.e., the *testimony* to God's eschatological saving activity in word and deed). For it is possible to bring God's eschatological saving activity to mind only in retrospect, and, in order to preserve the fundamental distinction between God's activity (revelation) and human activity (recollecting proclamation), this recollection requires no priestly or cultic representation but solely the word of the cross. This word, repeatedly called to mind, is a guiding principle for the Christian life, provided that it does not follow the religious or moral *do ut des* or *do quia dedisti* compulsions of the sacrificial logic—a logic that this word has rendered eschatologically obsolete—but simply adheres to what, given the proven love of God, is its self-evident and constant course of action in this world.

## 9. Dogmatic Implications

It should be clear from the above that the soteriological use of the mindscape of sacrifice in the New Testament differs significantly from its use in the Old Testament. Both follow fundamentally different grammars and therefore cannot be related to each other in unbroken continuity. The interpretation of Jesus Christ in the light of the traditional representational and conceptual category of sacrifice results in a fundamental reorganization of its sense structure, and it is in fact this reorganization, and not necessarily the category as such, that is meaningful in theological terms. Neither the category of sacrifice as such nor the fact that Jesus is declared to be a sacrifice are theologically illuminating and dogmatically relevant when taken in isolation. They simply demonstrate that Christians, too, express the experience of salvation using the thought and speech patterns that are culturally available to them for articulating salvation. What is much more theologically illuminating and dogmatically relevant is *how* they *use* these patterns; this becomes apparent from the *alterations* that are a feature of an image complex such as sacrifice when applied to Jesus Christ. For it is not the (often widely divergent) patterns, images, or ideas as such but rather the *alterations* to them in Christian usage that make the articulation of salvation with the aid of a specific image complex comparable with other articulations of the Christian faith. Taking the category of sacrifice as an example, however, something becomes clear that applies similarly to all complexes of images and ideas used by the Christian faith to articulate the salvific significance of Jesus's death on the cross and resurrection. This is that they are subjected to a fundamental *christological volte-face* or, as Luther put it, to a *baptism*,[177] through which they take on a *nova significatio* [new meaning][178] that can be understood when one pays attention to the breaks, alterations, and differences in its usage, rather than to the image and its semantic continuities.[179] From a theological point of view, it is worth tracking down these differences so as to uncover the soteriological content of the message of the christological confessions, and not simply, or primarily, the images and ideas used to formulate them. The latter are merely hermeneutical aids rather than what is important from a theological point of view: God's saving activity in and through Jesus Christ.

If one focuses theologically on these differences, however, it becomes evident that there are dogmatic implications that should be given further consideration. Thus, from the New Testament reorganization of the grammar of the category of sacrifice it follows *christologically* that it is not dogmatically adequate to conceive of Jesus Christ as a *persona privata*, an individual who becomes the bringer of salvation (Messiah, Christ, Son of God) only as a result of his work. From a theological point of view, he instead should be seen from the outset as an officeholder (Luther), "collective person" (Bonhoeffer), or "corporate Christ" (Moule). This is not—as in Kodalle's perfectly justifiable criticism of Bonhoeffer—because of a fatal bias toward the collective, an aversion to the individual as a hotbed of sin, or the exploitation of the one in the service of the species,[180] but rather because in dogmatic terms it is not about Jesus himself but about God's saving activity in and through him. Jesus therefore must be conceived of from the outset within the scope and context of this divine action as the one in whom God has linked himself with every human being and *has* incorporated them into his community (Rom. 5:18). Jesus Christ is the one in whom God has come as near to all of us as he comes to us time and again in the Spirit of Jesus Christ: as all-transforming love.

Accordingly, it follows for theological *anthropology* that the human person, too, is only adequately conceived of when he is considered not just as an individual or an example of the animal rationale or homo sapiens, but when he is viewed within a specific frame of reference, namely, his integration into the story of Jesus Christ. Neither does this have anything to do with collectivist thinking, but rather it concerns the insight that individuals,

177. WA 39:1, 229.
178. WA 39:2, 94, lines 17–18.
179. This is not to deny but rather to accentuate the fact that this understanding is possible only on the basis of the image itself insofar as one traces the grammar of its use before and after this "baptism" so that one is guided to the relevant distinctions and differences.
180. Cf. Kodalle, *Dietrich Bonhoeffer*, particularly chap. 3.

too, can be considered only within a frame of reference and that the proper frame of reference for their theological consideration is God's activity in the story of Jesus Christ. His story is the prehistory and the posthistory and thus the underlying history that is the basis of every human story, because it is the actualization of God's saving activity in and for his creation. It gives us a past and a future beyond the beginning and the end of our individual and collective story as human beings, and it demonstrates the truth of our humanness "archaeologically" (protologically) and "teleologically" (eschatologically), namely, that we are destined for personal fellowship with God and thus anchored in God's creative love. Individually and together, we live in our respective historical and individual ways not purely for ourselves alone, or just collectively with our earthly neighbors and our environment, but in and through the nearness and presence of God. This presence can be observed and experienced in the work of God's Spirit in numerous different ways with various degrees of clarity.[181] And it does not hand our earthly life over to the arbitrariness of our individual dispositions and their unpredictable (or, in fact, often predictable but nonetheless inalterable or unstoppable) collective consequences; instead, it ensures that what has the last word is not the consequences of our actions but the love of God in each individual life and in the life of the whole creation.

Both the christological and anthropological implications call for a departure from abstract concepts of individuality and experience-based generalizations and from thinking restricted to certain reference ranges and relational collective categories. The categories of theological doctrine, such as "creature," "sinner," "righteous one," "Son of God," "Messiah," "Lord," and so on, are not theological descriptions (valid alongside other types of description) of experiential circumstances of human life in general or of Jesus's life in particular.[182] As conceptual summations of the figurative language of faith, they are not descriptive but localizing predicates that position what they are alluding to within the frame of reference of God's activity and relate it to the latter in various ways. They do not say what something is; rather, they say that what it is can be truly recognized and appraised only when it is understood and appraised in its relationship to God as he has made himself manifest and accessible in the story of Jesus Christ. In this sense, theological doctrinal

181. Cf. M. Welker, *Gottes Geist: Theologie des Heiligen Geistes* (Neukirchen-Vluyn: Neukirchener, 1992).

182. The entire conceptual model that supposes there are certain facts that can be variously described, including in religious or theological ways, is profoundly dubious and indefensible from a hermeneutical point of view. Cf. Dalferth, "Stuff of Revelation," 130–33; Dalferth, "Christ Died for Us," esp. 315–25.

statements about Jesus Christ, God, humanity, the world, and everything
else are not descriptions of what they allude to; they are principles that lead
us to define and understand what is spoken of within the context of God's
saving activity so that we consider it not on its own but *coram Deo* and thus
*coram Christo*. Christian theological understanding and experience believe
that this process of consideration takes place properly when it is subject
to the grammar formulated, in its essential features, in the doctrine of the
Trinity.

This imposes no fresh theological requirements. In the field of Christology, both Augustinian/Lutheran sacramental Christology and incarnational/
two-natures Christology show the beginnings of this kind of thinking within
the trinitarian frame of reference that has to do with God's activity. When
such a Christology is liberated from the individualistic misapprehension that
it is a theory of the constitution of the *persona privata* of Jesus Christ, one
can hardly dispute that it seeks to conceptualize—whether successfully or
not—the proleptic and personal structure of the divine event of identification and incorporation that takes place on the cross. Similarly, in the field of
theological anthropology, one should bear in mind the doctrine of justification. The latter conceptualizes—albeit against the background of a different
(juridical) guiding metaphor—the proleptic incorporation of every human
being into a fellowship with God that is personally mediated by Christ, and
the response of faith to this being in Christ, and it conceives them entirely
properly as an activity undertaken exclusively by God to set up fellowship
with, liberate, and open up new life for his creatures. It is no accident that
both the attempt to conceive of God's activity of justification on the cross
in dogmatic terms and the attempt to conceive of the incarnation event as
God's universal saving activity lead to the doctrine of the Trinity. Where God
is concerned, the christological coincidence and the soteriological volte-face
of consecration and incorporation enacted on the cross make it necessary to
conceive in specific terms of a personal Trinity. For only in trinitarian terms
can the *solus Deus* be properly conceptualized, and only in trinitarian terms is
it therefore possible to fulfill the requirement that the genesis of the Christian
faith be described historically and reconstructed hermeneutically, and also
that a theological basis be established for its claim to validity.

The salvific significance of the death of Jesus is thus only apprehended (as
defined in the hermeneutical principle formulated above) if his death is considered dogmatically in an irreducible threefold context: in the context of the
life of Jesus, in the context of the life of God, and in the context of our own
individual lives. Jesus's death cannot be separated from the story of his life;
on the contrary, this story—and with it the story of Israel and of the human

race as a whole, with which it is integrated—is an essential context for under-standing his death.[183] The Old Testament complexes of images and ideas, which the New Testament employs in its christological and soteriological thought, provide impressive evidence for this. It must be added immediately, however, that Jesus's life story and its historical and hermeneutical backgrounds and corollaries are not the only context in which his death is to be understood. Otherwise, his death would be of individual, and perhaps historical, but in no way universal significance. It would be the death of one specific individual, who doubtless would have left his mark on history in the sense that he con-stitutes an *example*, recalled and imitated in numerous different ways, of a life of self-giving for others. But his death would be primarily the end of his life, and this life could be only an example for those who would live after him and know about him. Then his life would be an exclusive, closed story with historical effects but without universal, salvific significance.

But it is only this significance that prompts Christians, because of their faith in the nearness and love of the triune God, to take a historical interest in the story of the life and death of Jesus as well. Just as they do not know God without Jesus, neither do they know Jesus without God. As the proleptic saving activity of God, the story of Jesus Christ is not closed and exclusive but open and inclusive, because it is the eschatological coming of God to humanity. In the context of the life of God, Jesus's death marks God's arrival at the lowest point of human reality, as the Philippian hymn describes it. It is precisely through this divine self-mediation, effected under the conditions of death itself, that our reality, which has fallen victim to death, is transformed by God himself into its true identity of life in fellowship with God.

This transformation takes place proleptically in the openness and inclusivity of the story of Jesus Christ. It includes the story of each one of us, and each of our stories presupposes his story and is carried forward by it. Soteriologi-cally, the story of Jesus, culminating in his death on the cross, is thus only adequately recounted when it is affirmed as the beginning and the end of the story of every human person. Conversely, none of our stories can be given its true meaning unless it is integrated into his story. His story is the *pre*-story, the *underlying* story and the *post*-story *of every* human story—this, indeed, is the source of its universality.

But this does not blur the distinction between his story and our story, since his extends into ours and is continued by it and beyond it.[184] In fact,

---

183. B. Janowski, "Auslösung des verwirkten Lebens," esp. 55–56nn135–36.

184. This danger appears not to have been entirely avoided by Schillebeeckx (*Christus und die Christen*, 461).

this intimate link emphasizes the irreversible arrangement of these stories: his story includes ours, and ours is included in his. His story is the context that establishes and affirms the truth of our story; our story is the context in which the truth of his story is demonstrated. It is demonstrated as we learn to see the division, marked by sin, between his story and ours and the incorporation of our story into his in terms of pure grace, attributable to God alone and not to ourselves.

Christ is therefore not externally connected with us as our representative in a transaction between human beings and God. The confessional statement "Jesus *died for us*" does not mean that he died *instead of us* or *in our place* (in the sense of ἀντί), as one might say when speaking of someone who rescued a child from a burning house but lost his own life in the process. But it also does not mean that he died *for our sake* or *because of us* (in the sense of ὑπέρ), as one might say when speaking of someone who lost his own life in a (possibly unsuccessful) rescue attempt, or whose action set for his fellow human beings an inspiring example of selfless dedication on their behalf. Interpretations like these all imply a *vicarious action* or a *vicarious death*. If this idea is worked out within the framework either of a juridical conceptual model of law and penalty or of a cultic conceptual model of sacrifice and atonement, it is expounded as a *substitution* of one side for the other, as the replacement of the offender or victim by another living being (human or animal) that suffers the relevant consequences in his or her place. This in turn presupposes that those who participate in this substitutionary or vicarious action are understood ontologically as individuals who exist independently of the action and of each other, so that the action in turn can be apprehended merely as an external, exclusionary transaction between them. If we try to think of the salvific significance of Jesus Christ in this sense, we perceive him as a specific individual who, by his actions and suffering, accomplished a work from which other individuals can benefit by allowing the effects of this work to have an impact on them. But this quasi-causal thinking using the model of an acting subject and the consequences of his activity blurs the fact that the Christian resurrection confession attributes the accomplishment of *our* salvation not simply to Jesus's activity but to *God's* activity in and through Jesus Christ. It also entirely robs God's saving activity in Jesus Christ of its personal character, obscuring the fact that the issue is not merely, or even primarily, what Jesus did or suffered but what he *is* in his actions and suffering: the creaturely locus of the self-disclosing presence of God's creative and all-renewing love. The life-giving nearness of God's love, which Jesus proclaimed and Christians see manifest in Jesus's own life, death, and being raised from the dead as the ultimate eschatological reality of all life, is wholly inadequately described as the "work of Christ"; indeed, it is impossible to conceive of it using the concept of a "work." Jesus is not the producer of a work of salvation; he is the mediator who, in his own person, brings us before God and God before us; he is thus the locus at one and the same time of God's presence with us and our presence with God. The salvific significance of his death has nothing to do with a work he has performed from the earnings of which we can benefit. Our salvation is to be found in him as a person and in his story, not in a work that he has done: he is *in persona* the locus of the redeeming, liberating, and all-renewing presence of God. For precisely this reason Christ is not merely the *exemplum* but first and foremost the *sacramentum* of our salvation.[185] In him we are—indeed, each one of us is—in the presence of God: if in faith, then for our salvation, and if in unbelief, then for our judgment. So in his story we have a prehistory, an underlying history, and a posthistory, which entitles us to hope that what is true for him is and will be true also for us: ἀπέθανεν, ἐτάφη, ἐγήγερται [he died, he was buried, he was raised].

## 10. Christian Life after the End of Sacrifice

The dogmatic consequences identified arise out of the fundamental reshaping of the sacrificial field of imagery that I have described. This reshaping shows evidence of more than a merely semantic or hermeneutical modification of the grammar of the category of sacrifice. It is the linguistic reflex of the historical emergence of a new religion: the *Christian religion*. Given that Christians, appealing to the cross and resurrection of Jesus Christ, distanced themselves in a systematic way from the sacrificial cult of the temple and then from the synagogue as well, they broke away from their Jewish origins and also set themselves up in fundamental opposition to the Roman state religion. On the one hand, they refused, in the name of the one God, to participate in the emperor cult, as the Jews did too. On the other hand, they refused, in the name of Jesus Christ, to participate in the Jewish sacrificial cult, thereby forgoing the privileges of the Jewish *religio licita*. It is thus no accident that they were berated as atheists and persecuted by both the Jewish and the Roman authorities. If the practice of a sacrificial cult is the yardstick of a religion, then Christianity is not just noncultic but strictly *areligious*.[186]

185. Cf. E. Jüngel, "Das Opfer Jesu Christi als sacramentum et exemplum: Was bedeutet das Opfer Christi für den Beitrag der Kirchen zur Lebensbewältigung und Lebensgestaltung?," in *Wertlose Wahrheit: Zur Identität und Relevanz des christlichen Glaubens*, Theologische Erörterungen 3 (Tübingen: Mohr Siebeck, 1990), 261–82.

186. Conversely, this means that, from the Christian point of view, all religions that practice sacrifice are classed as false religions, on the grounds that they have a false understanding of

The consequences were and are considerable and even today still have not been thought through. It is no accident that they determine central areas of theological debate right up to the present. Thus, with their rejection of the cult of sacrifice, the Christians were withdrawing in principle as a religious movement from a classification that corresponded with the Hellenistic-Roman *theologia tripartita* [tripartite theology] and its underlying thought model involving myth and logos. In the same way their rejection of the cult of sacrifice separated them both from the folk religions and from the political state ideology, their worship practice also distinguished them from the academic nature-and-cosmos theology of the philosophical schools. Early Christianity appeared to its contemporaries in the ancient world as neither myth nor logos, as neither a religion nor an ideology or philosophy. This meant that it not only precluded the usual theological evaluation criteria; it also found itself confronted by two inescapable tasks. From a practical point of view it had to create for itself a *shared way of life* that was beyond the boundaries of folk religion and state ideology, cult, and civil religion and that was appropriate to its faith in Jesus Christ. From a theoretical point of view, it had to find a *theological form of reflection* beyond the boundaries of myth and logos. It achieved the first by forming principles governing its worship and communal life, and the second, in direct connection with the first, by developing its Christology and trinitarian theology.

Right up to the present day, both of these tasks have entailed a tightrope walk resulting in numerous crashes. Where the principles governing their worship and communal life were concerned, Christians, under pressure from late Roman requirements, fell back before long into the cultic organizational pattern of a religion of sacrifice.[187] Cultic ceremony and sacred assembly became the identifying marks of the Christians, not λογικὴ λατρεία [spiritual service], the fulfillment of God's will in one's whole life in the everyday world.[188] But,

---

God and a correspondingly false way of handling God's creation. Octavius asks, in M. Minucius Felix's dialogue of the same name (*Octavius*, ed. and trans. B. Kytzler [Darmstadt: Walter de Gruyter, 1993], 176–78), whether he should erect a temple for God, "since even the whole world, the work of his hands, cannot contain him[.] Should I seek to encompass such mighty majesty in a single small chapel, while I, a human being, inhabit a more spacious dwelling? . . . Should I bring God sacrifices from amongst the animals, whether small or large, that he has created for my use, thus throwing his gifts back in his face? That would be sheer ingratitude!"

187. There is no positive correspondence in the New Testament between Eucharist and sacrificial action (apart from the christological motif in Mark 14:24). The concept of sacrifice is first used in the context of the Eucharist in *Did.* 14.1. For the significance of the synagogue for the formation of the principles of Christian communal life, cf. J. T. Burtchaell, *From Synagogue to Church: Public Services and Offices in the Earliest Christian Communities* (Cambridge: Cambridge University Press, 1992).

188. E. Käsemann, "Gottesdienst im Alltag der Welt (zu Röm 12)," in *Judentum–Urchristentum–Kirche*, ed. J. Jeremias and W. Eltester (Berlin: A. Töpelmann, 1964).

as Paul set out in Romans 12 and underlined with his collection for the poor in Jerusalem, the worship of God as a human reaction to God's saving activity is not a sacral cult; it is the *testimony of the life*, serving one's neighbor in word and deed out of gratitude to God, doxology and *diaconia* in one. This testimony takes wholly concrete form in the collection of money, in standing up for justice, in a concern for the poor to be found in the Roman ports and trading cities, in a commitment, as Pliny reports, bearing out Romans 12:17–18, "not to any wicked deeds, but never to commit any fraud, theft, adultery, never to falsify their word, not to deny a trust when they should be called upon to deliver it up."[189] The creation and preservation of this coherence of doxology and *diaconia* in the life of the individual and within the community as an institution has been the fundamental practical challenge for the Christian way of life in every age, including our own.

And the same applies to theology. The difficult balance between philosophical speculation and popular remythologizing has only rarely been preserved in christological and trinitarian thought. Time and again Christians have allowed themselves to be seduced into celebrating these principles of thought, speech, and life as mysteries of the divine liturgy or presenting them as speculative truths (in the West), instead of understanding and following them as practical instructions for the λογικὴ λατρεία, the worship and service of God in the everyday world. But their function is not to communicate divine mysteries to human beings, secrets disclosed to Christians alone. Rather, they are intended to teach us to perceive God's nearness in the everyday context of our life by reminding us of the unstinting way in which God has come near to us in Jesus Christ, a reminder that is intended to give us a new and better understanding of ourselves and our world in the light of this, God's unstinting nearness, so that we are able to live our lives in a new (i.e., a *Christian*) way. To live Christianly, beyond the boundaries of traditional religion, ideology, morality, and philosophy, means at the very least that the religious distinction between the holy and the profane, the sacred and the secular, is obsolete for Christians. The consequences of this are and always have been considerable.

Now that there is an end to sacrifice, and the cult of sacrifice is a thing of the past, the distinction that has always been drawn on a cultic basis between religious and nonreligious spheres and conduct, has become fundamentally untenable for Christians. Christians know that the *whole of life* is lived in proximity to and in the presence of God—the whole life, in all its dimensions, of every single human being. Wherever that is ignored, we live in a state that

189. C. Plinius, "Lib. X, 96: C. Plinius Traiano Imperatori," in *C. Plinii Caecilii Secundi epistularum libri decem*, ed. R. A. B. Mynors (Oxford: Clarendon, ²1966).

the New Testament calls *sin*. Wherever, in contrast, God's Spirit sets us free
to perceive God's nearness and to allow ourselves to be drawn into it, we
live as sinners *in faith, in Christ, in the Spirit*; we are *new creations, justified*
and *set free*, or however else the cascade of images to be found in the New
Testament puts it.

If, however, it is true that each of us lives wholly before God and that this
is perceived only by those who know they are in God's presence and are not
caught in the position of a disinterested observer, and if a change of position
can be brought about neither by external pressure nor by a simple decision
of the will but only by free assent to the presence of God and by an equally
voluntary alteration of one's way of life, then a life lived in awareness of
God's nearness cannot be forced on anyone or demanded of anyone. It is only
when people see an example of such a life lived out before them that they are
enticed to allow themselves to be drawn into it.[190] So it is with good reason
that the words *request, invitation, offer*, and *acceptance* are among the basic
terms used in the proclamation of the gospel. The religious transformation
of the idea of sacrifice into a *moral challenge to others*, on the other hand,
is fundamentally obsolete and inconceivable for Christians: one can require
a sacrifice of oneself, perhaps, but never from someone else. A willingness
to suffer cannot be stipulated or imposed; it can only be practiced oneself.

So the ending of the cult of sacrifice radically changed Christians' *understanding of the worship and service of God*. What constitutes true worship
of God is not a certain class of actions, rites, or practices, as distinct from
other, profane practices, but simply the *grateful surrender of the whole person
to God* (Rom. 12:1).[191] *Every* Christian action must therefore be assessed and
measured according to whether it is carried out in the service of God (Rom.
15:16; Phil. 2:17), for God's praise (Heb. 13:15), and out of love for God as

190. Not by the example itself, but by what is manifest in and through it.

191. For—and this was the reasoning from the beginning—the human person is the image,
the *imago*, the *simulacrum* [likeness] of God. It is in the human life, not in some external place,
the limited space of a temple or an altar or an image of God, that true worship of God takes
place. To quote Octavius again: "Surely you do not believe that because we have no temples
or altars, we are concealing the object of our worship. By what image am I to represent God,
since, rightly considered, man himself is the image of God? What kind of temple should I erect
for him, since even the whole world, the work of his hands, cannot contain him? . . . Is not the
heart a better place for us to worship God, the soul a better sanctuary for us to consecrate to
him? . . . A good heart . . . , a pure mind, immaculate thoughts: these are the sacrificial gifts
that please God. Therefore, the one who protects his innocence prays to God; the one who
practices justice sacrifices to him; the one who abstains from fraud obtains his grace; the one
who rescues a human being from danger brings the most beautiful sacrifice to God. These are
our sacrifices; this is our worship: for us it is a person's righteousness that is the measure of his
piety" (Felix, *Octavius*, 176–79).

encountered in one's neighbor (Heb. 13:16). In other words, Christian life after the end of sacrifice means—to paraphrase Luther's first thesis—that *one's whole life is worship*, because Christians are to testify to God's Word as the salvation of the world with all that they do: with their private actions just as much as with their public activity, with their interpersonal conduct just as much as with their social and political actions.

This all-encompassing redefinition of the whole life changed, and is still changing, Christians' *understanding of the world*. The world is not a continuous battleground of demons, a purely temporal illusion before the bedrock of eternal being, or the scene of a struggle between good and evil powers whose outcome is still uncertain. In fact, the decisive new beginning has already taken place, even if it is not yet perceived everywhere. Thus, despite every contradictory tendency, the world in its temporal diversity and mutability can already be understood and acknowledged in faith as what it definitively is and ultimately will be: God's good creation. The consequences of this "disenchantment of the world" for the development of Western culture are well known and can hardly be overstated. Its negative aspects, the present cause of so many different complaints, are not the result of this disenchantment as such, since this would mean that it must be countered with a fresh enchantment (as is frequently and variously attempted today). Rather, they are the consequences of a failure to recognize and focus on the reverse side of this disenchantment with the same degree of emphasis: precisely because the critical turning point has already happened, there is no sphere of actual world reality that is not covered by God's good governance. The world is free from gods and demons but not without God. What is more, in all its dimensions it is God's creation and to be esteemed as such. We do this when we honor God as our creator, savior, and perfecter by strengthening those trends within the processes of the world that give God's love a recognizable form and by opposing those trends that obscure and undermine his love.

Of course, all of this alters Christians' *self-understanding*: if a person is required and destined to worship God in word and deed in the entirety of his or her life, and not just in parts of it, and if the life of every human being is essentially interrelated with that of others, then no one can live for himself or herself alone, and neither can just a few people practice this worship and service of God on their own. Instead, the life of every Christian and of the whole Christian community is intrinsically oriented toward humanity as a whole. If God lays claim to the entire life of a human being, then he also lays claim to the life of every human being. If the grateful surrender of one's entire person to God is the worship God desires, then the grateful surrender of every person to God is the worship he is waiting for. The claim of the Christian

faith to universality is therefore directly linked with the elimination of the
cultically based distinction between holy and profane, and both are grounded
in the fact that God alone has made salvation in Jesus Christ an eschatological
reality and is bringing it about pneumatologically.

What this means for our understanding of the *celebration* of Christian
worship in the narrower sense is that—correctly understood—*it resists any
reduction to a religious cultic ceremony*. Whatever we do in the act of worship
is a no less worldly business than everything else we do. "What," asks Jochen
Hörisch quite rightly, "is the everyday consumption of bread and wine when
compared with the ancient cults?" In contrast to "the terror and joy that the
Eleusinian Mysteries were able to provide," it was clearly "a venture of radical
aesthetic disenchantment."[192] And even if this contradicts the fashionable trend
toward symbol-laden holistic ritual, Christian worship ceremonies should be
*disenchantment events*, even today, in the sense that they should remind us in
word and sacrament that we all live from the secret of God's nearness, not
from our own resources.[193]

Conversely—and here is the point—this means that *nothing we do is necessarily excluded from being worship of God*. Every activity that combines
doxology and *diaconia* in conscious response to God's nearness and implicit
"service" to us is worship: not just liturgical ceremonies but equally everyday
activity. In a countermove to the fashionable segmentation and pluralization of
life, which threatens in its complexity to degenerate into a total free-for-all, the
essence of Christian existence after the end of sacrifice is that the *whole* life
of a Christian is *unqualified* worship of God. We are called to testify by our
lives in word and deed, for "*apud nos religiosior est ille qui iustitior* [among
us, the one who is most just is the one who is most religious]."[194] This is the
worship God expects from us.

This does not mean at all that everything we do must be dressed up to
look religious. On the contrary, *it means that our worldly activity is digni-
fied as worship of God*. This is the real point of our emancipation to the
"worldliness" that is rightly ascribed to the Christian faith. The world is not
a continuous battleground of demons or a comfortless vale of tears, and neither is it a disguised paradise; rather, it is the *sphere of this-worldly activity
before God*, in other words, *the activity of worship*. Inasmuch as Christians
live in such a way that they do what is natural, given the presence of God,
then even if in the sight of our world it does not seem at all obvious, they

192. J. Hörisch, *Brot und Wein* (Frankfurt: Suhrkamp, 1992), 72.
193. Cf. Kodalle, *Dietrich Bonhoeffer*, 124–29.
194. Felix, *Octavius*, 178.

are already holding the world in high esteem, regardless of all its undoubted ambivalences and opposing tendencies, as what it definitively is and ultimately will be: God's good creation.

Of all his creatures we alone are in a position to recognize and appreciate this. This marks us out, but it also imposes a specific responsibility on us. We can see how terribly wide the gulf is between our credal confession of the world as God's creation and the reality we experience. Hence it would be against our better judgment to evade the task of treating our this-worldly activity as service of God; we must therefore strengthen the trends that give God's love a recognizable form and oppose the trends that obscure and undermine his love. We need only do what is self-evident, if only we can learn to perceive this and allow it to govern our activity. Thus we will do all we can to counter wrong with right, rampant conflict with peace, widespread bondage with freedom, death with life—in other words, we will do all those self-evident things that are rightly expected of Christians but far too rarely done by them.

This also means that Christians cannot be content to be preoccupied with themselves. If we are destined to worship God in word and deed, not just in parts of our lives but in all its fullness, then we cannot be preoccupied with ourselves. For if the grateful surrender of one's entire person to God is the worship God desires, then the grateful surrender of every person to God is the worship he is waiting for. Christians are distinguished by the fact that they know this, and because of this they must do all they can to make this happen. The claim that the Christian faith makes to universality is therefore not an expression of a desire for religious dominance. It follows from the elimination of the cultically based distinction between the holy and the profane, and it spreads the good news that God is near *to all because* and *in the same way that* he stayed near to Jesus himself in his death on the cross.

Now that sacrifice has ended, this message will not be proclaimed properly if, despite everything, Christian faith sets itself up within the context of a given society as another religious cult or a societal civil religion. Christianity is permanently at risk of succumbing to cultic or ethical diminishment. Even so, Christians cannot force what they bear witness to on others, and neither can they make it a mandatory system of religious, moral, or political values. They must present it in such a way that it can be *freely accepted by others of their own accord*, because and to the extent that God himself bestows it on them: only thus will it achieve its purpose. No one can be compelled to carry another's burden; this must be recognized and done of one's own accord. And only a life lived as an example and a testimony can entice people into this kind of free acceptance.

On the other hand, if Christians present their message to society primarily or exclusively in the form of a religious cult, there will be a tendency, at the very least, for the fundamental removal of the distinction between sacred and profane areas of life to be called in question. *Christians must therefore make it clear, even in their worship ceremonies, that for them worldly activity is worship and worship is worldly activity.* Anything less would contradict the unqualified nearness and presence of God in all dimensions and areas of life. The special feature of liturgical worship as compared with worship as a whole is thus to be found in the verbal expression, the constant reminder and awareness we receive through the liturgy, of what is fundamentally true: there is no time, place, or area of life in which God is not present in his love.

This has consequences that are still highly controversial, even within Christianity. Since Christians' lives depend on God's nearness, there can be no Christian life without acts of worship in which this perception is presented in the words of the gospel and in ways that can be experienced, namely, the ceremonies of baptism and the Eucharist. However, given that Christianity is not a religion of sacrifice, it has no need of any related *cult*, with its differentiation between sacred and profane, its temples and altars, and its specialized *clergy* with their *cultic repertoire of rules and rites*. Admittedly, for understandable historical reasons, it soon developed all this, so that it metamorphosed into a form of religion that was recognizable even in the Roman context. It was probably as part of this process that it created for itself the preconditions without which it could not have advanced so far as to become within a few centuries the imperial religion of the Roman Empire. But from the perspective of the core and self-understanding of its own message, there is neither cause nor need for this. Despite all their evolution in practice and the theological development of doctrine in the course of church history, Christian worship ceremonies have no cultic or sacral import. They neither celebrate a sacrifice, nor are they a substitute for sacrifice; they require no clerical leadership by some priestly representative of Christ; they recognize no priests, or rather—since every believer is a "priest"—no distinction between priests and laity; they are not tied to specific places (temples) but take place wherever two or three are gathered in Christ's name; and although an order of service is indispensable for a Christian community, it has nothing to do with the cultic separation of holy from profane, clergy from lay, or the sacred from the secular sphere.[195] The particular task facing Protestant churches today is to affirm this unwaveringly within the ecumenical context

195. Cf. G. Ebeling, *Dogmatik des christlichen Glaubens*, vol. 1, part 1, *Der Glaube an Gott den Schöpfer der Welt* (Tübingen: Mohr Siebeck, 1979), 127–28.

as part of the debate concerning the understanding of ministry and the ordination of women.

Christian worship ceremonies are not an alternative to but a *special instance of* the testimony of the Christian life in the everyday world. In all their aspects they constitute a *practice of witness and reminder* by repeatedly calling to mind in word, action, and symbol God's ultimate saving activity in Jesus Christ and testifying to it before the world. Thus the word of the cross and the corresponding ceremonies of baptism and Eucharist call to mind in their respective ways the proximity of the saving and life-giving love of God made manifest in the cross and resurrection of Jesus. At the same time, they remind us that this reflective word of reminder is sufficient[196] and that there is no further need of sacrifice, sacrificial cult, or cultic priesthood, as well as reminding us why this is so: *because God has acted once and for all and has accomplished our salvation in Jesus Christ.* In other words, he *has* come near to us and draws near to us in his Spirit time and again. We can only ever refer back to this because with the remembrance the one remembered makes himself perceptibly present—*ubi et quando visum est Deo in his qui audiunt evangelium* [where and when it pleases God, in them that hear the gospel]. Christians have no advantage over other sinners except the perception of God's nearness because of the promise of the gospel. Paul called this *faith*. This is why Christian life after the end of sacrifice can be called, in a nutshell, a *life of faith*.

196. *Confessio Augustana* 7.

# Modern Author Index

# Subject Index